Comparing Political Thinkers

Comparing
Political Thinkers

edited by
Ross Fitzgerald

Pergamon Press
SYDNEY · OXFORD · NEW YORK · TORONTO · PARIS · FRANKFURT

Pergamon Press (Australia) Pty Ltd,
19a Boundary Street, Rushcutters Bay, N.S.W. 2011, Australia.
Pergamon Press Ltd,
Headington Hill Hall, Oxford OX3 0BW, England.
Pergamon Press Inc.,
Maxwell House, Fairview Park, Elmsford, N.Y. 10523, U.S.A.
Pergamon of Canada Ltd,
Suite 104, 150 Consumers Road, Willowdale, Ontario M2J 1P9, Canada.
Pergamon Press GmbH,
6242 Kronberg-Taunus, Pferdstrasse 1, Federal Republic of Germany.
Pergamon Press SARL,
24 rue des Ecoles, 75240 Paris, Cedex 05, France.

First published 1980

Copyright © 1980 Ross Fitzgerald

Cover design by Allan Hondow
Typeset in Australia by S.A. Typecentre Pty Ltd
Printed in Singapore by Singapore National Printers (Pte) Ltd

National Library of Australia Cataloguing in Publication Data:

Comparing political thinkers.

ISBN 0 08 024800 4
ISBN 0 08 024799 7 Paperback

1. Political science – Addresses, essays, lectures.
I. Fitzgerald, Ross, 1944-, ed.

320.5

All rights reserved. No part of this publication may be reproduced, stored in a retrieval system or transmitted in any form or by any means, electronic, electrostatic, magnetic tape, mechanical, photocopying, recording or otherwise, without permission in writing from Pergamon Press (Australia) Pty Ltd.

Contents

Preface — vii

Socrates and Plato — 1
Ross Fitzgerald
School of Humanities, Griffith University, Brisbane

Plato and Confucius — 19
Wu Teh Yao
College of Graduate Studies, Nanyang University, Singapore

Aristotle and Mencius — 40
Wu Teh Yao

Augustine and Hobbes — 54
Damien Grace
School of Political Science, University of New South Wales, Sydney

More and Socrates — 76
Conal and Averil Condren
School of Political Science, University of New South Wales, Sydney

Marsilius and Machiavelli — 94
Conal Condren

Hobbes and Locke — 116
Roger D. Masters
Department of Government, Dartmouth College, Hanover, New Hampshire

Rousseau and Hobbes 141
James MacAdam
Department of Philosophy, Trent University, Peterborough, Ontario

Rousseau and Hume 164
Paul Corcoran
Department of Politics, University of Adelaide

Hegel and Nietzsche 185
Wayne Hudson
Linacre College, Oxford

Calvin and Kropotkin 203
Vincent di Norcia
Department of Philosophy, University of Sudbury, Ontario

Rousseau and Marx 223
Patricia Springborg
Department of Government, University of Sydney

Mill and Marx 245
Graeme Duncan
Department of Politics, University of East Anglia, Norwich

Herbert Marcuse and Christian Bay 262
Ross Fitzgerald

John Rawls and Robert Nozick 285
M. W. Jackson
Department of Government, University of Sydney

Preface

Comparing Political Thinkers is a collection of fifteen original essays, written independently of each other, by political theorists from the English-speaking world. A primary aim of the book is to compare arguments advanced by different political thinkers – some ancient, some modern, some Eastern, some from the West. The list of thinkers dealt with is as follows: Socrates, Plato, Aristotle, Confucius, Mencius, Augustine, Hobbes, More, Marsilius, Machiavelli, Locke, Rousseau, Hume, Hegel, Nietzsche, Marx, Calvin, Kropotkin, Mill, Herbert Marcuse, Christian Bay, John Rawls and Robert Nozick. Thus this collection contrasts thinkers not only often across time, but also between very different social and cultural contexts. Some pairs of thinkers (such as Socrates and Plato) come from the same place and from very similar times; others (such as Plato and Confucius, Aristotle and Mencius) from roughly the same times, but from very different places and social environments. Others yet again (for example, Hobbes and St Augustine) come from very different times, places and environments. Despite the inevitable omission of key thinkers (names like Jeremy Bentham, Edmund Burke, Lenin and Mao Tse-tung readily come to mind) and despite the fact that essays of this length must, of necessity, simplify and compress often very subtle arguments, the student embarking on the study of political thought will be given a taste of seminal political ideas and also of the intriguing activity of comparing political arguments advanced by different thinkers. Such an activity raises very interesting and complex methodological problems, about comparison, which are dealt with by some of the contributors, especially focusing on the problem of thinkers employing a very different political vocabulary and language.

As with my previous academic collections, *Human Needs and Politics, What It Means to be Human* and *The Sources of Hope**, editorial intervention has been kept to a minimum. The essays within require neither brief nor abridgement. However, in the comparison of political thinkers certain key themes emerge. Despite all the differences in language and political vocabulary, all of the thinkers examined display specific (and specifiable) attitudes to human nature and human needs, to freedom, however that concept is conceived, and to how best to organize the good state or the good society – that is to say, how best to adapt institutional structures or arrangements to the nature of man.

To students embarking on the study of political thought, may I suggest that ultimately all explanation of political activity and all political recommendation is derived from a very basic attitude to, or set of assumptions about, what it means to be human. These conceptions of human nature are pivotal to political theory, empirical and normative. As Graeme Duncan writes, comparing the contemporaries Marx and Mill: 'At the heart of political theory lies the effort to establish a relationship between the state, or political institutions, or institutional arrangements, and man's nature, in whatever terms that might be expressed, and to engage in political advocacy – and perhaps more direct action – on that basis. Political theory is not pure, monastic, unsullied, but both arises out of particular social and political circumstances, especially situations of conflict, and advocates solutions or responses: it may be elevated, abstract, remote, learned, distinguished, but it is advocacy nonetheless, and it advocates on the basis of certain assumptions about the powers and limits of human beings. Crudely, a view of human nature is a view of what human beings actually – or normally or naturally – are, or what they distinctively, truly or ideally are, or what they are potentially.' However such views may be expressed or elaborated, any (and all) political theory implies a conception of what it means to be human. Primary among scholars' tasks are to fish or flush out such conceptions or assumptions.

It is, therefore, important for the reader to bear in mind whether the political thinkers being examined (or the political theorists doing the examining) make these attitudes or assumptions or conceptions of human nature explicit, or whether (as is so often the case) they remain implicit. But explicit or implicit, underlying all political thinking, such attitudes or assumptions are always there.

*All published by Pergamon Press, Australia.

Comparing Political Thinkers, among other uses, enables students to face and evaluate these basic assumptions about the most basic of all political questions: What is the nature of human beings and what are the political arrangements best suited to man in society?

I would like to thank all contributors for their co-operation in meeting what, for many was a difficult deadline. I would also like to thank the College of Graduate Studies, Nanyang University, Republic of Singapore, and Brian Reis of the Griffith University Library.

Ross Fitzgerald

For James Edward Jones
in Sydney

Socrates and Plato

Ross Fitzgerald

The person of Socrates comes down to us in the present shrouded in myth and disagreement. We know incontrovertibly that he lived, he spoke, and that he was tried and put to death. We know also that Socrates has profoundly affected the lives of others. Just as with Jesus, the Socratic problem is intractable in the sense that we are unlikely to achieve any consensus about the meaning and significance of his life and death. As with all important symbolic figures of the past, we create our own Socrates in the sense that our understanding of Socrates is refracted through our own personality in the time, place and culture in which we find ourselves. Indeed as thinking and feeling human beings we are obliged to do so. This does not mean that there are no 'facts' on which authorities agree. It is clear, for example, that Socrates, the son of a stone-mason or sculptor, was born in Athens in 470 or 469 B.C.; that he was given to taking trances; that at the time of his trial he was living with his reportedly shrewish wife Xanthippe; that he had three sons; and that he died at the age of seventy in the spring of 399 B.C. by taking hemlock. But while these and other biographical facts are generally the subject of agreement, as private persons and as philosophers we are still required to interpret Socrates for ourselves. As A. W. Levi has said, 'One can as legitimately ask a philosopher what stand he takes on the meaning of Socrates' life as one can ask what is his theory of the nature of sense-data or his belief about the objectivity of moral values.'[1]

Socrates wrote nothing: his life and character is known to us primarily from the account of his contemporaries, Aristophanes, Xenophon and Plato, and from Aristotle who did not write about him first hand. For practical purposes, these are our only sources of information about

---

[1] A. W. Levi, 'Idea of Socrates: The Philosophic Hero in the Nineteenth Century, *Journal of the History of Ideas*, 17: (Jan. 1956), 89–108.

Socrates' life and death.[2] Of these sources, the most extensive and important is Plato, who was approximately twenty-eight when Socrates died[3], but here the search for the 'real' Socrates is complicated by the fact that Plato used the character of his master Socrates to expound and advance his own views. Thus in reading the Platonic dialogues, we are faced with the problem of determining to what extent the ideas attributed to 'Socrates' reliably represent the views of the historical Socrates, and to what extent the ideas expressed are later additions or inventions of Plato.

Despite these problems, I maintain that it is both possible and necessary to separate the philosophy of Socrates from that of Plato and to extract a central core of Socratic doctrine. Moreover it is my contention that one can do so from a reading of Plato himself. This involves relying on what are now almost universally taken to be Plato's earliest dialogues[4], and especially the *Apology* which all critics concede is the most certainly 'Socratic' of all Plato's work. Although an imaginative reconstruction of an actual event, this account of Socrates' trial (ostensibly for corrupting the youth and worshipping false gods) could not have been radically in error as it was written soon after the trial – the essential elements of which were well known to all educated Athenians of the time, and certainly to those who later gathered around Plato's Academy.

A close examination of Plato's earliest dialogues, contrasted with his later works (especially the development of his Theory of the Forms and the notion of rule by a philosopher king), enables one to make a fundamental distinction between a 'Socratic' and a 'Platonic' way of thinking. The small group of Plato's earliest dialogues, particularly the *Apology*, *Crito* and *Euthyphro*, can be justifiably termed 'Socratic' in the sense that, as W. K. G. Guthrie argues, Plato is 'imaginatively recalling, in form and substance, the conversation of his master without as yet adding to them any distinctive doctrines of his own.'[5] To me, Socrates

---

[2] See W. K. C. Guthrie, *A History of Greek Philosophy*, Vol. III, Pt. 2: *Socrates*, Cambridge University Press, 1971, pp. 1–55.
[3] Plato went on writing until his own death at eighty in 347 B.C. when his massive final work, the *Laws*, was still unfinished. The trial and execution of Socrates turned Plato away from pursuing a practical political career to a full-time commitment to philosophy. For details of Plato's life, see chapter 2 in this collection.
[4] The most important of Plato's earliest dialogues are the *Apology*, *Crito*, *Euthyphro*, *Laches*, *Charmides* and *Lysis*. For a useful summary of the question of the chronology of Plato's works, see the table given in W. D. Ross, *Plato's Theory of Ideas*, Clarendon Press, Oxford, 1951, p. 2. See also J. E. Raven, *Plato's Thought in the Making: A Study of the Development of his Metaphysics*, Cambridge University Press, 1965, pp. 27–55.
[5] See W. K. C. Guthrie, *A History of Greek Philosophy*, Vol. IV: *Plato, The Man and his Dialogues: Earlier Period*, Cambridge University Press, 1975, p. 67.

and Plato represent two quite different positions about life and philosophy. Moreover, their opposing views have fundamental implications for human freedom. This difference in approach can be characterized as Socratic ignorance versus Platonic certainty. (Even though one can accept the admonition that there may have been no *concept* of personal responsibility in the vocabulary of fifth-century Greece, and that notions of freedom and authority were very different from our own[6], this in no way refutes the interpretation that Socrates, for example, placed personal responsibility and his obedience to God or the gods before anything else. Despite the objections of some contemporary linguistic philosophers and historiographers[7], there is, by definition, no other way of viewing the past than through the present, including the vocabulary and conceptual apparatus of the present. To believe otherwise is to be profoundly misled.)

Socratic ignorance versus Platonic certainty

One cannot separate the personality and character of Socrates from his philosophy, for Socrates' philosophy was a way of life.

Poor, extremely ugly (flat-nosed, pot-bellied, pop-eyed), but with a way of looking at people that many found fascinating and unforgettable, almost always dressed in an old coat, and often barefoot, Socrates was concerned with philosophical questions from an early age. He had also acquired a reputation for what today we would regard as mystical experience. In Plato's *Symposium*, Alcibiades relates how, whilst Socrates was a brave young infantryman serving in the Athenian army, he entered a fit of abstraction (some would say a trance) and stood motionless outside his tent all night, apparently wrestling with some philosophic problem, until at dawn he said his prayers and went inside. (Even more famous was Socrates' 'divine sign' or 'inner voice' which was with him from the early days of his childhood; we shall deal in detail with this later.)

Socrates' courage as a soldier and as a private person are well-attested. In 406 B.C., when it was his turn to help decide what business should be

---

[6] See Conal and Averil Condren, 'More and Socrates', in this collection. See also A. W. H. Adkins, *Merit and Responsibility*, Oxford University Press, 1962.

[7] See, for example, C. Condren, 'An Historiographical Paradox', in F. McGreggor and N. Wright (eds), *European History and its Historians*, University Union Press, Adelaide, 1977, p. 86; C. Condren, *Three Aspects of Political Theory*, Macmillan, Melbourne, 1979, chapter 1; and J. G. A. Pocock, *The Machiavellian Moment*, Princeton University Press, New Jersey, 1975.

brought before the Assembly, Socrates alone resisted the illegal demand of the democracy that a number of Athenian generals, charged with failing to rescue some men ship-wrecked in a victorious action, should be tried together instead of separately. Previously, in 408 B.C., he resisted an order from the newly established oligarchy of Thirty that he and four other citizens arrest a wealthy property owner, Leon of Salamis. The others obeyed, and Leon was arrested and tried. Socrates, who refused to arrest the man, was saved from severe punishment only by the counter-revolution, which restored the democracy. (Ironically, it was under this democratic regime that Socrates was eventually tried and sentenced to death.)[8]

Although like every Athenian citizen he served on the Council when required, Socrates deliberately avoided taking an active part in politics. He spent much of his time talking and questioning, and gathered around him a small circle of devoted followers, especially young men; these included Alcibiades and Critias who, as infamous traitors and oligarchs, were later to be partly responsible for his trial.

Most of Socrates' questions centred on practical matters and human problems. As a young man, Socrates had become disillusioned with the natural sciences of his time. Consequently he shifted his attention from physical inquiry (for example, about the origins of the world and the nature of matter) to a concern with the ends for which human beings ought to live and with how one can best take 'care of the soul'.[9]

When Socrates was in his early thirties, his earnest young friend Chaerephon consulted the Delphic oracle and asked whether anyone was wiser than Socrates. The oracle replied, 'No-one'. When Chaerephon reported this, Socrates was astonished and incredulous. In order to discover what the oracle meant, he set out to question people in every walk of life to find if anyone was wiser than he. Questioning politicians, poets and craftsmen, Socrates soon found that they did not know how ignorant they were. Those, like the politicians, who appeared wise, on close inspection were not so; poets had no understanding of what they had created; and artisans, although skilled in their specialized crafts, discussed matters they knew nothing about. Socrates realized that he was wise in the sense that he was aware of his ignorance. Predictably, many proud, vain, pompous people (and especially the old) were angered by

---

[8] See Guthrie, *Socrates, op. cit.*, pp. 59–61.
[9] See F. M. Cornford, *Before and After Socrates*, Cambridge University Press, 1968 (first published 1932), pp. 29–31.

Socrates' questions and he made many enemies. It is also not surprising that many of the intelligent young men of Athens were delighted with this process of questioning and, for better or worse, became his followers.

As a result of trying to decipher what the Delphic oracle meant, Socrates became aware that his mission in life (his service to God, or the gods) was to make himself and others aware of their own ignorance; and to encourage himself and others to question their previously unquestioned beliefs about, for example, man's place in the world, his duties to the state, and the nature of goodness and justice. Socrates' self-examination and the examination of others expressed a way of life; hence his famous statement, 'the unexamined life is not worth living'.

This constant questioning is the keynote of Socrates' approach to philosophy and to life; and as we shall see, it contrasts markedly with that of Plato.

Socrates constantly asked questions, but gave no answers. This is because he was aware that he *had* no answers (and also, I suspect, because he knew that, in the world of space and time, there were no fundamental answers to be found). Unlike the Sophists, Socrates was not a teacher, but a fellow-seeker. For this and other reasons, Socrates did not charge for instruction, if indeed what he engaged in could be termed 'instruction' at all.[10]

Socrates' profession of ignorance is tied to his description of himself as a midwife (rather than a bearer) of ideas. In Plato's *Theaetetus* the metaphor of midwifery is expounded thus:

> I am so far like the midwife, that I cannot give birth to wisdom; and the common reproach is true, that though I question others, I can myself bring nothing to light because there is no wisdom in me. The reason is this: heaven constrains me to serve as a midwife, but has debarred me from giving birth. So of myself I have no sort of wisdom, nor has any discovery ever been born to me as the child of my soul. Those who frequent my company at first appear, some of them, quite unintelligent; but, as we go further with our discussions all who are favoured by heaven make progress at a rate that seems surprising to others as well as to themselves, although it is clear that they have never learned anything from me; the many admirable truths they bring to birth have been discovered by themselves from within.[11]

---

[10] Aristotle makes the general statement that 'it was the practice of Socrates to ask questions but not to give answers, for he confessed that he did not know'. See *De Sophisticis Elenchis* 183b, lines 8–10.

[11] *Theaetetus* 150c-d, quoted in Guthrie, *Socrates, op. cit.*, p. 124. The translation is by Cornford.

In order to expose ignorance (in himself as well as others) Socrates primarily asked questions, especially 'what is . . . ?' questions about problems encountered in the human world. What is courage? What is piety? What is love or friendship? What is goodness or justice?

From Plato's earliest dialogues a typical pattern of Socratic cross-examination or questioning emerges. Rather than concern himself with problems of science or epistemology, Socrates invariably deals with problems of human life. Typically Socrates meets, in an informal social setting, a person who by virtue of his function or the actions in which he is engaged may be supposed to know the meaning of some important abstract term, for example, temperance (Charmides), piety (Euthyphro, who is prepared to accuse his father of lacking it), friendship (Lysis) and justice (Thasymachus). In the ensuing encounter Socrates and the respondent engage in what may be termed 'a search for definition'—a method that Plato himself adopted and, as we shall see, extended.

J. A. Elias summarizes a typical 'Socratic' dialogue:

> The respondent, called upon to give an account of the principle which justifies his belief and action, usually begins by enumerating examples of justice, piety, friendship, and so on, but Socrates makes plain that what he is after is a definition of what each of these examples has in common that enables it to be subsumed under the general term. The respondent then offers a first definition which Socrates examines in quasi-legalistic and even eristic fashion, misunderstanding where misunderstanding is at all possible, and forcing the respondent to refine his original position. Second, third, and subsequent definitions are then offered; all are subjected to criticism employing a variety of devices.[12]

These are some of the devices: (a) The definition is shown to be too broad or too narrow by citing examples which appear to fit, but which the respondent is unwilling to include or exclude. (b) Analogies and metaphors are employed to describe whether the concept to be defined is 'like' something more familiar among the arts and crafts. (c) Logical puzzles lead to one impasse after another.

A typical result of the cross-examination is that the respondent (who comes to realize that he doesn't really know the meaning of the key term) departs suddenly, confused and resentful.[13] Those cross-examined leave Socrates in what psychoanalysis terms 'a state of negative transference', angry with Socrates but also with themselves. Many, he says, 'are ready

---

[12] J. A. Elias, ' "Socratic" vs. "Platonic" "Dialectic" ', *Journal of the History of Philosophy*, 6: (July 1968), 205–16, the quotation is from p. 206.
[13] *Ibid*.

to bite me' when they see their cherished ideas discarded as phantoms and illusions.[14] To be forced to recognize one's ignorance is a disturbing and unpleasant process. Hence it is not surprising that other Athenians, especially the rich, the powerful, the old and the proud, were angry with Socrates' questioning (and also, one presumes, with his unwillingness to supply any answers).

Plato was not content with the essentially 'negative' result of Socratic interrogation. In his middle and later dialogues, the quest for the definition or essence of terms such as 'justice' led Plato to search for certain answers, based on the model of deductive mathematics and especially geometry.

The craving for certainty led Plato to posit the existence of eternal and unchanging Forms or 'Ideas' as a way out of what he perceived to be the epistomological impasse reached by the Socratic method. For Plato, his theory of the Forms provided the basis for a positive theory of truth.

In summary, the Platonic Forms or 'Ideas' comprise the world of ultimate reality which is independent of ordinary sensible experience. The Forms are timeless and unchangeable, and alone contain all that is truly real. Moreover, Forms or Platonic Ideas are not mere thoughts in a mind, not even in God's mind; they have a substantial and permanent existence of their own. The Form of 'Justice', for example, in itself is not a thought, but is an eternal *object* of thought. The world of the perfect Forms is thus the ultimate in abstraction.[15]

Plato's theory of eternal and unchangeable Ideas, which provide the ground for certain knowledge, is expounded through the mouth of 'Socrates' in Plato's dialogues such as the *Phaedo* and *Republic*. But the theory of the Forms, along with the notion of rule by a philosopher king, and of it being the task of the philosopher to *teach* others (as in Plato's Academy), are far removed from what I have termed Socratic ignorance.

Hans Meyerhoff's masterly essay, 'From Socrates to Plato', is extremely useful in comparing the 'Socratic' and the 'Platonic' approaches.[16] Meyerhoff first summarizes what Socrates did in the name of philosophy and how he did it.

•Unlike Plato, who philosophized in a formal academy, Socrates invariably discussed problems of life in an informal setting – for example,

---

[14] See Guthrie, *Socrates, op. cit.*, p. 82.
[15] See Raven, *op.cit.*, p. 215; and Cornford, *op. cit.*, p. 64.
[16] Hans Meyerhoff, 'From Socrates to Plato' in K. H. Wolff and B. Moore (eds), *The Critical Spirit*, Beacon, Boston, 1967, pp. 187–201.

at a banquet, at a rich merchant's house, by the bank of a river, at a court hearing or in prison.
• Socrates used a common type of evidence in support of his arguments, not evidence derived from any technical knowledge and unfamiliar to the lay person.
• He always discussed philosophical problems, not on an abstract level, but in the context of a concrete human situation – for example, a son prosecuting his father for manslaughter (as in the *Euthyphro*) or a friend trying to persuade Socrates to escape from prison after his trial (as in the *Crito*). In the words of Gabriel Marcel, he affirmed 'the primacy of the concrete'.
• The logic Socrates employed, rather than scientific or formal, was the informal method of cross-examination which (as we have seen) involves clarifying the meaning of a view that is advanced and then citing concrete counter-instances or pointing to logical flaws that refute this view.[17]

Meyerhoff rightly thinks that instead of refutation, it is more correct to say that view and counter-view are examined to show that both are defective, inadequate or deceptive. 'Socratic' logic consists of arguing back and forth, debating the pros and cons of a particular issue in an informal way. The Socratic 'dialogue' does not produce a formal proof or a formal refutation, as in logic or in mathematics.[18]

Meyerhoff asks why Socrates practised this kind of analysis, and answers 'to expose ignorance, or false beliefs, in others and in himself.'[19] Yet the process of self-examination (and cross-examination) is never completed. (As Freud said of some cases of psychoanalysis, it is 'interminable'.) Why, then, Meyerhoff asks, pursue a project that seems to be both frustrating and disappointing as far as the goal of attaining truth, or certainty, is concerned? The answer is that the process of examination is the only means of gaining self-knowledge which, though forever incomplete, is the only means of knowing what we are doing and how we are living. This conception of knowledge is existential in the sense *that truth is expressed in a way of life. It is not necessarily put into propositional form.*[20]

As Meyerhoff explains:

---

[17] *Ibid.*, p. 192.
[18] *Ibid.*, p. 193.
[19] *Ibid.*, p. 193.
[20] *Ibid.*, p. 193.

Truth refers to a correlation between consciousness and life. It means that theory and practice, consciousness and action are conjoined in a conception of life. Put differently, [true] knowledge in the primary sense is an attribute of life; it is not necessarily an attribute of beliefs or propositions as in later logic. Hence, Socrates could legitimately claim he was ignorant and still display [true] knowledge in life. That has been the perennial paradox, and fascination, he has presented to posterity.[21]

Seen from this perspective, Socrates' oft-quoted dictum 'Virtue is knowledge' is itself paradoxical, for to Socrates the only sure knowledge that the intellect can supply is knowledge of one's ignorance.

In marked contrast to Socratic ignorance, Plato believed that true knowledge can be firmly 'tethered' to the reality of the Forms. By this means Plato arrived at a definition of truth that consists in the correspondence between words and things or between reason and reality.[22] As we have seen, the only 'true' reality for Plato is the world of the Forms; ordinary sensible experience is regarded as being unreal and illusory.

Another distinguishing characteristic of Plato's approach is that, in the Academy, philosophy was practised in closest possible conjunction with the exact sciences – of which mathematics was the most advanced at the time. Meyerhoff notes that, according to Plato, the closest approximation to a knowledge of Forms is a knowledge of mathematical objects, relations, and equations.

Finally, in the last dialogues, Plato is increasingly preoccupied with a new problem. It is not the Socratic question 'what is . . . ?'. It is not even Plato's earlier problem of how things in this world participate in the Forms beyond. It is the new problem of how these Forms, or essences of things, are logically related to each other in an ascending order of abstraction. In contrast to the human world of time, change and history in which we live, act and suffer, the world of the Forms is a realm of abstract essences. In the scheme of the 'divided line' in Plato's *Republic*, it is the intelligible world comprised of mathematical and dialectical reasoning where true knowledge dwells and into which the philosopher ascends from the sensible human world of the 'cave' – that is, the place of shadows and illusions.[23] For Plato, the philosopher via education climbs from the darkness of ignorance and false belief (in which most men are 'prisoners') to the sunlight of true knowledge of the Forms.

[21] *Ibid.*, p. 194.
[22] *Ibid.*, p. 194.
[23] For Plato's simile of the cave, see Guthrie, *Plato, The Man and his Dialogues: Earlier Period, op. cit.*, pp. 350, 497 and 312–18.

The method of Plato's later dialogues is quite different from the Socratic method of mutual cross-examination. As Meyerhoff argues, in the *Republic* it consists of an inquiry into the foundations of mathematics, or the derivation of mathematics from 'first principles'. Thereafter, it is generally called the method of division (*diaeresis*). This is the method of studying the logical relations, both combinations and divisions, that are possible in the universe of Forms.[24] To Meyerhoff, Plato's purpose or goal in his later dialogues is obvious. It is not, as with Socrates, the search for self-knowledge. Rather, 'the aim is to convert philosophy into the "queen of the sciences", providing both the logical foundation and a supreme *Summa* of the exact sciences. Self-knowledge may still be a by-product of this inquiry, but it is not the main object. The primary task of philosophy is to reconstruct, in the form and language of a logical, or deductive, system, the body of general knowledge about man's place in the universe and in society. That was Plato's secret dream, as it were.'[25] It was part of his quest for certainty, to which we shall return.

Socrates was put on trial, not only for his life, but for his way of life. Despite the fact that the charges by his accusers Meletus, Anytus and Lycon did not explicitly mention his ceaseless questioning of morality, custom and religion, it was this above all for which he was tried. In the democratic reaction that followed the overthrow of the thirty tyrants, Socrates' guilt lay in undermining the fabric of established authority and thus in threatening the fragile stability of his native Athens, which was only just recovering from the disastrous effects of the Peloponnesian War and internal political turmoil. From this perspective, Socrates' constant concern about the ends for which we ought to live is much more important in explaining his trial, than his allegedly anti-democratic attitude and the charge that Socrates had been the educator of Alabiades and Critias and so was responsible for their misdeeds.

Socrates' accusers, indeed the whole Athenian establishment, would have much preferred not to have brought Socrates to trial, let alone to find him guilty and sentence him to death. It is most important to realize that in a fundamental sense Socrates forced the hand of his accusers. Had Socrates been prepared to keep silent (and refrain from questioning) he

---

[24] Meyerhoff, p. 195.
[25] *Ibid.*, pp. 195-6, his emphasis.

need not have been brought to trial. Had he accepted exile he need not have appeared in court. Had he played the accepted game in the courtroom (for example, by conducting a proper 'defence', by begging for forgiveness, allowing his wife and children to plead for mercy) he need not have been found guilty, and had he not further angered the jurors by proposing that as a punishment he be given free meals at the place reserved for Olympian heroes, instead of suggesting an acceptable fine, he need not have been sentenced to death. Finally, had he been prepared to accept the chance to escape (arranged, it seems, with full knowledge of the authorities) he need not have died.

But Socrates chose to obey the letter of the laws of Athens and, more importantly, to obey something that transcended merely civil obligation – namely God, or the gods.

Service to God or the gods
For Socrates it was only the good life, not life itself, that one should care about. Socrates' courage and his insistence on following what he took to be the truth, in spite of what others thought or what prudence would dictate, were already well known before his trial. For Socrates, the only thing that ultimately mattered was obedience to the truth. At his trial he said it would be shameful if after facing death in battle at the state's command (as a soldier), he should now through fear of death disobey his divine command to philosophize by examining himself and others. There is no doubt that after the pronouncement of the Delphic oracle Socrates took his vocation seriously, as part of his contact with and service to the divine. Significantly, at his trial Socrates refused to accept acquittal at the price of giving up his mission. In the event of such an offer, he said he would answer thus:

> Athenians, I hold you in much affection and esteem, but I will obey heaven rather than you, and, so long as breath and strength are in me, I will never cease from philosophy or from exhorting any of you whom I chance to meet, in my accustomed words: My good friend, . . . are you not ashamed to spend so much trouble upon heaping up riches and honour and reputation, while you care nothing for wisdom and truth and for the perfection of your soul.[26]

Socrates says that he shall question and cross-examine and test such a person and . . .

---

[26] *Apology*, 29d.

if I think he does not possess the virtue he affects, I shall reproach him for holding the most precious things cheap and worthless things dear. This I shall do to everyone whom I meet, young or old, citizen or stranger, but especially to you, my fellow citizens, inasmuch as you are my own people. For be assured that such is heaven's command; and I believe that no better piece of fortune has ever befallen you in Athens than my enlistment in the service of heaven.

For I have no other business but to go about persuading you all, both young and old to care less for your bodies and your wealth than for the perfection of your souls, and to make that your first concern.

With reference to the charge of corrupting the young (the other being worshipping false gods) Socrates continues:

If by saying this (i.e. care for your souls) I am demoralising the young men, so much the worse; but if it is asserted that I have anything else to say, then that is not true.

'Therefore Athens', I should conclude, 'you may listen to Anytus or not; you may acquit me or not; for I shall not change my ways, though I were to die a thousand deaths.'[27]

This speech and the rest of Plato's *Apology* is without any shadow of doubt faithful in spirit and in substance to the statement actually made by Socrates in his own defence. Later, he warns his hearers:

If you kill me you will not easily find a successor to me who will be, if I may use such a ludicrous figure of speech, a sort of gadfly, attached to the state by God, and the state is a great and noble horse who is rather sluggish owing to his very size and requires to be stirred into life. I am that gadfly which God has attached to the state, and all day long and in all places am always fastening upon you, arousing and persuading and reproaching you.

Socrates clearly believed that God had sent him to Athens for its good,[28] and that he had communion with the divine.

In his trial Socrates makes much of his divine sign or inner voice. To my mind, his relationship to the voice supplies a key to Socrates' life. For Socrates, the inner voice was *not* what we would call 'conscience' (or, following Freud, the superego) which being supplied by human agency was by its nature fallible. It is crucially important to realize that Socrates regarded it as an infallible voice from God. When Socrates delivers his 'defence' he describes it as follows:

At sundry times and in diverse places I experience a certain divine or daemonic something, which in fact Meletus has caricatured in the indictment.

[27] See Cornford, *op. cit.*, pp. 35–7. The translation from the *Apology* is Cornford's.
[28] When he claims (*Apology* 30c-d) that it is not permitted for a better man to be harmed by a worse, the forbidding agent referred to is not human but divine.

> It began in childhood, and has been with me ever since, a kind of voice, which whenever I hear it always turns me back from something I was going to do, but never urges me to act. This is what has prevented me being a politician. And rightly, as I think.[29]

Socrates continues:

> For I am certain, O men of Athens, that if I had engaged in politics, I should have perished long ago, and done no good either to you or to myself . . . Nor do I converse only with those who pay; but anyone, whether he be rich or poor, may ask and answer me and listen to my words . . . Now this duty of cross-examining other men has been imposed upon me by God; and has been signified to me by oracles, dreams, and in every way in which the will of divine power was ever intimated to any one.[30]

After his condemnation, Socrates addresses the jurors who voted for his acquittal:

> In former times my customary prophetic sign has opposed me assiduously even in quite trivial matters, if I was going to do anything amiss. Now there has befallen me, as you see, what would commonly be considered the worst of all evils; yet neither when I left my house nor when I was taking my place in the court nor at any point in my speech has it opposed me. On other occasions it has checked me in the middle of a sentence, but this time and in this affair it has not opposed me in a single word or action.

Therefore, Socrates concludes that what has happened to him must be something good and that the death which awaits him cannot be an evil.[31]

Socrates' 'daemon' is what links him with the divine (but it holds him back rather than commands him on). Whatever we in the late twentieth century may think of the inner voice, and however we may explain it (or try to explain it away), Socrates believed that it was a signification of his divine mission. To regard Socrates' inner voice as anything but central is to miss something essential about Socrates' life and his philosophy. One can only agree with W. K. C. Guthrie (who also tries to separate the Socratic from the Platonic) in his summing up of Socrates:

> He seems to have been a man who, as Aristotle said, applied the whole of his remarkable intellectual powers to the solution of questions of practical conduct. In higher matters I would suggest that he was guided by a simple religious faith. Certain problems were in principle soluble by human effort. To trouble the gods with these was lazy and stupid. But there would always be

---

[29] *Apology* 31c-d.
[30] *Ibid*.
[31] *Apology* 40a-c, and see Guthrie, *Socrates*, *op. cit.*, pp. 82–3. According to Xenophon, the voice or sign did intervene before the trial, by preventing him from preparing a defence in advance (Guthrie, *Socrates*, p. 83).

truths beyond the scope of human explanation, and for these one must trust the word of the gods, whether given in oracles or through other channels.[32]

Guthrie continues:

> There was no irony in the way he talked of his divine sign: he put himself unreservedly in the hands of what he sincerely believed to be an inspiration from heaven. He possessed the religious virtue of humility (which in others also has sometimes been taken for arrogance), and with it, despite his ceaseless questioning of everything in the human sphere, of unquestioning belief. There is nothing impossible or unprecedented in the union of a keen and penetrating insight in human affairs, and an unerring eye for humbug, with a simple religious piety. He cannot have laid such emphasis on the 'care' of the *psyche* as the real man, without believing that as it was both truly human and had some share in the divine nature, so also it was the lasting part of us, and that the treatment accorded it in this life would affect its nature and fortunes in the next.[33]

In short, Socrates believed that his mission was a spiritual or mystical one and that his life was linked to something that went beyond pure reason.[34] Above all things he had to be true to the transcendent source of his divine sign (even if it meant death).

An important difference between Socrates and Plato is that whereas Socrates, despite all his questioning of human affairs, was content to accept the spiritual reality as an article of simple faith, Plato felt the need to support it with reason and intellectual arguments.[35] In my language, Plato tried to intellectualize a spiritual experience. 'The Good' and 'the True', for example, thus substitutes for the *diamon*. Craving certainty and intolerant of ambiguity, he attempted to construct a philosophic system (encompassing both nature and the whole field of human life) that made, to him, rational sense of Socrates' experience.

Spiritual experience, philosophic system

In Plato's intellectual construct he made a fundamental distinction between the world of ultimate reality (the world of the perfect, changeless Forms) and the uncertain and illusory world of appearance. In Plato's philosophic system the world of the Forms was the only true

---

[32] Guthrie, *Socrates*, p. 163.
[33] Guthrie, *Socrates*, p. 163, quoting *Phaedo* 63c. (In contemporary understanding the word *psyche* is best translated as 'soul' or 'spiritual dimension'. Ed.)
[34] See Henri Bergson, *Two Sources of Morality and Religion*, Doubleday & Co., New York, 1954.
[35] *Cf.* Guthrie, *Socrates*, p. 163–4.

object of knowledge, as opposed to the world of appearance which yielded mere opinion or belief.

Further, only true philosophers could apprehend the Forms, and this only after a long and rigorous process of education. The world of the perfect Forms, which were independent of sensible things, was accessible only to a select few: the philosophers (literally 'lovers of wisdom'). Plato contrasted true philosophers with 'the lovers of sights and sounds' who dwelt not in the realm of knowledge but of mere opinion and belief (*doxa*). Plato believed that in an ideal society (that is, one that, in the world of appearance, most clearly corresponded to the world of the Forms) the few who have attained wisdom should rule, while the rest should do as they were told.

Plato strongly believed that the human race would never have rest from its troubles, and good government would be impossible, until either true and genuine philosophers gain political control or else those who are already governing states become, by some divine dispensation, real philosophers.

The notion of rule by the wise, and particularly by a philosopher king, is the central thesis of Plato's major work, the *Republic*, written in Plato's middle life.[36] How far this position is from Socratic ignorance is apparent. Further, Platonic epistomology is very different from the Socratic method of uncovering ignorance by constant questioning. Rather than knowledge being a process of discovery, Plato held to a theory of knowledge as recollection (or reminiscence). Plato's theory of reminiscence is most clearly explained by Cornford:

> Knowledge of the perfect Forms . . . is at all times present in the soul itself. The knowledge is there, but latent and unconscious. What is called 'learning' or the discovery of truth, is the recollection of this latent knowledge, raised to the level of consciousness. The soul is guided in the search by its own dim vision of a truth that is always present, needing only to be seen more clearly, and co-ordinated with other parts of the whole system of Truth.[37]

For Plato, his theory of knowledge is linked to an alleged *proof of immortality* – yet another example of his pursuit of certainty:

> Also if knowledge is at all times present to the soul, the soul must be immortal and independent of the body and its senses. It has seen all truth in some

---

[36] The three great dialogues of Plato's middle life, the *Phaedo*, *Symposium* and the *Republic*, were strongly influenced by the ideas of Pythagoras, the famous mathematician and mystic who founded at Croton, in southern Italy, a school of philosophy which united science and religion. See J. E. Raven, *op. cit.*, pp. 4–5, 66–7.
[37] See Cornford, *op. cit.*, pp. 71–2.

former state of existence before it came into the body. The truth has been forgotten, but it is stored in a memory from which it can be recovered. This memory is not what we commonly call the memory, not a register of the experience which flows in, during this bodily life, through the channels of sense. Its contents are impersonal, the same in all human beings, and they have never been extracted or distilled out of sensible experience.[38]

The whole point of Platonic education is by a variety of disciplines and means to uncover such latent knowledge. But Plato makes it manifestly clear that ultimate truths are accessible only to a few.

To facilitate the education of a true philosopher (essentially recruited from the guardian class) Plato founded the Academy – which was dedicated to scientific study based on the model of mathematics, and especially geometry. (We have noted that early in his life Socrates had shifted from an interest in natural science to a concern for the right ends for which humans ought to live.) Just as Platonic education was indicative of his pursuit after certainty, so too Plato's political philosophy was above all things devoted to order, stability and changelessness. The good society was static. Uncertainty and ambiguity he could not tolerate – hence his suggestion that artists and poets (sowers of discord and confusion) should be discouraged from his ideal republic. Most would in fact be banned.[39] (The only forms of poetry that would be allowed in the Platonic state are hymns to the gods and eulogies of good men. In the *Republic* (398a) Plato maintained that if a dramatic poet should attempt to visit the ideal state he should be sent back to the border; while in the *Laws* Plato proposed a detailed and rigorous system of censorship for the good of the state.[40]) Significantly Plato's other important political suggestions were all geared to establishing and maintaining unity and stability. For example, no private property or possessions among the 'guardians'; wives and children to be held in common; a strict hierarchical division of society between guardians, auxiliaries (soldiers) and the mass of the population who did as they were told.

To sustain social and political stability, Plato advocated that rulers disseminate the myth of the earthborn and the metals; that is, some people were by nature gold and therefore fit to rule (the guardians); some

---

[38] *Ibid.* See also Cornford, *Plato's Theory of Knowledge*, Routledge & Kegan Paul, London, 1935.
[39] See Guthrie, *Plato, The Man and his Dialogues: Earlier Period, op. cit.*, pp. 451-3, 545-53.
[40] See Iris Murdoch, *The Fire and the Sun: Why Plato Banished the Artists*, Clarendon Press, Oxford, 1977.

were silver (the auxiliaries); and some bronze and iron (the farmers and craftsmen).[41] The god who moulded men put these metals into different types of people. In general the distinction will persist, but since the metals are all closely related, golden parents may have a child alloyed with silver or bronze, or vice versa. If this happens the rulers must arrange a transfer between classes; in particular, if the 'guardians' detect signs of bronze or iron in their offspring they are to be immediately relegated to the farming and artisan class.[42] Plato, and the rulers of his ideal state, *know* that the myth is untrue (he does, however, believe that the classification symbolized by the metals corresponds to a difference in human nature [43]), but he advocates the use of 'the noble lie' for the good of the republic. It is a 'necessary falsehood' which is to be employed by the rulers to maintain order and stability. Under no circumstances could one imagine Socrates deliberately employing falsehood for reasons of state.

Unlike Socrates, who did not teach, the whole purpose of Plato's Academy was to *educate* and to *instruct*. In the Academy, Plato made the thorough and systematic study of exact mathematical science the foundation for all further philosophic instruction. Plato's ideal 'philosopher' receives an 'education' Socrates never had. In the final stage (that is, from the age of thirty to thirty-five) the philosopher studies arithmetic, plane geometry, solid geometry, astronomy and harmonics, before completing his course of study with the higher dialectics. After this long and arduous educational process the Guardians, who have been brought face to face with the Idea of the Good, the True, the Beautiful and the other perfect Forms, are forced to return to the people, and rule. This is a most unsocratic idea. Thus in the *Republic* the philosopher must be compelled to leave the Academy (and the contemplation of the ideal Forms) and return to the 'common' world in which Socrates, barefoot in the marketplace, was at home and asked questions all his life.[44] Plato's only attempt at putting into practice his educational theory with an actual ruler met with abject failure. In 367 B.C. when Plato had presided over the Academy for twenty years, at the request of an old friend and admirer, Dion of Syracuse, he attempted to instruct Dion's son-in-law, Dionysius II, the weak but impressionable young ruler of Syracuse, in

---

[41] See, for example, Alvin W. Gouldner, *Enter Plato*, Routledge & Kegan Paul, London, 1967, especially pp. 197–233.
[42] See Guthrie, *Plato, The Man and his Dialogues: Earlier Period, op. cit.*, pp. 462–4.
[43] *Ibid*, p. 462.
[44] See Meyerhoff, *op. cit.*, pp. 195–9.

the principles of good government and true philosophy. Plato's not inconsiderable attempts (one of his visits was for a period of twelve months) were quite without success.[45]

Plato's quest for certainty is the key to his attitude and approach to life and to philosophy, as the acceptance of ignorance and the awareness of the limitation of human reason is to Socrates. For Plato, true philosophy must be based on certainty and must, like mathematics, rest securely on foundations that are indubitable or infallible. Hence Plato's search for certain truths contained in the perfect and unchangeable Forms. When he attempted to construct his ideal republic, ideal in the sense that in the world of seeming and appearance it would be the one that most closely approximated the world of the Forms, the society he envisaged was fixed and unchangeable. Plato's desire for stability and order on earth is yet another manifestation of his yearning for certainty, as is his alleged 'proof' of the soul's immortality.

In stark contrast, Socrates' whole life (and philosophy) of constant questioning, and his ultimate reliance on a power or reality outside himself which he did not claim to categorize or understand, is clear testimony to the fact that to him there was no end to the existential project of pursuing the truth.

The search for self-knowledge, and for truth or truths, is interminable in human life; it is terminated only by death (or resignation). With regard to fundamental human concerns, with regard to the question of how we ought to live our lives, there is no final or absolute answer which reason can provide. Thus a 'Socratic' search for truth stresses human freedom and autonomy and places choice (and indeterminancy) in the forefront. Despite all the differences in society, culture and language, Socrates justifiably stands as a symbol for a person who places individual responsibility and service to God before power, status and physical survival, and before the demands of family, friends and the state.

Plato's dream of achieving certainty in life and philosophy signifies an absolutist yearning to escape human limitation, whereas Socrates' awareness and acceptance of his fundamental ignorance (despite all his powers of reason) affirms that which makes us human, rather than animal or divine, and at the same time makes place for the mystery that many still call 'God'.

---

[45] See A. E. Taylor, *The Mind of Plato*, University of Michigan Press, 1960, pp. 13, 16–17.

Plato and Confucius

Wu Teh Yao

Of Plato the man, little is known. He was born in 428–427 B.C. to one of the most distinguished families of Athens during the early years of the Peloponnesian War. He died at the ripe age of eighty or eighty-one in 348–347 B.C. As a young man he sat at the feet of Socrates, whose ideas, personality and death had a profound impact on Plato's own life and career. Instead of devoting his life to the pursuit of politics, perhaps as a legislator – a role that would have well suited him as a member of a family of prominent public figures in the Periclean Age – he chose to pursue philosophy. Socrates' death at the hands of the Athenian rulers in 399 B.C. forced Plato to the conclusion that the states and governments in existence then, without exception, were bad. In one of his letters he stated that: 'the human race will not see better days until either the stock of those who rightly and genuinely follow philosophy acquire political authority, or else the class who have political control be led by some dispensation of providence to become real philosophers.'[1]

In this letter one detects the germ of Plato's idea of the philosopher–king – an idea that was later developed in the *Republic*. Plato thought that rulers must be *educated* to be philosopher–kings. In his late twenties Plato had almost certainly conceived the idea of some kind of institution or school directed especially at the ruling class. Plato's famous Academy was actually founded when he was forty; the event was the turning point of his life. It was in this institution that Plato, as teacher and thinker, left a rich legacy for learning and made an imprint on Western culture and civilization that survives to this day.

The twenty years from the founding of the Academy until he was sixty were uneventful for Plato. One can imagine that besides his teaching

---

[1] Letter VII, quoted in George H. Sabine, *A History of Political Theory*, 3rd edition, Holt, Rinehart & Winston, New York, 1961, p. 37.

duties he was busy organizing and administering the Academy. The school attracted pupils from throughout the Hellenic world, and as far as is known it did not collect any tuition fees, although it might have had other ways of financing itself. To run such an institution would have been no easy task for any one. To have it running for forty years, under one continuous administration, was indeed a major achievement.

Little was recorded about Plato's teaching method. From his most famous and celebrated pupil, Aristotle, we know that Plato lectured without manuscripts or notes, on a wide range of topics, from mathematics to philosophy, music to gymnastics, and from education to politics. Plato placed great emphasis on the study of geometry. 'Let no one without geometry enter here' was inscribed over the portal of the Academy, where his lectures could have lasted for several hours, and the ensuring discussions continued for days. The marathon nature of the discourse in the *Republic* is an indication: the whole dialogue was supposed to have taken place in one session lasting late into the night.

At the age of sixty, Plato accepted the invitation of his friend of twenty years standing, Dion, to journey to Syracuse. Dion was the brother-in-law of Dionysius II, a man of thirty who had succeeded his father as ruler. Plato's mission was to educate him not so much to be a philosopher–king, but to be a good ruler who would make Syracuse strong in order to check the expanding power of Carthage, which had already reached Sicily. Plato's mission failed, because Dionysius II was not 'educable'. His early education had been neglected and given over to pleasures, ease of living and power. (Confucius would have passed judgement on Dionysius II as 'a piece of rotten wood that cannot be carved'.) Plato returned to Athens, but made another journey in 361-360 B.C. hoping to patch up the quarrel between Dionysius II and Dion whom he had exiled. This time his reception was less cordial, even hostile. Due to the mediation of Archytas of Tarentum, after complex negotiation, Plato was allowed to leave Syracuse and return to the Academy.

During his later years he wrote the *Statesman* and the *Laws*. Both these works were written after careful observation, and research into the actual political system of the times. Consequently they are more politically 'realistic' than the 'idealistic' but more daring thrust of, for example, the *Republic*. Throughout his life, Plato wrote thirty-six dialogues, and a number of other works such as the *Statesman* and the *Laws*. In most of his writing he did not use the first person, but rather attributed his words to Socrates.

Confucius was born in what is now the province of Shantung, in 551 B.C., about 125 years before Plato. He died at the age of seventy-two. Though of aristocratic descent, Confucius' family lineage, going back to the Shang dynasty of the fifteenth century B.C. is much less distinguished than that of Plato's. Confucius, a poor commoner, was forced to earn a living as a teacher, unlike Plato who had the advantages of wealth and family influence.

Confucius' comparatively low social status, but aristocratic descent, could have influenced his value judgements on politics and education. He did not have a high opinion of the aristocrats of his time, saying 'It is difficult to expect anything from men who stuff themselves with food the whole day, while never using their minds in any way at all. Even gamblers do something and to that degree are better than the idlers'.[2]

Unlike Plato, who had Socrates as a teacher, Confucius was largely self-taught. He was particularly interested to learn about old social institutions and customs of the Chou Dynasty, which lasted for nearly 900 years, and to study the political practices of its founder, the Duke of Chou. Often in his dreams Confucius met the Duke of Chou and thought of his ways of government. In this sense, the Duke of Chou was Confucius' spiritual teacher, as Socrates was Plato's intellectual guide.

Confucius married at the age of 19 and had a son named Li, the Carp, named after the fish given to him by a nobleman. Li's son, Tsze-sze, expanded on the teachings of his grandfather; *The Doctrine of the Mean*, one of the four Confucian classics, is attributed to him. The other three are the *Analects, The Great Learning* and *Mencius*. None were directly written by Confucius himself, but were compiled by his followers and disciples. Tsze-sze's work, put in writing, was passed on to Mencius so that the teachings of Confucius would not be lost or misquoted or misinterpreted by oral presentation.

Both Confucius and Plato harboured aspirations for public office. Such ambitions were natural for intellectuals of the time, in China as well as in Athens. As mentioned above, Plato initially wanted to be a legislator or administrator but gave up the idea in disgust after seeing his beloved teacher Socrates put to death by the 'politicians'. Plato himself became a teacher. Confucius, however, held public office in various capacities. For four years from 500 B.C., when he was about fifty years old, to 496 B.C. he was a magistrate of the town of Chung-tu, assistant superintendent of

[2] *Analects*, Book XVII, chapter 22. See James Legge, *The Chinese Classics*, Vol 1: *Confucian Analects, The Great Learning, The Doctrine of the Mean*, Hong Kong University Press, 1970 (first published Clarendon Press, Oxford, 1893).

works and then minister of crime in his native state of Lu. History records that he performed well, but his sovereign, the ruler of Lu, a man given to the pleasures of life, paid heed neither to his work nor to the sage's advice. Thereupon Confucius embarked on fourteen weary and sometimes harzardous years of travelling to the neighbouring states, trying to convince the rulers to govern in accordance with principles based on human values and virtue rather than on power and force of arms. At a time when power and intrigue were the prevalent practices, none of the rulers listened to him or took his words seriously. Disappointed, he returned to Lu. As recorded in the *Analects*, a stranger confronted his disciples and said, 'The world has been long without principles of truth and right; Heaven is going to use your Master as a bell with its wooden tongue.'[3] With these travels into neighbouring states, the 'political' life of Confucius came to an end. He was then in his late sixties. (Plato's political life ended when he was in his early sixties after two visits to Syracuse. Both Plato and Confucius were 'political failures' if judged by the standard of the times). Confucius returned to Lu, where in the last years of his life, he taught, selected and arranged ancient poetry, studied the *Book of Changes*, and wrote the *Chun Chiu*, known as *Spring and Autumn Annals*, the only major work directly attributed to him; unlike Plato, Confucius wrote very little. However, his career as a teacher was as long as that of his Western counterpart.

Although Confucius accepted tuition fees, he never refused to give anybody instruction, even though the payment might be a piece of meat or fish. In education, as Confucius saw it, there should be no distinction of class. All could become his students if they met certain standards of academic excellence; his admission standards were based on quality of mind and performance, not on birth and wealth. This was a revolutionary educational concept in the China of the sixth century B.C., when the haughty and the powerful ruled. Confucius' democratic concept of education provided the poorest farm boy with the social mobility to move upwards to become, as some have, ministers or prime ministers of China, and the Confucian educational tradition has persisted to this day. Plato would have subscribed to such an idea, though he might have excluded the slaves of Athens because, by custom, slaves did not participate in the process of government and politics; nor were they admitted into institutions of higher learning.

Unlike Plato, Confucius did not establish an academy. He taught

---

[3] *Analects*, Book III, chapter 24. All translations from the Confucian classics are from Legge, *op. cit.*

whenever and wherever he could, although his house served often as a school. Moreover as far as is known, he never gave a public lecture, but rather talked to small groups. Like Plato, Confucius was not known to use notes and his talks covered a wide range of topics similar to those of Plato's – with the notable exception of geometry.

Plato's teaching method was primarily the technique of 'dialogue' developed by Socrates. No full description of Confucius' teaching method is available, but if the *Analects* are any guide, one can safely assert that Confucius did not entirely use the lecture method, nor did he insist on memorizing by rote. The *Analects* in fact contain questions and answers from both teacher and students. The challenges and responses are not dialogues in the Platonic sense of the word, but mini-dialogues, very typical of the Chinese love of brevity. Here is one example:

> Tse Kung [a disciple] asked about government. The Master said, 'The requisites of government are that there be sufficiency of food, sufficiency of military equipment, and the confidence of the people in the rulers.' Tse Kung said, 'If it cannot be helped, and one of these must be dispensed with, which of the three must be foregone first?' 'The military equipment,' said the Master. Tse Kung again asked, 'If it cannot be helped, and one of the remaining two must be dispensed with, which of them should be foregone?' The Master said, 'Part with the food. From of old, death has been the lot of all men; but if the people have no faith in their rulers, there is no standing for the State.'[4]

Almost any incident could be used by Confucius as subject matter for a lesson: On the way home, after escaping from the hands of some assailants,

> Confucius passed a house where he had formerly lodged, and finding the master was dead, and the funeral ceremonies going on, he went in to offer condolences. When he came out, he told Tse Kung to take the outside horses from his carriage, and give them as a contribution to the expenses of the occasion. 'You never did such a thing', Tse Kung remonstrated, 'at the funeral of any of your disciples; is it not too great a gift on this occasion for the death of an old host?' 'When I went in,' replied Confucius, 'my presence brought a burst of grief from the chief mourner, and I joined him with my tears. *I dislike the thought of my tears not being followed by anything.*'[5]

On another occasion when his disciples reported that a fire had taken place at a stable for horses, the first question he asked was whether anybody was hurt. Confucius used this incident to stress the point that human life is of higher value than animal life or material losses.

[4] *Analects*, Book XII, Yen Yüan, chapter 7.
[5] Legge, *The Chinese Classics*, Vol. 1, chapter 5, 'The Life of Confucius', p. 77.

Confucius chose his teaching material from first-hand experience and from actual situations in the courts of rulers as well as from stalls on the roadside. During one of his travels he and his pupils were short of provisions and therefore very hungry. One of his outspoken pupils, Tse Lu, asked whether a *Tsun Tse*, a 'superior gentleman', had to endure in such a way. The reply was: the 'superior gentleman' might have to endure want, but the *Siao Ren*, the 'inferior small man', when in want gave way to unbridled license. The distress continued for seven days, but Confucius retained his equanimity. He even played his flute.[6] In this reported incident, Confucius not only taught a precept but also set an example.

As seen from their teachings, both Plato and Confucius were men of the highest moral principles. To Confucius, if rank, honour and wealth were not properly acquired, they were not to be accepted. He even advised his students not to aspire to public office if the state was in disorder. Plato gave up practical politics altogether because of the corrupt use of power by the governing body of officials. This does not mean that Confucius and Plato were not interested in society and government. Both men wanted to see well-governed states and both placed faith in education as the most enduring way to change man, society and government.

On the other hand, they differed in many important respects. Confucius loved poetry and undertook the task of selecting from an array of 3 000 ancient poems, some 306 which he set to music. Plato was critical of poets, including Homer. He thought poetry that aroused the emotions of men and portrayed the indecent behaviour of gods and goddesses was not suitable for the education of guardians. Confucius was basically a philosopher concerned with man and his relationship with his fellow men, while Plato aspired to be a scientist. To this difference can be ascribed the difference in values between the two civilizations – one emphasizing the study of science and therefore the growth and development of science and technology, the other emphasizing the understanding of man.

We know more of Confucius the man than of Plato. Besides the short and concise texts of the Confucian classics from which people quote abundantly, the Chinese know Confucius as a man who liked ginger, who did not indulge in excesses in eating, and who never allowed himself to get drunk. His dress, appearance and deportment were recorded in detail

[6] *Op. cit.*

in Book X of the *Analects*. His manner of speech and behaviour was also recorded in considerable detail:

> Confucius, in his village, looked simple and sincere, and as if he were not able to speak. When he was in the ancestors' temple or in the court, he spoke minutely on every point cautiously. When he was waiting at court, in speaking with great officers of the lower grade he did so blandly, but precisely. When the ruler was present, his manner displayed respectful uneasiness; it was grave but self-possessed . . . When he saw anyone in mourning dress, though it might be an acquaintance, he would change countenance . . .[7]

There are many other recordings of Confucius' reactions to various situations including the way he sat and ate at the dining table. These apparently trivial matters have had a tremendous impact upon the manner of behaviour of the Chinese for more than two thousand years. The moderation in drinking, the use of ginger in cooking and the way guests and hosts sit at a dining table are but a few examples which reflect the influence of the sage. These matters must also be read against the background of Confucius' teaching of *Li*, which for social purposes is a code of manners or etiquette for guiding the conduct of the people. To say a man is without manners to a non-Chinese is nothing but a slight rebuke. To say to a Chinese of old China that he was without *Li* was putting him to shame. It was an insult; it was like calling him a barbarian.

When Confucius lived during the sixth century B.C., the practices of *Li* as a code of conduct for guiding the whole nation had existed for centuries, as had the system of government with the emperor as head of the 'big family' which we now call nation or state. The family as a fundamental unit of society had also existed since time immemorial. But there were varying factions within China, and in Confucius' time there was neither political unity nor administrative centrality. The fabric of social solidarity was also shattered. Worse still, Confucius maintained that moral decay was eating into every aspect of society. It was a period of every man for himself: power and gain were the motivation of the rulers, and men switched their loyalties to serve the highest bidders. No one was to be trusted and flattery was the prevalent social practice. It was a period of great social and political disorder, and like other thoughtful and concerned individuals of his time, Confucius was searching for a way to bring order to society so that man could live in harmony with himself and in peace with his political and social environment.

---

[7] Quoted in Legge, *op.cit.*, p. 89.

Like the China of Confucius' time, Plato's Athens had inherited some influences of older civilizations, but unlike China, which was undergoing a period of decadence when Confucius appeared, Athens at Plato's birth was at the height of its glory as the cultural centre of Greek civilization. However, Athens was defeated in the Peloponnesian War. With this defeat the power of Athens declined. But even before this, Athens, the political, social, economic and educational model of the time, was already showing signs of decay. Men were expressing doubts about almost anything that had to do with human relationships. Good behaviour, it was argued, was dictated by selfish motives and for selfish ends. Some even said (as did Glaucon and Thrasymachus in the *Republic*), that doing wrong was not immoral and was certainly advantageous. And if one did something wrong, it would be better for a man not to be caught and punished. The worst thing would be if he were wronged and had no power or revenge. Revenge – an eye for an eye, a tooth for a tooth – was the standard of justice. Justice, argued sophisticated men of the time, was for the strong, manipulated by the strong, and dispensed by the strong.

These prevailing ideas, together with the unjust execution of Socrates, stirred Plato's imagination to create a form of government in which justice could prevail over injustice so that the citizens of the state could live a harmonious life.

Neither Confucius nor Plato could entirely escape the political realities of his time. Confucius spoke of 'all under heaven' when he referred to the Chinese political and social structure; this is understandable because China had always been an immense political entity or empire. Plato, in the geographical environment of Greece, could not have conceived of a polity much larger than a city state. According to Plato, an ideal state would be composed of 5040 citizens, with slaves and aliens doing the daily manual work. The idea of a classical Greek democracy was based on direct participation in some form, however minor, by all genuine citizens; slaves and aliens were excluded. This participating role, basic to the idea of Athenian democracy, was expressed by Pericles who said, 'An Athenian citizen does not neglect the state because he takes care of his own household, and even those of us who are engaged in business have a very fair idea of politics. We alone regard a man who takes no interest in public affairs, not as a harmless, but as a useless character; and if few of us are originators we are sound judges of policy.'[8] However, could such a

---

[8] Quoted in *Sabine, op. cit.*, p. 14.

democratic system work if the state were a vast one with hundreds of thousands of inhabitants like the China of Confucius' time? Confucius had to look at the problems of politics both quantitatively and qualitatively, whereas Plato was more concerned with only the qualitative aspect of government.

It is interesting to note that in his concern to create a polity in which man could live in harmony with his fellow man, neither thinker advocated revolution, although many of their ideas were revolutionary in the context of their time. Confucius accepted the principle of the Mandate of Heaven as legitimating a ruler. If the Mandate is withdrawn – for example, when the country is badly administered – only then is a change justified. Such a change can be accomplished only by force of arms, as no ruler wanted to give up the Mandate. Every ruler claimed to have the Mandate of Heaven to continue his rule, however bad he might be in the eyes of the people. Changing the Mandate was a very difficult task. Confucius did not advocate the overthrow of a government by force but advised his pupils to work for a good government and refrain from participation in public life when the government was bad.

Like Confucius, Plato did not advocate the use of force to overthrow the existing political systems – the so-called 'democratic' government which had executed Socrates. Instead he formulated an ideal republic, still the same size as a city state, but with a different structure and content. In this sense, his approach was revolutionary; in this sense, also, the *Republic* is the most comprehensive and revolutionary political treatise in the history of political thought, and the inspiration of all subsequent political utopias.

In the opening chapters of the *Republic*, Plato, through the mouth of Socrates, champions justice against the prevailing belief that injustice was the more powerful force in society and that those who used unjust means obtained and kept power and influence. As though directly pointing his finger at the rulers of the time, Plato laid down his fundamental principle of government: 'the best should rule'. But who is the best? This leads to Plato's most daring and revolutionary thought: the concept of a philosopher–king who has the wisdom and the knowledge to govern a state. But how is a man to become a philosopher–king, or 'guardian' as Plato called him? By a rigorous process of education, was Plato's answer. Moreover, the guardians' children should be brought up in a community practising common ownership and sharing so that private ownership, which encouraged selfishness, would be abolished. Where would the guardians come from? Plato did not answer the question, at least not directly in the *Republic*. But in a state where the philosopher–king ruled, there was certainly no place for the kind of 'democracy' like that prevailing at Athens. Democracy, in Plato's mind, was not the best form of government. Only the talented few should rule.

Confucius did not write a treatise like the *Republic* and his political ideas recorded in the *Analects* were set down by his students and later propounded by them in *The Great Learning* and the *Doctrine of the Mean*. These ideas were less systematic than Plato's, though were quite revolutionary in the context of his time. Confucius stressed loyalty as a desirable political virtue, because in China at the time there was practically none; ministers were murdering their sovereigns. He advocated government by the virtuous qualities of a ruler because the rulers of his time were morally bad; he championed the government of humane consideration because all rulers were only interested in power and gain, sometimes using torture to achieve their own ends. Unlike Plato, who went from one extreme to another (as reflected in the 'idealistic' *Republic* which was written in his early manhood and the 'realistic' *Laws* which was written in old age), Confucius adopted the doctrine of the mean or of moderation even in regard to politics. Instead of creating a philosopher–king to be the ruler, he stated that his ideal rulers were the Emperors Yao, Shun and Yu of antiquity. These emperors were said to be men of great virtue and wisdom, who reigned and did not rule. They all had the Mandate of Heaven, and thereby also possessed the trust of the people. By extolling the virtues of the great rulers of antiquity, Confucius was suggesting that the current Chinese rulers should emulate them.

Both Confucius and Plato paid a great deal of attention to education as a means to bring about the kind of polity they wanted. Because of this primary emphasis and the importance attached to it, the *Analects* and the *Republic* can be regarded as treatises on education. Both are intended to educate men, with the *Republic* emphasizing educating the rulers, and with the *Analects* stressing the education of the ordinary individual in how to behave. Confucius believed that in education there should be no distinction of class, and when he was asked what to do when a state was rich and had many people, his answer was, 'educate them'. One can say that Confucius was one of the early teachers of mankind who advocated democracy in education.

When Plato thought of the rulers for his own utopia described in the *Republic*, he also first thought of education.

He wrote:

> If our citizens are well educated, and grow into sensible men, they will easily see their way through all these [illusions] . . . For good nurture and education implant good constitutions, and these good constitutions taking root in a good education improve more and more, and this improvement affects the breed in man as in other animals.[9]

Both Confucius and Plato believed that education could change human behaviour. 'In the beginning', Confucius said, 'human nature is about the same. It is the environment [social] that makes the difference.'[10] Education can change people from being small and mean to becoming superior or even saintly.

In their approaches to the realization of a republic, Plato and Confucius have similar as well as dissimilar ideas. There is, however, one fundamental difference in approach between the two thinkers: When Plato set out to construct his republic, he came to the conclusion that in order to understand the individual, one has to understand the nature of the state first, because the state is the larger of the two. To understand the nature of justice affecting individuals, one has to understand justice as dispensed by the state – to start with the greater and proceed to the lesser. The following passage illustrates the point:

> Justice, which is the subject of our enquiry, is, as you know, spoken of as the virtue of an individual, and sometimes as the virtue of a state. And is not a state larger than an individual? Then in the larger, the quantity of justice is likely to be the larger and more easily discernible. I propose therefore that we enquire into the nature of justice and injustice, first as they appear in the state, and secondly in the individual, proceeding from the greater to the lesser and comparing them.[11]

Plato went on to 'construct' a state, starting with needs and division of labour and the selection and education of the guardians or philosopher-kings.

Confucius adopted exactly the opposite approach. He could not accept the idea that by knowing and understanding the state, one would know and understand the individual. To him, the state was an abstract entity, too far above the individual for him to perceive it. On the contrary, Confucius' idea was that if one knows and understands the individual, and individuals make a state, one therefore understands the nature of a state, which reflects the collective nature of individuals. To Confucius,

---

[9] Plato, *Republic*, eds B. Jowett and L. Campbell, Arno Press, New York, 1974, pp. 121 and 294.
[10] *Analects*, Book XVII, Yang Ho, chapter 2.
[11] Plato, *Republic*, *op. cit.*, pp. 51-2.

good government starts from a good individual person, and the cultivation of the individual person, regardless of rank or status, is the most important social as well as political value. Therefore to understand the state, one has to proceed from the 'lesser to the greater'. Confucius starts with the individual, then the family, then the nation, and then the world. This is well illustrated by these extracts from *The Great Learning*:

> The ancients who wished to illustrate illustrious virtue throughout the kingdom, first ordered well their own states. Wishing to order well their states, they first regulated their families. Wishing to regulate their families, they first cultivated their persons. Wishing to cultivate their persons, they first rectified their hearts.
>
> Things being investigated, knowledge became complete. Their knowledge being complete, their thoughts were sincere. Their thoughts being sincere, their hearts were then rectified. Their persons being cultivated, their families were regulated. Their families being regulated, their states were rightly governed. Their states being rightly governed, the whole kingdom was made tranquil and happy.
>
> From the Son of Heaven down to the mass of the people, all must consider the cultivation of the person the root of everything besides.[12]

From such a process of reasoning, Confucius attempted to construct his idea of an ideal state, a commonwealth, a 'republic'.

While environmental factors had a major influence upon the thought of Confucius and Plato, it is nevertheless difficult to explain convincingly why their fundamental approach differed so radically. Confucius' idea was that all systems should begin with people, whereas Plato's idea was to build a system first and see where people could fit into it, and who should be selected and educated to be the guardians. (It is important to realize that various schools of thought existed in Athens at that time, as they did in China in Confucius' time. In Athens there was Isocrates*, who had a school of his own, teaching young men to become orators in order to win political office. In China there was Lao-tze, a slightly older contemporary of Confucius, propounding a different philosophy and approach for men to live in contentment as a means to achieve peace of mind and human happiness.)

Confucius emphasized the rule of and by man as the fundamental theory of politics. He accepted the idea that the ruler, the emperor, was chosen by heaven and thus had the Mandate. He could therefore be removed only by heaven, the supernatural force governing the affairs of

---

[12] The English translation is from Legge, *op. cit.*, p.355ff.
* Isocrates, who was some years older than Plato, was head of a rival school founded before Plato's Academy. (Ed.).

man and nations. It was therefore necessary to educate the head of state to be a good ruler. For instance, in politics, if the ruler is upright, who dares not be upright? If the ruler sets examples by devotion and hard work, his countrymen will try to emulate him; if he governs by means of virtue, his government may be compared to the north polar star, which keeps its place while all the stars turn towards it.[13] This emphasis on the rule of and by man has been a major characteristic of the theory of government in East Asia ever since.

In the West, ever since Plato's time, government has proceeded from the 'greater to the lesser', from the state to the individual, from the 'larger justice' of the state to the 'lesser justice' of the individual. The West has emphasized systems of government such as that to be formed in accordance with a constitution or charter of some kind. This emphasis on the system or the rule of law above the rule of man is best exemplified by the Constitution of the United States of America. In this constitution the executive power of government is checked and balanced by the powers of the legislative and the judiciary. This principle of restraining the power of the ruler has been behind the development and practice of all Western and Western-influenced forms of government. Theoretically, the governing power comes from and lodges with the people.

In the East Asian political tradition, as stated above, the right or legitimacy of the ruler as sovereign comes from heaven. But heaven's choice of ruler must also be pleasing to the people, and what is pleasing to the people is also acceptable to heaven. Therefore the Mandate of Heaven and the wish of the people are one. However, such a theory of government carries with it an inherent weakness. Who is to restrain the actions of the sovereign ruler, as there is no constitutional system that will restrain or guide his conduct? Such a system of government can easily give rise to authoritarian rulers, as has happened in China's history. Again, if the emperor is wicked, how shall the people get rid of him? Revolution or violent dynastic change have been the answer. In practice, of course, wicked emperors were few, bad emperors were many and incompetent emperors were perhaps most common. However, like all systems of government, there were certain built-in restraints on the ruler, such as custom and tradition, which acted as counter-balances to the theoretically unlimited power of an emperor. Other restraining forces were elder statesmen, and accountability to heaven, which could also temper the inclinations of the sovereign toward authoritarianism; in as

---

[13] *Analects*, Book II, chapter 1; Book XII, chapter 14; and Book XIII, chapter 1.

much as if he provokes the people to revolt, and they do so successfully, the Mandate is withdrawn. It must also be remembered that the constitutional and legal restraints imposed on the ruler in the West have not prevented some rulers from becoming authoritarian or even totalitarian.

It is difficult to compare the 'republics' conceived by Plato and Confucius. Plato's *Republic* defies classification – it combines politics, economics, education, eugenics and sociology. In the same way one has to comb through the *Analects, the Great Learning* and *The Doctrine of the Mean* in order to sieve out the political ideas of Confucius and arrange them into a system of thought, and from it construct a polity, a republic.

However, it is possible to single out three areas of thought which are basic to the foundation, structure and nature of the 'republics' postulated by the two thinkers. To both, ethics are above politics, and the practice of politics consist of doing what is right and just, not what is possible and expedient. To Confucius the duty of somebody involved in politics is to be morally upright, and to do what is righteous. Virtue is the highest qualification expected of the ruler. Confucius' 'republic' can be regarded as an ethical–moral state, ruled by a person of the highest moral character and ethical ideals. Thus he compared a government by virtue to the polar star which acts as an example and a guide.

To Plato, also, ethics are above politics. His republic was set up in search of justice. The inquiry that prompted him to write the *Republic* was: 'Which is more profitable, to be just and act justly and practise virtue, whether seen or unseen of gods and men, or to be unjust and act unjustly, if only unpunished and unreformed?'[14] Who is happier, the man who obtains his wealth and enjoys his high position by acquiring them through unjust means, or he who does not possess great wealth nor hold a public office of importance but who has always acted justly? The answer given in the *Republic* is that the latter is a happier man. Furthermore, it was Plato's conviction that it is better to suffer injustice than to do injustice. And the final counsel is that 'we hold fast ever to the heavenly way and follow after justice and virtue always.'[15] Such expressions are certainly ethical in nature, and can also be regarded as moral.

Though to both men ethics are above politics, in structure their ideas differ radically. When Confucius was asked about government he

---

[14] Plato, *Republic, op.cit.*, Book 4, p. 150.
[15] *Ibid.*, Book 10, p. 367.

replied, 'The prince is prince, and the minister is minister; when the father is father, and the son is son.'[16] In other words, a ruler should behave like a ruler, a minister like a minister, a father like a father and a son should behave like a son. He also remarked, 'A prince [ruler] should employ his ministers according to the rules of propriety [*Li*]; ministers should serve their prince with faithfulness [loyalty].'[17] Confucius thus laid down the concept of status–obligation going down all the way to the fundamental unit of society, the family. In the family, the status–obligation concept is upheld and propagated by the concept of filial piety. This value concept penetrates deep into the heart of society and status–obligation is still a social and political value-concept in the East.

Plato said that the state originated from varying needs of humanity in regard to food, clothing and shelter. When providers, partners and helpers are gathered together in one habitation, the body of inhabitants is termed a state; its citizens include husbandmen, builders, weavers, carpenters, smiths, shoemakers, herdsmen, merchants, retailers, warriors and, finally, the guardians, whose sole duties are to rule and administer the state. From a simple organization to meet the needs of its citizens, the state becomes complex because of new needs and more refined tastes and wants. Because it is formed on the basis of the division of labour and specialization of functions, it conveys a horizontal concept that every profession is as important as every other because all professions are needed to make a society functional. This horizontal concept, different from that of status–obligation can be regarded as basic to the development of democratic states in the West. This together with the emphasis on institutions over the importance of man, gave rise to the contract–right agreement between the ruler and the ruled; whereas the tradition of a 'social contract' does not apply in the East.

The two 'republics' differ in nature because of their structural differences. The state or republic envisaged by Plato must expand because of the new needs and demands of its citizens. He said: 'Then we must enlarge our borders . . . Then a slice of our neighbour's land will be wanted by us for pasture and tillage, and they will want a slice of ours.'[18] War ensues, and warriors are needed to protect the nation and to go to war. Plato's republic is a dynamic, expanding state at odds and at war with neighbouring states all the time, and by discussing the necessity of war, he was reflecting the political environment of the ancient Greek city

---

[16] *Analects*, Book XII, chapter 11.
[17] *Analects*, Book III, chapter 19.
[18] *Plato's Republic, op. cit.*, Book 2, p. 58.

states. Confucius also grew up at a time of instability, but all wars were fought by the Chou vassals. Therefore, China was basically 'unified' in the name of Chou, a situation quite different from that of Greece in the fifth century B.C. Confucius was interested in preserving the imperial order of Chou, and therefore his state or republic was static in nature and he opposed the expansion of existing 'states'. To him it was not the size of the state that mattered, but the virtue and righteousness of its ruler.

There is another difference in the nature of the two 'republics'. Plato was very concerned with the broad problems and understanding of politics, as perceived and practised by the Greeks of his time. Politics was the overriding concern of all qualified citizens and concern for participation in politics was a noble pursuit. Plato was less concerned with the methods of actual government, although in the *Republic* some principles are touched upon. For instance, he wrote a great deal about the principles and subjects that were to form the guardian's education, but did not include instructions on how actually to govern a state. In other words, Plato was more interested in the theory of politics than the practicalities of government. He also discussed the growth, change and decline of the various forms of government – for example, how timocracy (the government of honour) arises out of aristocracy (government of the best). Then follows oligarchy, a form of government which teems with evils, then democracy which naturally follows oligarchy although it is very different. Lastly comes tyranny which is the worst form of government.

The *Republic* also provides penetrating insights into human nature and human institutions. Plato described oligarchy or government by the elite as 'a government resting on a valuation of property, in which the rich have power and the poor man is deprived of it. And then one, seeing another growing rich, seeks to rival him, and thus the great mass of the citizens become lovers of money. And so they grow richer and richer, and the more they think of making a fortune, the less they think of virtue . . . And so at last . . . men become lovers of trade and money; they honour and look up to the rich man, and make a ruler of him, and dishonour the poor man.'[19] If this state of affairs is prolonged, there will be more poor than rich, and the time will come for a change by revolution, when the majority poor will wrest power from the rich few. Democracy then becomes the form of government. Such a state will be full of freedom and frankness, said Plato. 'A man may say and do what he likes . . . Then in

[19] *Ibid.*, Book 8, pp. 277–8.

this kind of state there will be the greatest variety of human natures . . . just as women and children think a variety of colours to be all things most charming, so there are many men to whom this state, which is spangled with the manners and characters of mankind, will appear to be the fairest of states . . . These and other kindred characteristics are proper to democracy, which is a charming form of government, full of variety and disorder, and dispensing a sort of equality of equals and unequals alike.'[20]

To Plato, freedom in a democracy ends in anarchy. 'Freedom as they tell you in a democracy is the glory of the state . . . But the excess of liberty, whether in states or individuals, seems only to pass into excess of slavery.'[21] Since excessive increase of anything often causes a reaction in the opposite direction, another form of government will step in to restrict the unlimited freedom that the people are accustomed to enjoy. This he calls tyranny, the worst form of government. Of a tyrant, Plato says: 'At first, in the early days of his power, he is full of smiles and he salutes every one whom he meets; . . . liberating debtors, and distributing land to the people and his followers, and wanting to be kind and good to everyone! But when he has disposed of foreign enemies by conquest or treaty, and there is nothing to fear from them, then he is always stirring up some war or other, in order that the people may require a leader . . . And the tyrant, if he means to rule, must get rid of them [his bravest and boldest followers].'[22] In other words, he must put his friends to death and use slaves (who were looked down upon as socially undesirables) as bodyguards. But the tyrant is not free. 'He who is the real tyrant, whatever men may think, is the real slave . . . He has desires which he is utterly unable to satisfy . . . Moreover . . . he grows worse from having power: he becomes and is of necessity more jealous, more faithless, more unjust, more friendless, more impious than he was at first; he is the purveyor and cherisher of every sort of vice, and the consequence is that he is supremely miserable . . .'[23] What Plato said twenty-four centuries ago is still applicable today.

To Confucius, the problem of politics was a simple one. He knew of only one system, the rule of an emperor who had the Mandate of Heaven. There were tyrannical rulers and bad ministers; the form of government under which they functioned had been the same for centuries. When

[20] *Ibid.*, Book 8, pp. 286–8.
[21] *Ibid.*, Book 8, pp. 293–5.
[22] *Ibid.*, Book 8, pp. 299–300.
[23] *Ibid.*, Book 8, pp. 315–6.

talking about political systems, Confucius' idea was to follow the customs and traditions of the Hsia, Shang and Chou dynasties. He never claimed to be an originator, but a 'synthesizer' of past cultural traditions. He concentrated more fully on government and administration than on political theorizing, although in his mind theory could not be separated from practice.

What then are Confucius' ideas on government and administration? The heart of his ethical–political thinking is the practice of *Ren*, the human-hearted qualities – especially of compassion, which should pervade all areas of administration from the emperor to his ministers and down to the magistrates at the county level. The first requirement of a ruler is to be a man of human-heartedness.[24] Then he must be just and impartial, working hard at all times for the public good. He must also be trustworthy, because without trust his reign will not last, and his ministers will seek crooked ways to administer his government. Above all else, a ruler must love his people and be an example to them in every way. For it was Confucius' belief that 'When a ruler's personal conduct is correct, his government is effective without the issuing of orders. If his personal conduct is not correct, he may issue orders, but they will not be followed.'[25]

The general policy of all rulers should be guided by nine standard rules, namely: the cultivation of their own characters; the honouring of men of virtue and talents; affection towards their relatives; respect towards their great ministers; kind and considerate treatment of the whole body of officers; dealing with the mass of people as they would their own children; encouraging all types of artisans; indulgently treating foreigners; and kindly cherishing the princes and dukes. It follows then that in the cultivation of the ruler's character, a way of life is established. By honouring men of virtue and talents, he is less likely to err in judgement. By showing affection to his relatives, there is no grumbling or resentment among his uncles and brothers. By respecting the great ministers, he is kept from errors in the practice of government. By kind and considerate treatment of the whole body of officers, he leads them to make the most grateful return for his courtesies. By dealing with the mass of the people as his own children, he leads them to encourage one another in doing what is good. By encouraging all types of artisans, his resources for expenditure are rendered ample. By indulgent treatment of men from a distance, others will like to come and stay in his country. And by his

[24] *The Great Learning*, chapter 3.
[25] *Analects*, Book XIII, chapter 6.

kindly cherishing the princes and dukes, the whole kingdom is brought to revere him.[26] About particular guidelines of administration, Confucius had this to say – let the administrator honour the five excellent things and banish the four bad things. The five excellent things are: when the person in authority is beneficent without great expenditure; when he lays proper tasks on the people without their repining; when he pursues what he desires without being covetous, securing benevolently what he deserves; when he maintains dignified ease without being vain, not indicating disrespect to anyone; and when he is majestic without being fierce, always maintaining an air of dignity in all his acts and appearance. In contrast, the four bad things are: putting the people to death without giving them any education – this is called cruelty; suddenly requiring the people to do a full work-load, without giving them warning – this is called oppression; issuing orders as if they are not urgent at first and later insisting on them with severity – this is called injury; generally, when giving pay, or rewards to men, being niggardly – this is called acting the part of a mean bureaucrat.[27] In administration, Confucius praised the dignified air and respectfulness of the administrator as excellent qualities. This is, of course, in line with his philosophy of education and government that the behaviour of the individual person in action and in words, in outward appearance and in the heart, must not be separate but be one in harmonious unity.

Confucius' ideal ruler is a different individual from Plato's philosopher–king. He would be a man of great virtue, full of dignity and warmth of heart, but nevertheless wise in handling men and dealing with affairs of state. However, his wisdom will not show. Plato's guardian or ruler is a supremely wise man who also has virtuous qualities, but his wisdom is felt by those who come in contact with him and reaches all branches of government and all parts of the republic. Confucius' ruler reigns, whereas Plato's ruler rules. Confucius' ruler would be a family man, a model father and devoted husband. Plato's ruler would live in community with his fellow guardians, sharing wives and children. Both rulers will be devoid of selfishness and both 'republics' will be governed by devoted individuals, that of Confucius, chosen by heaven from the best among men, and that of Plato chosen by men from the best of men. Confucius in the tradition of the Chinese sought after virtue, whereas Plato in the tradition of the Greeks sought after wisdom.

[26] See *The Doctrine of the Mean*, chapter 20.
[27] *Analects*, Book XX, chapters 2 and 3.

In his old age, Confucius is said to have expressed his idea of his republic in the following words:

> When the Great Way prevails the world is a commonwealth; men of talent are selected for office; sincerity is emphasized and friendship is cultivated among men. Men do not love only their own parents, nor do they treat as children only their own children. A competent provision is secured for the aged till their death, employment for the able-bodied, and a means of upbringing for the young. Kindness and compassion are shown to widows, orphans, childless men and those disabled by disease, so they all have the wherewithal for support. Men have their proper work, and women have their homes. Man hates to see the wealth of natural resources undeveloped, but does not hoard wealth just for his use. Man hates not to exert himself, but does not exert himself only for his own benefit. Thus schemings are repressed and find no development. Robbers, filchers and rebellious traitors do not show themselves, and hence the outer doors are left open. This is called the Great Unity (of mankind).[28]

In 2500 years, the republics of two of the world's greatest minds have never come into existence. The rule of perfect virtue has never appeared in China, although virtuous rulers have ruled. The philosopher–king has yet to exist, although many wise kings have ruled over kingdoms and empires. Complete justice and a completely harmonious order have never prevailed, but just and harmonious societies of various degrees have from time to time appeared in the history of mankind. A fair sharing of resources and wealth has never been achieved, but attempts are being made to narrow the gap between individuals as well as between nations. Only men of talent should be selected for public office; this ideal has never been achieved, but the examination system, imperfect as it is, has been devised for the purpose.

Imperfect is the republic created by man; its imperfections are those of man himself. In view of the imperfections and weaknesses that are the maladies of man, he has to settle for the second best, the third best and even the fourth best form of government to anchor his ship of state. These 'bests' were realistically summed up by Confucius:

> Now the Great Way does not show itself, man's heart centres in the family. Man only regards his relatives as relatives, his children only as his children and accumulates wealth for his own use. Man builds walls and moats to protect his city . . . creates institutions for the buying and protection of property, praises the brave and claims achievements and success for himself. Therefore schemings and intrigues arise and wars have their beginnings.[29]

[28] *Li Chi*, (The Record of Rites), chapter 21.
[29] *Ibid*.

And there is no end in sight. The kind of society that existed more than 2500 years ago, when those great thinkers, Confucius of the East and Plato of the West, constructed their noble republics, is still with us–there is the modern timocratic man, the democratic man, the oligarch and the tyrant. Man, supposed to be the most intelligent of all species, has to live in the state of his own creation, and the possibility of a Platonic or Confucian republic seems very far away.

Aristotle and Mencius

Wu Teh Yao

'Green comes out of blue' is an Asian saying to describe the relationship between the teacher and the student. Blue mixed with yellow becomes green, yet green is neither yellow nor blue; it is a distinct and different colour. Without the blue there is no green – the original colour, blue, is the master, and yellow is the raw material that when mixed with blue becomes green, the finished product. In the same way, the student has a distinct contribution of his own, different from what he learns from his master.

This blue-green metaphor can be used to describe the relationship between Plato and Aristotle. Plato was the master, the head of the Academy which he founded, and Aristotle was the student who attended the Academy for a period of twenty years, leaving it only after Plato's death in 347 B.C. Twelve years later, he opened his own school, the Lyceum, and there he taught, researched and did most of his extensive writing in his own distinctive way. However, he made many references, particularly in the *Politics*, to Plato's ideas, though more in criticism than in agreement. His teaching method differed from that of Plato, in that Aristotle was a lecturer, not an initiator of dialogues.* Aristotle was empirically inclined, making a study of 158 constitutions of Greek city states before formulating his theories of government, while Plato's *Republic* is a treatise on political theory created by the daring imagination of an original thinker. Aristotle, the empiricist, introduced his *Politics* by saying, 'Observation shows us, first, that every polis (or state) is a species of association, and secondly, that all associations are instituted for the purpose of attaining some good, for all men do their acts with a view to achieving something which is, in their view, a good'.[1]

* For a contrasting interpretation, see 'Socrates and Plato' in this collection. (Ed.)
[1] Aristotle, *Politics*, translated and introduced by Ernest Barker, Clarendon Press, Oxford, 1961, Book I, page 1.

The blue-green metaphor cannot, strictly speaking, be applied to Mencius' relationship with Confucius. Mencius (372-289 B.C.) was a close contemporary of Aristotle (384-322 B.C.) and both men were living, as far as is known, in two great cultural centres of the world unaware of each other's existence. But Mencius did not study under Confucius as Aristotle did under Plato. Mencius was born about 175 years after Confucius, and it is said that he studied under the disciples of Confucius' grandson, Tsze-sze. It can therefore be said that Mencius was a believer or follower of Confucius' teachings. However, it can also be said that Mencius was a student of Confucius, because a student of Confucius' students' students can claim that he was also a student of the master. To the contemporary Western mind, such a claim sounds incomprehensible, even farcical. But to one who is familiar with the Eastern intellectual tradition, a scholar who claims to be a student of the master assumes moral authority in teacher-student relationships.

It would be extremely difficult for one who is immersed in the Sino-Confucian tradition to conceive that a student should criticize his teacher as Aristotle did Plato. Aristotle criticized the *Republic* as impractical, especially the passages suggesting that guardians share their wives in common. Aristotle said that in a state such as Plato postulated, parents would not know their children, nor would the children know their parents. There would be no real feeling between them, therefore at best such a society would be only a fraternity. 'The cause of the fallacy into which Plato falls must be held to be the wrong character of the premise [about the nature of unity*] on which he bases his argument. It is true that unity is to some extent necessary, alike in a household and a polis; but total unity is not.'[2] Plato's *Laws* came also under Aristotle's severe criticism. He said: 'The whole system [of government proposed in the *Laws*] tends to one neither of democracy nor of oligarchy, but rather an intermediate form, of the sort which is usually called "polity": the citizens, for example, are drawn only from those who bear arms . . . The constitution depicted in the *Laws* has really no element of monarchy, but only the elements of oligarchy and democracy, with a particular inclination towards oligarchy.'[3] Aristotle often quoted Plato out of context and even put words into his mouth. Even more surprising to one

---

* Plato's prime aim in the *Republic* was to produce a stable and totally unified state. Thus he rejected all intermediate associations, such as monogamous marriage and the family, which could divert the loyalty of the guardians away from the state. (Ed.)
[2] Aristotle, *Politics*, op. cit., p. 53.
[3] Ibid., pp. 60 and 61.

brought up in the Eastern tradition is the fact that Aristotle, in constructing his ideal or practical state, did not hesitate to borrow ideas from the *Laws* and suggestions from the predecessor whom he criticized.[4]

In contrast, Mencius quoted and evoked the authority of Confucius to prove or disprove various points, but never directly criticized or refuted his master. In the seven books of Mencius, Confucius is quoted or referred to many times. He invoked the authority of Confucius to put across his own views. He said that Confucius hated a semblance that was not a reality, the glibness of tongue that could be confounded with righteousness, and the sharpness of tongue that could be confounded with sincerity.[5] He even singled out Confucius as an epoch-making personality, saying: 'From Confucius downwards until now, [that is, the fourth century B.C.] there are only 100 years and somewhat more. The distance in time from the sage is far from being remote, and so very near at hand was the sage's residence. In these circumstances, is there no one to transmit his doctrines? Yea, is there no one to do so?'[6]

This does not mean that Mencius was merely regurgitating what Confucius taught and said. Mencius expanded upon the teachings of Confucius. For instance, Confucius dealt at length on the humane principle of *ren* (benevolence) and only touched upon the principle of *yi* (righteousness). *Ren* is the heart of the whole system of Confucian thought. Mencius, however, expanded on the principle of *yi* and according to him, the two concepts are of almost equal importance; so much so that the two words *ren* and *yi* always go together in Mencius' writings. Confucius implied that human nature is good; Mencius boldly stated that it is good. The master in preaching his doctrine of *ren* had a love of the people in his heart, but Mencius categorically stated that the people are the most precious resource of a state. While Confucius extolled virtue as the requisite for government, his student declared: 'Virtue alone is not sufficient for the exercise of government; laws alone cannot carry themselves into practice.'[7] Mencius' views on government therefore differed from those of his Master. However, he did not single out Confucius' views for criticism, but said that virtue, though necessary for government is not enough. Neither is law alone enough to sustain

---

[4] *Ibid.*, p. 62 (footnote).
[5] *The Works of Mencius*, transl. James Legge, Hong Kong University Press, 1970 (first published Clarendon Press, 1895), Book VII, chapter 37, para. 12.
[6] *Ibid.*, Book VII, chapter 38, para. 4.
[7] *Ibid.*, Book IV, part 1, para. 3.

government, but both are to be used simultaneously. Mencius went a step further; while Confucius stated that only the virtuous man should govern, Mencius said that a non-virtuous ruler should be overthrown.

The question of whether or not a student should criticize his teacher may appear irrelevant to the Westerner. After all, the pursuit of truth should be the primary concern of the scholar. This independent spirit of inquiry is deeply embedded in Western culture and civilization, just as respect for the teacher was already a tradition when Mencius appeared in the fourth century B.C. The inquiring spirit of Western man is exemplified by the myth of Prometheus, who defied the authority of the gods by giving fire to man. This revolt against authority, from whatever source, is a strain that comes out vividly in the intellectual history of the West. As a result, there is richness in Western political thought, just as there is variety in every other aspect of Western life and culture. In criticizing the ideas and theories of his teacher Plato, Aristotle was saying that the free spirit of inquiry spares no man, whether he is or was one's teacher. And to many people, this is proper and good.

To an Eastern traditionalist, such an attitude would be anti-traditional and therefore intolerable. While the quality of Chinese political thought represented by Confucius, the Legalists, Lao-Tze or Moh-Tze is in no way inferior to that of the Western thinkers, Chinese political thought cannot measure up to that of the West in variety. Perhaps the spirit of the Eastern man is different; there is no Prometheus in Chinese mythology. In fact, in the Sino-Confucian tradition, the Eastern man is brought up to respect authority and to respect the teacher. For example, as long as a ruler has the Mandate of Heaven, he rules; only when he has violated the Mandate by misrule can he be overthrown. One may not defend one's teacher if he is wrong, but one certainly does not single out his ideas for adverse criticism.

To Mencius, Confucius was a man of perfection. He said that no-one had measured up to Confucius, either in character or intellect. Aristotle made no such acknowledgement to Plato in his writings, although he did say in the *Politics*: 'All the writings of Plato are original: they show ingenuity, novelty of view, and a spirit of inquiry.'[8] This much Aristotle conceded to his teacher, but without the ideas set forth in the *Republic* and the *Laws*, would there have been the *Politics*? In the opinion of this writer, Plato is the more original thinker of the time, although Aristotle also made original contributions to the political thought of mankind.

[8] Barker, *op. cit.*, p. 57.

With Confucius and Mencius, the problem as to who is the greater man does not arise. Without the *Analects*, there would have been no *Works* of Mencius, as the latter is the continuation and expansion of the former's basic ideas, although Mencius puts forward new theories and concepts. He introduced one outstanding concept not mentioned by Confucius – that of tyrannicide. To Mencius, unlike his master, the people were justified in overthrowing a tyrannical emperor. Yet despite his contributions (especially with regard to the nurturing of the individual to attain self-reliance, dignity and greatness) most Chinese, when comparing him to Confucius, only accord Mencius the status of a 'lesser sage'.

Let us now compare the political ideas of Aristotle and Mencius. Aristotle began the *Politics* by saying that the *polis* or political association belonging to the order of things that exist in nature is the most sovereign and inclusive association for men. It was inconceivable to Aristotle that a man could be dissociated from such an organization – he must be either a god or a beast. By nature, man is a political animal intended to live in a *polis*. Mencius, less of a scientist but certainly no less astute an observer of the social and political institutions of his time, began his discussion on politics by enunciating a principle for government. In answer to a query by the King of Hui, he said that his only purpose was to talk about benevolence and righteousness, not about profit. If profit be the motive for life, everyone, including nations, would struggle and fight for what the individual or a nation would consider to be his or its profit or interest. Mencius then went on to compare good and bad government, though the only form of government he knew was rule by a monarch or an emperor, unlike the political systems of ancient Greece.

In his treatment and study of the household, Aristotle pointed out the differences in the composition of the units that make up a family – the master and slave, husband and wife, father and children – and the units that make up a state. In the family, the emphasis is on unity, where the father rules, whereas the nature of a state is pluralistic. If unity is the principle, then in tending to greater unity the state becomes a family. The family is said to be more than the state, and the individual is more than the family. This contradicts Aristotle's premise (which underlies his concept of a *polis*) that the state exists by nature prior to the family; to Aristotle, the whole (the *polis*) must come first before the parts (the family and individuals).

Mencius' concept, which is the Confucian concept, is exactly the opposite. He said that people have a common saying, 'the kingdom, the state and the family'. To him, the kingdom is rooted in the state, the state is rooted in the family and the family is rooted in the individual person. From such a premise, one infers that the individual exists prior to the family and family prior to the state.

There is yet another basic difference that affects and influences both men's ideas about politics. Aristotle had a pessimistic and cynical view of human nature, with no faith in democracy. He thought that democracy (rule by the superiority of number) was the type of government that could easily deteriorate into mob rule. To Aristotle, some men were slavish by nature, and therefore they were born to be ruled by others. He also had a low opinion of the ability of women. On the other hand, Mencius had an optimistic view of human nature, saying that it is good, as no human being can bear to see the sufferings of others. Who can stand by when a child falls into a well? Does a person consider whether the child is of rich or poor parents before he tries to save it? Who does not have the feeling of shame, the dislike of evil doings such as committing murder?

These basically different views on the nature of man certainly influenced political ideas that exist to this day. In the West for instance, influenced by Aristotle, the trend has been to limit and control the power of the ruler, given the belief that human nature is evil; in the East, the practice has been to place unlimited power in the hands of the ruler, according to the belief that human nature is basically good.

While both men differed in their ideas about human nature, their views on the size of the ideal state are quite similar. Aristotle used the states of Athens and Sparta as examples; his ideal state was smaller. He said that the territory should be large enough to enable its inhabitants to live a life of leisure, combining liberality and temperance. It would be well for the citizens to know each other and it would be wrong to judge greatness by the size of the population. A great state is not the same as a populous state, and it is the capacity to govern that counts. Mencius was also unimpressed by size. He said that a state of a hundred *li* square (about 575 square metres) could achieve kingly greatness in its rule, such as had been achieved by the great emperors of antiquity whose territorial domains were not larger than a hundred *li* square. The criterion of good government was the practice of the principle of *ren*, not the size of a state's territory or population. If the state is governed according to the principles of benevolence and righteousness, then it will be tranquil and the people will be happy.

Like Aristotle, Mencius who lived towards the end of the Chou

Dynasty when fightings between the warring states were cruel and frequent, believed that large states were difficult to govern. He advocated small states with small self-sufficient populations, believing that such states would be more peaceful.[9] This may be a little different from Aristotle's concept of a small state. To Aristotle a small state was the most effective instrument for his ideal *polis*, with citizens actively participating in the process of government. Both men, however, favoured small states that were more or less self-sufficient in food and comparatively easy to govern and defend. Mencius went so far as to see evil in big states. According to him, a man who uses force and merely pretends to be benevolent usually becomes a leader of princes, and such a leader requires a big kingdom which is often the result of military conquests.

Aristotle wrote at considerable length about defence, the advantages and the disadvantages of a *polis* near the sea and the necessity of having a navy to protect it. He stressed the physical requirements for the defence of a state, such as the location and size of the territory and its fortifications, as well as the economic life-lines. Mencius' concept of defence was different. He singled out three factors – timing, geography and man – which he thought were most important in defending a state. He gave as an example a city under siege. It could not be taken because of its geographical position. Yet, another city had high walls, deep moats, good weapons and plenty of food in stock, but was overcome and taken. Why? Because the people were dissatisfied and revolted against the ruler. Therefore, a state is made secure not by the strengths of mountains and rivers and the sharpness of arms, but by the strength of the union arising from the accord of men. This belief that men are more important than weapons is typically Eastern and it still has considerable weight in modern Chinese defence strategy. In the West, however, more emphasis has been placed on weaponry.

Who are to be the inhabitants of a state such as that favoured by Mencius and Aristotle? Mencius knew only one type of political system–a state ruled by emperors and kings on a feudalistic basis. Their subject people were the intelligentsia, the farmers, warriors, artisans and merchants. They were all inhabitants of the land, with more obligations than rights, although by custom the intelligentsia were supposed to have certain privileges because of their special intellectual talent. There was

---

[9] *Lao-Tze*, a contemporary of Confucius, was also in favour of a small state when the sounds of barking dogs and crowing cocks could be heard across the borders.

no class distinction between citizens and slaves, such as defined and classified by Aristotle in his *Politics*. And it is on the issue of 'citizenship', the problem of who are to be classified as the real citizens of a *polis*, that Aristotle the political scientist excelled. His definitions of citizen and citizenship make fascinating reading. He said, '. . . a state is a compound made up of citizens, and this compels us to consider who should properly be called a citizen and what a citizen really is. We may leave out of consideration those . . . naturalized citizens. A citizen proper is not one by virtue of residence in a given place: resident aliens and slaves share a common place of residence [with citizens], but they are not citizens. Nor can the name of citizen be given to those who share in the civic rights only to the extent of being entitled to sue and be sued in the courts. The citizen . . . is best defined by the one criterion, "a man who shares in the administration of justice and in the holding of office".'[10]

This sharing is interpreted to mean sharing in deliberative or judicial office. Such definition is exclusive; with such a definition, many of the inhabitants of Aristotle's state cannot qualify for citizenship, although many other inhabitants – the resident aliens, the traders, the craftsmen and particularly the slaves – are necessary supporting elements for the functioning of the state. Aristotle then went on to say that the citizen of one kind of state is different from those of another in the way that oligarchy is different from aristocracy.

However, Mencius made no such distinctions, and in this sense he is closer to the modern concept of citizenship than is Aristotle. To Mencius, the people make up the state, and all can qualify for political office provided that they have talent and good moral character. This inclusive concept of political participation based on talent and virtue, not on class distinction, is typically Confucian.

According to Aristotle the basis of citizenship is the constitution of the state; it is the political framework and the legal instrument by which a state operates. The kind of constitution to a great extent determines the kind of state. But the principle of a constitution is its conception of justice, and conceptions of justice differ. For instance, democrats say that if men are born equal they should, in justice, have equal rights. Oligarchs, on the other hand, say that the degree of wealth is most important, and that unequal wealth therefore means, in justice, unequal rights. From such hypotheses Aristotle went on to describe in perceptive detail the forms, merits and demerits of the various types of constitutions

---

[10] Barker, *op. cit.*, p. 93.

such as those pertaining to kingship, aristocracy and the right form of constitution called 'polity'. He also discussed the three perverted forms: democracy (the least bad), oligarchy (worse) and tyranny (the worst). Each form of government is again divided. Kingship, for instance, had five forms: the Spartan form; that which existed among uncivilized people; the tyrannical type; that of the Heroic Age of Greece; and finally the absolute type, such as the kingship of Persia. Aristotle went on to state that 'the best form of political society is one where power is vested in the middle class, and good government is attainable in those states where there is a large middle class – large enough, if possible, to be stronger than either [the extreme rich and the destitute poor] of them singly; for in that case its addition to either will suffice to turn the scale, and will prevent either of the opposing extremes from becoming dominant'.[11]

While Aristotle concentrated his study and investigation on institutions that make up a state, Mencius concentrated his efforts on trying to understand man – again a reflection of the difference between the Western and Eastern traditions in the approach to politics. And it was in the study of man that Mencius excelled; in this approach, he was following the Confucian school of thought that the cultivation of the moral person is at the root of everything. In Mencius' opinion a moral person should be not only benevolent but also righteous. *Ren* is man's heart (mind) and *yi* (righteousness) is man's path. The literal meaning of *ren* is 'man'. Since *ren* is the heart of man, it is also *in* the heart of man. The feeling of sympathy thus belongs to all men. This feeling implies the principle of benevolence; that of shame and dislike implies the principle of righteousness. These feelings are in men.[12] According to Mencius human nature is basically good. His idea of politics is therefore to draw out the good that is inherent in the nature of man, rather than to build a political association based upon the premise that human nature is evil.

The ultimate strength and courage of the individual person, however, depends upon the choice between life and death. It is at such an hour of decision that one sees the full stature of the man of benevolence and righteousness. As Mencius said: 'I like fish, and I also like bear's paws. If I cannot have two together, I will let the fish go and take the bear's paws. So, I like life, and I also like righteousness. If I cannot keep the two together, I will let life go and choose righteousness.'[13] Countless people have sacrificed their lives over the centuries in order to let life go and

[11] *Ibid.*, p. 182.
[12] *Works*, Book VI, in Legge, *op. cit.*, Vol. 2, p. 402.
[13] *Ibid.*, p. 411.

choose righteousness. Perhaps Mencius' most uplifting testimonial to the human spirit and dignity of man is this oft-quoted passage:

> To dwell in the wide house of the world, to stand in the correct seat of the world and to walk in the great path of the world; when the desire for office is obtained, to practise the principles for the good of the people; and when that desire is not achieved, to practise them alone; neither wealth and honours can dissipate the will, nor can poverty and mean condition change the belief in a principle. Even power and force will not make him bend. These are the characteristics that constitute a great man.[14]

In summary, then, one can say that Aristotle has made a permanent contribution to the study and development of political science, whereas Mencius has provided a standard and inspiration for the development of individuals as they ought to be.

Aristotle the political scientist is very much concerned with revolutions, which usually involve constitutional changes. His analysis of the general and particular causes of revolutions are most perceptive. According to him, the root cause of revolutions is the different interpretation of justice by the people. Justice always involves the concept of equality and man has a passion for equality, but the problem is that the inferiors become revolutionaries in order to be equals, and equals in order to be superiors. Democrats insist on numerical equality, but oligarchs want proportionate equality because of their wealth, which is the source of their power. In a democracy, revolution tends to be caused by demagogues attacking the privileged rich; in an oligarchy revolutions could take place because of unjust treatment of the masses and dissension from within the ruling circle; in aristocracies revolutions are mainly due to a policy of narrowing the circle of government to the few. In modern political language, such a government, originally in the hands of a creative minority, by the nature of its structure and progress becomes a dominant minority, intent on pursuing its narrow and exclusive aims.

But Aristotle was not merely a political theoretician. At the Lyceum, he taught and advised young men from all over the Greek world who would one day hold political office. Some would become rulers. He advised that it is better to award small honours over a period of time than to give great honours rapidly; it is very important to prevent magistrates from using office for their own benefit. In other words, a ruler must prevent corruption among the officials of the government.

---

[14] *Ibid.*, p. 265.

Among the most 'machiavellian' of Aristotle's comments are those about the preservation of a tyranny. His 'advice' about doing this includes the elimination of outstanding men and the removal of men of high ideals and independent thought. A second measure is to prohibit organizations for cultural purposes and to adopt every possible means of making every subject as much of a stranger as possible to every other. Every resident in the city should be required to constantly appear in public and hang about the palace gates, so that he or she can be watched; thus people will be moved to humility by a habit of daily slavery. A fourth line of policy is that of endeavouring to get regular information about every man's sayings and doings – this entails the creation of a secret police. Finally, people should be kept so busy earning a daily pittance that they have no time for plotting. A tyrant should be a war-monger so that his subjects are constantly occupied with war hysteria and are continually in need of a leader. Sowing distrust should be a special characteristic of tyrants.

One would search in vain to find such utterances in the *Works* of Mencius. The closest he comes to such advice is saying that to rule a country is not difficult. One must not antagonize the powerful families; though this policy is understandable in a feudal society, it does not necessarily mean good government. As a matter of fact, Mencius always spoke of government as it ought to be, not as it was; the latter was the idea followed in Aristotle's *Politics*. To Mencius the state and government should be like those of the famous emperors of antiquity such as Yao, Shun, Tang and Wen. These emperors had the qualities of benevolence and they were always with and liked by the people: 'King Wen [the founder of the Chou Dynasty] used the strength of the people to make his tower and his pond, and yet the people rejoiced to do the work calling the tower, "the marvellous tower", calling the pond "the marvellous pond", and rejoicing that he had his large deer, his fishes, and turtles. The ancients caused the people to have pleasure as well as themselves, and therefore they could enjoy it.'[15] Such a state of affairs was quite different from that which prevailed at his time when all princes, rulers and tyrants were indulging in luxurious ways of living and self-indulgence.

Mencius even categorically stated that a tyrant should be overthrown. It is interesting to note here that Aristotle, who regarded tyranny as the worst form of government, did not hesitate to point out ways and means for a tyrant to stay in power and continue his rule by deception. On the

[15] *Ibid.*, p. 128.

other hand Mencius regarded a tyrant as a robber, not a king; such a person should meet the fate of a robber – to be executed.

Aristotle did not state specifically what should be done if a king turns into a tyrant – it is here that Mencius made a major contribution to political thought. One of his challengers, the ruler of the state of Chi, asked, 'Was it so that Tang [the founder of the Shang dynasty] banished Chieh [the last ruler of the Hsia dynasty] and King Wu [the second ruler of the Chou dynasty] smote Chiou [the last ruler of the Shang dynasty]?' Mencius replied, 'It is so in the records.' The challenger, the ruler of Chi, said, 'May a minister then put his sovereign to death?' Mencius replied 'He who outrages the benevolence proper to his nature, is called a robber; he who outrages righteousness, is called a ruffian. The robber and the ruffian we call a mere fellow. I have heard of the cutting off of the fellow Chiou, but I have not heard of putting a sovereign to death, in his case.'[16] This is now known as the doctrine of tyrannicide, which laid the theoretical foundation and justification for revolutions and chopping off the heads of bad sovereigns, much to the dislike of some later rulers of China.

Let us now return to Aristotle's original concept that all associations are instituted for the purpose of attaining some good. The most sovereign and inclusive association is the *polis*. As such is the nature of the polis, it is capable of attaining the highest good, and good of the state is the same as that of the individual. Aristotle argued that 'the men who believe that a state as a whole is happy when it is wealthy . . . This man who grades [the felicity of] individuals by their goodness, will also regard the felicity of states as proportionate to their goodness . . . the same way of life which is best for the individual must also be best for the state as a whole and all its members.'[17] To this line of argument, Mencius would agree; such was the way of politics that he also espoused. According to Confucian thought, the cultivation of the individual's good character is at the root of everything. What is good for a state – that is, a well-ordered state – must also be good for the individual; such examples existed when the country was ruled by wise, virtuous and talented emperors.

Aristotle and Mencius differed, however, in their views of how the highest good could be achieved. Aristotle placed his faith, as an empirical political scientist would do, in constitutions which are the legal instruments that establish states. In other words, he emphasized the rule

---

[16] *Works*, Book I, chapter 8 in Legge, *op. cit.*, Vol. 2, p. 167.
[17] Barker, *op. cit.*, p. 283.

of law rather than the rule of man. On the other hand, Mencius, influenced by the Chinese political environment of his time, had to make the point that examples of goodness, virtue and therefore good rule must come from the ruler himself as an example to his people.

While the state is a political association for the highest good of its members, by whom shall be it governed in order to attain such good? Mencius was in favour of government by the most virtuous and talented men. Said he: 'If a ruler gives honour to men of talents and virtue and employs the able, so that offices shall all be filled by individuals of distinction and mark . . . then all the scholars of the kingdom will be pleased to wish to stand in his court.'[18] He went even further to say 'Some people labour with their minds, and some with their strength. Those who labour with their minds govern others; those who labour with their strength are governed by others. Those who are governed by others support them; those who govern others are supported by them. This is a principle universally recognized.'[19]

Aristotle would agree that government ought to be carried out by the best possible people, because the office holders of his state or *polis* are the selected few from the general body of citizens. But as a political realist, he recognized the fact that some states were not governed by the most talented men. He made allowance for such a state of affairs, even enumerating ways to retain and perpetuate a tyrannical state, as mentioned above.

From his description of the nature of a state, of master and slave, of ruler and ruled, one can conclude that Aristotle, like Mencius, believed that those who labour with their minds govern those who labour with their strength. By affirming this 'universal truth', both Mencius and Aristotle have come under considerable criticism. In this age of egalitarianism and proletarianism, it is a very distasteful concept, although it states a social truth.

In assessing Aristotle's and Mencius' ideas of politics, as seen from the *Politics* and the *Works* of Mencius, one inevitably comes to the conclusion that the two works are not closely comparable. The former is a work of political science, treating in detail the history, growth and changing nature of states from one form of government to another, including the decline and fall caused by revolutions. The philosophical foundations of the state are discussed; Aristotle points out in detail how the *polis* is to be run by a concerned citizenry supported by the traders, the craftsmen and

[18] Legge, *op. cit.*, Vol. 2, p. 199.
[19] *Ibid.*, pp. 249–50.

the workers, including the slaves, who were to be regarded as the lowest class of human beings. The *polis* is the highest type of association that man can achieve, and it is in the *polis* that he can also contribute his best. Therefore, man has to belong to a *polis*. If he does not participate in such a life, he is either a god or a beast; by nature, man is a political animal.

On the other hand the *Works* of Mencius do not deal exclusively with politics, but postulate a philosophy and way of life. Unlike Aristotle, Mencius believed that political institutions were to be subordinated to the existence of the individual; to him the people are the most important components of a society. One never finds the statement in the *Works* of Mencius that man is by instinct a political animal. However, it must have been obvious to him that man could not escape from being a member of society. Like his 'teacher', Confucius, Mencius is concerned with the problem of how to bring out the best in man. This is in accord with his belief that human nature is basically good, and that man can become a good and useful member of society.

Politics is the work of a great, perhaps the greatest, political scientist, and a great political philosopher. Mencius is basically a political moralist, and a stern one too, but he is less a political scientist than Aristotle. The *Politics* can be used as a practical handbook by statesmen and politicians; the *Works* of Mencius, however, can serve as an inspiration and a guide in government to statesmen and politicians when they want and are able to be reflective. The power and influence released by the ideas of Aristotle and Mencius, like those of their teachers Plato and Confucius before them, are certainly far greater than those of any collection of generals, statesmen or rulers.

Augustine and Hobbes

Damien Grace

St Augustine of Hippo 354-430 A.D. and Thomas Hobbes 1588-1679 stand like two great portals at either end of the Christian era. Augustine leads us from the classical world to the Christian; Hobbes from the Christian to the modern. Augustine, a brilliant rhetor, theologian and Father of the Church, could not have imagined that his writings would form so sturdy a foundation for a world which, if not always Christian in spirit, was so in identity. Hobbes was born after that identity had collapsed in senectitude, and was instrumental in forming its successor. A political philosopher of the very front rank, he witnessed the passing of a specifically Christian ordering of the world and its replacement by the perspectives of empirical science. A wide intellectual and political gulf, then, stands between these two thinkers.

Not only were Augustine and Hobbes separated by the life of a Christian civilization under which neither of them lived, but their modes of reflection upon politics and society differed markedly. For Augustine, philosophy had little to offer, and speculation was fruitful only in so far as it lead to God. For Hobbes, philosophy was a habit of mind as much as a means of reaching certitude about the world. How, then, is the fifth-century African bishop, concerned with the spiritual welfare of his flock, to be compared with the seventeenth-century English philosopher intent on firm conclusions about matters mundane; is there enough common ground between them to permit comparison of their political theories?

Only a crude sense of history would allow one to assume that both men were concerned with the 'same' intellectual and political problems. Nevertheless, the general category of political theory is broad enough to allow the inclusion of writers of diverse preoccupations and styles, despite their differences in time and culture. Such common classification is not in terms of their activity as theorists of politics – such activities may

range from the writing of philosophy to the production of cliché – but in terms of that to which they turn their attention, political conduct.[1] Politics is an abstraction without clear semantic boundaries. To look for its essence, to ask what it is, is already to mistake its character. If 'essentialism' – as Karl Popper calls it[2] – is a distraction from real problems, this is especially true of the search for an adequate definition of 'politics'. Politics occurs where there is the possibility of change through conflict and compromise, where a given structure of authority has not altogether pre-ordained the types of conflicts and solutions that are possible within a society. As a social activity it involves a sense of belonging, the recognition of certain rules of conduct and the acknowledgement of the right of designated authorities to enforce them. Political life is an artifice that permits the genesis, development and resolution of conflicts without the destruction of order. It allows the application of power bounded at one end by consensus and at the other by anarchy. Between these extremes it may offer vast or limited possibilities for persuasion. Politics is not simply a matter of mechanics or technical skill or animal cunning, an activity concerned merely with force or rules. The possibility of persuasion means that it is a linguistic activity and potentially an intellectual activity as well. Behind the complexity of politics there is the central feature described by de Jouvenal as the 'systematic effort, performed at any place in the social field, to move other men in pursuit of some design cherished by the mover'.[3]

A political theory can be understood as an attempt to state or recommend the conditions upon which this effort to move another is made. Within this understanding there is room for comparing the theories of Augustine and Hobbes as set forth in their great books, *Concerning the City of God Against the Pagans* and *Leviathan*.[4]

Initially comparison yields some obvious similarities and contrasts. Both men are concerned with fundamentals, with the principles underlying human conduct. Both base their theories of politics upon human nature about which both are pessimistic. Both wrote at times of

---

[1] For a lucid and important discussion of political theory under its various species see Conal Condren, *Three Aspects of Political Theory*, Macmillan, Melbourne, 1979, chapter 1.
[2] See, for example, Popper's attack on 'what is' questions and essentialism in *Unended Quest*, Fontana, 1976, pp. 17–30.
[3] Bertrand de Jouvenal, *The Pure Theory of Politics*, Cambridge, 1963, p. 30.
[4] The texts used are Augustine, *Concerning the City of God against the Pagans*, transl. H. Bettenson, Penguin, Harmondsworth, 1972; Thomas Hobbes, *Leviathan*, ed. M. Oakeshott, Oxford, n.d. All page citations refer to these editions.

political crisis, and both expressed an overriding concern for peace. Both argued that the subject was obliged to obey those who ruled, whether they were tyrannical or benign.

They differ, however, in the fundamentals to which they address themselves. Augustine reduces all things to their relationship with God and assesses them according to whether they have kept their place in God's scheme of things; God is the source of all that is and all that happens in Augustine's world. For Hobbes, God is in the background. He has set up the universe on certain principles and left it running. Hobbes, then, is able to leave God out of his explanation of human behaviour and his theory of ethics. He is a materialist who reduces all that is and happens in the world to matter in motion. All events, whether wholly external, like a rain storm, or internal, like feelings of fear, ambition or love, may be explained in terms of matter in motion.

Moreover, despite a shared pessimism, and to some extent a shared individualism, the theorists diverge on the nature of human society. Augustine effectively distinguishes between society and polity; Hobbes observes no such distinction. For Augustine man is naturally social, although political domination is not natural but the product of the Fall of Man. For Hobbes society cannot persist without political authority to keep order. This authority is not natural and must be created and continually sustained because man is naturally unsociable. State and society in Hobbes' theory are, then, artificial.

What is not obvious in any simple arrangement of two thinkers in terms of extraneous organizing principles such as 'their views of . . . man, society, polity, authority, etc.' are their central concerns and intentions, their peculiar textures of thought and argument, in short, their distinctive understandings of politics.

The *City of God* is commonly described as a *livre de circonstance*, an apologetic work designed to defend Christianity against charges by pagan Romans that it had enfeebled the empire and lost for Rome the protection of its traditional gods. In 410A.D. Alaric the Goth had forced the capitulation of Rome and sacked the city. Unwelcome as this event was to the inhabitants, its significance was far greater than the fall of a once great city: to civilized people throughout the empire it signalled the passing of the world of familiarity, of security and stability. Confronted with Christian and pagan refugees from Rome, Augustine had to deal not simply with an enlarged flock but with an identity crisis which threatened the fidelity of his North African diocese. But the *City of God* is not simply a response to this challenge. Peter Brown in his brilliant biography of Augustine argues that the germ for the book had earlier settled in Augustine's mind and once there was not to be dislodged. The effect of the fall of Rome is better understood in the shape taken by the work than in its genesis and central theme. For the refugees who had settled in Carthage provided Augustine with a highly literate, cultivated and intelligent audience, and a potentially exegetical work became a sophisticated demolition of paganism.[5]

Augustine commenced writing in 413 and laid down his pen in 426, when he was seventy-two, four years before his death. The work was planned on a vast scale in twenty-two books. The first ten are explicitly directed against old pagan practices and beliefs. The succeeding twelve are more oblique on these matters, for they are concerned with the working out of Augustine's central theme, man's place in the universal order and his destiny in the city of God. No summary could do justice to the range of topics it covers, but this is of small moment: the inclusiveness of the work matters less than its end, which is to show the audience that they have a vital choice before them which is inescapable. They can love God and serve Him and thereby find their way to His city; or they can love the things of the world and be damned. Given the overriding importance of this theme, it is hardly surprising that political questions should have to take their place beside discussions of more mundane matters. But this does not mean that Augustine's political theory is insignificant: in the context of the *City of God* it cannot be central, but must assume its proper place not only in God's but in the author's scheme of things.

The problem of Augustine's political theorizing, however, is not simply that it is embedded in theology, but that its style does not present us with clearly defined issues and solutions, such as we find in Hobbes. Augustine is writing for a highly literate audience, using authorities like Cicero to great effect, showing his erudition and literary skills in an array of rhetorical devices. In so doing he at once incorporates and transcends the literary heritage of the past, using it to break down the defences of his audience only to win them to his conclusions. He is not simply concerned either with abstract speculation or with the formal treatment of the political questions of his day. For this we might be grateful, for what has come down to us, almost incidentally to his great project, is a theory of political life that combines the coherence of a world-view and the immediacy of a response to urgent problems.

[5] See P. Brown, *Augustine of Hippo*, London, 1967, chapters 25–7.

Central to Augustine's thinking in the *City of God* is an insistence on man's dependence on his maker. It is the tension between this reality and mankind's denial of it that gives impetus to the work. In his youth, before his conversion to Christianity, Augustine had been attracted to philosophy through reading Cicero. He had sought in Manicheism and Platonism to rise by the power of his own intellect to the understanding of wisdom and truth. Even after his conversion there remained in him some confidence in the unassisted powers of an educated man. In the *City of God*, however, all such notions are abandoned.[6] In order to understand Augustine's attitude to politics it is necessary to appreciate the grounds of this rejection.

For Augustine, creation has been radically disordered by the Fall of Adam. God created man 'as a kind of mean between angels and beasts', destined for immortality if he obeyed his maker. But if he used his free will 'in arrogance' against the will of God, then he should be condemned to live like the beasts, to have no command of his desires, and finally to die.[7] As a consequence of the disobedience of Adam and Eve, their flesh became disobedient, the will was no longer master of the passions. 'The soul, in fact, rejoiced in its own freedom to act perversely and disdained to be God's servant; and so it was deprived of the obedient service which its body had at first rendered.'[8] The disorder of the original sin was transmitted genetically through the offspring of our first parents. Hence all 'mankind is led from that original perversion, a kind of corruption at the root' to everlasting damnation, unless saved through the grace of God.[9] Original sin is a defect, not chiefly of the flesh, but of the soul. The things of the world are in themselves good, as are the desires which lead men to their use. Evil is simply the absence of a fitting good: it has no existence of itself. So when the things of the world are enjoyed for themselves, displacing God in the affections of man, this preference of a relative good to an absolute one is evil.

> Greed . . . is not something wrong with gold; the fault is in a man who perversely loves gold and for its sake abandons justice, which ought to be put beyond comparison above gold. . . . Pride is not something wrong in the one who loves power, or in the power itself; the fault is in the soul which

---

[6] R. A. Markus traces this change of attitude in *Saeculum: History and Society in the Theology of St Augustine*, Cambridge University Press, 1970, chapter 4.
[7] *City of God*, XII, 24, p. 502.
[8] *Ibid.*, XIII, 13, p. 522.
[9] *Ibid.*, XIII, 14, p. 523.

perversely loves its own power, and has no thought for the justice of the Omnipotent.[10]

Evil, then is the product of a perverse will, one that turns in upon the self rather than towards the Creator: its root is pride.

The intervention of God's grace in the affairs of men, however, offered the possibility of salvation. It also meant that mankind could be divided into those who received this grace and those who did not. In this fundamental division within mankind is the basis for two societies or, as Augustine calls them, cities. One city chooses 'to live by the standard of the flesh', the other 'by the standard of the spirit'.[11] They are the product of two incompatible loves: God or self. Love itself is an orientation of the will, so that 'a rightly directed will is love in a good sense and a perverted will is love in a bad sense'.[12] The earthly city 'was created by self-love reaching the point of contempt for God, the heavenly City by the love of God as far as contempt of self'.[13] Those who belong to the former have their reward – such as it is – in this life; members of the latter await their reward in God.[14] For even righteousness will not bring happiness on earth. The righteous person will treat his earthly existence as a pilgrimage towards something infinitely greater. Thus, although he shares with members of the earthly city all the assaults that the flesh is heir to, and the cares, fears and woes that attend human existence, his attitude to them will make them light. For what are these burdens when compared with the glory to come? Those owing allegiance to the earthly city find the turmoils of life less tolerable for there is nothing beyond them to give consolation. Yet, such frustrations cannot be amended in this life: they are the legacy of the Fall. Classical authors, such as Plato, who believed that loosening the bonds of the flesh would allow the ascent of the soul, were mistaken. According to Augustine, it is the disordered soul of man that produces the vicissitudes of the flesh.[15] Hence, ancient doctrines that teach the elevation of the soul through release from the imprisoning body offer no true peace. One cannot through one's own powers remove the defects of original sin.

This doctrine has important consequences for politics. The life of the *polis* or *civitas* cannot be an end in itself. It cannot satisfy the longing of

[10] *Ibid.*, XII, 8, pp. 480–1; *cf.* XIV, 13, p. 573.
[11] *Ibid.*, XIV, 1, p. 547.
[12] *Ibid.*, XIV, 7, p. 557.
[13] *Ibid.*, XIV, 28, p. 593.
[14] *Ibid.*, XV, 1, p. 595.
[15] *Ibid.*, XIV, 3, pp. 550–1.

the human heart, nor alleviate the anxiety of the human condition. This has already been illustrated with respect to Rome when Augustine begins Book XIX of the *City of God* with a devastatingly pessimistic attack on classical doctrines of human felicity. Philosophy, family, friendship, society – nothing earthly can remedy the fearful condition of temporal existence. Children suffer inexplicably; sincere men judge wrongly and the righteous are tortured and executed unjustly; wars fought even for just causes are a source of grief.[16] Such is man's changeable and uncertain life in the *saeculum*. Peace, which he seeks above all, eludes him.[17] Yet members of the city of God already enjoy a peace of soul denied to those who belong to the earthly city, for they refer all in this world, both pains and pleasures, to the will of God.[18] Now, although it will be clear to members of the city of God that the only peace worth the name is the peace of God's order, yet even the perverted peace of the temporal order, the *saeculum*, is connected with true peace or it would not bear the name.[19] This temporal peace, which 'consists in bodily health and soundness, and in fellowship with one's kind', is God-given, and is to be enjoyed by members of both cities alike.[20] It is, however, the end of the members of the earthly city and is thus sought by them for itself; but it is not to be despised by those whose end is the peace of God. Although the two cities are divided spiritually, they are mingled in the *saeculum* and may find agreement at least on the limited peace of the temporal domain and the political arrangements needed to secure it.[21] Where they will differ is in their attitudes to the peace provided by political measures.

Political domination is an unnatural state of affairs for Augustine. It is a necessary institution to keep order in society, but only because of the disordered wills of men. It is, then, a consequence of sin and a punishment for it. It is closer to slavery than to the family, for the family belongs to the order of nature. The father who is just will give orders to his wife and children in love, not in power, and these orders will be obeyed in love, not in fear.[22] Of course, the Fall has distorted even this fundamental order, but the family still provides the paradigm for rule by Christian authorities. Like the good father, or *paterfamilias*, they should

[16] *Ibid.*, XIX, 1– 9; see P. Brown, Saint Augustine in his *Religion and Society in the Age of St Augustine*, Faber, London, 1972, pp. 25–45, especially p. 37.
[17] *City of God*, XIX, 12.
[18] *Ibid.*, XIX, 27, p. 892.
[19] *Ibid.*, XIX, 12, p. 869.
[20] *Ibid.*, XIX, 13, p. 872.
[21] *Ibid.*, XIX, 17, p. 877.
[22] *Ibid.*, XIX, 14, p. 874.

regard themselves as servants of their charges rather than as masters. For God did not intend that man should rule over man. 'He did not wish the rational being, made in his own image, to have dominion over any but irrational creatures, not man over man, but man over beasts. Hence the first just men were set up as shepherds of flocks, rather than as kings of men . . .'[23] Domination is rather the characteristic of the earthly city, as Augustine makes clear at the very beginning of his great work: 'The city of this world . . . aims at dominion . . . is . . . dominated by that very lust of domination.'[24] It was this lust to dominate, to rival God, which led to the fall from grace of the Devil and caused him to seduce Adam and Eve from the love of God.[25] God's original order has been freely rejected by the will of man, however, and along with the other inconveniences which attend his pilgrimage through life is that of coercion. Although remaining naturally sociable, man's natural capacity for harmonious relationships is vitiated by sin: 'the human race is, more than any other species, at once social by nature and quarrelsome by perversion.'[26] But, just as a proclivity to conflict cuts away at man's capacity for sociability, so it provides the means for checking conflict and providing a minimum of order. For the love of domination gives rise to the political structures imposed upon society and thereby secures a 'precarious peace'.[27]

Augustine is not, however, advocating a despotism. On the contrary, he urges the identification of the ruler with the *paterfamilias*, assures the pious ruler of his eternal reward and deprecates the tyrant as a slave to his vices. Moreover,

> It is beneficial that the good should extend their dominion far and wide . . . with the worship of the true God by genuine sacrifices and upright lives. This is for the benefit of all, of the subjects even more than the rulers.[28]

Yet it is idle to seek justice or fulfilment in the temporary order of cities and kingdoms. Any peace that may be enjoyed in this world 'is such that it affords a solace for our wretchedness rather than the joy of blessedness'.[29]

---

[23] *Ibid.*, XIX, 15, p. 874.
[24] *Ibid.*, I, Preface, p. 5; *cf.* XIV, 28, p. 593.
[25] *Ibid.*, XIX, 12, pp. 869–70; *cf.* XI, 13, p. 445; XIV, 11–13.
[26] *Ibid.*, XII, 28, p. 508.
[27] Markus, *Saeculum*, p. 95.
[28] *City of God*, IV, 3, p. 138. On this, see H. A. Deane, *The Political and Social Ideas of St Augustine*, New York and London, 1963, p. 129ff.
[29] *City of God*, XIX, 27, p. 892.

Augustine enjoins obedience to civil authorities upon those who follow the true God whatever the customs, laws and institutions of the polity. For these arrangements are, in themselves, matters of indifference to the city of God; they have their ephemeral value in the order and peace they provide, and this need not conflict with the spiritual orientation of that city. An overriding allegiance to God, then, can be the occasion of conflict only when temporal rulers issue commands contrary to piety. When such a conflict arises, the martyrs are to serve as models for the godly. That is, the city of God is prepared to endure persecution; its purpose is not to overthrow tyrants or organize resistance. On the contrary, 'it does not hesitate to obey the laws of the earthly city by which those things which are designed for the support of this mortal life are regulated.'[30] That these laws will often be repressive or unjustly administered is not surprising. The actions of men are infected by ignorance and perversity of will. In this variable world the most one may hope for is the shadow of justice. In the midst of so much wickedness, however, even this shadow is welcome to the children of light.

Because the political domain is concerned with the minimum order necessary to sustain life – that is, with the external requirements of the body – the city of God can attend to it without compromise. This city will measure the benefits of living in political society not from its approximation of true justice or goodness but from the degree of order that facilitates their pilgrimage.

Augustine explicitly denies the possibility of true justice being realized in this world. The point is intended generally, but Rome is the immediate target of this denial. Hence, upon a remark of Sallust* – 'Justice and morality prevailed among them by nature as much as by laws' – Augustine comments sardonically, 'I imagine that the Rape of the Sabines arose from this "justice and morality".'[31] If a commonwealth is to be defined in terms of justice, as Scipio† asserts, then Rome was never

---

[30] *City of God*, XIX, 17, p. 877.

* Sallust, or Gaius Sallustius Crispus, (86–c.35 B.C.), was a Roman statesman and historian who concentrated on critical stages in the decline of the Roman Republic. His *Histories* cover the critical period from the death of Sulla in 78 B.C. to Pompey's rise to power in 67 B.C.; unfortunately only fragments of these five books survive. His earlier historical monograph, *The Conspiracy of Cataline*, is noted for brilliant speeches and character sketches. Sallust was judged by Quintilian to rival Thucydides, and Martial ranked him as Rome's foremost historian. (Ed.)

[31] *City of God*, II, 17, p. 66.

† *Publius Cornelius Aemillianus Scipio Africanus Minor (185/4–129 B.C.)* was a Roman official and general in Africa and Spain. He was also the brilliant leader of the so-called Scipionic Circle, a group of pro-Hellenic philosophers, poets and politicians. (Ed.)

a commonwealth. Augustine demonstrates that 'true justice is found only in that commonwealth whose founder and ruler is Christ'[32], and argues for a definition of the political community that makes no reference to transcendent values. According to this revised definition, 'A people is the association of a multitude of rational beings united by a common agreement on the objects of their love.'[33] Within this morally neutral definition it is possible to conceive of the coexistence of the two opposed cities. For they have only to agree on the limited matters of civil order. A people may have a history of bloodshed and corruption, yet Augustine will 'not make that a reason for asserting that a people is not really a people or that a state is not a commonwealth'.[34] True justice, then, is reserved for a higher form of association which takes its scale of values from the love of God.

The consequence of Augustine's argument is the secularization of political life.[35] It becomes a matter of regulating the behaviour of men, of securing agreement on a limited range of objectives amongst people with a variety of loves and opposed ends. Politics is separated from the domains of morality and religion. There is an indifference, at times almost an hostility, towards political life: 'Remove justice and what are kingdoms but gangs of criminals on a large scale? What are criminal gangs but petty kingdoms?'[36]; Augustine applies to such gangs a definition similar to that applied to a 'people'. The city of God leads 'a life of captivity in this earthly city as in a foreign land.'[37] Though its peace be welcome, it exercises no hold on the righteous. The disposition of the individual towards this peace is what really counts: 'virtue rightly uses the blessings of peace, and even when we do not possess that peace, virtue turns to a good use even the ills man endures.'[38] By severing the connection between civic and religious consciousness, Augustine brings to its culmination his attack upon Rome and paganism.

Augustine's very choice of title for his work is political. He self-consciously draws attention to his peculiar usage of the term 'city',

---

[32] *Ibid.*, II, 21, p. 75; XIX, 21–3.
[33] *Ibid.*, XIX, 24, p. 890; *cf.* Deane, *op.cit.*, chapter IV and conclusion.
[34] *Ibid.*, XIX, 24, p. 890.
[35] This theme is strongly developed in the works of Deane and Markus; *cf.* H. Caton, 'St Augustine's Critique of Politics', *New Scholasticism*, 47 (1973): pp. 433–57.
[36] *Ibid.*, IV, 4, p. 138.
[37] *Ibid.*, XIX, 17, p. 877.
[38] *Ibid.*, XIX, 10, p. 865.

citing Psalm 87 for his authority.[39] Peter Brown points out that his usage is 'technical' and J. O'Meara is emphatic that 'the essential, if not sole, significance that Augustine wishes us to grasp from his use of the term "city" is quite simply the idea of association itself . . .'[40] This is too simple: Augustine uses the term ambiguously.[41] Yet it is true that the main sense in which the word is used is politically neutral, or rather not political at all. This itself is politically significant in a society where political and theological discourse had a tendency to coalesce and where the Roman *civitas* in particular had been endowed with theological significance by some influential Christians.[42] Augustine, however, deliberately distances himself from conventional attitudes towards the political community, from the *civitas* as a quasi-mystical focus of loyalty which might obscure a clear view of one's obligations to God. Rome holds no privileged position in God's plan of salvation. Thus the course of Roman history, its triumphs and failures, may be explained entirely in secular terms without recourse to the favour of the pagan gods or the grace of the true God.

Thomas Hobbes' political thought differs in style from Augustine's and is based upon different foundations. What is surprising, perhaps, is the number of similarities between them, at least within the broad framework adopted here. Of several works devoted to politics, including *De Cive* (1642) and *De Corpore Politico* (1650), *Leviathan* (1651) remains Hobbes' greatest achievement. Like the *City of God* it is a response to a world in disorder yet is also a working out of an argument whose

---

[39] *Ibid.*, II, 22, p. 75. Augustine uses the term 'Christ's commonwealth' here, but as 'commonwealth' is 'so commonly used elsewhere with a different sense', he substitutes 'city', presumably because its biblical provenance dissociates it from common usage. *Cf.* xv, 1, p. 595: 'I also call these two classes the two cities, speaking allegorically" etc.

[40] Brown, *Religion and Society*, p. 25; J. O'Meara, *Charter of Christendom*, New York, 1961, p. 41; *cf.* pp. 39–43.

[41] Although the polity is supposed to provide common ground for the co-existence of the heavenly and earthly cities, the political order seems to belong to those who love to dominate – that is, the earthly city. On Augustine's assumptions, the two should only be identified if the political *civitas* is the centre of love for its inhabitants. If it is treated merely in a functional sense, it will not distract those intent on the city of God. At times, however, Augustine seems not to be attacking an attitude but temporal cities as such. Rome, for example, is all but identified with the *civitas terrena*. And, in debunking Sallust's praise of Rome, Augustine moves from a political sense of 'city' to a religious one (III, 17, pp. 111–12). Similarly, Cain is marked out not simply for his worldliness but as the founder of cities (xv, 2, p. 596). *Cf.* Markus, *Saeculum*, pp. 56–61, and J. N. Figgis, *The Political Aspects of St Augustine's 'City of God'*, Gloucester, Mass., 1963, first published 1921, pp. 46–7.

[42] Notably by Eusebius, a fourth-century bishop and adviser to Constantine. See Markus, *Saeculum*, at length but especially p. 50ff.

conception antedates and transcends immediate pressures. Hobbes was born into an age of political strife – his very birth was brought on by the approach of the Spanish Armada – which persisted either domestically or internationally for the duration of his ninety-one years. But many lesser writers were moved to write by contemporary disturbances, and, indeed to advance the same conclusions as Hobbes without producing a rival to *Leviathan*. Hobbes' claim to pre-eminence – or infamy – lies in his method of reaching his conclusions.[43]

The genesis of Hobbes' method probably occurred some time in 1629 when he chanced upon a volume of Euclid.[44] The rigorous demonstrations of geometry from clearly defined premises were seized upon by Hobbes as the paradigm for scientific enquiry. This was no less a conversion than Augustine's acceptance of Christianity upon reading St Paul. And like Augustine, Hobbes proceeded to pour scorn upon the ideas and practices of his former mentors from the strength of his new position.

In Euclid Hobbes found what had hitherto been lacking in moral and political argument – a method for rigorously deducing certain conclusions from self-evident and simple premises. The method of geometry contrasted sharply with the nonsense of the Aristotelians, befuddled by the obscurity of their own terms. Confusion about the meaning of terms was a source of uncertain opinion. As opinions are apt to vary, they serve as an incitement to civil strife; a clear method of proceeding to certain conclusions, however, replaces opinion with knowledge and removes a potential source of civil discord. Hobbes tried out his new approach to political questions in the *Elements of Law*, circulated privately in 1640, and in *De Cive*, published in 1642. The audience for the Latin work was even then limited and, under pressure of 'questions concerning the rights of dominion and the obedience due from subjects', Hobbes embarked upon a new work in English. It was *Leviathan* and its appearance was timely. The disturbances of the English Civil War had culminated in the execution of Charles I in 1649, and the question of allegiance to his sucessors was still not settled.

---

[43] For a concise treatment of Hobbes' life and works, see R. S. Peters, *Hobbes*, Penguin, Harmondsworth, 1956. On Hobbes' ideas in their ideological context, see Q. Skinner, 'The Context of Hobbes's Theory of Political Obligation' in M. Cranston and R. S. Peters (eds), *Hobbes and Rousseau*, New York, 1972. D. D. Raphael's *Hobbes, Morals and Politics*, London, 1977, contains a handy guide to recent interpretations of Hobbes.
[44] For Hobbes' method and its background, see J. W. N. Watkins, *Hobbes's System of Ideas*, 2nd edition, London, 1973, chapters 2–4.

But the book was timely in another sense as well. Just as Augustine's political theory belongs to a wider theological view of the world, so Hobbes' belongs to a general conception of philosophy. For Hobbes, philosophy offered the prospect of integrating all sciences under the same classification of causes. Hitherto the sciences had been held back 'by succeeding philosophers strangled with the snares of words'.[45] In recent times, however, Copernicus, Galileo, Kepler and Harvey had made great strides in the advancement of astronomy, physics and physiology. More recently still, Hobbes noted, civil philosophy had been properly begun in his own book, *De Cive*. This was because what had previously passed for philosophy was so imprecise that it could yield only absurdities.[46] Definition of terms is the indispensible requirement for the removal of confusion and the attainment of truth.[47] Hence *Leviathan* begins with definitions of the terms upon which Hobbes will build his case. Where with Augustine one could talk of the style of the argument, with Hobbes one is faced not simply with a powerful style but with explicit claims about method. For Hobbes, it is the correctness of this method which makes his conclusions sound.

The method consists not only in definition and in proceeding logically to conclusions, but in establishing the relevant items to be defined. This Hobbes achieves by a process of analysis that owes much to the resolutive–compositive method of the Paduan school and its most famous exponent, Galileo, and to the anatomical investigations of Hobbes' friend Harvey. The idea behind the resolutive–compositive method is to arrive at first principles by resolving the object of enquiry into its constituent parts and then recomposing them. In the first part of *Leviathan*, Hobbes treats of man, who is both the constituent and the maker of the state. In the second part he recomposes the state giving an account of its nature. In the third and fourth parts Hobbes turns his attention to religion and politics.

Applied to man, the method resolves all his emotions, his imagination, reason and volitions into matter in motion, to tiny imperceptible movements within him.[48] Hobbes is a materialist. He lays out the components of human nature and invites us to test the aptness of his analysis by introspection.[49] His view of man is pessimistic but not

[45] Quoted from *De Corpore* by J. Kemp, *Ethical Naturalism: Hobbes and Hume*, London, 1970, p. 3.
[46] *Leviathan*, chapter 5, pp. 25–30.
[47] *Ibid.*, chapter 4, p. 21.
[48] *Ibid.*, chapter 6, p. 31.
[49] *Ibid.*, Introduction, p. 6.

moralistic; he shares Augustine's sober attitude towards human inconsistency and self-regard, but he does not judge. Man is described as nature fashioned, not as sin afflicted him. He is governed by two main types of 'endeavour': 'appetite or desire', and 'aversion'. Those things he moves towards are desired, those he moves from are repugnant. These appetites and aversions are constantly changing, not only from person to person but within the same person.[50] Neither Hobbes nor Augustine believes a person may confidently vouchsafe his actions in the future; each holds a view of human nature that emphasizes changeableness.[51] For both, this inherent instability is a potential source of civil discord.

Unlike Augustine, Hobbes defines good and evil in nominalistic terms. While for Augustine there is a divinely ordained order of things according to which the appetites may be properly or improperly followed, for Hobbes 'whatsoever is the object of any man's appetite or desire . . . he . . . calleth *good:* and the object of his hate and aversion, *evil:* and of his contempt, *vile* and *inconsiderable.*' Whatever pleases us we call good, whatever displeases us we call bad, 'there being nothing simply and absolutely so'. Moral principles cannot be inferred from the nature of man or the world. They are the product of civil society in which there is a power to overawe each man and force him to subscribe to the laws of the society.[52]

The importance of a common power to maintain order is not far from Hobbes' mind even as he proceeds, with great economy, through an inventory of the 'voluntary motions', the desires and aversions that animate mankind. Having defined the emotions, desires, fears and faculties pertinent to his discussion, Hobbes enquires which of them conduce to peace and obedience to a common power, and which incline men to the contrary. For the voluntary motions of men are never at rest: there is no *summum bonum* (supreme good) which will satisfy them.[53] Augustine too had considered the rapaciousness of the appetites but had concluded that they could find their final satisfaction only in God.[54] For Hobbes, however, the constant striving of each man for felicity presented a political problem. In order to secure felicity for himself, not only in the present, but in the future, a person must have power, which is the means to felicity. Hence Hobbes postulates 'for a general inclination for all

---

[50] *Ibid.*, chapter 6, p. 32.
[51] *Cf.* Brown, *Religion and Society*, pp. 28–9.
[52] *Leviathan*, chapter 6, pp. 32–3.
[53] *Ibid.*, chapter 11.
[54] See his *Confessions*, I, 1.

mankind a perpetual and restless desire of power after power, that ceaseth only in death.'[55] In competing to satisfy their desires, men engage in violence. But their desires should not only be thought of in terms of ease, luxury or competition for honour. Hobbes takes as many pains to exorcise intellectual vices, verbal absurdities and religious misconceptions and anxieties as Augustine does the bogus gods and demons of Rome. For misconceptions and ignorance of the causes of things can be as dangerous as competing desires for scarce resources.[56] It is Hobbes' intention to disclose these errors and abolish the ignorance that infects the body politic and produces the sickness of war. He has found the germs of this sickness in the nature of the individual.

What makes the natural condition of mankind dangerous is not the pursuit of felicity or the avoidance of misery as such, but that this pursuit or avoidance must be in competition with others. The danger results from the fact that, according to Hobbes, men are very nearly equal. This equality applies both to 'the faculties of the mind' and 'to the strength of the body'. For there is none so strong that he might not be killed by stealth or 'by confederacy with others'. As for intellectual qualities, most of these are not innate and may be acquired over time. When men compete, they do so as near equals and this encourages them to have their own way. No man, then, may trust another, and this distrust Hobbes calls 'diffidence'. Similarly, social life is poisoned with enmities when there is no common power present to check them. For each would have his fellows esteem him as highly as he esteems himself and even though this were by extortion. In the nature of man Hobbes has found 'three principal causes of quarrel. First, competition; secondly, diffidence; thirdly, glory. The first, maketh men invade for gain; the second for safety; and the third, for reputation.'[57]

Left to themselves, with no 'common power to keep them all in awe', men would be in a state of war. 'For War, consisteth not in the battle only, or the act of fighting; but in a tract of time, wherein the will to contend by battle is sufficiently known . . . All other time is Peace.' This condition of war is intolerable. No-one is able to rely on his own strength and wit for security, and the consequences that must ensue from this

---

[55] *Leviathan*, chapter 6, p. 39; chapter 10, p. 56; chapter 11, pp. 63–4.
[56] Hobbes justifies his discussion of essences, for example, on political grounds, so 'that men may no longer suffer themselves to be abused, by them, that by this doctrine of *separated essences*, built on the vain philosophy of Aristotle, would fright them from obeying the laws of their country, with empty names.' *Ibid.*, chapter 46, p. 442.
[57] *Ibid.*, chapter 13, pp. 80–1; but *cf.* chapter 17, especially pp. 111–12.

radical insecurity are set forth in what is probably the best-known passage in *Leviathan*. Learning, commerce, technology, the arts, letters and society, all would be lost in a state of war. But the worst aspects of this condition are 'continual fear, and the danger of violent death'.[58] Yet men may be delivered from the misery of their natural condition by their fear of death, their desire to live well and the hope of doing so. For they will thereby be inclined to peace, and reason will provide them with the means to attain it.[59]

The conclusion of reason is that every man should lay down his right to all things, claiming only as much liberty for himself as he would allow to any other.[60] Thus, each man freely contracts with every other man for their mutual protection to transfer their natural rights to a common representative or power. For although both fear and desire incline men to observe the covenant they have made, such dispositions are not in themselves adequate guarantees of order. As Hobbes observes, 'covenants, without the sword, are but words, and of no strength to secure a man at all'.[61] The only way to ensure security is for the many to unite in one will in concluding a contract to transfer all their power to the sovereign 'to the end he may use the strength and means of them all, as he shall think expedient, for their peace and common defence'. Thus is formed from many natural men a greater artificial man, 'that great Leviathan . . . that mortal god, to which we owe under the immortal God, our peace and defence'. Hobbes does note that contract is not the only way a sovereign can be instituted. He may also be established by way of 'natural force' or conquest.[62]

In either case the power of the sovereign is to be considered absolute. For however harsh conditions of life may appear under a sovereign, they will not match the misery of the state of nature from which he is absent. In a comment reminiscent of Augustine, Hobbes points out that 'The condition of man in this life shall never be without inconveniences; but there happeneth in no commonwealth any great inconvenience, but what proceedeth from the subject's disobedience . . .'[63]

It is hardly surprising that in matters of religion, which had been the cause of violence during the gestation of Leviathan, Hobbes should argue

---
[58] *Ibid.*, chapter 13, p. 82.
[59] *Ibid.*, chapter 13, p. 84.
[60] *Ibid.*, chapter 14.
[61] *Ibid.*, chapter 17, p. 109.
[62] *Ibid.*, chapter 17, pp. 112–13.
[63] *Ibid.*, chapter 21, p. 136.

for a uniformity decreed by the sovereign. For the church cannot be a rival authority where the sovereign is absolute. The commonwealth being 'but one person . . . ought also to exhibit to God but one worship'.[64] The sovereign is the final authority on scriptural interpretation, and is to ensure obedience to its commands. Before their conversion to Christianity, heathen sovereigns 'had the name of pastors of the people, because there was no subject that could lawfully teach the people, but by their permission and authority'. This right, asserts Hobbes, was not lost upon their conversion and, as Christians, they retain the power 'to ordain what pastors they please' and 'to teach the Church'.[65] This position rather weakens the force of Hobbes' earlier statement that 'subjects owe to sovereigns, simple obedience, in all things wherein their obedience is not repugnant to the laws of God.'[66]

Hobbes has demonstrated to his satisfaction the generation of political order in the commonwealth, and the conditions for its maintenance or destruction. He has deduced from natural principles why men obey this order and recognize those who enforce it. But he has not simply presented a set of conclusions that may be persuasive to some while obnoxious to others; he has provided with his conclusions a way of knowing. And given that 'all men by nature reason alike, and well, when they have good principles', the provision of such principles may be presumed to be salutary. Hobbes has provided for those capable of appreciating it, not a disinterested piece of theorizing, but a means of healing the recent wounds of the Civil War.

The intellectual gulf separating Augustine and Hobbes will now be clear. Augustine is a realist who belongs to a world in which the earth is the centre of creation, and man its crowning masterpiece.[67] For him there is an objective order according to which actions are right or wrong, just or unjust. It is a transcendent order, but is no less real for that. On the contrary, it is more real, for it is not affected by the imperfections, flux and decay of the temporal world. While Augustine lays stress upon the individual in his attitude towards God, he never doubts that man is naturally sociable.

---

[64] *Ibid.*, chapter 31, p. 240.
[65] *Ibid.*, chapter 42, p. 355. For an elaboration of this theme, see P. Springborg, 'Leviathan and the Problem of Ecclesiastical Authority', *Political Theory*, 3 (1975): pp. 289–303.
[66] *Leviathan*, chapter 31, p. 232.
[67] For a concise account of Augustine's realism, see M. H. Carré, *Realists and Nominalists*, Oxford University Press, 1946.

Hobbes, however, is a radical nominalist, an individualist, ethical naturalist and materialist. Motion rather than rest permeates his vision of the world. The earth is no longer the centre of the universe for thinking men. Relations among things have replaced essences as the basis of enquiry. What was previously an attribute is now a perception, something activated in the perceiver, not present in the object perceived. There is no objective moral order according to which justice may be measured, and there is no transcendent pattern after which the world is fashioned.

But we have before us not simply two different understandings of politics, but understandings of different scope. Augustine eschews the completeness attempted by Hobbes. The phenomenalism of the latter restricts what is knowable to what is observable, thereby circumscribing experience and offering the prospect of completeness. Augustine's world, however, is populated with good and evil spirits, and man's knowledge of God's intentions is a realm of infinite ignorance. In Hobbes' world view, reason is the appropriate instrument for guiding action. In Augustine's it is faith, for without knowledge of the divine plan, only the right attitude towards God's law can provide a measure of serenity. As Peter Brown has observed, a seventeenth-century theorist could

> ... imagine how reason, and a necessity assessed by reason, would lead [man] to found a state; and to derive from this 'mythical' rational act of choice, a valid, rational reason for obeying, or reforming, the state as it now is. By contrast, medieval thought ... regard(s) it as impossible to extrapolate and isolate man in such a way ... Above all, the link between the individual and the state cannot be limited to rational obligation. As it exists it is mysterious.[68]

Whether Brown's observation holds true in general or not, it expresses a truth about Augustine and Hobbes. It is a profound truth reflected in their procedures of argument. Where Hobbes seeks to be inclusive, to leave no obstacle in the way of securing peace, Augustine is more concerned that men will be deluded into believing they have powers they do not possess. The philosophical argument is designed to free men from the state of nature, to make them independent by showing them how to control a dangerous environment. The theological argument is designed to destroy man's sense of independence, the possibility of his making gods dance, his achievement of felicity through 'creative politics'.[69]

[68] Brown, *Religion and Society*, pp. 26-7.
[69] The phrase is Markus', *Saeculum*, p. 83.

Hence, the psychological, moral and metaphysical principles from which the Augustinian and Hobbesian political theories derive differ markedly. Ostensibly one may detect analogies between terms like 'peace', 'justice' and 'pride', or in shared concepts such as the equality of mankind. But such analogues and equivalences may be due more to the effects of translation than to a substantive overlap in meaning. Even allowing for the inevitable semantic differences between, say, *pax* and 'peace' disguised by translation, it is clear that these terms belong to quite distinct ideological contexts. Hobbes himself is at great pains to ensure that his readers should not mistake his usage for that of his predecessors. He takes to task the schoolmen for erecting a transcendental metaphysics upon linguistic confusion, and carefully defines his terms to establish clearly the difference between his type of theorizing and theirs. Certainly he differs from Augustine. Whereas for Augustine a term such as 'peace' has mystical associations, for Hobbes it is defined positivistically as the absence of war. Augustine has a much more positive – rather than positivist – conception of peace as the tranquillity of God's order upon creation. It is nothing less than eternal life, the Ultimate Good of the city of God.[70]

Similarly, Hobbes' use of the term 'pride' seems to resemble Autustine's. In the theories of both, pride is a source of social disorder. And for both, pride involves the exultation of self. Hobbes, however, defines this exultation solely in terms of the relation of the individual to others: pride is the denial of the equality of all. Augustine views pride as the fundamental sin against God. It is not simply something natural to humanity, a want of reason in the estimation of a common equality, but a defect of the will. Augustinian man not only fails to acknowledge the power of God but supposes himself able to exercise powers that are not his. Again the difference is not merely one of usage but of assumption and intention: Augustine's metaphysics are transcendental; Hobbes' materialist.[71]

Yet intimations of similarities between the two theorists are not unfounded. Augustine's realism issues in much the same theoretical consequences as Hobbes' nominalism. The doctrine of original sin no less than the doctrine of nominalism removes absolute virtue from the domain of the sublunary world. Augustine's replacement of true peace, justice and other virtues with earthly simulacra parallels Hobbes'

[70] *City of God*, XIX, 27, p. 892.
[71] *Ibid.*, XIV, 13; *Leviathan*, chapter 15, p. 100.

derivation of a moral code from civil society. They are not the same thing, for Augustine's simulacra are at least shadows of a real order, but their political implications are similar. Because true peace, order, justice and concord cannot be attained in this life, they offer no enticement to members of the city of God to resist their temporal rulers. Even tyrants have their usefulness as a test of virtue. Thus obedience is enjoined even for the minimal peace that is afforded under a harsh or corrupt regime.

Augustine's minimal definition of the commonwealth, stripped of a moral or religious legitimation, agrees closely with Hobbes'. For both, its function is to maintain order. Whereas Hobbes would dismiss accusations of tyranny as statements, not about the sovereign, but about the dispositions of the accuser, Augustine might concede their validity but would deny that this made any difference to the subject's obligation to obey. Both are theorists of *de facto* power: whoever rules is to be obeyed so long as he preserves some order, or, in the case of Hobbes, for so long as he is able to defend his subjects.

Hence, despite their differences, both theories have similar consequences. Both Augustine and Hobbes end up by separating out political from moral and religious discourse. Paradoxically, Augustine does this within the structure of a theological argument. Politics is removed from the realm of the particular – the myth of Rome – and its identity transposed to the universal where it takes its place in God's scheme for the salvation of man. Hobbes too removes politics from the realm of controversy by changing its identity from one fashioned from law, custom, religion and history to one derived from science. Both Augustine and Hobbes separate political discourse from matters that give rise to crisis by shifting the level of argument and changing its terms. They do this not by adopting a wholly new political language – this would simply be an irrelevance – but by redefining conventional terms in their respective political vocabularies. Hence Augustine Christianizes terms like 'peace' and 'justice'.[72] No longer may they apply properly to earthly kingdoms. The similacra that take their place will not distract the pilgrim in his journey to God. Augustine has revealed a new *civitas* as deserving loyalty exclusively, and has plundered the earthly city of its lustre to show better the sovereignty of God. Hobbes, with his philosophical method, performed a parallel operation twelve hundred years later by redefining the current political vocabulary to free it of opinion and bring it under the control of science.

[72] *Cf.* Markus, *Saeculum*, pp. 64–5.

Bertrand de Jouvenal has characterized political problems as essentially unsolvable: 'What makes a problem "political" is precisely that its terms admit no solution properly so called.' While political problems may not be solved, they may be settled, which is another matter altogether: 'While it is the very definition of a solution that it satisfies in full all the terms of the problem, the settlement does not do so. It cannot do so, since, as in bankruptcy, there is no possibility of meeting all claims in full.'[73] If this distinction is extended to the intellectual realm of politics, to political argument, Augustine and Hobbes can be seen to have framed their theories not as solutions to political problems but as settlements. Neither pretends that political arrangements will change the nature of man. As the diversity of human pursuits and attractions lies at the bases of the first problem of politics – how to secure peace – the theories of Augustine and Hobbes propose to harness rather than abolish socially incompatible elements in the human make-up. If those who belong to the earthly city wish to project their final satisfactions into the shapes of earthly empires, argues Augustine, then those who belong to the city of God may make use of the consequent benefits. But there is no reconciliation possible between them. The case is similar with Hobbes. When the fundamental principle of self-preservation within men is unmatched by their means to secure it individually, then rationality dictates that they surrender individual rights of self-protection to someone who can. But because the competitive drives are only contained, not transformed, Hobbes' theory is a settlement, not a solution.

Yet the *City of God* and *Leviathan* are not simply or wholly about politics. The former is a work of theology, the latter one of philosophy. If de Jouvenal is right in his observation that political problems, *qua* political, are insoluble, then it may be expected that problems in theology and philosophy, where there is coherence and agreement on terms, are amenable to solutions that satisfy and not merely settle. Indeed, it seems that of settlements only one is possible in politics, whereas in theology and philosophy, as in quadratic equations, there is room for more than one solution. While Augustine and Hobbes may not have found solutions to political problems, perhaps this spurious bankruptcy would not have troubled even Hobbes: both theorists remained solvent within their specific activities, that is, where it counted. And it is upon the authority of those activities that their political theorizing stands.[74]

[73] *Pure Theory of Politics*, pp. 206–7.
[74] I have adapted freely here from Condren, *Three Aspects of Political Theory*, chapter 1.

Politics, then, is a secondary problem for both theorists. Although each is confronted with questions about violence, peace and order and with the nature of arrangements to deal with them, such questions are made tractable within the primary activity of theorizing theologically or philosophically. The irony of comparison is to reveal in the differing assumptions and procedures of Augustine and Hobbes a substantial agreement on conclusions. But such agreement could only be a settlement, never a solution.

More and Socrates

C. and A. C. Condren

I Amongst the symbolic graffiti embedded in the floor of Siena Cathedral, is one of the mythical Hermes Tristmegistus conveying pagan learning to the Christian world; and one of the world under the sway of fortune in which an unlikely looking Socrates is being handed the palm of victory. The presence of Hermes and Socrates in the floor of Il Duomo pointedly invites consideration of the relationships between history and myth that pivot around the Christian awareness of pagan civilization, which ambivalently was both an encumbrance and an inheritance.

That there was a problem of relationship between, as it were, the ages of light and dark was a direct consequence of several things: a belief in a Christian dispensation; a linear conception of time; and, partly, a polemical desire to separate the pagan from the Christian.[1] On the one hand there was postulated theologically a fundamental gulf between the two worlds; on the other the existence of the pagan world could hardly be theologically redundant, and there was much potentially born in the age of dark that might be of service in the light – a view that the children of crepusculus,* such as St Augustine, could hardly avoid.

To simplify drastically, one may say that the problems raised were answered in terms of religious pragmatics. The pagan was transmitted insofar as it could be translated into Christian terms. In principle its value was a function of its figurative power and its symbolic resonance. As

---

This essay is adapted from a paper given at the Thomas More Quincentenary Congress, St John's College, University of Sydney, 17 August 1978.

[1] Gerald A. Press, 'History and the Development of the Idea of History in Antiquity', *History & Theory*, 16(1977): No. 3, 281–96. See also Joseph Levinson, *Confucian China and Its Modern Fate*, chapter 3, Vol, III, Routledge and Kegan Paul, London, 1965, on the separation of past and present in modern China, and his conclusion (especially pp. 113–15) where an early Christian parallel is drawn.

* The twilight. (Ed.)

Petrach had said, his studies of antiquity were made in order to bring the ancient to the feet of the modern church.[2] Hermes on the floor, who brings wisdom by the grace of God, is himself a symbol that joins light to dark. Socrates is perhaps the most powerful example of an ancient pagan figure becoming something of a *figura*, and something of a myth – a man becoming a representative symbol to be used variously in the light of another world.[3] Christianity has hardly lacked an ability to generate symbols of its own, which, as it were, act as paradigms for the assimilation of the ancient world, the most notable species of which are the saints – people exemplifying acutely Christian ideals and providing a link between this world and the Christian afterlife. Their existence sharpens the qualities of the pagan virtuous in Christian eyes, whilst the pagan virtuous add a diachronic† depth to the saintly class, hence the letters between St Paul and Seneca. Together the possibilities of virtue resonate across the great divide, like bright beads along a single string of time.

II It is in this context that some general comparison between Socrates and More as men, and as symbols, may be illuminating and not entirely arbitrary. Methodologically, however, we must try to tread a path between two extremes. At one, comparisons may easily enough become too general to have any substance. At the other, by a covert process of translation, one can easily present as a specific and direct point of comparison that which has been prejudiced or even manufactured by the terms we choose to use. Thus, for example, Edward Freeman quite properly censures Grote for translating *demagogue* as 'opposition speaker' and so employing and connoting political and institutional categories which permit purely spurious comparisons between nineteenth-century England and ancient Athens. Again, once Emerton has rendered the term *Ciompi* as 'bolshevik', he has not so much uncovered a point of

---

[2] Cited in J. Huizinga, *Men and Ideas*, trans. J. S. Holmes and Hans van Marle, Meridian, New York, 1965, p. 273.
[3] The evidence of the use of Socrates in the ancient world is patchy, but it appears to have been both persistent and varied – a vital means by which men came to terms with their troublesome inheritance. Quintillian and Cicero make extensive use of him; he loomed large in Stoic and Cynic pedigrees; he was widely used by Christian writers, most notably Jerome, Augustine, Tertullian and John Chrysostom; and he was available equally for apostate polemic, see Libanius, *De Socratis Silentio Opera*, trans. E. J. R. Forster, Vol. v, Stuttgart, 1909. In English much valuable documentation is provided by John Ferguson, *Socrates: A Source Book*, Macmillan, London, 1970.
† Diachronic = historical, as opposed to synchronic. (Ed.)

comparison between medieval and twentieth-century tyranny as manufactured a comparison through a categorical anachronism[4], and on which dubious basis he then feels able to explain Salutati's *de Tyranno* (1400) with reference to the career of Musollini (*sic*).[5] It is this interesting and insidious process of conceptual translation (a species of mythologizing masquerading as comparison) that we shall meet with respect to the trials and the deaths of both men.

A median way requires the use of a general classificatory vocabulary to which neither man is assimilated, but in terms of which each can be similarly located with respect to his own society. Along this way there are a number of generally valid if indirect points of comparison between Socrates and More:

• Both men lived in societies that exhibited not singular but dual senses of political identity. Athenians, Corinthians and Spartans were all also Hellenes, and commitment to a notion of *Hellas* could cut across loyalty to *polis*, its rhetoric channelling and justifying what might also be seen as the fermentation of *stasis*. Commitment to *polis* was always a fragile flower, torn at its roots by family and locality, at its branches by a ramified sense of Hellenic identity. Similarly an Englishman, or an Italian, was also a member of Christendom, recognition of which could, as it did with Becket, qualify allegiance to *regnum*.[6] So too, the rhetoric of the peace of Christendom could cloak family and local aspirations that could tear at the fabric of society. Socrates' sense of identity as an Athenian was probably misunderstood, qualified less than his accusors feared; More's qualified loyalty to his prince understood too well.

• Both men, as needs no labouring, had an uncompromising sense of moral absolutism, a not uncommon phenomenon but particularly significant when we note that both lived in societies in which the received moral vocabularies were unstable. Socrates lived through the period in which the inherited moral vocabulary of Homer's world and archaic Greece was collapsing and was beginning to be replaced by a new range of moral sensibilities, requiring a transformed moral and political

---

[4] For further comment and more formal elaboration, see C. Condren, 'An Historiographical Paradox', in N. Wright and F. McGreggor (eds), *European History and its Historians*, University Union Press, Adelaide, 1977, p. 86.

[5] Edward Freeman, *Historical Essays*, Second Series, London, 1800, p. 154; E. E. Emerton, *Humanism and Tyranny*, Peter Smith, Gloss. Mass., 1964, pp. 53 and 63 respectively.

[6] This point is expanded in the essay 'Marsilius and Machiavelli', in this collection.

language.[7] The situation of Sir Thomas More (1477/8-1535) was similar; there is a sense of *fin de siècle* that permeates much of the writing of the late fifteenth and early sixteenth centuries, which has improperly surprised some historians blinded by such labels as 'the renaissance', the 'rise of the modern state', 'the age of discovery'.[8] But this sense of decline was well founded. Christendom seemed to be fragmenting and to be externally threatened; no longer the world, it was struggling to maintain its place within the world.[9] A perceptive pessimism is found in thinkers who parenthesize More's life: In *Aeneas Sylvius*, Piccolomini's famous letter to Rome of 1454 lamenting the lack of loyalty to church and empire alike[10]; and a generation later, though less prophetically, in the astrologer Pomponatius' belief in the imminent collapse of Christianity itself.[11] The so-called rise of the modern state was in effect the collapse of Christendom, it replaced a dual with a singular sense of political identity, and with it came a change in the vocabulary of politics. Indeed, like the collapse of the Homeric honour code which could not survive the emergence of the classical *polis*, this collapse was principally one of a field of moral and political *clés mots* which abridged Christendom and its parts' sense of the purpose and qualities of political life.

If Socrates stands between the old Homeric honour code and the new co-operative conception of the *polis* intimated by the great tragedians and defined by Plato and Aristotle, More may be seen as standing between the *regna* of Christendom and the European state intimated by Machiavelli and defined by Hobbes. As we are dealing with ethico-political conceptions, both Socrates and More are better located with respect to linguistic change than to institutional change. In such periods of conceptual transformation, a sense of the morally absolute is apt to look out of touch, and is certainly difficult to maintain insofar as the very elements of moral discussion are too often unstable. Socrates and

---

[7] See, at length, A. W. H. Adkins, *Merit and Responsibility*, Oxford University Press, 1962.
[8] For example, M. Gilmore, *The World of Humanism*, Harper & Row, New York, 1952, pp. 1–4.
[9] This was the main significance of the term 'Europe' being extended from the esoteric realms of cartography to those of social and political awareness. It was only as Christendom failed as an abridgement of political experience that the term 'Europe' took on political reference. See Denys Hay, *Europe: The Emergence of an Idea*, Edinburgh University Press, 1955.
[10] Quoted in Gilmore, *op. cit.*, p. 1.
[11] Cited in C. S. Lewis, *A History of English Literature in the Sixteenth Century (Excluding Drama)*, Oxford University Press, 1973 edn, p. 5.

Gorgias, More and Machiavelli, share parallel communities of different problems. Further, both Socrates and More drew on parallel aspects of their inheritances in order to maintain some sense of the absolute. Socrates drew on an inheritance of the importance of the oracles and possibly shamanistic wisdom in evoking his notion of the *daimonion* – the inner voice. More's behaviour and sense of moral purpose came from his belief in a knowable Christian God whose purposes for mankind were mediated through the head of Christendom. Both, in short, relied upon similarly universal contexts of their political identities in order to express a sense of moral absolutism with respect to the possibilities of proper action.

• It is not surprising that both appear to have shared similarly ambivalent attitudes to political activity, though both were very much political animals. Socrates, as citizen of Athens, was perforce a political animal, in the only way that made sense to the Athenians. When called upon he performed his political duties, the very proof of his being *eleutheros* ('free'). He was, however, by no means totally committed to the politics of his society, as both Plato and his accusors make clear. The political arena was not the only, or necessarily the most suitable, stage on which man should exhibit his virtues. If the arena was inescapable and the most natural setting for the *agathos* ('the good man'), it also provided a constant source of corruption. As Socrates is made to lament in the *Republic* (a latish work but the comment seems in character), how much more dangerous is man of philosophic potential if corrupted by his political society.[12] In Shakespeare's image, 'lillies that fester smell far worse than weeds'. If More's society afforded something of a genuine choice concerning political participation, More's own decision to hazard the life at court was patently marked by ambivalence. For men of More's world, the possibilities of a-political citizenship clearly pointed the character of political life, especially life in the ambit of a prince.

In a world of monasteries and universities one could hardly be an unselfconscious political citizen. Thus the familiar *topoi* and maxims of the ancient world concerning politics and moral corruption had different points for Socrates and More; the *Epigrammata* are translations in at least two senses of the word. If he did not like the heat the citizen *could* leave the hothouse. Equally few were called to enter a world of rapid growth

---

[12] Plato, *Republic*, 495a.

and sudden decay, wherein the King's displeasure could signal death.[13] Lillies could fester, lillies could bloom, and this was precisely why the good man should make the effort to enter courtly life. For the good man to quit the hothouse, despite the dangers of death and corruption, the whole world became a worse place. Such grounds were shared possibly by Machiavelli, certainly later by Clarendon.[14]* But if the grounds were plausible enough, lacking a Guicciardini's praise of ambition as a political virtue, they could be little more than a covert justification for self-seeking, and self-deception, and there may be just a touch of such self-deception in More, as there was in Clarendon when he tried to serve too many masters for too long.[15] But if both More and Socrates shared ambivalent attitudes to political activity and the dangers of corruption, their awarenesses can hardly have had the same metaphysical grounding. For only in a Christian, post-Augustinian world is political life necessarily entangled with human corruption; politics, having no *finalis intentio*, is a product of the expulsion from Eden, and by augmenting the temptations of private life is doubly dangerous for the fallen. For a Socrates such beliefs would seem absurd, but for all the inheritors of the conception of Christendom, such as More and Machiavelli, they provided the *a priori* warning that needed fleshing out only with historical examples.

• Given a superficially similar but differently rooted political ambivalence, it is not surprising that both More and Socrates can easily be read

[13] 'And so they said that these matters be Kings' games, as it were, stage plays, and for the more part played upon scaffolds, in which the poor men be but the lookers-on.' (More, *The History of King Richard III*, R. S. Sylvester (ed.), Yale University Press, 1976, p. 83.) The pun on scaffold is vital here. Adages concerning the uncertainty of life of men in public politics were common; William Roper cites one, *'Indignatis principis mor est.'*, ('Life of Sir Thomas More, Knight', in E. E. Reynolds (ed.), *Lives of St Thomas More*, Dent, London, 1963, p. 35), and More's *Epigrammata* sporadically explores the theme.

[14] Machiavelli, *Il Principe*, chapters 22 and 23; and Clarendon, *Contemplations and Reflexions on the Psalms*, on which see I. Coltman, *Public Men and Private Causes*, Faber, London, 1962, especially parts I and II. The theme is perhaps ultimately rooted in Plato, for example in *Republic*, 519C–8.

* Edward Hyde, 1st Earl of Clarendon, historian and autobiographer, (1609–1674) was a strong influence on Charles I on matters of legality and constitutionalism, but when his advice went unheeded, and civil war broke out in England, he remained loyal to the king. He was expelled from Parliament. Charles appointed him Chancellor of the Exchequer and a privy councillor, and in 1658 he became Lord Chancellor for Charles II; in 1660 he was made Baron Hyde of Hyndon, and in 1661 Viscount Cornbury and 1st Earl of Clarendon. After the monarchy was restored in England, he became Chancellor of Oxford University and speaker of the House of Lords.

In the course of his career he made bitter enemies on all sides. In 1667 he was accused of treason and banished. (Ed.)

[15] See Coltman, *op. cit.*, pp. 116–21.

as critics of their respective societies. Xenophon notwithstanding, Socrates' life and death are unintelligible except as sustained acts of social criticism. More, from his fanciful exploration of tyranny in *The History of King Richard III*, to his imaginative fear that sheep will eat men, was a critic of the society to which he was also committed.

Further, with both, the force and direction of their criticisms is somewhat elusive. For Socrates this is principally the case because he did not write but was interpreted through his diverse followers and critics. We can do little better than explore the compound image created, each for his own purposes, by Aristophanes, Xenophon and Plato; of direct evidence there is none. With More the elusiveness is the result of his mode of writing – his persistent, perhaps his deliberately defensive indirection.[16] Thus with the *Epigrammata* the points at which More speaks and More seeks to translate are often obscure. With the *Richard* and the *Utopia*, the general categories of time and geographical space are used to achieve a potential distance between the written works and the force of what More has to say.[17] Disingenuous perhaps, cautious certainly, and from this, an ambiguity, like the *de facto* ambiguity of the evidence surrounding the real Socrates, which results in a diversity of possibility for interpretation and use. In a certain ambiguity we can see with both men a factor in each one's symbolic resonance.

We may, however, go a little further; More, it seems, had an unambiguous respect for law and custom, and so too apparently did Socrates. Richard's disrespect is one of the principle marks of the tyrant; the Utopians' respect for law *per se* one of their unquestionable virtues. But here there is a danger. We must be careful not to convert this respect into clear evidence for a shared social conservatism. More lived in a world in which the rhetoric of law and custom was *de rigueur*; even the most revolutionary of statutes (*Quia Emptores*, the *Constitutions of Clarendon* and the *Acts of Succession and Supremacy*) were all defensible in terms of custom. Whatever a man respected he could justify through the idiom of custom; whatever he abhorred could be its breach. Custom and law were thus highly prescriptive terms, they were a part of every apologist's

---

[16] On More's intellectual caution and indirection, see D. G. Grace, The Political Thought of St Thomas More, 1509–1521, unpublished Ph.D. thesis, University of New South Wales, 1980.

[17] So too with the *Dialogue of Comfort*, but with this and the other works mentioned the indirection also functions to disperse and augment his points of reference beyond England – a direct consequence of More's dual sense of political identity. G. Elton makes this point with respect to the *Dialogue* in reviewing the Yale edition of *The Tower Works*, (*English Historical Review*, April 1978).

armoury. That More in fact lived in a period of considerable legal change merely complicates our problems of understanding.

Again the parallel with Socrates is pointed but indirect. He lived in a similarly confusing period of legal change and, if we are to be guided by Plato's earliest dialogues, he espoused an absolutist respect for the forms of law. This respect, however, would have been grounded less in a sense of tradition transmitted over time, than in a belief that *nomos* ('law') was embedded in a vibrant *physis* ('nature'). During Socrates' lifetime, however, the precise scope of *nomos* and its relationship to *physis* were both matters of doubt – and there appears to have been something of a free-floating rhetoric of *physis* and *nomos* as there was of custom and law in More's time. In short, in times of legal transition both could still call on rhetorics of legal establishment, and it is thus perhaps less ironic than it might seem that both more or less through due process of law were tried and executed.

III Thus far we have outlined some general lines along which the comparison of figures such as Socrates and More can proceed: that is, given a general classificatory vocabulary, we can, as it were, delineate a set of parallel taxonomies. But to repeat; this process of indirect comparison is not to be confused with seeing Socrates and More as sharing the same problems, confronting the same issues and ideas, being in the same camp, being prominent beads on the same string. There is a difference between a vocabulary deployed to get to grips with a variety of problems, and the reduction of any one set of problems to the terms of another.

It is this particular confusion that is a great temptation in dealing with what seems to provide the most obvious and significant point of comparison between the two men – the meaning and underlying issues of their trials and deaths. What we understand to be the common conspectus may be abridged as follows:

> Both Socrates and More were public men of high moral principle whose consciences required them in the name of a higher law to refuse to do what the authority of the state demanded. Both, as Wilde might have put it, played Antigone to different Creons in the name of liberty, conscience and the moral order. As neither would compromise, both were tried, and with the aid of perjury, malice and dubious charges, were similarly condemned, and died upholding their principles, despite the attempts of others to persuade them to comply with the requirements of the state.

All this seems to be very plausible, but a large part of its plausibility arises through shifting from general classificatory categories to a community of specific issues, which were not Socrates', nor strictly speaking More's, but are rather ours in terms of which the trials of both men may be translated to make common and reassuring sense to us.

Our own political experience is characterized by a distinctive vocabulary, which provides the 'problems' in terms of which we see political action; the criteria of political judgement; and an attendant rhetoric of political eristics. It functions somewhat, though not as neatly, as our received field of chromatic discrimination divides our palette into the spectrum of colours by which we appraise the hues and tincture of the world around us.

A large part of the political field of terms is constituted by such reciprocally related *clés mots* as 'conscience', 'authority', 'state', 'freedom', 'public', 'private', 'right', and 'obligation'. To use this vocabulary is to be engaged in some form of political speculation. What we must remember, however, is the historical contingency of both the political and 'chromatic' fields of terms we nowadays normally employ. Between the sixteenth and twentieth centuries, there have been changes both subtle and significant, though as is usually the way with language none have been easily discernible or predictable in their ramifications. New words have come into political prominence (state, nation, totalitarian); old words have fallen into political desuetude (loyalty, custom, piety); and continuingly significant terms have greatly changed in denotation, connotation and emotional resonance (democracy, rhetoric, right, conscience, and class).

We are not saying, for example, that people are no longer loyal, pious, and so forth; but that the vocabulary through which issues are formulated and the political world understood has changed, not totally, but significantly; not with respect to individual words acting as independent variables, some of which may retain some permanent residue of fixed meaning; but with respect to a whole reciprocally related field of terms.[18] And if the language that structures political discourse and awareness has changed between More's world and ours, we can hardly hold our political problems in common. These points, however, are easily overlooked because of the superficial continuity of many terms since the sixteenth century, and because of the positive desire to press the past into the shape of the present. The floundering world of

---

[18] The problem is not strictly speaking one of whether human nature has changed (as, for example, Erwin Panowsky would have it); it is a question of how it is conceptualized and appraised.

sixteenth-century Christendom may thus easily be translated into the terms that characterize the modern industrial nation–state, a process of translation that is categorically anachronistic, and systematically distorting; for any account of More's trial that trades in terms of 'state', 'individual' and 'conscience' (in a modern sense) delineates the political world and its problems as More never did. At the beginning of the sixteenth century 'state' was hardly a part of western political vocabulary; 'family' and functional 'class' were more significant abstractions than 'individual'; and 'conscience' – a word much favoured by More – was by no means clearly everybody's right of appeal, any more than it was unequivocally a witness to a fact, or a judge of right, or almost on occasions an opinion or view that could simply be changed.[19] Indeed, before the term came to refer uniformly to everyone's belief as to what it was right for them to do as individuals, it hardened into the very different Miltonic sign of an infallible and exclusive moral knowledge.[20] In short, of the main meanings found in the sixteenth century, one achieved a dominance in the seventeenth century and the other, in a very extended sense, has become normal in the twentieth. When More spoke of his conscience we cannot be certain he entertained our meaning of the word, but we can be sure that he was aware of meanings we have all but forgotten, in a very different context of lexical associations, and that it did not assume the importance we have much later attached to it.[21] Thus the recent acknowledgement by the Anglican Church that More is one who died for conscience sake would seem to have more ecumenical charity than historical validity: his virtue thus becomes unquestionable without evoking problematic connotations of Roman authority.

With Socrates the continuities are even more severely fractured. Between him and More were not only interposed the civilizations of Rome and Christendom: we now employ terms that owe much to both, and little or nothing to Greece. The notions of public and private, power and authority we owe to Roman political awareness; those of redress and representation, largely to medieval Christian society. Indeed the field of political terms with which the Greek was at home is now remarkably alien

---

[19] See C. S. Lewis, *Studies in Words*, Cambridge University Press, 1974 edn, p. 181ff, who discusses the first two senses at length. For all three of these, at times bewildering senses of the term, see the letter from Margaret Roper to Alice Alington, (August 1534), item 206 in *Correspondence of Sir Thomas More*, E. F. Rogers (ed.), Princeton University Press, 1947.
[20] John Milton, *Areopagitica*, a fine discussion of which is to be found in W. Kendall, 'How to Read Milton's *Areopagitica*' in *Journal of Politics*, XXII (1960): 439–73.
[21] See Lewis, *op. cit.*, pp. 202–4.

to us. Notions of pollution, appearance, personal honour, impiety, courage and cunning were of paramount importance. Justice, until Plato, had an uncertain status[22]; there was no clear concept of authority[23]; the notions of freedom and representation almost the reverse of our understandings[24]; whilst a notion of individual moral responsibility seems to have been quite absent.[25] In this context there is no place for a conscience in a modern sense, and Socrates' *daimonion* is certainly not 'conscience' as we understand the term. Lewis quite properly does not associate *daimonion* with conscience, his starting points in Greek being *oida* (I know) and *sunoida* (I share knowledge with). Liddell and Scott's *Lexicon* circumscribes the area of reference for *daimonion* as divine operation, and associates *daimonia* with a lesser class of demons. *Genius*, in the latin sense is probably closer than conscience. Ironically, when Tertullian understood the Socratic *daimonion* to be a form of demon, and contrasted all such *demonia* with Christian wisdom, he was, despite his apologetic motivation, much closer to the historical and linguistic truth than the contemporary association of *daimonion* with conscience.[26] Similarly, it is little wonder that we search in vain in Plato's account of Socrates' trial and death for a satisfying defence of individual freedom from the authority of the state, or conversely for a doctrine of unqualified obedience to what it decrees.[27]

Because Homer wrote of wine dark seas, flowing black blood, and other fancies, when we all know that the sea is but occasionally red with blood and for all its effects wine is never blue, grey or green, it has been

[22] See Adkins, *op. cit.*, at length.
[23] J. L. Myers, *The Political Ideas of the Greeks*, Greenwood, New York, 1967 edn, p. 142, remarks that it could refer to the end of a piece of rope, a cause, a foundation, a beginning, as well as referring to public office and to initiation.
[24] Representation was the mark of the slave. On *eleutheria*, see Myers, *op. cit.*, p. 319ff.
[25] It is this and its consequences for understanding Greek society that is Adkins' starting point. His position here is hardly idiosyncratic amongst classical scholars – especially those concerned with the understanding of Greek tragedy – but it is a position we do well to ignore, or consider to be free of any significant repercussions, whenever we wish to appropriate the Greeks to ourselves. See, for example, John Jones, *On Aristotle and Greek Tragedy*, Chatto & Windus, London, 1962, p. 15, where he notes that *hamartia* had no overtones of moral error.
[26] See Lewis, *op. cit.*, p. 181; and Tertullian, *De Anima*, J. H. Waszink (ed.), Amsterdam, 1947, 12–6. For Waszink's detailed notes, see pp. 83–98. See also Tertullian, *Apology*, XXII 1–3; and Minucius Felix, *Octavius*, XXIV 9, who writes of the command and will (*ad natum et arbitrium*) of Socrates' attendant/besieging demon (*adsidentis sibi daemonis*). Such an association is blithely asserted, for example, by C. J. Friedrich, *An Introduction to Political Theory*, Harper & Row, New York, 1967, p. 86.
[27] See, for example, Rex Martin, 'Socrates on Disobedience to Law', *The Review of Metaphysics*, 24 (1970): 21–38, and also references p. 21.

held that the Greeks were colour-blind. What was overlooked was that the Greek chromatic field was not ours, nor its discriminations replicas of ours by any other set of names.[28] That is true, though more clearly of Attic political vocabulary at the time of Socrates' death; it is true, though less completely, of English political vocabulary at the time of More's. To equate the issues of Socrates' fate with More's, and both with our problems and the issues defined by our language, is to suffer a sort of conceptual colour-blindness, to perpetuate a chromatic reductionism, a grey on grey which is the mark of historical blindness. Above all it is the mark not of historical interpretation but of symbolic elaboration and translation, and it is in this respect above all else that More and Socrates may be directly compared.

In ceasing to be living men with their own experiences and problems, they both became symbols, passive coins in the exchange and reckonings of others. But this general point itself needs cashing and the term 'symbol' unpacking.

In his discussion and delineation of symbolism, Northrop Frye draws a useful working distinction between archetypal and monadic symbols.[29] Archetypal symbols are those that function within the common literary inheritance of a given society or civilization. They are significant images (metaphors, similes) which encapsulate a wide range of ideas and associations. The image of blood on the hands of Lady Macbeth thus draws on associations of blood, red, and guilt, which, in English, we can take largely for granted. Such imagery is archetypal and provides the well-worn literary currency of a civilization included in which may be personified images both poetic (Father Time) and historical (Richard III as the archetypal wicked uncle).[30] When the associations of these personified images become sufficiently laudatory the names may come to have the sort of resonance and authority which Dodd called the *auctoritas*

---

[28] Consider the term *glaukon* which covered the chromatic range light blue, grey, green, greyish–green. It could also mean bright and gleaming.

[29] N. Frye, *Anatomy of Criticism*, Princeton University Press, 1975, 2nd essay 'Ethical Criticism: Theory of Symbols', pp. 71–128.

[30] We do not know how quickly Richard became the symbol of the wicked uncle, but a ballad, dated 1595, called 'Children in the Wood' ('Babes in the Wood') tells the story of an uncle who murdered his niece and nephew in order to get their property and was punished by God with the loss of his own sons, goods and life. This looks very like an oblique reference to Richard. There is also a play, dated 1601, dealing with the same story. Shakespeare's Richard III was first performed in 1593. In this play both murderers repent after they have killed the children. Shakespeare probably took much of his plot from *The History of King Richard III* attributed to More.

of the master.[31] The words, actions and beliefs of such persons (images) with respect to a given field of experience, become eminently usable and co-optable, because of who they were, or are alleged to have been.

When such archetypal images are able to function across different societies *qua* cultures they become monadic. At this point, in this context, two aspects of this delineation of symbolism need to be stressed:
(1) Archetypal and monadic symbols are not mere ornamentation; rather they are a means of imposing some conceptual order upon the world.[32] That is, they structure and convey a sense of that structure to the reader, albeit in a shorthand form. This is especially so with sets of closely entangled problems. MacLeish once remarked, with respect to his own use of Job as symbol: 'When you are dealing with questions too large for you, which, nevertheless, will not leave you alone, you are obliged to house them somewhere . . .'[33] Symbols, archetypal and monadic, at the concrete level, or by means of personification, help to supplement abstract fields of terms used to similar ends. Thus the archaic Greeks used a genealogical relationship between the goddesses Themis and Dike to express or to house an understanding of the relationship between *themistes* (ordinances) and *dikaiasune* (justice).[34] It was in fact this ability to move from the symbolic (archetypal) ordering of the world to an abstract conceptualization of it that Vico saw marking the limits of the primitive (poetic) and the rational mind.
(2) The distinctions between archetypal and monadic symbols that Frye makes suggest a means of plotting symbolic significance on the axes of increasingly complex (extensional) and decreasingly specific (intensional) reference. That is, the more general and widely used are symbols, the less they have specific force or the ability to delineate and abridge any precise understanding. Any symbol used by an author, even if widely used within his or her work, will in that context carry more discriminate associations than the same symbol used archetypally by the whole community. In the same way a symbol used archetypally by one community will have more intention than that, or any symbol, functioning at the monadic level. Thus the monads 'light' and 'dark'

---

[31] C. H. Dodd, *The Authority of the Bible*, Fontana, London, 1960 edn, pp. 33–4.
[32] See Peter Munz, *When the Golden Bough Breaks*, Routledge & Kegan Paul, London, 1973, pp. 74–5. Munz argues that symbols are the only way of expressing some kinds of experience, especially the religious.
[33] Archibald MacLeish, cited in *Myth and Symbol*, Berenice Slote (ed.), University of Nebraska Press, 1963, p. 79.
[34] On these relationships, see Myers, *op. cit.*, p. 183.

function as images of 'good' and 'evil' or 'knowledge' and 'ignorance'.[35] What is subsumed under these less pictorial terms (that is, the understanding of what constitutes 'evil' or 'knowledge') may, however, vary considerably.[36] Concomitantly, what archetypal and monadic symbols lose in denotation they gain in extensive, if vague, suggestiveness.

The use of such symbol structures in practical and religious discourse is particularly common. Such usage identifies the speaker with his or her audience as sharers in a common experience and awareness (what makes a cliché is an excess of mutual familiarity). In this process of identification the manipulation of resonant symbols is a principal rhetorical strategy.

This consideration of types of symbols and their various usage and force has now placed us in a position to make some direct comparison between More and Socrates as symbols. Both are, of course, personified as historical figures with the *auctoritas* of the master; that is, both have laudable resonance. Socrates functions in the monadic dimension, and it can be argued that More does also, but this depends upon where, and according to what criteria, one draws the lines between specific cultural groups or distinctive civilizations.

Secondly, both function in the same symbolic nexus; within the world of political and moral discourse, each houses the same sort of problem. Both, as symbols, personify the same cluster of contemporary abstract world-ordering conceptions: integrity, individuality, humanity, principled self-sacrifice and wisdom, which have connotations of the individual on the side of rights versus the state. This means more than just that they are both personifications of 'good' as opposed to 'evil'; Socrates and More are both symbols ranged against the potential misuse of political authority, figures at the gates of a higher moral realm. They are thus as symbols less available to established authority than to those who wish to identify with the subjects of the state's authority or who wish to stress that authority's responsibility. Consequently, the simple association of Socrates and/or More with a contemporary situation, say involving conscientious objection, the persecution of intellectuals or

---

[35] C. S. Lewis remarks in *The Allegory of Love*, Galaxy, New York, 1964 edn, p. 44, that it is more sensible to ask how these associations became severed rather than to try to trace their initial joining.

[36] Consider Plato's imagery of the cave, the difficulties of unravelling precisely what he wished to convey by it, and the ease with which it could be made to subsume Christian notions that were expressed in similar imagery.

dissent on religious grounds, evokes an immensely resonant inheritance. Thus when they are used as symbols, the writer is writing not about them but about the present trailing a coat of suitably lineal colours–a situation that often requires scant de-coding because of such expressions as 'we have a lot to learn from the life of . . .' or 'the death of . . . is a warning to us all . . .' This we suggest may help explain why politicians were so willing to speak on More during the recent and extensive quincentenary celebrations. They praised the symbol and thereby identified themselves with the qualities it houses and the audiences who hold it dear. In trading in a traditional symbolic currency they made a sort of down payment on political respectability – there but for the Grace of God go all politicians of integrity. We cannot imagine a similar willingness to talk on Hobbes or (outside Italy) on Machiavelli.

Thirdly, if both are typically tokens in the currency of moral and political discourse, there are similar barriers in the way of making either an effective literary symbol, and in the way of untangling the historical truth about them. The dead weight of moralizing cliché is apt to limit their literary potential; to adopt a thoroughly aestheticist position, moral investment is an enemy of art.[37] It is true that Plato was able to make Socrates a figure of considerable literary power in his early dialogues, but then the mythical Socrates was still to be defined; Plato achieved this, and it was above all his work that defined Socrates as a *topos* for future reference–one taken up by Demosthenes and his rival Aeschines, for example, and possibly even by the writers of Greek New Testament, who may have made aeretological use of Socrates in their accounts of the crucifixion of Christ.[38] Certainly the possible association of Socrates and Christ was given brilliant, if brief, expression by Voltaire who called Christ the Socrates of Galilee. But the Socratic image is usually more banal. When Graves sees the hemlock as a poison fit for a male chauvinist, one finds only an ingenious flippancy[39]; and when Fowles

---

[37] Here aestheticist needs some unpacking. We are not referring to aestheticism as a rule of conduct for life (*à la* Walter Pater, and Wilde ambivalently), which is itself a moral position. Here aestheticism refers to certain standards and vocabulary (concerning form, style, imageric unity, metre, etc.) which are logically distinguishable from moral categories of appraisal, and which are the means by which we assess phenomena as artistic constructs *per se*. The danger, then, that moral judgement brings is that of intellectual confusion as to which standards of appraisal we wish to apply in the consideration of an artefact.
[38] See H. C. Kee, *Jesus in History*, Harcourt Brace, New York, 1970, p. 121.
[39] Robert Graves, *The White Goddess*, Faber, London, 1962 edn, p. 11.

speaks of Socrates as the philosopher who preferred hemlock to the lie[40] it is only a tired vulgarization of a now age-old and well-worn cliché.[41]

Even more has St Thomas been mewed up in the cliché-ridden realms of moral enthusiasm; the didactic invariably triumphs over the poetic; the play *St Thomas More* virtually an unperformed item of Shakespearean apocrypha; *A Man for all Seasons* a noble failure.

That moral investment in both has hampered historical understanding of either can be seen in a number of ways. The reactions of eighteenth and nineteenth (and even some twentieth) century classicists to the death of Socrates is a fair guide to their opinions about the French and American revolutions and/or modern democracy. If, as Professor Elton would have us believe, More was sexually unbalanced, there is no shortage of those who would reject his views, and not only because of the lack of firm historical evidence. Or when Sir Clements Markham argued that More was a dishonest historian, an historiographical reaction is the last thing one gets. One gets reactions less appropriate to historical activity than to actions of libel. The image is more important to many than the man, which has not proved an abundant help to scholarship.

There is a sense that with respect to both Socrates and More we are living in a pre-Darwinian universe; one in which the truths of religion appear to be balanced upon the shoulders of Adam. If, however, Adam does not exist, that is if our images of Socrates and More do not stand firmly in historical truth, then there are too many who think that the standards of the present are thus threatened. If one's world stands upon Adam and Adam upon an elephant, it may seem vital not to look for the turtle underneath.

With respect to both men's symbolic significance, the differences, as Frye's nomenclature would suggest, are only of degree, and their status is supplementary. Socrates has been in use for much longer, transcending the age of darkness, not least because he was blessed not simply with a mythographer of talent but with a disciple of surpassing genius. More has been used less extensively, but with an intensity with which few other

---

[40] John Fowles, *Daniel Martin*, Little Brown & Co., Boston, 1977, p. 178.
[41] Boethius, *The Consolation of Philosophy*, Book I, 3, 15–20 and 30–35, makes the appropriate allusions in the context of asking of his own fate whether this is the first time that wisdom has been exposed by the wicked (*improbos*) to ruin/death (*periculis*). The graffito in Siena Cathedral in which Socrates is handed the palm of victory may contain an allusion to Boethius' comment concerning Socrates' victory over an unjust death; see also Tertullian, *Apology*, XIV 7; and Ferguson, *op. cit.*, p. 30, who cites Origen, *Against Celsius*, 9, 7.

such well-established symbols can compare. A synthesis of the two would give us a figure of the potency of Christ, in whose shadow, in their different ways, both stand. But the fusion of the two is not entirely at one remove; there is a sense in which a Socratic image of More may well stand behind his *Dialogue of Comfort Against Tribulation*; a Platonic image stands behind the mythography of William Roper.[42] The reports of the conversations in the tower aimed at persuading More to change his 'conscience' and make his peace with his king may have been consciously modelled on Plato's dramatic account of Crito's equally unsuccessful attempts in the cell to persuade Socrates not to die.[43] Whilst in the reports of their final crises both Socrates and More are seen to comfort their comforters – Crito and Sir William Kingston, respectively.[44] If this is so, one reason why the historical Socrates and the historical More seem so comparable is because the Socratic symbol, embedded in the floor of the church, was already available as a housing for the problems that in his final months would not leave More alone, and that could add such resonance to the cries of his apologists. Harpsfield's testimony is enough:

---

[42] Consider the question of More's second wife, Lady Alice, whose reputation on very little evidence is that of a shrew treated with tolerant amusement by her husband; the character is beautifully drawn by William Roper. Nicholas Harpsfield, 'Life and Death . . .', in *Lives of St Thomas More*, E. E. Reynolds (ed.), Dent, London, 1963, p. 107, recalls her 'aged, blunt and rude' and provides some suitably shrewish dialogue. Socrates also allegedly had two wives, the second of which, Xanthippe, had a reputation for shrewish bad temper and was treated with tolerant amusement by Socrates when, as some said, he could not get out of her way (see especially the *Socrates* of Diogenes Laertius). The similarities could just be coincidence, but it seems possible that the character of More's wife is something of a myth modelled on a Xanthippean image to extend and refine the image of More himself. (J. H. Marsden, *Philomorus*, London, 1878 edn, p. 56, writes of Alice playing Xanthippe to More's Socrates.) Certainly, Jerome's anecdote from Diogenes Laertius, cited in Ferguson, *op. cit.*, p. 312, could fit both couples: Having been abusing Socrates at length Xanthippe finally poured dirty water over him. 'He simply dried his head, saying "I always knew there would be rain after all that thunder."' (*Against Jovinianus*, I 48). The anecdote was much cited throughout the sixteenth century. See Sir John Harrington, *The Metamorphosis of Ajax*, Elizabeth S. Donno (ed.), London, 1962, p. 153, where the rain is appropriately the contents of a chamber pot, and footnote 254 for other uses.
[43] See the letter from Margaret Roper to Alice Alington (1534) in *Correspondence, op. cit.*, which Chambers thinks might even have been written by More and in which Margaret seems clearly cast in the role of Crito.
[44] Compare the opening passages of Plato's *Crito*, especially Crito's breaking the news to Socrates of the arrival of the ship from Delos, with Roper: ' "In good faith, Master Roper, I was ashamed of myself, that, at my departing from my father, I found my heart so feeble, and his so strong, that he was fain to comfort me, which should rather have comforted him."' William Roper, 'Life of Sir Thomas More, Knight', in Reynolds, *op. cit.*, p. 47.

O noble and worthy voice of our noble, new, Christian Socrates! The old Socrates, the excellent virtuous philosopher, was also unjustly put to death; whom, when his wife at that time following, outrageously cried, 'Shall such a good man be put to death?' 'Peace, good wife,' quoth he, 'and content thyself; it is far better for me to die a good and true man than as a wretched malefactor to live.'[45]

---

[45] Harpsfield, 'Life and Death . . .', in Reynolds, *op., cit.*, p. 164.

Marsilius and Machiavelli

C. Condren

In that remarkable monument to academic fantasy, 'The Tradition of Classical Political Theory' (which starts with Plato and ends in the vicinity of Marx), Marsilius and Machiavelli stand in singular relationship to each other. On the one hand they are as close as successive chapters in the same book; on the other they seem separated by epochs – so near and yet so far. Marsilius (1275/80-1342, uncertain) is the last great mediaeval theorist, Machiavelli (1469-1527) the founder of modern political thought who decisively broke with the mediaeval tradition. So runs the common image, one result of which is that comparison between the two thinkers is apt to run only at the level of *ad hoc* counterpoint. The mediaeval Marsilius may be briefly contrasted with Machiavelli to show how modern the Florentine is[1]; or a passing doctrinal similarity may serve to emphasize how revolutionary Marsilius of Padua was for his time.[2] The barriers erected by the sense of epoch inherited from Jacob Burckhardt* have in fact been of systematic disservice in understanding both thinkers, who share important intellectual continuities.

This essay is adapted from a paper delivered at the 21st A.P.S.A. Conference, 27–29 August 1979. My thanks are due to the various discussants, especially R. N. Berki (A.N.U. and University of Hull), Paul Corcoran (University of Adelaide) and Harry Redner (Monash University).

[1] For example, F. Raab, *The English Face of Machiavelli*, Routledge & Kegan Paul, London, 1964, pp. 1–2.

[2] For example, F. Battaglia, 'Sul *Defensor Pacis* di Marsilio da Padova', *Nuovi studi di Diritto Economia e Politica*, 2 (1929): 145-6. Allan Gewirth, *Marsilius of Padua and Medieval Political Philosophy*, Vol. 1, Columbia University Press, New York, 1964 edn, pp. 35–7, has a few more substantive comments.

* The Swiss historian Jacob Christoph Burckhardt (1818–1897) was a philosophical historian whose books dealt with cultural and artistic history and whose lectures examined the forces that had shaped European history. Burckhardt's masterpiece, *The Civilization of the Renaissance in Italy*, was published in 1860. (Ed.)

This, of course, is not to imply an identity of concern or of conception. Comparison exists on a sliding scale from assertions of strict identity to assertions of specific contrast, between which there is an area of identifiable similarity. It is within this region that the comparisons here must be located; within this region the comparisons are direct (a is like b) rather than indirect (a is to b as c is to d), but within this region also there is particular danger of comparisons being vitiated through the use of insufficiently stable covering terms. That is, comparative statements require an answer to the question 'comparable when seen as a what?'. If this *what* is indiscriminate, comparisons made under its auspices may be vacuous if not misleading. The point would possibly not be worth making but for the fact that political theory itself is such a porous classifier, and thus to compare Marsilius and Machiavelli as political theorists requires some minimal specification. We need to know at least what sort of political theory in terms of which they seem comparable, and how it is related to politics.

Here I wish to suggest no more than a rudimentary distinction between theories extrinsic and theories intrinsic to the political activity of a society.[3] The first, although recognizably having politics as a subject matter, are not controlled by what in a given society are political criteria of judgement; and they do not conform to conventions of political discourse or have their terminus in effecting the possibilities of political action. In contrast, the second are generated by and are directed towards discernible political problems. They are, as Dante put it, theories for the sake of action.[4] Under the auspices of such theories we may place manuals for advice, ideologies, manifestos, and statements of political principle.

Both Marsilius and Machiavelli may be placed clearly within this latter category. Thus, and most pertinently, neither tailored his arguments to the requirements of sustained philosophical discourse nor, more generally, let the winds of argument (in Plato's expression) take him where they will. In Machiavelli's case these negative delineations of his theory probably require little argument. Except in the loosest sense, he cannot be called a philosopher, by the formal standards of either his time or by those of ours. He never defined; he was never much concerned with logical sequences of argument; he used virtually no formal philosophical

---

[3] For further explication, see C. Condren, *Three Aspects of Political Theory: On Confusions and Reformation of an Expression*, Macmillan, Melbourne, 1979, chapter 1.
[4] *De Monarchia*, I.ii.35.

vocabulary; all this is expressed in his famous statement that he is interested in the effective truth of things.[5]

Marsilius' position bears a strong resemblance to Machiavelli's. Despite his use of philosophical terminology, and his abstract and technical scholastic tone, he was not interested in pursuing philosophical questions further than he believed necessary to make an effective political case. Indeed in exhibiting a passable knowledge of philosophical and theological issues he was adhering to some of the accepted conventions of political and religious rhetoric in his own society, which sometimes involved the wholesale translation of philosophical issues and terminology into a range of political imperatives.[6] He too may be seen to have been interested in the effective truth of things, though the philosophical idiom he used (was constrained to use, perhaps) is absent in Machiavelli. Despite some idiomatic differences then, which are further explored below, both Marsilius and Machiavelli may be located in the same region of political theory – a preliminary point that provides a fundamental basis for valid comparison, inasmuch as in going on to specify some substantive points of similarity we are not obliged to translate the theoretical concerns and preoccupations of one into the currency of the other – a process that could be nothing but distorting.[7]

It is, however, possibly more contentious to suggest that there is some continuity in the conception of political society under the auspices of which both lived, and to the understanding and condition of which they directed their theories. This political society was Christendom. The term *christianitas* is one of a distinct family of political conceptions (such as *polis*, state and nation) which have been employed or invented by a people in order to abridge their distinctive and respective senses of political identity. Such senses of identity would invariably cover institutional arrangements, ideals and characteristic idioms of political discourse. With this

---

[5] *Il Principe*, chapter 15. All references are to the Feltrinelli edition of *Il Principe e i Discorsi sopra la prima deca di Tito Livio*, Milan, 1973 edn. (Henceforth, *P* with chapter number is used for reference to *Il Principe*; *D*, book number and chapter number for *I Discorsi*.) Good translations are to be found in A. Gilbert, *Machiavelli: The Chief Works and Others*, 3 vols, Duke University Press, North Carolina, 1965.

[6] This is a more contentious view than the one expressed on the location of Machiavelli's theory. For further elaboration of my position, see, 'Marsilius of Padua's Argument from Authority: A Survey of its Significance in the *Defensor Pacis*', in *Political Theory*, 5 (1977); and 'Marsilius of Padua and the Poverty of Traditionalism', in *Il Pensiero Politico* 3 (1978): 393ff. For an opposing view, see Gewirth, *op. cit.*, at length.

[7] For further remarks concerning conceptual translation *qua* comparison, see 'More and Socrates', in this volume.

understanding, summation terms such as 'Christendom' cannot be replaced by others (such as the anachronistic 'mediaeval state') without our running the risk of importing alien political problems and awareness.

The term 'Christendom' was invented around the ninth century and gradually fell into political disuse in the seventeenth century. Thus its political life spans more than the lives of Marsilius and Machiavelli. In its simplest terms the conception of Christendom entailed and abridged both a sense of being Christian and of being Roman. Christendom, and the various individual societies encompassed by it, shared a religion that legitimized and informed political life, defining moral priorities and political ideals, sanctioning institutions and laws, and providing a distinct vocabulary of political issues. Similarly all societies that saw themselves as a part of Christendom under a Christian God (and thus suspended in a legitimate universe) also believed themselves to be the inheritors of Roman civilization, which it was important to pass on to future generations. Dante once complained of the lack of Romans in Florence; Bruni spent much time on the politically important task of proving that Florence had been founded by Republican Rome; and even in England the Brutus foundation myth died hard and late. Anyone who lived within Christendom was then the beneficiary of a resonant sense of identity, and indeed such a person would enjoy a dual sense of identity as, say, a Paduan, a Florentine, or an Englishman, as well as being a member of Christendom.[8] This dual sense of identity necessitated a balance of concern. Even the most parochial of writers employed the vocabulary and established idioms of political discourse to be found in Christendom as a whole; even the most universalistic made reference to, or assumed, the specific communities of which Christendom was comprised.

With Marsilius the emphasis is firmly upon the macrocosm. Although many of his political preoccupations (not least the political aspirations of the clergy) were common in the Italian communes, and although many of

---

[8] In neither Marsilius' nor Machiavelli's time was Italy an object of political allegiance; it was rather a geographical frame for cultural association, having reference principally to the middle and north of what is now Italy. Machiavelli as an Italian nationalist (or even patriot) is an invention of nineteenth-century Italian nationalists. The myth lives on in much Italian scholarship (the mythologies invented by English-speaking commentators are somewhat different). A good survey of much recent work is to be found in J. H. Geerken, 'Machiavelli Studies Since 1969', *Journal of History of Ideas*, 37 (1976): 351ff. A more extensive study with special reference to Italian interpretation and with extensive quotations from nineteenth and early twentieth-century interpretations is to be found in Franco Fido, *Machiavelli*, in the series *Storia della Critica*, S. Petronio (ed.), Palumbo, Palermo, 1975.

his institutional recommendations and terminology are strongly reminiscent of the politics of Florence and Padua, there is an unmistakeable drive towards appealing to Christendom as a whole.[9] He may start from typically communal concerns, but he universalizes them and translates them into abstractions relevant to the whole of Christendom to which he appeals.[10] Only once does he allude to his Paduan origins.[11] He is informed and concerned with the politics of France, Germany and England; he deals with what has happened in Italy as a prelude to what he sees as happening in the rest of Christendom.[12] A portion of his experience may come from the part, but the concern is principally with the whole.

With Machiavelli this emphasis has shifted. He is of course aware of an extensive political community beyond the confines of his *patria* and he is informed on matters French, German, Argonese and Swiss, but his political focus is northern Italy and Florence. Appropriately, whereas Marsilius wrote in the *lingua franca* of scholastic Latin, Machiavelli chose to write in his local dialect. More significantly, Machiavelli's awareness of a larger political community is mediated through a more fragmented and various vocabulary. Thus in *I Discorsi* I.12, he writes not of a singular *christianità*, but of a plurality of Christian states and republics: *gli stati e le republiche christiane*. This expression from a seminally important section of *I Discorsi* is symptomatic of significant changes in political awareness between Marsilius and Machiavelli. Between the fourteenth and early sixteenth centuries Christendom as a geographical area had been increasingly threatened by exterior foes – its status being changed from a

---

[9] On the communal background to his thought, see Gewirth, *op. cit.*, pp. 23ff and 196ff; and N. Rubenstein, "Marsilius of Padua and the Italian Political Thought of his Time' in *Europe in the Late Middle Ages*, J. R. Hale, J. Highfield and B. Smalley (eds), Faber, London, 1965; and J. K. Hyde, *Padua in the Age of Dante*, Manchester University Press, 1966.

[10] Thus although the title, *Defensor Pacis*, is reminiscent of the oath that a *podestà* would take on accepting office in a city, the rhetoric of peace had a much wider significance and explicitly biblical sanction. Although the *legislator humanus* encompasses the grand councils of the republican communes, it is a sufficiently generalized concept to apply to almost any political community within Christendom. I have further discussed this concept and the pointlessness of searching for an explicit institutional background in *Three Aspects of Political Theory*.

[11] *Defensor Pacis, Dictio* I.i.6. My references are to the Horst Kusch edition, Rütten and Loening, Berlin, 1958. (*Defensor Pacis* is referred to as *DP* with *Dictio*, chapter number and section numbers following.) The Gewirth translation, *Marsilius of Padua, The Defender of Peace*, Columbia University Press, New York, 1956, I have found to be valuable and generally reliable; the E. Lewis translations in *Medieval Political Ideas*, 2 vols, Faber, London, 1954, to be significantly less so.

[12] *DP* I.i.6 and 7; *DP* I.xix.4ff.

theoretical equation with the whole world to a physical location within it.[13] Moreover, internally there had been an increasing sense of fragmentation, discord and impending doom. Put simply, the summation term 'Christendom' was ceasing to abridge political awareness, and was becoming irrelevant to it. The increasing emphasis on the part rather than the whole was not restricted to Machiavelli, any more than was the phenomenon of using the vulgar tongue for political theorizing.[14] If we can see the beginnings of erosion in the status of the term 'Christendom' around Machiavelli's lifetime, then we can also see it being replaced by other terms providing more appropriate abridgements and refining a changed political awareness – the most notable being 'Europe' and 'state', the former being transferred from the confines of cartography to take on political and social reference appropriate to Christendom's becoming just a place within the world[15] and the latter being extended metaphorically from legal, administrative and agricultural frames of reference into political ones, fittingly encapsulating a sense of political society's being, in effect, like estates, discrete geographical areas of effective or legal control.

The results of these gradual supplementary shifts in vocabulary were to be very great for the whole political vocabulary of western society – but where Machiavelli stands in this process is difficult to determine. He was acutely aware of Europe threatened, and of Christian societies living a threatened and precarious existence, and he makes frequent use of the term state (*lo stato*) in a political context. But the use of a metaphor is still a long way from the belief in or elaboration of what would one day become a formal concept. States for Machiavelli are like estates, areas of effective, legal and/or administrative control[16]; thus rather than seeing in him the beginning of modern state theory, he is better seen as coping with the demise of Christendom theory, developing metaphors and images from whence he may, in order to make some effective sense (truth) of a world he sees as endangered and essentially unstable.[17]

---

[13] D. Hay, *Europe: The Emergence of an Idea*, Edinburgh University Press, 1955, at length.
[14] Fortescue's *On the Governance of England* was written in English a good generation before *P*. and was explicitly concerned with only two parts of Christendom. Political theory written in Tuscan goes back also a considerable way before Machiavelli.
[15] Hay. *op. cit.*
[16] I am drawing here on J. H. Hexter's brilliant essays republished in *The Vision of Politics on the Eve of the Reformation*, Allan Lane, London, 1973, especially chapters 3 and 4.
[17] See Hexter, *op. cit.*, pp. 150–78. In this context, see the expression already cited from *D* 1.12 referring to '*gli stati e le republiche*'.

We may thus suggest a continuity of concern under the auspices of a shared conception of political society. When Marsilius wrote, a conception of Christendom could provide a clear criterion of political legitimacy. The variety of his many attacks on the Church and the evils of the present could all be subsumed by the single claim that the institutionalized Church was at odds with Christendom. When Machiavelli wrote, however, the term Christendom no longer connoted clear incontestible criteria of political assessment. This raised at least three problems: (1) Can the world be made to cohere with the ideal of Christendom? (2) How is it now possible to categorize and assess political relationships and behaviour? (3) What are the problems for those working beyond the troublesome conceptions of political propriety and behaviour subsumed by the idea of 'Christendom'?

The first of these questions preoccupied the mind of Sir Thomas More; the second could not be answered at an abstract level without first developing an alternative to the conception of Christendom, and this was not done until the seventeenth century; the third question informs the whole of *Il Principe*, a work that directly confronts the radical disjunction between new princes and their lack of legitimacy. Machiavelli, then, wrote in a period of the demise of 'Christendom'; but it was a demise that Marsilius seemed to fear, and it is this that gives the Paduan something of the air of a prophet. What one feared the other was obliged to accept, and this in turn required that each amend his perspective accordingly.

The picture of the relationship between the two men's theories that I have so far sketched can now be elaborated by considering their treatments of religion and history.

Religion as an idiom of discourse

We may view the politics of religion in two ways: in one way religious belief provided a distinctive discursive idiom, which structured political awareness and formulated political issues; in another way, because the Church was such a vital part of social life, religion itself was an important subject of political discussion. Christendom's religious idiom of discourse comprised biblical allusions and reference, which themselves could carry imperative force; religious metaphors (especially organic ones), which gave significance to the phenomena to which they were applied[18]; and theological terminology, which in being transferred into

---

[18] See, for example, John of Salisbury, *Policraticus*, 5.1; and Nicholas of Cusa, *De Concordantia Catholica*, 3.1. This is not to say, as Weldon would have it, that there was

the political arena became imperative metaphors – that is, metaphors about what ought to be done.[19] Such an idiom dominates most of the *Defensor Pacis* and is striking inasmuch as it is turned uncompromisingly against the established Church. The peace that Marsilius would defend is Christ's on earth, and its enemies are more related to Judas than to St Peter. Marsilius' references to biblical and patriotic writings are both copious and central; they are taken as statements that speak directly and (in the case of the New Testament) with inescapable authority for the present. Organic imagery is less well developed than it had been by John of Salisbury, or was to be by Nicholas of Cusa, but where found it is striking. In *Dictio* I.xi.3 he refers to the law as an eye made of many eyes (*lex sit oculis ex multis oculis*), which should surely be read not as a prefiguration of 1984, nor even as a result of Marsilius' alleged medical training, but rather as an allusion to an Old Testament conception of justice.

More significantly, the whole of *Defensor Pacis* is organized around the theological distinction between faith and reason as epistemological categories, the arguments derived from one being designed to supplement those derived from the other.[20] Moreover the distinction between faith and reason is used by Marsilius to considerable political effect. His position is not entirely consistent, but the main force is that not only do faith and reason provide different forms of knowledge, but also that they are directed towards different ends, and that contradictions between the two forms of knowledge can be tolerated. What is true according to faith need not be so according to reason, and recognition of this fact does not require that we necessarily in all contexts opt for the truths of faith. This form of argument was an effective recognition of the difficulties of reconciling received Christian belief with the thought of

---

an expression of an organic theory of the state (*States and Morals*) but that there was a common but variously negotiable currency. Even maps of Christendom could be drawn in the shape of a man, as a figure of Adam (*figura* of Christ). See M. J. Wilks, *The Problem of Sovereignty in the Later Middle Ages*, Cambridge University Press, 1963, p. 32, note 4. Familial father and son relationships were also used (for example, by Hugh of Fleury and by Dante); the Church was often pictured as the bride of Christ; Christendom sometimes as his seamless robe. E. Kantorowicz, *The King's Two Bodies*, Princeton University Press, 1955, explores the English parliament as understood through the image of the Trinity, but permutations are legion.

[19] Clear outlines of this phenomenon and the ideological possibilities to which it gave rise are to be found in Wilks, *op. cit.*, and in Peter Munz, *The Place of Hooker in the History of Thought*, Routledge & Kegan Paul, London, 1952, though in both cases (pp. 17 and 3 respectively) the connections are read as logical rather than as metaphorical.

[20] *DP* I.i.8.

Aristotle, and was an attempt to justify holding to both by restricting the authority of each to a separate world of discourse.[21] The Church never found this 'two truths' theory theologically respectable, but although the theory was initially generated by a desire to embrace cherished incompatibles, it could make sound philosophical sense. For it provided some formal recognition of the fact that what we call 'truth' is very often neither absolute nor independent of the intellectual conventions in which truth statements are enmeshed. What assertions we regard as true are a matter of what coheres with what else we accept, and the criteria of assessment we consider most relevant. In Marsilius, there is neither a non-contentious desire to accept both the Bible and Aristotle as true, nor any sustained philosophical interest in a notion of conventional truth or (to use an anachronism) in a coherence theory of truth. In Marsilius, the allusions to, and the use of, a 'two truths' theory become political averroism*: briefly, the abstract conceptions are cashed directly into political referents.

The object of reason and reason itself are taken to refer to the secular world and the wisdom through which existence in this world is understood. The object of faith and faith itself are taken to refer to the after-life, Christian wisdom concerning this and the Church in its role as purely otherworldly guide. Mankind, for Marsilius, thus seeks two forms of happiness, one in this world and one in the next; political society serves one, the Church the other.[22] As an institution, however, the Church exists only in this life, and is comprised (he evokes the original sense of *ecclesia*) of living believers. It thus exists within the domain, and comes under the authority, of reason (political society). In this world then, the institutional Church has no political authority. Consequently, with respect to law, what might have binding authority in and for the after-life has no authority in this life unless it is also given binding force according to reason (political society). In short, terminology drawn from theology and philosophy is used to argue not only that the Church *qua*

[21] The two truths theory was probably developed by Siger of Brabant whose works were banned in 1277 and are now lost. It was perhaps the most significant of the concepts that make up the loose notion of averroism, and one not to be found in Averroes himself.

* Political averroism means the complete separation of theology and philosophy, as a corollary of the separation of Church and State. Averroists had a 'double-truth' theory, where the same statement could be true philosophically, yet false theologically. The doctrine is conventionally, but falsely, associated with the name of Averroes, a twelfth-century Arab philosopher. (Ed.)

[22] See, for example *DP* I.iv, v and vi. Gewirth's discussion in *Marsilius*, Vol. I, *op. cit.*, is very good. A succinct statement of the practical consequences is to be found at *DP* II.xi.7.

institution (the vessel of faith) has no political authority, but also that secular society (the analogue of reason) has a rationale independent of religious sanctions and values.

If we now turn to Machiavelli, we can see that on the one hand there are only remnants of a distinctive religious idiom of discourse in his political theory; on the other hand, much of what has been held to be most distinctive about him seems predicated on the *ad hoc* acceptance of political averroism. Indeed the remnants have to be searched for before we find a reference to heaven or the scrap of a biblical story.[23] The major exception is the final and striking chapter of *Il Principe*[24]; whilst the most significant casualty perhaps, is the inherited notion of *fortuna*. Fortune is no longer a sign of God's concern for his world, nor a mediation between a God and the actions of his people. Rather it is, in Machiavelli, although occasionally associated with God or heaven, a disembodied metaphor for the contingency that marks political affairs.[25]

The claim made for Machiavelli, that he is the first modern political scientist, is often thought to reside in what Croce termed his discovery of the autonomy of politics; that is, the discovery that political life has rules and a momentum independent of private, moral and Christian considerations.[26] Such an understanding of Machiavelli needs much

---

[23] See *P* 14; *D* III.1.
[24] This point could afford considerable elaboration and illustration. In *P* 26 Italy is feminine in more than grammar, and a feminine image is developed from Italia into that of the female Christian martyr ravished and despoiled and awaiting redemption. God is an immediately active force, he has given portents and signs, manna has fallen, water has come from the rock. But says Machiavelli, God will not do all for us, less he interfere with free will (a nice rhetorical twist on a theological problem). The passage is reminiscent of Savanarola, Dante (*Epistola* 5) and, above all, Marsilius (*DP* II.xxvi.20). Machiavelli was clearly capable of resorting to and using effectively the traditional theological idiom of Christendom.
[25] The metaphors he uses for *fortuna* (the word is never defined) have at least this underlying force – that the political world is unstable and uncertain, and in this lies the fundamental problem. The belief in a radical contingency in human affairs was widespread. Consider Guicciardini, *Ricordi*, 161 (Garzanti edition, Milan, 1975) where he reflects upon all the accidents that can befall us and how many things must conspire to produce one good harvest; hence 'nothing makes me marvel more' (*mi maravigli più*) than to see a good year or an old man. On the importance of contingency in the political thought of Machiavelli and Guicciardini, see J. G. A. Pocock, *The Machiavellian Moment*, Princeton University Press, 1975. One can contrast Machiavelli's usual use of *fortuna* with Commynes' gloss on the term (cited in A. Gilbert, *Machiavelli's Prince and its Forerunners*, Barnes & Noble, New York, 1968 edn) as *une fiction poétique* for the loss of God's grace. As such, the term could be an unambiguous form of shorthand when firmly embedded in the context of a religious idiom of discourse.
[26] B. Croce, 'Machiavelli e Vico – La politica e L'etica', *Elimenti di politica* (first published 1925), cited in *Opere di Benedetto Croce*, Vol. 4, Laterza, Rome, pp. 204–9.

qualification. Here it is enough merely to note, firstly, that a number of Florentine writers had been concerned with the discrepancies between political life and received Christian mores: Bruni and Palmieri were both prepared to accept such discrepancies[27]; and Valla, making a related case, argued that the religious life was inferior to the active political life, which is to go further than Machiavelli.[28] Secondly, in this whole family of arguments concerning the *vita activa politica*, and the standards quintessentially represented by the *vita contemplativa*, there is a distinct echo of political averroism: thus political life has a discernible character which cannot be reduced to a mere shadow of monastic rules of Christianity and is not co-extensive with private Christian ethical considerations. Throughout the late fifteenth century, faith and reason remained important coins in the currency of Florentine political debate[29], and what is now clear is that there is a tradition of speculation that accepts their mutual irreducibility. I am not saying that it was really Marsilius who discovered the autonomy of politics, but rather that Machiavelli inherited, took for granted and presented a species of argument divested of its formal trappings, which was ultimately located in a religious idiom of thought and which had proved, certainly since Marsilius, to be of service to the politically active anti-clerical.

Religion: The topic

Marsilius' attack on the established Church was the apotheosis of anti-clericalism, but it was much more than this. He argued that from the perspectives of both this and the next life, the Church must be condemned and reformed; it was an enemy of peace and salvation. The proper role of the Church rested upon a clear conception of the role of religion *per se* and of Christianity in particular. In a passage that some have seen as pre-figuring Marx, he suggested that all religions have a social role. Pagan religions, by means of false stories concerning salvation

---

[27] See H. Baron, "Franciscan Poverty and Civic Wealth as Factors in the Rise of Humanist Thought', *Speculum*, 13 (1938), especially (on Palmieri's *Della vita civile*) p. 23ff.

[28] *De professione religiosorum*, *Opera Omnia*, Turin, 1962, pp. 287–322, on which see C. Trinkhaus, 'Humanist Treatises on the Status of the Religious, Petrach, Salutati and Valla, *Renaissance Studies*, 5 (1964). See Gaines Post, 'The Medieval State as a Work of Art', reprinted in B. Tierney *The Middle Ages*, Vol. 2: *Readings in Medieval History*, Knopf, New York, 1974 edn, for the practical legal background of 'state' theory, to which political averroism may be seen as giving a formal expression.

[29] F. Gilbert, 'Florentine Political Assumptions in the Period of Savanarola and Soderini', *Journal of the Warburg and Courtauld Institutes*, 1957, p. 187ff.

and damnation, made the citizens of communities more disposed to tranquillity.[30] The priests were the pedlars of political opiates, and for this there is praise. Marsilius' brief account of the social function of formalized religion both explains the existence of priestly castes in society and, in the context of his argument, condemns his own Church in comparison with the pagan ones it has superseded.

The continuities between Marsilius and Machiavelli are marked, but there is a changed emphasis. Whereas the anti-clericalism of the Paduan is unrelenting, that of the Florentine is sporadic, and almost intellectually orthodox.[31] Both men lament the impiety of their respective ages, and both hold the papacy largely responsible; but whereas Marsilius holds the Italian province up as a warning to Christendom[32], Machiavelli regards Italy as only the worst example of widespread decay.[33] Whereas Marsilius is persistently intent on returning Christendom to its first principles, Machiavelli employs a more occasional reference to return and renovation.[34] By the end of the fifteenth century, the acceptance of a situation putatively feared by Marsilius had enabled a shift of emphasis, and thus what in Marsilius are a few remarks about the politically cohering function of religion become in Machiavelli an elaboration of a theory. Such a theory we find clearly set forth in *I Discorsi* 1.9 – 15, and it results in a dilemma for Machiavelli symptomatic of his ailing society. Again his vocabulary is illuminating; instead of referring to the faith, he refers to *religione*, the Tuscan derivative of the Latin *religio*, to bind or hold together. *Religione* is a bond that provides the common ethos without which society must collapse. This insistence upon the primacy of *religione* is symbolized by his elevation of Numa over Romulus in the heroic charter of Rome.[35] Such a bond overcomes and turns to advantage internal class divisions; helps resist external threat; and can always be used as a source of appeal and a means of manipulation by those who have authority in society. There is a sense in which the kind of manipulation we call 'Machiavellian' is, for Machiavelli, predicated upon widespread piety.

---

[30] *DP* I.v.11–12.
[31] See, for example, Guicciardini's remarks on Machiavelli's attack on the papacy (*D* 1.12) in his *Considerazione*, XII, in *Selected Writings*, transl. C. Grayson, Oxford University Press, 1965, p. 81.
[32] *DP* I.i.2; and II.xxvi.20.
[33] *D* I.12.
[34] *D* III.1 provides an explicit appeal for such return.
[35] *D* I.11.

These postulates enable him to make a number of specific comparisons between his own society and that of the Romans. His own society is irreligious and therefore weak and riddled with destructive class warfare. The Romans were pious and strong and in Roman society class tension merely heightened the virtues of the people because a common religious sense modified its extremities. Widespread piety permitted the Romans to argue through religion with political effect. In short, with religion come all the virtues; with its collapse comes political disaster.[36] When the Greeks disregarded their oracles the Greek *poleis* began to fall. Machiavelli's interest, however, is closer to home, and he remained haunted by the Savanarolan experiment which briefly united Florence in a grim religious piety and which, collapsing with the death of Savanarola, provided a microcosm of the poverty and potentiality of religious enthusiasm.[37]

There is then a discernible theme in Machiavelli that stresses the socially cohering functions of religion above all else. Certainly society requires good arms (with which he is much concerned) and good laws (with which he is little concerned), but good arms are built upon good order and discipline and this can only be maintained through religion.[38]

If religion provides coherence for society then it is a short step to comparing the sort of ethos provided by religion, with its political consequences; but here a dilemma becomes manifest. *Nostra religione*, which, as for Marsilius, is the truth, is also a political failure. Rome provides political and military models for the present, but to do so it must be a religious model also. In *I Discorsi* II.2 Machiavelli confronts the problem of explaining Christian failure by the standards of this world. He begins by blaming Christianity *per se* for providing an ethos inferior to the Roman, but ends by blaming only the interpreters of Christianity. The equivocation is reflected elsewhere.[39] A clearer and more persistently theoretical mind would have taken refuge in thorough-going political averroism; an atheist would have seen no dilemma, and would have been unlikely to have equivocated; a man of deeper religious

---

[36] D I.12, '. . . *nessuno maggiore indizio*' (there is no greater indication) of the ruin of a provincia (in the sense of a political community), than to see its religion scorned ('*dispregiato il culto divino*').

[37] On the haunting importance of Savanarola for Machiavelli and his generation of Florentines, see J. H. Whitfield, *Machiavelli*, Oxford University Press, 1948.

[38] D I.11.

[39] Although Machiavelli sometimes laments the cheek-turning ethos of Christianity, he also explicitly attributes the strength of the Swiss to their remaining close to religious principle.

sensibility would not have been so concerned with the failure of 'truth' in this world, he could escape to contemplate the next. But Machiavelli was some sort of Christian living in the wreck of a Christian society, to the political dimension of which he was deeply committed. His failure to decide between the reasons he suggested for his religion's failure is symptomatic of the world he lived in. He extends a species of reflection used initially to explain the existence of pagan religion to a point at which a range of paradoxical and quite unpalatable possibilities becomes apparent in a society in which Christianity fails to do what Christians believed pagan religions did. In so doing he reflects upon, illuminates, and exacerbates the religious crisis of his times.

If we look briefly beyond him we find that the religious idiom of discourse was reformulated along the sort of martial lines of which Machiavelli may well have approved. The cosmic order became increasingly one of war between God and the Devil; religious groups became armies of salvation, and in seventeenth-century England, where there was so much rhetoric of Christian warfare, Machiavelli was much read and approved of.[40] Theoretically it is possible to locate him retrospectively as the most central figure in a virtual tradition of speculation concerning the political role of religion in society. It runs certainly from Marsilius through Bacon, to Hobbes, Rousseau, Mandeville and Marx and ends (?) in the systematic study of the sociology of religion.

History

It is now a commonplace that political societies rely on an awareness of the past for a sustained sense of identity in the present. Initiation into the 'history' of a society is a mode of political education; understanding the political rhetoric of a society requires that we understand its past. Even historians, dismissive of school textbooks, suspicious of official histories and mythologies, will now, albeit with qualification, stress the practical relevance of the past. For centuries we have been told that the main point of studying the past lies in the wisdom that can then be brought to bear upon the present.

Now when a practical attitude to the past is well developed it results in what we may call an historical idiom of political discourse. There are two common features:

---

[40] See M. Walzer, *The Revolution of the Saints: A Study in the Origins of Radical Politics*, Harvard University Press, Cambridge, Mass., 1965.

(1) Although the past is invariably thought of as being true, factuality *per se* has no ultimate or undisputed authority. This is so, because if the purpose is to guide the future, then the past, real or imagined, has significance only insofar as it can be made an effective handmaid.

(2) Since what matters is that which impinges on the present, the practical needs of the present provide the principal criteria of selection. Thus from the perspective of any given society the history of other societies appear as appendices. Within this received history, some areas take on great potency. These amount to what can be called 'authority centres', reference to which can become the principal means of appraising the present, and the possibilities of future action.

Christendom provides an almost paradigmatic example of this, as historical idiom of political theory. The words of specific figures from the past became authoritative in the present – not so much because of what they had said (meanings were constantly disputed) but because of who they had been. There was an explicit and heavy emphasis on custom: what was established was legitimate, what was older was better. There was thus a pronounced immemorial drift to political argument; a propensity to search back and invest authority in what seemed to come from 'time immemorial'. Laws were discovered rather than made, and the most revolutionary proposals were alleged to be customary. The drift was weakened, however, beyond a clear 'authority centre' constituting the Christo–Roman nexus from the life of Christ to the death of St Augustine. It was from here that Christendom's belief in its Christian and Roman inheritance emanated. Anything discrepant with the received image of this period therefore needed careful justification in terms of both the religious and the historical idioms of discourse. Theoretically we can distinguish two idioms (two elements in a synthesis), but in practice separating them from their normal supplementary use is more difficult. As it becomes easier (with Machiavelli contra Marsilius), we are presented with further evidence of a decline in a style of political discourse.

With both Marsilius and Machiavelli we can see an extensive and expert use of an historical idiom, a point that immediately enables us to draw some negative conclusions about the general characters of their theories. Neither, as has sometimes been claimed, used an inductive method of reasoning – even if, as it is normally understood, such a claim makes logical sense. Neither was trying to be an historian, in the modern sense. On the contrary, for both, the past was illustrative of general truths about the present, and was malleable in the interests of those 'truths'. Marsilius was prepared to cast doubt upon the *Donation of Constantine*,* but was also prepared to accept it when convenient.[41] Machiavelli reported and romanced on the Battle of Anghiari in a way he must have known to be totally untrue.[42] These instances do not reflect historical incompetence but simply that the historical idiom of political theory is not history, as it is understood – although, as I shall suggest, the two are ultimately connected. Further, both relied heavily on the authority of the past, and it is in large part each man's ability to orchestrate the voices of the past into an impressive and distinctive chorus on the present that is so striking. Moreover, with both, one can detect a distinct immemorial drift to their arguments: Marsilius explicitly evokes custom as a criterion for determining one of his most central conceptions[43]; while Machiavelli admits to being well disposed to certain things simply because of their antiquity.[44] Finally, this immemorial drift flows into a distinct 'authority centre', and in both cases this is carefully specified and elevated to the level of an ideal in contrast to which much of the present is condemned. Thus both men largely disapprove of modern times, and are revolutionaries in that they wish to return to first principles. This, of course, makes neither of them unusual. Christendom's historical idiom made revolutionaries of many in this sense, just as it might make them seem reactionaries in the modern sense, or simply conservative because they approve of 'custom'. It is best

---

* *Donation of Constantine*, a document that discusses the supposed grant by the emperor Constantine the Great to Pope Sylvester I (314-335) and his successors, of spiritual supremacy over the other great patriarchates and over all matters of faith and worship, as well as of temporal dominion over Rome and the entire Western Empire. It was claimed that the gift was motivated by Constantine's supposed gratitude to Sylvester for miraculously healing his leprosy and converting him to Christianity. Now universally admitted to be a forgery, it was regarded as genuine by both friends and enemies of the papal claims to power throughout the Middle Ages.

From the early eleventh century the document was increasingly employed in support of the papal claims, and from the twelfth century onward it became a weapon of the spiritual powers against the temporal. Although the validity of the document was sometimes questioned, its genuineness was first critically assailed during the Renaissance. In 1440 Lorenzo Valla proved that it was false and began a controversy that lasted until the end of the eighteenth century. (Ed.)

[41] See *DP* I.xvi.8 (doubting the authenticity of the Donation, which Ockham apparently proved to be a forgery on lines similar to those for which Valla is now famous); and see *DP* II.xi.8 and xvi.9 for his acceptance of it.
[42] See Sydney Anglo, *Machiavelli: A Dissection*, Paladin, London, 1969, p. 167, who cites Machiavelli's *Florentine History*, Vol. V, and points to this as evidence for Machiavelli forgetting to be a good empirical historian.
[43] *DP* I.xii.4.
[44] *P* 20.

to avoid such epithets, as they are indiscriminate or misleading when imported into an alien world of discourse.

There are significant differences between them. For Marsilius the authority centre acts as a model for theology and for ecclesiastical institutions. The areas of social experience discussed in the light of this model concern administration, law and economics. Marsilius was acutely aware of the close relationship between political power, economic power, administrative omnipresence and effective legal coercion. The emphasis in Machiavelli is quite different. He is more concerned with warfare, class antagonism and the personal strategies of political survival.

Marsilius' authority centre is unquestionably the Christo–Roman nexus. More important than precise chronological delineation, however, is the fact that he develops a scale for weighing authority along two parallel lines of words and actions. Carrying most authority are the words and actions of Christ, next those of the Apostles, and then the Early Fathers; these together provide him with both a razor against named opponents, who might use other authorities (such as Papal Bulls and Decretals), and a means of anticipating future objections.[45]

Machiavelli writes in no such combative mood: there is no scale of hierarchy of authority, as he does not have to fight for those he uses. Moreover the authority centre has shifted back and acquired more fluid dimensions. Crucially it has shifted across the great ideological divide, on which Christendom's sense of identity chiefly depended, to pagan republican Rome. This shift, as needs no labouring, is intimately tied up with the society's sense of religious crisis.

Marsilius is altogether more unselfconscious in his use of his authority centre. Despite its distance in time he never exhibits any doubt as to its immediate, and generally literal, relevance to his own world. Machiavelli is more defensive. He justifies in terms of human nature and of what others have learned with respect to human experience, drawing systematically upon the Romans.[46] Moreover he has frequent buttressing recourse to more modern examples, and even to more ancient ones.

---

[45] I have discussed this in *Three Aspects of Political Theory*, pp. 208–9.
[46] Thus, echoing a saying attributed to Pittacus of Mytilene, Machiavelli writes (*D* III.43): not without reason have wise men said that if one wishes to see the future one must know the past, for all events resemble those of past times ('*gli antiche tempi*'). This is because all men are animated by the same passions; therefore the results of their actions must be the same. (See *D* I. Introduction, for the imperative to codify Roman wisdom for the benefit of the political present).

The first difference between the thinkers, being principally a matter of supplementary areas of interest, simply disguises an idiomatic continuity. The second and third differences are of more significance and general interest. There is something of a crude dialectic at work with respect to historical idioms of political theory, to which Pocock has drawn attention.[47] Interest in the political past is a part of dealing with present political problems; as these become exacerbated, the past as a source of wisdom is pursued further. As the past is revealed in more detail, it is shown to be more alien, more complex and less amenable to the present than was thought. The messages coming from it are more diverse and contentious, and hallowed myths can be reduced to the status of broken straws in the winds of rhetoric.[48] In short, the extensive use of an historical idiom, especially where it focuses on a distinct authority centre, is apt to become self-destructive. Such a process as this perhaps helps to explain the weakening of the Christo–Roman nexus as an authority centre between the times of Marsilius and Machiavelli, and the drift towards even earlier times as the authoritative past (searched for, and fought over) is revealed as irrelevant or inconclusive.

The Christo–Roman authority centre had indeed been revealed in great detail, and the picture of society that Marsilius had drawn showed irreparable discrepancies with the present. So in the fifteenth century, Lapo da Castiglionchio, wanting to defend the institutional existence of the Church and realizing he could not do so in terms of the ancient Church, shifted back to the age of pagan Rome in search of a more relevant or palatable authority.[49] The modern world was being severed from the world of Christ and the Roman Empire, which it was supposed to have inherited; and the pagan was a model for the Christian. When Machiavelli wrote, a single stable authority centre was little in evidence; the common cry for a return to first principles was becoming empty; and those for whom *l'áutorita de' Romani* was enough were being put on the defensive.[50] Machiavelli boldly proclaimed a new route, but it was arguably not new, and to increasing numbers it must have seemed like the old route to nowhere.

---

[47] J. G. A. Pocock, 'The Origins of the Study of the Past: A Comparative Approach', *Comparative Studies in Society and History*, 5 (1962–63); and *The Ancient Constitution and the Feudal Law*, Cambridge University Press, 1957.
[48] This Pocock illustrates well in both of the above works with reference to the Ancient Constitution.
[49] See Baron, in *Speculum, op. cit.*, on *De Curias Romanae Commodis*, a work that in the context of Marsilius and Italian political thought requires more discussion.
[50] Consider the combined force of Guicciardini, *Ricordi*, 6, 69, 110, 117, 143.

Two forms of criticism of this whole idiom are discernible and both are equally relevant to Marsilius and Machiavelli; perhaps they are equally worth mentioning for what was to come out of them. The first amounted to an implicit criticism of the propriety of using the past to establish guiding principles – and men have been prone to do this when the past is not sufficiently available to promote the principles they favour. It is to be found in Salutati's remark that John of Salisbury showed only that tyrannicide had been common, not that it was justified; the principle had to be established independently of the authority of the past.[51] Even Marsilius employs such an argument briefly and precisely when he is finding the voice of St Augustine difficult to manipulate.[52] It is to be found in Sir Philip Sidney's defence of poetry which involves an attack on the claims of 'history' to guide us to truth.[53] It is to be found in Hobbes – who could find no place for witnesses or authorities, in contrast to his opponents who relied on them and used them to considerable effect.[54] Finally it can be seen as providing the ideological background out of which came Hume's famous philosophical caveat concerning the shift from matters of fact to matters of value.[55]

The second form of criticism seems much less common; it is not so much the beginnings of a formal refusal to countenance an historical idiom as a scepticism born of the failure to use one with adequate success, and it stops well short of deserting an interest in the past. It is to be found in Guicciardini's masterly reflections on Machiavelli and in some of his *Ricordi* where he could well have been writing of Marsilius; thus, judging by (historical) examples is falacious, for unless things are alike in all respects we can be sure of nothing, a change in detail may have consequences beyond our expectations, for (in effect) the variables of history are never entirely independent. 'How mistaken', he writes 'are those who cite the Romans at every turn.'[56] The past, in short, is alien, infinitely complex and difficult to employ in the present, and it is seeing

---

[51] *De Tyranno* (On Tyranny), II.
[52] *DP* II.xix.8–10, where he suggests the difference between a fact of a statement (written or verbal) and its value, truth or usefulness (*quod aliud est credere sermonem aut scriptorum aliquam esse tradicionem alicuius seu ad aliquo factam, et aliud est credere illam esse verum*).
[53] *An Apology for Poetry* (1595), in *English Critical Essays, Sixteenth to Eighteenth Centuries*, ed. E. D. Jones, Oxford University Press, 1956 edn.
[54] Thomas Hobbes, *Leviathan*, Review and Conclusion.
[55] David Hume, *A Treatise of Human Nature*, III.i.1.
[56] *Ricordi*, 110.

the differences that takes 'the keen and perspicacious eye'.[57] Defeat has been turned into a virtue; the impractical past is not to be abandoned but enjoyed.

In looking beyond Machiavelli, as we did briefly with respect to religion, we can see that these two themes of criticism, both in their different ways generated by the difficulties of the historical idiom, coalesce in the tenets of nineteenth century historicism, have become as it were the credo, and have provided the criteria of judgement for twentieth-century professional history. Historicism is an ideology of failure. It did not emerge triumphantly, as the result of the combined attempts of proto-historians such as Marsilius, Machiavelli and Guicciardini to throw off the yoke of practical history and political mythology; to write objective history; and to treat the past on its own terms and for its own sake. These may be proper ideals, but they struck no-one as on a road to Damascus.[58] They amount to the rationalization of failure, possibly inevitable, to do something that most of those who have written about the past have regarded as more important, namely to use it as a form of intrinsic political theory.

Conclusion

Under the flexible headings of religion and history it has been possible to organize some of the continuities that link Marsilius and Machiavelli. Together, these continuities, and also the differences that I have indicated between the two theorists, indicate a political crisis of much broader significance. A sense of religion and tradition helped, as did nothing else, to cohere and define the political civilization of

---

[57] This is Grayson's translation of *'vuole buono e perspicace occhio'*; see also *Ricordi*, 6, where the detection of differences between cases is said to require *'la discrezione'*. E. Pasquini's comments in the Garzanti edition draw attention to similarities with La Rochefoucault in this context. Quentin Skinner, *The Foundations of Modern Political Thought*, Cambridge University Press, 1978, sees Cornelius Agrippa's *De vanitate* as an intensification of Guicciardini's attitude. As *De vanitate* is an indiscriminate attack on all human understanding, however, this reading is perhaps misleading.

[58] The image is not gratuitous. Road imagery (evoking purposeful journeys, paths, thresholds, even marches) is part of the stock-in-trade of historians of history. It functions as a field of metaphors for the progress and advance of historical thought towards modern historical writing. I have discussed the logic of this elsewhere. I am aware that historicism is a difficult and vague term. Here I have in mind the doctrine that historical understanding is distinctively non-ideological and non-scientific, and above all centred on recovering the past as it was. This meaning of the term is not to be confused with that popularized by Karl Popper in *The Poverty of Historicism* and *The Open Society and Its Enemies*, both published by Routledge & Kegan Paul, London.

Christendom. As these became increasingly problematic so Christendom collapsed, and the politically reflective were left in need of a largely re-ordered political vocabulary to cohere their experience. The point may be made simply by reference to the underlying force of the *Defensor Pacis* and *Il Principe*.

Il Principe is explicitly a work for new princes, who, by virtue of that fact alone, are likely to have trouble in maintaining their political estates. They, like no other rulers, are naked and need guidance, living as they do without recourse to the legitimizing effects of being clothed in tradition, custom or religious sanction.[59] The absence of these legitimizing trappings defines, like axes, the new prince and his problems. Where, conversely, the prince can claim the sanction of custom or religion his problems are fewer; so Machiavelli discusses neither hereditary nor ecclesiastical principalities, except to indicate that they do not need his advice.

Marsilius on the other hand is preoccupied with the greatest of all ecclesiastical principalities, and the force of his argument is precisely that as a principality, a political phenomenon *per se*, it lacks that sanction of religion and custom that hedges legitimate rulers. Thus whereas Marsilius uses and explores Christendom's sense of tradition and religion to discredit what he portrays as a *de facto* political phenomenon, Machiavelli accepts and works within the widening area where tradition and religion no longer apply with certainty.

It remains only to return to a first principle: the distinction between the Middle Ages and the Renaissance. In the light of what I have argued here, this distinction, with one theorist on either side of it, is both misleading and spurious. It is not that there are mediaeval elements in Machiavelli or modern elements in Marsilius, but that all such sentiments (and they are widely accepted) are mere modifications of the Burckhardtian model, and it is this that we need to abandon. The distinction itself, initially elaborated in respect to art and architecture, is irrelevant to the political theories of both men. I am not suggesting a new location of either thinker along the curve defined by the Mediaeval and Renaissance axes: I am asking for a new graph. Obviously people never

---

[59] I associate this understanding of 'the prince' as a figure cut off from the legitimizing force of tradition with a comment of Michael Oakeshott's in *Rationalism in Politics and Other Essays*, Methuen, London, 1962. This view is elaborated in Pocock, *The Machiavellian Moment, op. cit.*, as also to some extent is the importance of the absence of religion. I have made the point with specific reference to *P* 11 in *Three Aspects of Political Theory*, chapter 3 and note 22.

saw themselves as living in the Middle Ages[60], but the period covered by this anachronism had a great faith in social rebirth, the rhetoric of which was a barometer of political crisis. The rhetoric of *renascità*, together with significant changes in political vocabulary necessitated by the cracking and straining of old terms in the uncertain drift of language, and the changes in the characteristic idioms of political discourse, indicate a widening and deepening sense of crisis. This crisis was not the decline of the Middle Ages or the attempt to develop the modern state; consequence does not imply intention. The crisis concerned the ideological conception of society, which Marsilius saw as threatened; which yet others saw him as threatening; and the collapse of which Machiavelli accepted as part of the effective truth of things, even if his own writings, in dealing with its ramifications also reflect it.

---

[60] On the early uses of the expression 'middle ages', see N. Edelman, 'The Early Uses of Medium Aevum, Moyen Age, Middle Ages', *Romanic Review*, 29 (1938): 3. The best accounts I know of the history of the distinction are to be found in W. K. Ferguson, *The Renaissance in Historical Thought*, Boston, 1948; and especially in J. Huizinga, 'The Problem of the Renaissance' in *Men and Ideas*, transl. J. Holmes and H. van Marle, Meridian, New York, 1959 edn.

Hobbes and Locke

Roger D. Masters

Today, we are accustomed to discuss politics in terms of 'rights': people speak of 'civil rights', 'human rights' and 'property rights'. In foreign policy, nations and ethnic groups claim the 'right to self-determination'. Within most civilized societies, individuals claim equal 'rights' to free speech, employment, health care – and of course to vote. For example, the issue of abortion often takes the form of a conflict between the foetus' presumed 'right to life' and the mother's 'right' to control her own body.

To understand this way of approaching politics, it is useful to study the political theorists who first developed these ideas in our tradition. Usually, the Anglo-Saxon conception of the 'rights to life, liberty, and estate' is traced to John Locke (1632–1704). But Locke himself was preceded by an equally illustrious thinker – Thomas Hobbes (1588–1679). For Hobbes, as for Locke, political life can only be understood in terms of the 'natural rights' of all humans. For both thinkers, political communities are based on a social contract; Hobbes, like Locke, taught that all legitimate political institutions rest on the consent of the governed.[1]

At first, however, it seems strange to discuss Hobbes and Locke as similar thinkers. For Hobbes, the sovereign is 'absolute'; for Locke, men have a right to revolution. Hence it is usually assumed that Hobbes is an exponent of absolute monarchy. In contrast Locke openly favours limited government: he explicitly defended the Glorious Revolution of 1688 (which brought William and Mary to the throne and established the modern tradition of constitutional monarchy in England), and his doctrine of natural right inspired the Declaration of Independence (which led to the founding of the United States as an autonomous and free republic).

---

[1] See Leo Strauss, *Natural Right and History*, University of Chicago Press, 1953.

It is, of course, dangerous to discuss a political theorist apart from the context within which he wrote. Although Hobbes is often treated in historical isolation, he represented an important intellectual current in his own times. As recent research has shown, Hobbes was anticipated by some, cited or followed by others, and often criticized precisely because his works were viewed as both popular and dangerous.[2] Whatever Hobbes' genius and individuality, therefore, it is hardly necessary to assume that his thought emerged *ex nihilo*. Quite the contrary, any full account of Hobbes must take into consideration his relation to Bacon – not to mention other leading thinkers of his day in England and in Europe (ranging from Galileo to Descartes). For present purposes, however, it is sufficient to say that Hobbes' writings constitute a great synthesis of seventeenth-century thought.

Among Hobbes' English contemporaries and immediate successors, perhaps the most influential was John Locke. It is probably impossible to prove whether – or at what time – Locke read Hobbes' works. But Locke's extraordinary reticence, which led him to publish his *Two Treatises of Government* anonymously, cannot be entirely ignored; because Locke lost his teaching position in Oxford for suspect views and participated in 'subversive' political activity, his failure to cite Hobbes could have been to avoid the ill-repute of being considered a 'Hobbist'.[3]

In any event, the parallels between Locke's fundamental principles and those of Thomas Hobbes are striking. To be sure, Locke draws different *conclusions* from Hobbes. In particular, Locke teaches the importance of a limited form of government, with a division of powers between legislative and executive; although probably first drafted

---

[2] See especially Quenton Skinner, 'The Context of Hobbes' Theory of Political Obligation', in Maurice Cranston and Richard Peters, (eds), *Hobbes and Locke*, Anchor Books, New York, 1972, chapter 5.

[3] That such a repute was feared by Locke – and that even one of his friends had assumed Locke's principles to be Hobbesian – can be inferred from Sir Isaac Newton's apology for the fact that 'I took you for a Hobbist.' (Letter from Newton to Locke, 16 September 1693, quoted in Skinner, 'The Context of Hobbes' Theory of Obligation', p. 116.) Some scholars claim that Locke scarcely read Hobbes, but merely echoed themes that were common knowledge: see Peter Laslett's edition of Locke's *Two Treatises of Government*, Cambridge University Press, 1963, especially pp. 71–4. But others have argued for extensive and direct study of Hobbes, carefully hidden to avoid disrepute: for example, Richard Cox, *Locke on War and Peace*, Clarendon Press, Oxford, 1960. Although the thesis presented here does not depend on proof that Locke had read Hobbes' writings, the frequency with which Hobbes was discussed by the authorities Locke did consult (notably Grotius and Pufendorf) indicates some degree of direct and conscious influence.

between 1679 and 1683, Locke's *Treatises* were published in 1689 as a defence of the Glorious Revolution and the principle of government based on popular consent.

To appreciate the differences between any two thinkers, however, one must also consider their similarity. To do so, it is useful to begin with a statement of the basic issues we can expect to encounter when studying any position in political thought. All political theorists develop a conception of *human nature*. But all thinkers also elaborate a view of *history*. Hence, in order to situate Hobbes and Locke in the context of Western political thought, it is first necessary to clarify how attitudes toward human nature and history form the underlying dimensions on which political ideas can be compared.[4]

At first, the concept of human nature seems to imply expectations about human history. As a result, it is often presumed that 'optimism' and 'pessimism' are generalized attitudes towards the world. In fact, however, it can be shown that optimism or pessimism about *human nature* (are people basically selfish, or naturally 'good'?) is quite distinct from optimism or pessimism about *history* (will the future be an improvement on the present, or decline and corruption?).

In more philosophical terms, one can say that every political theorist answers at least two fundamental questions: first, what is the relationship between human nature and society (that is, are humans naturally social and co-operative, or are individuals basically egoists?). And second, what is the relationship of human knowledge and action to nature (that is, is science limited to a contemplation and understanding of nature, or does it permit control and mastery of natural scarcity?). These questions are, of course, merely formalizations of optimistic and pessimistic assessments of human nature and of history. But they show that attitudes on one dimension cannot be reduced to the other. Hence there are good grounds to assert that these categories are fundamental elements of all political thinking.

This structural framework generates four major forms or 'archetypes' of political thought. First, one can be pessimistic about both human nature and history (other humans are naturally selfish – and this condition is inevitable, leading to the impossibility of resolving the problem of political conflict). This position is characterized by the

---

[4] For an outline of this approach, which constitutes an application of 'structuralism' to political thought, see Roger D. Masters, 'Nature, Human Nature, and Political Thought', in J. Roland Pennock and John W. Chapman (eds), *Human Nature in Politics – Nomos* XVII, New York University Press, 1977, chapter 3.

Pre-Socratics and Sophists in ancient Greece, who can be said to have founded the tradition of Western political thought.

Second, it is possible to be optimistic about human nature but pessimistic about history (humans are naturally sociable and capable of co-operation, but history does not fundamentally improve). This position is well illustrated by Aristotle's teaching, which represents one of the most persistent modes of political thought in the West.

Third, one can be pessimistic about human nature but optimistic about history (other humans are naturally selfish, as the Sophists had claimed – but knowledge of this fact when combined with knowledge of natural science can lead to a conquest of natural scarcity and a resolution of political conflict). As will be shown below, Hobbes, Locke and the modern thinkers following them elaborate this type of political theory.

Finally, some thinkers are optimistic about both human nature and politics (humans are naturally capable of co-operation, and scientific mastery of natural necessity can lead to historical progress). Marx presents, in the clearest possible way, this perspective on political life.

From this perspective, Hobbes and Locke illustrate one of the basic approaches to political thought. Their perspective differs sharply from classical political philosophy, in good part because the ancients did not believe that scientific knowledge would make possible political or social progress. And they differ from Marxists and related points of view, because both Hobbes and Locke see human beings as naturally selfish individuals.

In the form or 'archetype' of political thought represented by Hobbes and Locke, politics is understood in terms of the 'natural rights' of human beings, the formation of governments by popular consent, and the conscious design of effective constitutions that insure the self-preservation of citizens. A comparison between Hobbes and Locke is therefore useful as a means of understanding the contemporary approach to political life in terms of individual 'rights'.

The similarity between Hobbes and Locke:
Human nature, selfishness and the social contract

Hobbes has been described as a 'pessimist' with regard to human nature who was 'optimistic' about history. More precisely, a pessimistic view of human nature assumes that humans are by nature egoistic and hedonistic – that is, that humans are not naturally sociable, so that the 'state of nature' is a condition of conflict between selfish individuals. Hobbes' view of the natural selfishness and conflict among men is well-known; he argues that 'during the time men live without a common power to keep them all in awe, they are in that condition which is called war; and such a war as is of every man, against every man.'[5] But Hobbes also teaches that science, when used to direct human industry, can effectively resolve the conflicts that have destroyed all previously existing political systems. For example, he claims that it is entirely possible to construct a commonwealth that will be 'eternal'.[6] His 'optimism' concerning historical progress could best be defined as the assumption that science makes possible the conquest of natural scarcity, thereby overcoming political conflict and social discontent.[7]

To see how Locke compares with his predecessor, it is best to begin from their conceptions of human nature. The root of Hobbes' position appears, at the outset of the *Leviathan*, as a radical reinterpretation of all human life in terms of matter in motion; after summarizing Galileo's revolutionary conception of inertia, Hobbes describes all thoughts as the result of sense impressions.[8] Locke is best known as a philosopher for his *Essay Concerning Human Understanding* – a work that begins with an extended demonstration that 'neither principles nor ideas are innate'.[9] Locke's philosophy is thus based on the famous proposition that the human mind is naturally 'white paper, void of all characters, without any ideas' and that all reason and knowledge come from 'experience'.[10] This assertion reminds one of Hobbes' remark that 'the common people's minds . . . are like clean paper, fit to receive whatsoever by public authority shall be imprinted in them'.[11] Like Hobbes, therefore, Locke bases his thought on what has come to be known as the *tabula rasa* theory

---

[5] Thomas Hobbes, *Leviathan*, edited by Michael Oakeshott, Blackwell, Oxford 1960, chapter 13, p. 82.
[6] *Ibid.*, chapter 30, p. 220.
[7] *De Cive*, Dedicatory Letter, in Thomas Hobbes, *Man and Citizen*, edited by Bernard Gert, Anchor Books, New York 1972, p. 35ff.
[8] *Leviathan*, chapter 1, pp. 7–8.
[9] John Locke, *Essay Concerning Human Understanding*, edited by Alexander Campbell Fraser, Dover, New York, 1959. Although first published in 1691, two years after the *Two Treatises of Government*, the *Essay* was probably begun before Locke wrote on political topics. In the Epistle to the Reader, Locke indicates that the impulse to examine 'human understanding' came from a meeting that recent scholarship dates in the winter of 1670–71; apparently, 'difficulties' which Locke and five or six friends discovered when discussing 'principles of morality and revealed religion' led him to write a first draft of the *Essay* in the 1670s. As early as 1671, Locke wrote: 'all knowledge is founded on, and ultimately derives itself from Sense, or something analogous to it; and may be called Sensation.'
[10] *Essay*, II.i.2, volume 1, pp.121–2.
[11] *Leviathan*, chapter 30, p. 221.

of knowledge, according to which all ideas can be traced to sense-impression or reflection on prior experience.[12]

One of Locke's main arguments against innate ideas lies in the variability of human customs from one society to another; in the *Essay*, he is at pains to show that some peoples have condoned if not praised virtually every conceivable action, from cannibalism to parricide.[13] In so doing, Locke asserts: 'Robberies, murders, rapes are the sports of men set at liberty from punishment and censure.'[14] This argument surely seems akin to Hobbes' doctrine that the state of nature is a 'war of all against all'. Such an impression is confirmed by the sole explicit reference to Hobbes in the entire *Essay*, which occurs just before this passage:

> That men should keep their compacts is certainly a great and undeniable rule in morality. But yet, if a Christian, who has the view of happiness and misery in another life, be asked why a man must keep his word, he will give this as a reason: – Because God, who has the power of eternal life and death, requires it of us. But if a Hobbist be asked why? he will answer: – Because the public requires it, and the Leviathan will punish you if you do not. And if one of the old philosophers had been asked, he would have answered: – Because it was

---

[12] Locke's argument in the *Essay*, when stripped to its essentials, seems remarkably close to that of Hobbes. For example, since there are no 'innate' standards of good and evil, for Locke – as for Hobbes – 'things then are good and evil, only in reference to pleasure and pain'. (*Essay*, II.xx.2, volume 1, p. 303; *cf.* II.xxi.43, volume 1, pp. 340–1) This 'utilitarian' view leads not only to a redefinition of the passions (II.xx.4–17, volume 1, pp. 303–7) but to relativism in judgements of what is good and bad: 'the philosophers of old did in vain inquire, whether *summum bonum* consisted in riches, or bodily delights, or virtue, or contemplation . . . the greatest happiness consists in having those things which produce the greatest pleasure, and in the absence of those which cause any disturbance, any pain. Now these, to different men, are very different things.' (II.xxi.56, volume 1, p. 351). As Hobbes said, 'there is no such *finis ultimus*, utmost aim, nor *summum bonum*, greatest good, as is spoken of in the books of the old moral philosophers.' (*Leviathan*, chapter 11, p. 63). Since preferences are caused by individual experience, freedom or liberty must consist in *power* to act: 'liberty is not an idea belonging to volition, or preferring; but to the person having the power of doing, or forbearing to do, according as the mind shall choose or direct'. (*Essay*, II.xxxi.10, volume 1, p. 317) Hence the will can be subject to material determination, yet an act can be free; the question of 'free will' is, strictly speaking, 'unintelligible'. (*Essay*, II.xxxi.14, volume 1, p. 319) On each of these fundamental propositions, Locke follows Hobbes closely. It is curious that many discussions of the relationship between Hobbes' *Leviathan* and Locke's political teaching ignore the *Essay Concerning Human Understanding*. For the exception that proves the rule, see Laslett's introduction to the *Two Treatises of Government*, *op.cit.*, pp. 79–91.
[13] I.ii.9–10, volume 1, pp. 72–4.
[14] I.ii.9, volume 1, p. 72.

dishonest, below the dignity of man, and opposite to virtue, the highest perfection of human nature, to do otherwise.[15]

In other words, Locke first asserts the difference between Christian, Hobbesian and classical accounts of moral obligation, and then uses an example confirming the empirical accuracy of Hobbes' account.

This kinship between Hobbes and Locke has not always been noticed by commentators who begin by comparing the Hobbesian state of nature with Locke's *Second Treatise of Government*. According to Locke, it would seem that the state of nature is peaceful — and that Hobbes erred in describing it as a war of all against all:

> And here we have the plain difference between the State of Nature and the State of War, which however some Men have confounded, are as far distant, as a State of Peace, Good Will, Mutual Assistance, and Preservation, and a State of Enmity, Malice, Violence and Mutual Destruction are one from another. Men living together according to reason, without a common Superior on Earth, with Authority to judge between them, is properly the State of Nature. But force, or a declared design of force upon the Person of another, where there is no common Superior on Earth to appeal to for relief, is the State of War.[16]

As most critics have not failed to point out, Hobbes would appear to be one of the men who 'have confounded' a peaceful state of nature with a state of war.

While Locke's formulation is more palatable than that of Hobbes, however, it is not clear whether there is any effective difference between the two authors. Immediately after the apparent criticism of Hobbes, Locke goes on to say that

> . . . in the State of Nature, for want of positive Laws, and Judges with Authority to appeal to, the State of War once begun, continues, with a right to the innocent Party, to destroy the other whenever he can . . .[17]

Hence civil society originates, for all practical purposes, due to the lack of a 'common power' in the state of nature.

> To avoid this State of War (wherein there is no appeal but to Heaven, and wherein every the least difference is apt to end, where there is no Authority to decide between the Contenders) is one great reason of Mens putting themselves into Society, and quitting the State of Nature.[18]

---

[15] I.ii.5, volume 1, p. 69.
[16] *Second Treatise*, chapter iii.19, in *Two Treatises of Government*, Peter Laslett (ed.), *op. cit.*, p. 298.
[17] *Ibid.*, iii.20, p. 299.
[18] *Ibid.*, iii.21, p. 300.

By an 'appeal to Heaven,' Locke clearly means violence – as the remainder of the passage and numerous other passages make clear.

That Locke's 'state of nature' almost inevitably degenerates into a state of war has been obscured by his description of the 'law of nature':

> The State of Nature has a Law of Nature to govern it, which obliges every one: And Reason, which is that Law, teaches all Mankind, who will but consult it, that being all equal and independent, no one ought to harm another in his Life, Health, Liberty, or Possessions . . . Every one as he is bound to preserve himself, and not quit his Station wilfully; so by the like reason when his own Preservation comes not in competition, ought he, as much as can, to preserve the rest of Mankind . . .[19]

But Hobbes too had spoken of a rational 'law of nature' conducive to peace.[20]

As Locke's *Essay* (not to mention our common experience) proves abundantly, however, 'all Mankind' do *not* naturally 'consult' their 'reason'; for Locke (as for Hobbes), the law of nature is not self-enforcing, like the law of gravity. Admitting that 'confusion and Disorder will follow' from the fact that each individual enforces the law of nature, Locke adds that 'civil Government is the proper Remedy for the Inconveniences of the State of Nature, which must certainly be Great, where Men may be Judges in their own Case . . .'[21]

Locke's 'law of nature' thus has exactly the same status and character as that of Hobbes: beginning from the natural right to self-preservation, both authors develop a rational law of nature including each man's obligation to seek peace 'when his own Preservation comes not in competition.' While Hobbes puts the argument more brutally than Locke – no doubt because for Hobbes it is crucial to sustain the fear of renewed civil war – both thinkers give the right to self-preservation priority over the rational obligation to peace whenever the two conflict.[22]

---

[19] *Ibid.*, ii.6, p. 289.
[20] *Leviathan*, chapter 14, p. 84.
[21] *Second Treatise*, ii.13, p. 294.
[22] *Cf.* Strauss, *Natural Right and History*, chapter 5. It should be added that, like Locke, Hobbes also distinguishes between the state of war which inevitably arises in the state of nature, and a primeval, *peaceful* stage of the state of nature. What Hobbes calls 'the natural condition of mankind' is *not* the historical origin of human existence; on the contrary, 'it was never generally so, over all the world.' Among the 'savage people' in America, Hobbes admits that there is 'concord' within 'small families' even though 'they have no government at all'; such a state of nature can be peaceful, but life in it is 'brutish'. See *Leviathan*, chapter 13, p. 83; and compare Jean-Jaques Rousseau, *Second Discourse*, Part 1, R.D. Masters (ed.), St Martin's Press, New York, 1964, pp. 105–37.

To escape the 'incommodities' or 'inconveniences' of the state of nature, men agree to a contract that establishes civil society. Hobbes had defined this social contract as follows:

> A commonwealth is said to be instituted, when a multitude of men do agree, and covenant, every one, with every one, that to whatsoever man, or assembly of men, shall be given by the major part, the right to present the person of them all, that is to say, to be their representative; every one, as well he that voted for it, as he that voted against it, shall authorize all the actions and judgments of that man, or assembly of men, in the same manner, as if they were his own, to the end, to live peaceably amongst themselves, and be protected against other men.[23]

Locke obviously shares the Hobbesian view that civil society is the result of a social contract, by which free and equal men lay down natural rights in order to escape the dangers of a war of all.

> Men being . . . by Nature, all free, equal, and independent, no one can be put out of this Estate, and subjected to the Political Power of another, without his own Consent. The only way whereby any one devests himself of his Natural Liberty, and puts on the bonds of Civil Society is by agreeing with other Men to Joyn and unite into a Community, for their comfortable, safe, and peaceable living one amongst another, in a secure Enjoyment of their Properties, and a greater Security against any that are not of it.[24]

Like Hobbes, Locke believes that *all* civil society is based on 'consent'; like Hobbes, the social compact creates a community 'with a Power to Act as one Body'.[25] Locke even speaks of the body politic as 'the mighty Leviathan'. He stresses that his social contract must establish the principle of majority rule: 'When any number of Men have so consented to make one Community or Government, they are thereby presently incorporated, and make one Body Politick, wherein the Majority have a Right to act and conclude the rest.'[26] Without this, the social contract would have to be absolutely unanimous, and 'such consent is next impossible ever to be had' because some would miss the assembly and others would disagree. If one insisted on absolute unanimity, Locke adds,

> the coming into Society upon such terms, would be only like Cato's coming into the Theatre, only to go out again. Such a Constitution as this would make the mighty *Leviathan* of a shorter duration, than the feeblest Creatures . . .[27]

---

[23] *Leviathan*, chapter 18, p. 113.
[24] *Second Treatise*, viii.95, pp. 348–9.
[25] *Ibid.*, viii.96, p. 349.
[26] *Ibid.*, viii.95, p. 349.

In the decisive respect, Hobbes and Locke agree on the principle of majority rule.

Locke's transformation of Hobbes:
Historical optimism and the doctrine of limited government

To be sure, Locke's teaching differs from that of Hobbes. For Locke, the social contract is an explicit agreement to be bound by majority rule in subsequent decisions. In contrast, Hobbes argues that majority rule is 'tacitly covenanted' by all those who 'voluntarily entered into the congregation of them that were assembled'[28] and that the social contract properly so-called is a *subsequent* decision, naming the sovereign. Locke's social contract engages 'every individual that united into it'; Hobbes' social contract is an agreement between all the *subjects*, to which the sovereign is *not* a party.

Locke therefore rejects the notion of an 'absolute ruler' who remains in the state of nature and is not bound by the social contract. Indeed, Locke very clearly describes such a Hobbesian contract, and dismisses it–albeit without mentioning Hobbes. Although sharing Hobbes' basic principles, Locke insists that social contract refers to what Hobbes called the 'tacit covenant' to abide by the majority, and not – as for Hobbes himself – to the decision of which individual or group should have political power. The result is that Locke is able to convert Hobbes' doctrine into a defence of limited, constitutional government.

This difference between Hobbes and Locke was of course of momentous import in English politics, since Locke's *Treatise* could be used to legitimate the 'Glorious Revolution' bringing William and Mary to the throne. But the philosophical depth of the disagreement between Hobbes and Locke should not be exaggerated; Hobbes had explicitly endorsed any form of government, whether by a man or an assembly of men.[29] In *A Dialogue between a Philosopher and a Student of the Common Laws of England* (published in 1681), Hobbes suggests that 'there is no King in the World, being of ripe years and sound mind, that made law

---

[27] *Ibid.*, viii.98, p. 351. Even Laslett, who is otherwise sceptical of Hobbes' direct influence on Locke, admits that this is a 'deliberate invocation of the language of Hobbes'. (See *Leviathan*, p.351, note.)
[28] *Leviathan*, chapter 18, p. 115.
[29] See *Leviathan*, chapter 18, p. 213.

otherwise' than by having 'called together the Lords and Commons, in such manner as is used at this day in England.'[30]

Hobbes' *Dialogue* is an extremely interesting practical application of his principles, which deserves more attention. In this work, Hobbes flatly asserts that 'God made Kings for the People, and not People for Kings'.[31] He explicitly accepts the 'Statutes that restrain the Levying of Money without consent of Parliament' and even remarks that 'those statutes are in themselves very good for the King and People' as long as they do not prevent 'Kings from the use of their armies in the necessary defence of themselves and their People'.[32] Nor is this a total departure from Hobbes' earlier work, since he refers to *'rex in parliamento'* in the *Leviathan*.[33]

Locke's conception of the 'executive' and 'federative' power, as distinct from 'legislative' power[34], should be compared to Hobbes' remarks on the inability of the parliament to defend citizens 'from the domineering of Proud and Insolent Strangers . . . that seek to make us Slaves', especially since the crisis could occur 'when there is no Parliament sitting, or perhaps none in being'.[35] But whereas Hobbes, here as elsewhere, stresses the dangers of foreign attack and civil war, Locke merely touches in passing on the risk of 'disorder and ruine' and the resulting need to leave powers of 'great moment . . . to the Prudence and Wisdom of those whose hands it is in.'[36]

As the editor of Hobbes' *Dialogue* puts it, Hobbes 'instantly and violently alienated' the kind of readers whose active support was necessary for the political success of his doctrine.[37] In the words of another careful scholar, Hobbes' 'influence on thought about politics has been enormous, but his purchase over what men do politically has been negligible' . . .; after Hobbes wrote, political philosophy 'became entirely different, but the political habits of his countrymen were changed not one little bit . . . and insofar as Hobbes has done that, it is through Locke that he has done it.'[38]

---

[30] Thomas Hobbes, *A Dialogue between a Philosopher and a Student of the Common Laws of England*, edited by Joseph Cropsey, University of Chicago Press, 1971, p. 166.
[31] *Ibid.*, p. 61.
[32] *Ibid.*, pp. 63-4.
[33] *Leviathan*, chapter 26, p. 175.
[34] *Second Treatise*, xii.147-8, pp. 383-4.
[35] *Dialogue*, p. 61.
[36] *Second Treatise*, xii.147-8, pp. 383-4.
[37] Cropsey, 'Introduction' to Hobbes' *Dialogue*, p.18.
[38] Laslett, 'Introduction' to Locke's *Two Treatises*, pp. 90-1.

To show the extent to which Locke transformed the Hobbesian teaching into a more palatable doctrine of limited government, it is necessary to consider Locke's approach to human history. As was noted above, optimism toward the future reflects an expectation that human action can control nature and alleviate natural scarcity. On this score, Locke elaborates Hobbes' historical optimism into a powerful political doctrine.

Among the teachings of Locke, the so-called 'labour theory of value' is particularly well known:

> For 'tis Labour indeed that puts the difference of value on every thing . . . I think it will be but a very modest Computation to say, that of the Products of the Earth useful to the Life of Man $9/10$ are the effects of labour; nay, if we will rightly estimate things as they come to our use, and cast up the several Expences about them, what in them is purely owing to Nature, and what to labour, we shall find, that in most of them $99/100$ are wholly to be put on the account of labour.[39]

'Land that is left wholly to Nature' is merely 'waste' and has a 'benefit' which amounts 'to little more than nothing'; without human labour, natural materials 'in themselves' are 'almost worthless'.[40]

One of Locke's main examples is the condition of the Indian tribes encountered by English colonists in North America. For Locke, 'in the beginning all the World was America'[41] and 'in the wild woods and uncultivated wast[e] of America' the inhabitants are 'needy and wretched'.[42]

> There cannot be a clearer demonstration of any thing, than several Nations of the Americans are of this, who are rich in Land, and poor in all the Comforts of Life; whom Nature having furnished as liberally as any other people, with the materials of Plenty, i.e. a fruitful Soil, apt to produce in abundance, what might serve for food, rayment, and delight; yet for want of improving it by labour, have not one hundreth part of the Conveniences we enjoy: And a King of a large and fruitful Territory there feeds, lodges, and is clad worse than a day Labourer in England.[43]

Hobbes implicitly encourages men to abandon political conflict in favour of the comforts and conveniences of life derived from economic activity;

---

[39] *Second Treatise*, v.40, p. 314.
[40] *Ibid.*, v.42–3, pp. 315–6.
[41] *Ibid.*, v.49, p. 319.
[42] *Ibid.*, v.37, p. 312.
[43] *Ibid.*, v.41, pp. 314–5.

Locke makes this teaching explicit and clear.[44]

In context, Locke's discussion of the labour theory of value is used to establish a natural 'right' to property. Since this right is not secure in the state of nature, men form civil society to preserve not only their right to life, but their right to property. Or, in Locke's phrase, the 'Rights and Privileges of the Law of Nature' rest on the natural 'power' of every man to 'preserve his Property, that is, his Life, Liberty, and Estate'.[45] Hobbes' concept of the natural right to self-preservation is thus rephrased as a right to 'Life, Liberty, and Estate'; the 'chief end' of civil society 'is the preservation of Property' in this enlarged sense.[46]

Whatever the technical differences between Hobbes and Locke, it should be evident that the Lockean formulation rests on the notion that human labour and industry – based on scientific knowledge or technical art – transform virtually worthless natural materials into 'conveniences' taking the form of valuable property.

> Man (by being Master of himself, and Proprietor of his own Person, and the Actions or Labour of it) had still in himself the great Foundation of Property; and that which made up the great part of what he applyed to the Support or Comfort of his being, when Invention and Arts had improved the conveniencies of Life, was perfectly his own . . .[47]

Although this passage refers explicitly to the right of the individual against others in the state of nature, it also applies to humans collectively: 'God gave the World . . . to the use of the Industrious and Rational' and commanded men 'to subdue' the Earth and 'appropriate' it.[48] One is

---

[44] Hobbes' endorsement of economic activity is more obvious if his famous description of the state of nature is read, without the negatives, as a statement of the goals to be achieved in civilized society: 'there is . . . place for industry, because the fruit thereof is . . . certain; and consequently . . . culture of the earth; . . . navigation; . . . use of the commodities that may be imported by sea; . . . commodious building; . . . instruments of moving and removing, such things as require much force; . . . knowledge of the face of the earth; . . . account of time; . . . arts; . . . letters'. (*Leviathan*, chapter 13, p. 82). If read with great care, Hobbes' *Leviathan* establishes the groundwork for industrial society, laissez faire economics and representative government. (*Cf.* Aristotle, *Politics*, I.1256a–1259a.)

[45] *Second Treatise*, vii.87, p. 341.

[46] *Ibid.*, vii.85, p. 341; and ix.123, p. 368. On the continuing relevance of Locke's concept, see Ramon M. Lemos, 'Locke's Theory of Property', *Interpretation*, V (Winter 1975): 226–44. Although Hobbes insists that property only comes into existence within civil society (whereas Locke argues that labour provides a natural claim to property even in the state of nature), for both there is no assured and protected right to property prior to the social contract.

[47] *Second Treatise*, v.44, pp. 316–7.

[48] *Ibid.*, v.34–5, pp. 309–10.

reminded of Hobbes' assertion that 'Plenty dependeth, next to God's favour, merely on the labour and industry of men.'[49]

The effects of 'invention and arts' are thus a form of industry which can multiply the 'conveniences' of life a thousandfold. In this sense, the development of science and industry appear to control – or, in Locke's own words, to 'subdue' – nature for the 'convenience' and 'comforts of life'. Elsewhere, Locke is explicit on the power of science to serve 'for the common use of human life':

> Of what consequence the discovery of one natural body and its properties may be to human life, the whole great continent of America is a convincing instance: whose ignorance in useful arts, and want of the greatest part of the conveniences of life, in a country that abounded with all sorts of natural plenty, I think may be attributed to their ignorance of what was to be found in a very ordinary, despicable stone, I mean the mineral of *iron*. And whatever we think of our parts or improvements in this part of the world, where knowledge and plenty seem to vie with each other . . . the use of iron lost among us, we should in a few ages be unavoidably reduced to the wants and ignorance of the ancient savage Americans, whose natural endowments and provisions come no way short of those of the most flourishing and polite nations. So that he who first made known the use of that contemptible mineral, may be truly styled the father of arts, and the author of plenty.[50]

The labour theory of value, which Locke emphasizes in the *Second Treatise*, can lead to the production of objects making life comfortable and pleasant – but for this to occur, there must exist 'useful arts' and therewith science. Like Hobbes, therefore, Locke sees the application of scientific method to human problems as the key to a resolution of political conflict.[51] While Locke warns against taking 'doubtful systems for complete sciences', he points out that the 'study of nature . . . if rightly directed, may be of greater benefit to mankind than the monuments of exemplary charity that have at so great charge been raised by the founders of hospitals and almshouses'; in place of Christian charity or classical philosophy, the 'knowledge of bodies' gotten by 'our senses, warily employed in taking notice of their qualities and operations on one another', is a 'surer way to profitable knowledge'.[52] In short, Locke – like Hobbes – was a political thinker who combined a

---

[49] *Leviathan*, chapter 24, pp. 160–1.
[50] *Essay*, IV.xii.11, volume 2, p. 351.
[51] See *De Cive*, Dedicatory Letter, p. 91; and *Leviathan*, chapter 30, p. 220.
[52] *Essay*, IV.xii.12, volume 2, pp. 352–3.

'pessimistic' assessment of human nature with an 'optimistic' view of progress, using human science to overcome natural scarcity.

The Anglo-Saxon political tradition: Liberalism and the American regime

Whether by direct influence or parallel development, both Hobbes and Locke represent a tradition that long dominated Anglo-Saxon thought and profoundly influenced continental European thinkers. Although sometimes described as the 'modern natural right' teaching, this position is better understood as the combination of attitudes towards human nature and towards scientific or historical progress (especially since some of its exponents, such as the 'utilitarians', abandoned the concept of *natural* rights). Whether one considers Hume, Adam Smith, Bentham, and both James and John Stuart Mill, or includes such French thinkers as Voltaire, Diderot and Helvétius (to mention some obvious names), the juxtaposition of 'pessimism' about human nature and 'optimism' concerning the future of science and industry clearly characterized a major epoch of Western thought.[53]

Rather than trace this historical tradition in detail, however, it would probably be more useful to indicate a practical political consequence of the thought of Hobbes and his successors: namely the Constitution of the United States. As is generally known, Thomas Jefferson's draft of the Declaration of Independence was inspired by Locke's *Second Treatise*; insofar as Locke's principles are viewed as part of the Hobbesian strand in Western thought, it would follow that Jefferson and the Declaration are likewise in this tradition. But since it is unwise to trust to such superficial syllogisms, let us look at the evidence.

As early as 1768, the Massachusetts House of Representatives protested against British policies on the grounds that 'it is an essential, natural right, that a man shall quietly enjoy, and have the sole disposal of

---

[53] See Strauss, *Natural Right and History*, chapters 5 and 6; Christopher Hill, 'Thomas Hobbes and the Revolution in Political Thought', in *Political Theory and Ideology*, Judith Shklar (ed.), Macmillan, New York, 1966, pp. 35-48; and C. B. Macpherson, *The Political Theory of Possessive Individualism*, Oxford University Press, 1962. Little has been said of the great influence of Hobbes and Locke in the epistemology and metaphysics of thinkers ranging from Berkeley and Hume to Kant. For the example of Hobbes' influence on Liebnitz, and therewith on the development of physics, see J.W.N. Watkins, 'Liberty', in *Hobbes and Rousseau*, Peters and Cranston (eds).

his property.'[54] While every American student is taught that the colonists claimed such rights, there was another principle behind the protest:

> At the expense of their blood, at the hazard of their fortunes, without the least charge to the country from which they [our forefathers] removed, by unceasing labor, and an unconquerable spirit, they effected settlements in the distant and inhospitable wilds of America, then filled with numerous and warlike nations of barbarians . . . It is universally confessed, that the amazing increase of the wealth, strength, and navigation of the realm, arose from this source.[55]

The colonists thus echo Locke's argument that 'labour . . . puts the value on every thing' and is the source of the right to property. Since 'God gave the world . . . to the use of the Industrious and Rational', and the Indians did not improve the 'rich' lands of North America 'by labour' the settlers were only reasonable in taking credit for displacing the Indians and converting 'the distant and inhospitable wilds of America' into a source of 'wealth' and 'strength' for Great Britain. In short, prerevolutionary colonial declarations presume both the individualistic doctrine of natural rights developed by Hobbes and Locke *and* the assertion that human action can overcome the scarcity of 'nature'.

The text of the Declaration of Independence, as drafted by Jefferson and adopted on 4 July 1776, is justly famous for its assertion of inalienable or natural rights:

> We hold these truths to be self-evident, that all men are created equal, that they are endowed by their Creator with certain unalienable Rights, that among these are Life, Liberty, and the pursuit of Happiness. That to secure

[54] Letter of the Massachusetts House to the Agent of the Province in England, 12 January 1768, in *The Federal Convention and the Formation of the Union of the American States*, Winton U. Solberg, (ed.), Liberal Arts Press, New York, 1958, p. 8. The colonists began their remonstrances from the position that 'his majesty's liege subjects in these colonies are entitled to all the inherent rights and privileges of his natural born subjects within the kingdom of Great Britain.' (Declaration of Rights of the Stamp Act Congress, 19 October 1765, in Solberg, *op. cit.*, p. 6) The shift from claiming the 'rights and privileges' of British 'subjects' to arguing on the basis of 'natural right' was therefore a radicalization of colonial opinion – but even the first colonial views fall conveniently within the framework of Locke's teaching. (*Second Treatise*, xix. 223–4, pp. 432–34) Hence the 'Declaration and Resolves' of the First Continental Congress derived the right to 'life, liberty, and property' from 'the immutable laws of nature, the principles of the English constitution, and the several charters and compacts'. (14 October 1774, in Solberg, *op. cit.*, p. 11) One is reminded of Hobbes' statement that 'the law of nature, and the civil law, contain each other'. (*Leviathan*, chapter 26, p. 174).

[55] 'Declaration of the Causes and Necessity of Taking Up Arms', 6 July 1775, in Solberg, *op. cit.*, p. 17.

these rights, Governments are instituted among Men, deriving their just powers from the consent of the governed. That whenever any Form of Government becomes destructive of these ends, it is the Right of the People to alter or to abolish it, and to institute new Government, laying its foundation on such principles and organizing its powers in such form, as to them shall seem most likely to effect their Safety and Happiness.[56]

As is often noted, these 'self-evident' truths reflect Locke's teaching. What is not so frequently realized, however, is that Jefferson's formulation could also be derived from Hobbesian principles.

For Hobbes, the laws of nature and of nature's God are the basis of any social contract; for Hobbes, all men are created equal and the rights to life, liberty and the pursuit of happiness are unalienable; for Hobbes, governments are instituted to secure the life of men and rest on the consent of the governed. More to the point, Hobbes teaches that, since the end of obedience is protection, when a government becomes destructive of its subjects, their obligation ceases:

> The obligation of the subjects to the sovereign, is understood to last as long, and no longer, than the power lasteth, by which he is able to protect them. For the right men have by nature to protect themselves, when none else can protect them, can be no covenant be relinquished . . . The end of obedience is protection; which, wheresoever a man seeth it, either in his own, or in another's sword, nature applieth his obedience to it . . .[57]

The catalogue of the 'long train of abuses and usurpations', that constitutes the largest part of the Declaration of Independence can be described accurately as a statement that the colonists 'seeth' that the British Crown is no longer able to protect their life, liberty and property.[58]

Even if the Declaration of Independence could not be interpreted in Hobbesian terms, it is clearly an example of the social contract theory of government. From this point of view, the last sentence, concluding with the ringing 'we mutually pledge to each other our Lives, our Fortunes and our sacred Honor', is most important. In addition to resting on a contractual theory of government, however, the Declaration of Independence also rests on the assumption of historical progress. King George's acts are 'Cruelty & perfidy scarcely paralleled in the most barbarous ages, and totally unworthy of the Head of a civilized nation'.

---

[56] In Solberg, *op. cit.*, p. 34.
[57] *Leviathan*, chapter 21, p. 144.
[58] For example, 'He has plundered our seas, ravaged our Coasts, burnt our towns, and destroyed the lives of our people.' (In Solberg, *op. cit.*, p. 36)

Not only has the King encouraged the 'merciless Indian Savages' but he 'has endeavoured to prevent the population of these States; for that purpose obstructing the Laws for Naturalization of Foreigners; refusing to pass others to encourage their migration hither, and raising the conditions of new Appropriations of Lands.'[59] In short, Jefferson's famous text combines a natural right contractual theory with the assumption that the colonists, coming from a 'civilized nation' which represents progress over 'the most barbarous ages' can legitimately displace the 'merciless Indian Savages' by 'New Appropriations' of their lands.

It would be easy to show that not only the Declaration of Independence but the American Constitution itself rests on this combination of 'pessimism' about human nature and 'optimism' about the progress of science, industry, and human history. At the Constitutional Convention in 1787, the terminology of Hobbes and Locke was generally taken for granted. For example, the issue of how powerful to make the national government was debated in terms of whether or not 'the separation of G.B. placed the 13 States in a state of Nature towards each other.'[60] Indeed, one delegate sought to prove his interpretation of the 'state of nature' doctrine by reading passages from Locke, as well as from Vattel, Lord Somers and Priestley – but not from Hobbes.[61]

Although the Founding Fathers cited Locke's formulation of natural rights, their descriptions of human nature were frequently close to Hobbes': 'The question is not what rights naturally belong to men; but how they may be most equally & effectually guarded in society.'[62] 'Pride is indeed the great principle that actuates both the poor and the rich . . . The Rich will strive to establish their dominion & enslave the rest. They always did. They always will. The proper security agst them is to form them into a separate interest. The two forces will then controul each other . . .'[63] 'Give the votes to people who have no property, and they will sell them to the rich who will be able to buy them.'[64] 'The love of fame is the great spring to noble & illustrious actions.'[65] 'The people are uninformed, and would be misled by a few designing men.'[66] 'If a

---

[59] In Solberg, *op. cit.*, pp. 35–6.
[60] 'Madison's Notes of Debates in the Federal Convention', in Solberg, *op. cit.*, p. 157.
[61] *Ibid.*, p. 180.
[62] *Ibid.*, p. 185.
[63] *Ibid.*, p. 200.
[64] *Ibid.*, p. 271.
[65] *Ibid.*, p. 232.
[66] *Ibid.*, p. 234.

Constitutional discrimination of the departments on paper were a sufficient security to each agst encroachments of the others, all further provisions would indeed be superfluous. But experience had taught us a distrust of that security; and that it is necessary to introduce such a balance of powers and interests, as will guarantee the provisions on paper.'[67] The Constitutional principle of a separation of powers to be maintained by 'checks and balances' is thus but a means to guard natural rights equally and effectually against selfish or 'designing' men.[68]

Combined with this 'pessimistic' view of human nature, however, is a striking optimism about the historical progress open to the world. To be sure, both Madison and Hamilton expressed the judgement that the success of the Convention would 'decide for ever the fate of Republican Government' – with Hamilton adding that 'if we did not give to that form due stability and wisdom, it would be disgraced & lost among ourselves, digraced & lost to mankind for ever.'[69] This sense of uniqueness was nonetheless an opportunity; a new regime was possible because, as Pinckney asserted, 'the people of this country' are the 'most singular' of any in the world, being 'very different' from all others in both the 'modern world' and 'among the antients'.[70] As a result, in Gouverneur Morris' words, 'the whole human race will be affected by the proceedings of this Convention'.[71] Not only was it said that 'this Constitution will be much read and attended to in Europe'[72] but several of the Founding Fathers explicitly asserted that 'we are laying the foundation for a great empire'[73] and 'framing a system we wish to last for ages'.[74] When Madison sought to convince the delegates from small states, he asked them 'to renounce a principle [which] . . . if admitted must infuse mortality into a Constitution which we wished to last forever'.[75] The mechanisms to secure 'a mutual check and mutual security'[76] were thus intended to 'control' the conflict between rich and poor that had

[67] *Ibid.*, p. 239.
[68] See Alexander Hamilton, James Madison and John Jay, *The Federalist*, Modern Library, New York, 1941, especially Nos 10 and 51. For a good commentary, see Martin Diamond, 'The Federalist', in *History of Political Philosophy*, Leo Strauss and Joseph Cropsey (eds), Rand McNally, Chicago, 1963, pp. 573–93.
[69] *Ibid.*, p. 177.
[70] *Ibid.*, pp. 167–9.
[71] *Ibid.*, p. 203.
[72] *Ibid.*, p. 277.
[73] *Ibid.*, p. 286.
[74] *Ibid.*, p. 176.
[75] *Ibid.*, p. 189.
[76] *Ibid.*, p. 200.

destroyed other known republics, resulting in ancient as well as modern tyranny. In short, the Constitutional Convention was an attempt to achieve a radical 'progress' in human history.

The argument that Locke's principles of natural right have characterized the American regime from its outset is, of course, hardly original. What is more important for our purposes is the confirmation that a distinct combination of views concerning both human nature and human history, which has been found in the writings of both Hobbes and Locke, can also be traced in the founding of the United States. It is thus not necessary here to prove direct 'influence' by Hobbes as the cause of American political principles, though some scholars have begun to discuss this possibility; rather, it suffices to point out that the Founding Fathers are an impressive illustration of the practical effects of joining a modern view of science and progress with an individualistic concept of human nature.[77]

It might be thought that the parallels between American political thought and the tradition of Hobbes and Locke follow necessarily from their shared source in the Anglo-Saxon political tradition, and especially

---

[77] The classic work on the influence of Locke on American political thought is Louis Hartz, *The Liberal Tradition in America*, Harcourt Brace, New York, 1955. See also Roger D. Masters, 'The Lockean Tradition in American Foreign Policy', *Journal of International Affairs*, XXI (1967): 253–77. For a recent analysis of the links between Hobbes and the American regime, see Frank Coleman, *Hobbes and America*, University of Toronto Press, 1977. Given James Madison's role at the Constitutional Convention, not to mention his contribution to *The Federalist*, the books he read as a student at Princeton are especially good evidence of the intellectual influences on the American Founding Fathers. When Madison went to Princeton, the library there included 'more of Locke's writings than those of any other theorist on the reading list . . . Witherspoon's lectures repeat, without attribution, many of Locke's arguments from the *Second Treatise*, chs. V and VIII, and the critique of Filmer from the *First Treatise*, especially§ 105.' (Dennis F. Thompson, 'The Education of a Founding Father: The Reading List for John Witherspoon's Course in Political Theory, as taken by James Madison', *Political Theory*; IV (November 1976); 523–9.) The syllabus for 1771, when Madison took Witherspoon's course, read: '. . . Grossius (Grotius), Pufendorf, Barberach (Barbyrac), Cumberland, Seldon, Burlamaqui, Hobbs (Hobbes), Machiavel, Harrington, Locke, Sidney (Sydney), and two late books, Montesquieu's Spirit of the Laws and Ferguson's History of Civil Society.' Witherspoon discussed in the lectures two authors not on the reading list: Hume and especially Hutcheson. Of the authors on the reading list, therefore, the most frequently cited was apparently Hobbes: '. . . in his politics lectures Witherspoon refers to Hobbes more often than any theorist except Hutcheson. According to Witherspoon, Hobbes is "an author of considerable note but of very illiberal sentiments in politics," and "Few are of his sentiments now, at least in Britain" . . . In his "Commonplace Book" (1759-72), Madison paraphrases a passage from Hobbes (*Papers*, Vol. 1, pp. 16, 27n). Madison evidently purchased a copy of *Leviathan* in 1782 . . . He recommends in 1783 that Congress acquire "Hobbes' Works" . . .' (*Ibid.*, p. 526.)

in the common law. But granted that neither seventeenth-century British political thought nor eighteenth-century colonial experience emerged *ex nihilo*, one must beware of simplistic historical accounts: the common law by itself could hardly provide a complete 'explanation' of *both* sides of the English civil wars or of *both* sides of the American revolution.

Hobbes and Locke appear to have taken different positions in the political conflicts of their time, yet neither uses the common law tradition as a necessary and sufficient ground of their preferences. Locke's reliance on natural right might seem surprising if the common law is taken as a symbol of constitutional restraint on arbitrary government; it is more reasonable if one focuses on the incompatibility between historical 'progress' based on science and an independent (often socially conservative) tradition of legal interpretation. Similarly, the American 'rebels' did not long base their position solely on the 'rights of Englishmen'; at the American Constitutional Convention, the common law was rarely discussed explicitly, though it was presumed that judges would rely on its concepts.[78] While English political experience was doubtless a necessary condition for the emergence of the tradition of political thought discussed here, the latter can hardly be equated with the former.

Hobbes, Locke and contemporary social science

Since my objective is to show the persisting influence of the kind of political thought epitomized by Hobbes and Locke, no further attempt will be made to demonstrate how their position developed into utilitarianism, laissez faire liberalism, or positivism. Instead, it will be instructive to conclude by suggesting some of the intellectual parallels between Hobbes' theories and contemporary social science. In a number of fields, twentieth-century research has been based – albeit often unconsciously – on principles that are astonishingly close to those found in Hobbes or Locke. Perhaps this similarity should be no surprise in the field of psychology. As two distinguished scholars, one a psychologist and the other a philosopher, recently put it:

> There are many candidates to the title of 'the father of modern psychology'. But the claims of Thomas Hobbes can be pressed very strongly in that he was not only the first to suggest that human beings are machines, but also the first

---

[78] For example, 'Madisons Notes of Debates in the Federal Convention', in Solberg, *op. cit.*, p. 293.

to attempt a systematic explanation of *all* human actions in terms of the same principles as were used to explain the behaviour of inanimate bodies. Descartes and others thought that animal behaviour and the *involuntary* actions of men could be mechanically explained, but not distinctly human actions, involving reason and will. Hobbes ruthlessly extended Galileo's assumptions into the innermost sanctuaries of human thought and decision. He claimed originality for his civil philosophy on this account. Indeed, he hoped that his name would be as famous in this history of psychology and social science as that of Harvey who extended the new science of motion to physiology.[79]

But apart from Hobbes' 'claims' or 'hopes', what does this tell us about modern psychology and its political implications?

The similarity between Hobbes and modern psychology – particularly of the 'behaviourist' school – is hardly accidental. Both attempt to apply the experimental methods of modern physical science to the explanation of human as well as animal behaviour; both seek the deductive certainty of geometric proofs or *laws* of behaviour. Like Hobbes, experimental or behavioural psychologists have generally taken an individualistic and hedonistic view of human nature: behaviour is analyzed in terms of the individual organism's learned responses to pleasant or painful stimuli. This 'Stimulus-Response' model not only ignores instinct as a major factor in human behaviour, but has sometimes been used to deride the study of instinct in other species as well. Given the stress on individual environment and life-history as the cause of behaviour, much psychological research was focused on learning theory; in the search for 'behavioural laws' that would apply to all organisms, it was often assumed that the natural history or inheritance of a species is not a major factor in animal behaviour.[80]

So-called 'behavioural' psychology, particularly in Anglo–Saxon

---

[79] R. S. Peters and H. Tajfel, 'Hobbes and Hull – Metaphysicians of Behavior', in *Hobbes and Rousseau*, Cranston and Peters, (eds), p. 165.

[80] Peters and Tajfel cite C. L. Hull's attempt to elaborate 'the basic molar behavioral laws underlying the "social sciences"' by starting 'with colorless movement and mere receptor impulses as such, and from these build up step by step both adaptive behavior and maladaptive behavior.' (*Ibid.*, p. 166, citing Hull's *A Behavior System*, Yale University Press, 1952, pp. 25–6.) For additional examples, see B. F. Skinner, *Science and Human Behavior*, Free Press, New York, 1965; S. C. Ratner and M. R. Denny (eds), *Comparative Psychology*, Dorsey, Homewood, Ill., 1964; Zing-Yang Kuo, *The Dynamics of Behavior Development*, Random House, New York, 1967. On the difference between the 'Stimulus–Response' theory long dominant in Anglo–Saxon psychology, and the study of animal behaviour by European ethologists following Konrad Lorenz, see Roger D. Masters, 'The Impact of Ethology on Political Science', in *Biology and Politics*, Albert Somit (ed.), Mouton, The Hague, 1976, pp. 199–207.

universities, thus shared Hobbes' views toward both science and human nature. One consequence is that specialists in the field have long tended to attribute human problems to the environment – and therewith to propose educational or social reform as the solution to political or economic conflict. Although B. F. Skinner's utopian *Walden Two* is a striking example, one could also point to industrial psychology (attempts to discover an environment increasing workers' productivity and contentment), educational psychology (manipulation of students' learning environments in order to improve performance), or various forms of therapy (seeking to condition the individual to a better 'adaptation' to his personal situation).

Similar tendencies could be found in economic theory and practice. It is possible that economics as a distinct discipline could be traced to the writings of Hobbes' contemporary and friend, Sir William Petty, whose *Essay in Political Arithmetick* (1686) seems to symbolize one consequence of Hobbes' teaching, and whose *Treatise of Taxes and Contributions* (1662) was owned by Locke and may have influenced his view of property.[81] In any event, Locke himself not only wrote on economics, for example, *Some Considerations of the Lowering of Interest and Raising the Value of Money* (1691), but also played a direct role in British economic policy-making in the 1690s.

But it is the parallel of basic principles between contemporary economics, and Hobbes or Locke, rather than the circumstances linking them with Adam Smith, Nassau Senior or James Mill, that is of interest here. Non-Marxist economists generally share both an individualistic or 'pessimistic' view of human nature *and* a progressive or 'optimistic' view of history. Hence Western economic theories have long assumed that, since individuals are the best judges of their own 'utility', the competitive market is the most efficient way to allocate goods and services; like Hobbes, economists usually believe that 'the value of all things contracted for, is measured by the appetite of the contractors: and therefore the just value, is that which they be contented to give'.[82] But most economists have also felt that the process of industrial 'development', as it took place in Europe and North America, could (or at least should) be followed elsewhere in the world; like Hobbes, economic theory – at least until very recently – has presumed that 'plenty dependeth . . . merely on the labour and industry of men' without regard

[81] *Second Treatise*, p. 305 note.
[82] *Leviathan*, chapter 15, p. 98

to natural 'limits to growth.'[83]

Parallel examples could readily be given from political science, not to mention more specialized fields such as game theory, statistics, etc. But the reader may well be asking a quite different question at this point. If the combination of 'pessimistic' views of human nature with historical 'optimism' is so widespread in contemporary social science, and can be found in the American Constitution as well as in the writings of an absolute monarchist like Hobbes, hasn't the argument proven too much rather than too little? The family of approaches to human life which could be classified as akin to Hobbes seems bewildering in its variety. Could it be that the principles used to classify Hobbes, Locke and other political thinkers are so vague as to be meaningless?

I would suggest that this question could only be posed from *within* the Anglo–Saxon tradition. In the United States, for example, the Hobbesian–Lockean position seems ubiquitous, both in politics and in academic social science, because our regime was explicitly based on Locke's teaching. As Louis Hartz put it, when explaining the impotence of socialist movements in the United States:

> A society which begins with Locke, and thus transforms him, stays with Locke, by virtue of an absolute and irrational attachment it develops for him, and becomes as indifferent to the challenge of socialism in the later era as it was unfamiliar with the heritage of feudalism in an earlier one.[84]

To gain perspective on the American version of Western liberalism, therefore, it is necessary to contrast it with forms of political thought that rest on different premises.

---

[83] *Leviathan*, chapter 24, p. 161. For a clear statement of the presumed efficiency of the competitive market, see Paul Samuelson, *Economics*, McGraw-Hill, New York, 1951, especially pp. 13–24 and 50–58. As evidence of the assumption of continued historical progress, consider W. W. Rostow, *The Stages of Economic Growth*, University Press, Cambridge, 1960. Indeed, the characteristic assumptions of Western economists are so widely shared today that they can best be revealed by citing dissenting views – which tend either to reject the individualism underlying the preference for a competitive market, as do Marxists, or to reject the optimistic view of history, as does E. F. Schumacher in *Small is Beautiful*, Harper & Row, New York, 1973. To be sure, it could be objected that English economic theory from Adam Smith to Malthus and John Stuart Mill was haunted by the problem of natural limits to economic growth. But a fuller consideration of liberal economics would indicate that these thinkers were reacting to an exaggerated version of historical optimism, which went beyond Bacon's dictum ('Nature to be commanded must be obeyed') to the unlimited or romantic optimism of Condorcet ('the perfectibility of man is indefinite'). For a thoughtful discussion, see Sheldon Wolin, *Politics and Vision*, Little, Brown, Boston, 1960, pp. 314–25.

[84] Hartz, *The Liberal Tradition in America*, p. 6.

Both Hobbes and Locke share a 'pessimistic' attitude towards human nature (individual 'hedonism' or egoism) and an 'optimistic' view of history ('progress' can resolve social conflict). Ultimately, the adequacy of these premises can only be tested by carefully considering such thinkers as Aristotle and Marx (who insist that humans are naturally sociable) or Rousseau (who stresses the inevitability of historical decay).[85] As such comparisons reveal, the writings of great thinkers are considerably illuminated when contrasted to each other in this way.

Ultimately, a comparative approach is especially fruitful because it forces us to confront the perennial issues of political philosophy. Does science make possible historical progress? Is selfishness the foundation of human nature? Can we discover the deepest truths through science and human reason, unaided by divine revelation? Since all of us must address these questions in our own lives, it is important to consider how they were analyzed by the best minds of our tradition.

---

[85] See Masters, 'Nature, Human Nature, and Political Thought', *op. cit.*; and Introduction, *Rousseau's Social Contract, with Geneva Manuscript and Political Economy*, Roger D. Masters (ed.), St Martin's Press, New York, 1978, pp. 5–25.

Rousseau and Hobbes

James MacAdam

It is a mug's game to compare, in the space of one essay, two of the greatest political philosophers of modern times. Ripe judgements, placing them at extremes, abound. Hobbes is the defender of the absolute right of kings; Rousseau is the apostle of democracy. Hobbes' philosophy is individualist and Rousseau's collectivist. Hobbes is a radical liberal (or an authoritarian), Rousseau a radical democrat (or an anarchist) – and so on. Slogans have something to be said for them. But it is my desire to find a basis of comparison which is less broad, closer to Hobbes' and Rousseau's own concerns, and yet meaningful to the contemporary reader. I think I have found such a basis in a passage from a letter written by Rousseau to the Marquis de Mirabeau on the twenty-sixth of July 1767.

Apparently Mirabeau had sent Rousseau a book that espoused 'legal despotism' and had requested an opinion of the work from Rousseau. Here, in part, is Rousseau's reply.

> Your system is very good for the men of Utopia; it is worth nothing to the sons of Adam.
>
> Here, in my previous ideas, is the great problem of politics, which I compare to that of squaring the circle in geometry ... *to find a form of Government which places the Law above the man* ... If unhappily it cannot be found, and I acknowledge candidly that I believe it cannot, my advice is that one must pass to the other extreme, and put straightaway the man as much above the law as can be; in consequence, establish arbitrary despotism, and the most arbitrary possible ... In a word, I see no supportable position between the most austere democracy and the most perfect Hobbism [*Hobbisme*]: for the conflict between men and laws, which places the state in

---

Research for this essay was supported by funds from the Canada Council and Trent University. I am indebted for criticisms — not all of which were accepted — to my colleagues Michael Neumann and Bernard Hodgson.

continual intestinal war, is the worst of all political conditions.

But the Caligulas, the Neros ... my god! I fling myself writhing to the earth and curse my fate in being a man.[1]

As a basis of comparison, this passage has much to commend it. It is a comparison made directly by Rousseau. Hence, we know that at least he believes the issue is central. The comment is made at a time and in a way that is significant; Rousseau's major writings in political philosophy (*Discourse on the Origins and Foundations of Inequality*, *Political Economy*, *On the Social Contract* and *Emile*) are now behind him and the tone suggests reflection on the value of them. The passage suggests that Rousseau is prepared to divide the world of politics between himself and Hobbes so that either he is right or Hobbes is. It raises a fundamental problem which, as Hobbes notes, is at least as old as Aristotle:

> ...this is another Errour of Aristotles Politiques, that in a wel ordered Common-wealth, not Men should govern, but the laws.[2]

Finally, although Rousseau is the author of the comparison, it is not one in which he misrepresents the thought of Hobbes, as he was wont to do. Hobbes believed it essential to good politics that the sovereign person be above the law, in the sense of not being subject to it. This belief coincides with Rousseau's description of a despot in *On the Social Contract*: 'the despot is one who puts himself above the laws themselves'.[3]

But although the question whether the law should be above man or vice versa establishes a suitable ground of comparison, it is itself in need of clarification and determination. I propose to satisfy this need by considering in what terms and for what reasons Hobbes believes that the sovereign person must be superior and then Rousseau's terms and reasons for reaching the conclusion that law must be. That accomplished, I propose to examine their reasons, reject some, and develop those that seem of the greatest importance. I very much doubt whether I can be impartial counsel for both, as perhaps in the circumstances I

---

[1] J.-J. Rousseau, 'Lettre à M. Le Marquis de Mirabeau, le 26 juillet 1767', in *Jean-Jacques Rousseau: The Political Writings*, Vol. II, edited by C. E. Vaughan, Blackwell, Oxford, 1962, p. 160 (my translation).

[2] Thomas Hobbes, *Leviathan*, edited by C. B. Macpherson, Penguin, Harmondsworth, 1968, p. 699.

[3] J.-J. Rousseau, *On the Social Contract, with Geneva Manuscript and Political Economy*, (henceforth referred to as '*Contract*') edited by Roger Masters and translated by Judith Masters, St Martin's Press, New York, 1978, p. 98. (The editions of the texts of Hobbes and Rousseau have been chosen on the basis of their availability to students. Those pertaining to Rousseau include important minor pieces.)

should be; my sympathies in the end are with Rousseau, but I have great respect for both. It is to be hoped that I can be fair enough to permit the reader to judge; not so much the merits of their cases on the issue, but the qualities of their philosophies as read through it.

Hobbes: Man above law, How understood

In the preface to his work *The Citizen*, Hobbes states that he circulated copies of it privately to get some reactions, so that 'if any things appeared erroneous, hard, or obscure, I might correct, soften and explain them'. He then reports:

> These things I found most bitterly excepted against. That I had made the civil powers too large; but this by ecclesiastical persons. That I had utterly taken away liberty of conscience; but this by sectaries. That I had set princes above the civil laws; but this by lawyers. Wherefore I was not much moved by these men's reprehensions, as who in doing this, did but their own business.[4]

Hobbes is less than just, in suggesting, as he seems to, that these objectors are merely looking out for their own interests. But he does, in his pithy fashion, set forth in this passage the principal schools of opposition to his view and the centrality of the issue in his time. The ecclesiastical powers were concerned that men should not be commanded to do that which is contrary to divine and natural law. Supremacy of natural law was also the majority opinion of political philosophers. But Hobbes was opposed too by Protestant sects who held that men must not be obliged by the sovereign to do that which is contrary to moral conscience. Milton's 'priesthood of all believers'[*] presumably includes the notion that each individual is capable of knowing what he is morally obliged to do and should not be forced to do otherwise. Lastly, the lawyers held that the law was not the prerogative of the sovereign person but was instead established in the common law by precedent and by courts.[5] All these views had powerful protagonists and a long history.

---

[4] Thomas Hobbes, *Man and Citizen*, edited by Bernard Gert, Anchor Books, New York, 1972, p. 105.

[*] The 'priesthood of all believers', a doctrine emanating from Martin Luther, denied the necessity for any intermediary between God and human beings (for example, a special priestly caste) and so elevated the role of individual conscience. In this sense, all believers are priests. (Ed.)

[5] For discussion of the views opposed to Hobbes', see John Laird, *Hobbes*, University Microfilms, Ann Arbor, Michigan, 1966, pp. 56–81; Miriam Reik, *The Golden Lands of Thomas Hobbes*, Wayne State University Press, Detroit, 1977, pp. 98–112; and Ross, Schneider and Waldman (eds), *Thomas Hobbes In His Time*, University of Minnesota, Minneapolis, 1924, pp. 8–30.

What was the view that Hobbes put against them all? It is that the sovereign power must be absolute and undivided. The sovereign power should include every conceivable political power. 'The sword of war is in the same hand, in which is the sword of justice'.[6] He is the legislator: he can make, repeal and interpret all law. He can declare war. He appoints the judiciary and all government officials are responsible to him. He is a party to no covenants, compacts or oaths and is obligated only to obey natural law. He is unpunishable. In a memorable passage in *Leviathan*, Hobbes describes the sovereign's power by means of verses from Job:

> There is nothing ... on earth, to be compared with him ...He seeth every high thing below him; and is King of all the children of pride.[7]

In his earliest work, *The Elements of Law, Natural and Politic*, Hobbes summarizes sovereign power:

> It is an error therefore to think: that the power which is virtually the whole power of the commonwealth, and which ... is usually called supreme or sovereign, can be subject to any law but that of God Almighty.[8]

The same claim, that the sovereign should not be subject to civil law, is repeated, several times, in lengthy passages throughout *The Elements of Law, The Citizen* and *Leviathan*.[9]

Hobbes' reasons

They seem to be four in number. Three express the view that subjection of the sovereign to law is incomprehensible. The first attacks Aristotle's thesis that 'not Men should govern, but the Laws'. 'What man', Hobbes asks, 'that has his naturall senses ... beleeves the Law can hurt him; that is, Words, and Paper, without the Hands, and Swords of men?'[10] The claim, I take it, is that government by laws is practically, and not logically, incomprehensible; it is contrary to common sense. The second reason is that just as no man be bound or obliged to himself so neither can the lawmaker be bound or obliged by his laws.[11] The third reason is that if the sovereign is subject to law then he is not absolute and unlimited.[12]

---

[6] Thomas Hobbes, *The Elements of Law, Natural and Politic*, edited by F. Tonnies with an introduction by M. M. Goldsmith, Frank Cass & Co., London, 1969, p. 107.
[7] *Leviathan*, p. 362.
[8] *The Elements of Law*, p. 172.
[9] See *The Elements of Law*, pp. 172, 183 and 187; *Man and Citizen*, pp. 173, 183, 187, 247 and 248; *Leviathan*, pp. 313, 367 and 699.
[10] *Leviathan*, p. 699.
[11] See *Man and Citizen*, pp. 183, 247 and 248; *Leviathan*, p. 313.
[12] See *The Elements of Law*, p. 117; *Man and Citizen*, p. 187; *Leviathan*, p. 367.

'To be chief and subject are contradictories.'[13] The fourth reason is that the sovereign is the representative (and agent) of every citizen's interest in security.[14] His being above the law is necessary for their security.

Of these four reasons, the first three seem to be weak, at least unless they are allied with the fourth. Hence, my procedure will be to criticize the first three reasons and leave the fourth, and strongest, for consideration later.

The first reason appears to be an *argumentum ad populum*, a cheap shot, unworthy of Hobbes. No philosopher who claims that men should be governed by laws holds, or at any rate needs to hold, that all laws should operate without sanctions or penalties. The concept of enforceable laws is not inconsistent with government by laws. It might still be argued that Hobbes means that ultimately the obligation to obey depends on the awesome fear caused by the sovereign. But Rousseau and H. L. A. Hart agree that 'being obliged to do X' and 'having an obligation to do X' are logically independent notions.[15] A thief can oblige me, through fear, to hand over my purse but it does not follow that I have an obligation to do so. Contrariwise, I may be under an obligation to do X but not feel obliged to do it from fear of the consequences.

The second reason seems to turn on the logical oddness, or even the logical incomprehensibility, of binding or obliging oneself to oneself. It does appear logically odd to talk of having an obligation to oneself, for who is obliged to whom? And it might even be argued, to take the stronger case, that such notions as obliging oneself, having a duty to oneself or making a promise to oneself are logically parasitic on uses of these terms which apply externally to the self. One can be obligated or have a duty or make a promise to another person. But not, strictly speaking, to oneself.[16] Hence, it is only by a kind of tolerance, amounting to logical sloppiness, that such notions as being obliged to oneself get any currency at all.

I am unclear which, if either, of these arguments is the one intended by Hobbes. But it doesn't matter. One can give him both or either and still hold that his conclusion doesn't follow. To the extent that Hobbes' argument has force, it runs on the claim that there is no significant

---

[13] *Man and Citizen*, p. 258.
[14] See *The Elements of Law*, pp. 105 and 179; *Man and Citizen*, pp. 151, 173, 176, 258 and 259; *Leviathan*, pp. 228, 232 and 268.
[15] See *On The Social Contract*, pp. 48–9; and H. L. A. Hart, *The Concept of Law*, Clarendon Press, Oxford, 1961, p. 80.
[16] See *Man and Citizen*, p. 247.

difference, in the required respect, between a private and a public person – and this is dubious. In chapter 16 of *Leviathan*, Hobbes takes great care in building a complex argument to the effect that the sovereign is, and must be, a public person. His acts are not the effect of *force*, rather they are *authorized* by the consent of the people. He has the authority of the commonwealth to make, abrogate and interpret law. No private person has this authority, as Hobbes himself argues. In this sense he is a public person, an official, albeit supreme, of the state. Let us suppose then that he makes laws prohibiting rape, libel, assault and theft. Would it follow from the mere fact that the sovereign makes such laws that he is entitled (or that the people intended him) to commit 'when he pleaseth'[17] rape, libel, assault and theft? Of course, the sovereign could on occasion except himself from such a law because he has the power. But this, of itself, does not show he is then authorized, in Hobbes' sense. Without further explanation, there seems no contradiction in holding that he who makes the laws is subject to them.

The third reason, that if the sovereign is subject to law then he is not absolute, supreme and unlimited, seems intended by Hobbes to be tightly logically such that its denial is self-contradictory. Like statements about God, either the sovereign is omnipotent or he is not. If his power is limited then he is not omnipotent (or absolute, supreme, unlimited), and if he is not omnipotent then he is not sovereign. Rather the limiting power is sovereign. But this argument depends upon a fallacy of ambiguity. Sovereign power can be limited in either of two ways: by another human or by laws. A person could be sovereign of a state, in the first sense, in that there is no other person or official capable of overruling him, but his power could still be restrained or voided by law. Hobbes seems to think that by showing the illogicality of a sovereign superior to the sovereign, which is the first sense, he has shown the illogicality of the sovereign being subject to law, which is the second. But he has not. Indeed, in a constitutional system, 'sovereign power' can logically be supreme *and* limited. It may be such, for instance, that only the judiciary can interpret the law and only the legislators can make it. Each can be supreme, in not being subject to a higher power, and yet limited, in having their powers voided by acting outside their competence.[18]

---

[17] *Leviathan*, p. 313.
[18] In criticizing Hobbes' third reason, I am indebted to H. L. A. Hart, *The Concept of Law, op. cit.*, pp. 64–70.

Rousseau: Law above man, How understood

There is an eloquent passage in the essay on *Political Economy* in which Rousseau expresses his view that law should be supreme:

> How can it be that they obey and no one commands, that they serve and have no master, and are all the freer . . . These marvels are the work of law. It is to law alone that men owe justice and freedom. It is this celestial voice . . . that teaches [man] to act according to the maxims of his own judgment and not to be in contradiction with himself. It is also through the law alone that leaders must speak when they command . . .[19]

However, to understand Rousseau it is best to turn to the first two books of *On the Social Contract*, and especially to chapters 4 and 6 of Book II; there Rousseau identifies sovereignty, legislation, the general will of the people and civil law. The meanings and relationships of these concepts are too complex to consider in this place[20]; it may be enough for our purposes to emphasize Rousseau's conception of law. Sovereignty is restricted to legislation. The sovereign is the general will and, for us, this dark saying may be understood in terms of the formula that the law expresses the general will if 'the law comes from all equally and applies to all equally'. When all the people, as legislators, enact a rule for the good of all, then the people are sovereign, and the rule is obligatory law. In other words, the citizen is viewed under a double aspect: as sovereign, he is a maker of the law, as subject, he is obligated by laws so made. Each takes part in the making of the rules to which each is subject. Rousseau summarizes:

> Given this idea, one easily sees that it is no longer necessary to ask who should make the laws, since they are acts of the general will, nor whether the prince is above the laws, since he is a member of the State; nor whether the law can be unjust, since no one is unjust to himself; nor how one is free yet subject to the laws, since they merely record our wills.[21]

---

[19] *Contract*, p. 214.
[20] The reader unfamiliar with Rousseau's concept of the general will in relation to law might start with this simple notion: Think of an association, perhaps a club, wherein all members agree that all should take part in the making of the club rules, and such that the rules are to apply to all and benefit all equally. This is an approximation of laws made by the general will. One of the best accounts of the general will is found in J. C. Hall, *Rousseau: An Introduction to his Political Philosophy*, Macmillan, London, 1973, chapter 5.
[21] *Contract*, p. 190.

Rousseau's reasons

Rousseau seems to have five reasons, the first three of which are defeasible, the fourth good but not good enough, and the fifth worthy of extended treatment. The first reason is that any representative, be it a man or an assembly, who is given control over the laws will act in his or their own interests. The second is that the people will not so act; the voice of the people is the voice of God. The third is that since the law applies equally to all, it must apply equally to the prince or the government or any official. The fourth is that sovereignty of the general will necessitates a rule for the good of all. The fifth is that sovereignty of the people is necessary to the development of citizens as moral agents.

The first reason is a popular one with Rousseau. Thus in *Political Economy* he writes:

> Abuses are inevitable and their consequences disastrous in all societies, where the public interest and the laws . . . are continuously assailed by the personal interest and passions of both leader and members . . . Whether the magistrates belong to the people or the people to the magistrates . . . in general it would be sheer madness to hope that those who are in fact masters will prefer another interest to their own.[22]

In *On the Social Contract*, Rousseau argues again that the representative, be it man or assembly, either has or, in the case of a group, develops a will for his or its own good.[23] Now, it is not plain to me whether or not Rousseau is deliberately turning Hobbes' own principle against him – namely, the principle that 'by necessity of nature every man doth in all his voluntary actions intend some good unto himself.'[24] What does seem important is not so much an argument against legally unregulated representative legislative power; but rather that any representative of anybody will always act for the good of the representative himself and not for the good of the other. From this, Rousseau draws the conclusion that no representative can be trusted[25] to act for the public good. What he does not acknowledge is that the conclusion 'all representatives act for their own good' follows from (or at any rate I cannot find any other premise) 'each person acts for his or her own good'. In other words, 'acting for one's own good and not for the common' follows not from

---

[22] *Contract*, pp. 210–11 and 213.
[23] See *Contract*, Book II, chapter 3, and Book III, chapters 1 and 2.
[24] *The Elements of Law*, p. 84.
[25] Rousseau believes that trust is a function of control and hence advocates close regulation of government. In this he differs markedly from Hobbes. But he doesn't seem to mean that once the governors are the agents of the sovereign they will cease to act in their own interest or in that of the government.

being a representative but from being a person. No-one, whether representative or no, can be trusted to act for the public good.

This conclusion effectively undermines his second reason. Rousseau states it as follows:

> But unfortunately personal interest is always found in inverse ratio to duty, and it increases in proportion as the association becomes narrower and the engagement less sacred – invincible proof that the general will is always the most just, and that the voice of the people is in fact the voice of God.[26]

Rousseau's argument is not an invincible proof that the voice of the people is the most just, or even more just than that of a representative sovereign, if his first reason is correct. At the most, it suggests that *if* the people will for the good of all, then the sovereign will of the people is just: that is, *if* their will is the general will. The general will is always just, but Rousseau is aware that does *not* mean that the will of any individual citizen or of all together is always the general will. For that to be the case, the object of willing must be the common good.

In *On the Social Contract*, Rousseau indicates that the two reasons – every person acts for his own good, and the voice of the people is most just – are incongruent in the sense suggested above. At least, this is the way in which I can make some sense of Rousseau's obscure comments that:

> The people that is subject to the laws ought to be their author ... By itself, the people always wants the good, but by itself it does not always see it ... Private individuals see the good they reject; the public wants the good it does not see.[27]

At least a part of what Rousseau seems to mean is that although the people are sovereign *de jure* (by right), their rule would be no different from any other. Until they learn to legislate for the good of all, each would seek his or her private good. Hence, in fact the private citizen as such is no different, as a potential sovereign, than any representative. From here, one could suggest a canon of interpretation for the difficult chapter 'On the Legislator' which follows immediately the passage quoted above: 'The people *ought* to be author of the laws which they obey'. But by Kant's dictum, 'ought implies can'. In order for them to be able to properly author the laws, Rousseau claims that their nature must

---

[26] *Contract*, p. 213.
[27] *Contract*, p. 67.

be transformed[28]: they must learn to prefer the good of all over the good to each.[29]

Rousseau's third reason is that since the law applies equally to all, it applies equally to any representative of the people. Citizen or ruler should be equally subject to law. However, this argument is open to an appeal to Aristotle's other dictum that the law should treat equals equally and unequals unequally. That is, it could be argued that it is to the benefit of all that some persons in a state should have unequal (different and privileged) powers by law. Policemen, judges, civil servants, members of government and doctors in emergency situations should be treated unequally by law for the general good. Rousseau himself is committed to this position with regard to members of government and to the legislator. Had he considered the argument more carefully, his commitment to it might have been more extensive. Rousseau could perhaps meet this criticism, and I don't mean to suggest that being unequal under law is equivalent to being above law. My point is that Hobbes' argument is not destroyed merely by appealing to the principle that everyone is equal under the law. What needs to be explained is the difference between 'the law applies equally to all' and 'all are equally under law'. Magistrates, etc, can be treated unequally and still be subject to law.

The fourth reason is that sovereignty of the general will necessitates a rule for the good of all. The emphasis should be placed on 'necessitates'. According to Rousseau's scheme each citizen is a legislator: each must make rules for all. But in order to satisfy the requirement that each *can* subscribe to the rule made for all, any rule must be *acceptable* to all. As I understand Rousseau, the point can be understood as follows: Even if I, as a citizen-legislator, seek to have a rule for all that embodies a good for myself then I must, if the rule is to be acceptable to all, support a good of mine which is acceptable to others.

This argument has two features of interest. First, it 'forces one to be free' in the sense that it necessitates consideration of what others judge good and incorporation of one's own goods with those of others. Second, the argument undoubtedly applies elsewhere than in Rousseau's scheme of popular sovereignty. Anyone who is a member of any association governed by rules which all partake in the making of, be it a social club or parliament itself, can realize the compromise involved in getting a rule

---

[28] *Ibid.*, p. 68.
[29] *Ibid.*, p. 67.

acceptable to everyone and yet embodying a good to oneself.

But I personally doubt whether Rousseau would rest his case on this argument. As I interpret him, it is a half-way house; at best a way of being rationally self-interested. It is not a method of decision-making whereby one is genuinely considerate of what is best for one's fellows, but one of getting what is best for oneself in the circumstances. It is an argument that is compatible with a morality of individualistic rational egoism, one of cutting one's losses to obtain the best personal good available. Hence, I am inclined to think that Rousseau's fifth reason, that sovereignty of the general will is necessary for moral development, is the important one.

Possible misunderstandings averted

Before we consider the remaining and more important reasons of Hobbes and Rousseau, there are certain common misconceptions of both arguments that need to be cleared away so that they can be properly opposed to one another. They are as follows: One, Hobbes opposes democratic sovereignty. Two, Hobbes advocates arbitrary despotism. Three, Rousseau denounces representation. Four, Rousseau is a democrat who rejects absolute monarchy. Five, Rousseau does not accept absolute sovereignty. Six, according to Rousseau, the rule of law presupposes that the people are subject without qualification to the laws which they make. All six, unless properly restated, are misleading.

Hobbes goes out of his way in all his major writings to make clear that the sovereign person or power can be democratic. When the sovereign is democratic then the sovereign power would be represented by the will of the majority of the citizens. Hobbes thinks he has good reasons, which he gives, to prefer monarchy over democracy, but that is another matter. It is one thing to say that democratic sovereignty is a foolish choice; it is another to exclude it. Hobbes does not. Hobbes would deny Rousseau's charge of 'arbitrary despotism' if that is taken to mean, as reasonably it might be, that Hobbes' sovereign rules without the consent of the people or in defiance of natural law or in the absence of a legal system. Hobbes stresses that the consent of the people authorizes the sovereign, that he has a duty to obey natural law, that law applies equally to all subjects, must be put in clear language and be widely promulgated.

It is also misleading to suggest that Rousseau denounces representation. The sovereign power of legislation belongs solely and wholly to the people and must never be represented or delegated. However, the government, which executes the law, must be the representative of the sovereign. It is the agent of the sovereign, applying and executing what has been decided by the general will of the people. It is in terms of this attempt to sharply distinguish sovereign and government that the fourth misunderstanding is removed. Rousseau is pragmatic on the type of government most suitable for a particular people.[30] The best type is a function of population, economy, natural resources, tradition, etc. In general, a democratic state must be small, whereas absolute monarchy may be best in large states. That is to say, if democracy and monarchy are considered as forms of government, the choice is to be made on the basis of circumstances. But if they are considered as forms of legislative sovereignty then only democracy, rule by the laws of the general will, is legitimate and obligatory. Further, when the sovereign is the popular will then Rousseau argues that the sovereign ought to be absolute. Its sovereign power is unlimited, indivisible and inalienable. Such claims have aroused the opposition of later liberal thinkers, such as J. S. Mill and Benjamin Constant[31], but Rousseau believes that rule by the people for the people through laws ensures the enjoyment of freedom, justice, equality, property and self-preservation.

Finally, it is misleading to say that the people are subject to the law that they make. In one sense, this is true. Rousseau distinguishes between the citizens associated either as a state or as sovereign. As members of the state, the totality of the citizens is passive, they are simply subjects of the law. But as members of the sovereign, the people are active, making the laws to which, as subjects, they are obligated. As citizens of the state, all are equally obligated to obey. But as citizens of the sovereign, the people are not subject to the law if this is understood to mean that they cannot change the law. If the law is judged contrary to the public good, which might come about through changing circumstances, then the people are justified in altering it. No law, Rousseau asserts, binds the sovereign will, 'not even the best'.[32] But it is plain that the saying 'the sovereign people are not subject to law' is open only to the narrowest interpretation – that is, when all the people will the good of all, it can alter a law judged inconsistent with the good of all. With these misunderstandings averted, we can now turn to exposition of the final reasons of Hobbes and Rousseau, beginning with that of Hobbes.

---

[30] *Contract*, pp. 92–5.
[31] See J. S. Mill, *On Liberty*, edited by D. Spitz, Norton, 1975, chapter 1; for a statement of Benjamin Constant's views on Rousseau in this connection, see J. MacAdam, 'Rousseau and the Friends of Despotism', *Ethics*, October 1963.
[32] See *Contract*, pp. 76, 164 and 192.

Hobbes and the right to life

Hobbes' justification for the right of the sovereign not to be subject to law seems to rest fundamentally on the subject's right to life. Unfortunately the nature of this right is obscure. One of the obscurities can be brought to light through reference to a distinction Rousseau makes about natural law, rather than about natural right. Rousseau remarks on the difference between Roman and modern conceptions of natural law.[33] For the Romans, natural law tended to be *descriptive*; the catalogue of what humans *naturally do*, irresistibly, instinctively, motivated by inclination and passion, etc. For the moderns, natural law is *prescriptive*, setting forth universal, rational, moral principles of what all humans, given their common nature, *ought* to do.

Hobbes' concept of the right to life seems to combine what Rousseau distinguishes. On the one hand, man's strongest passion is the fear of his own death. Correspondingly, his strongest desire is to preserve his life at all costs. This view corresponds to the Roman view, and is presented by Hobbes as irrefutable empirical truth about humans: 'the natural right of preservation, which we all receive from the uncontrollable dictates of necessity'.[34] In this sense, self-preservation is an irresistible human drive over which moral and positive law are powerless. On the other hand, self-preservation is also characterized prescriptively; as a matter, not of fact, but of right.

> The Right of Nature . . . is the Liberty each man hath, to use his own power, as he will himselfe, for the preservation of his own Nature; that is to say, of his own Life . . .[35]

In the second sense, preservation of one's own life is a universal moral right. One is morally justified in doing whatever is necessary to save one's own life. Self-preservation is unconditionally morally permissible. The significance of Hobbes' concept of the right to one's life can be seen by applying it to the famous case of The Queen v. Dudley and Stephens (1884).[36] After several days adrift in a lifeboat without expectations of being rescued, Dudley and Stephens killed and ate a cabin boy. Other theories of the natural right to life would hold that one's moral right to one's own life entails a moral duty to respect the life of another. Hence,

---

[33] J.-J. Rousseau, *First and Second Discourses (Discourse on the Sciences and Arts, Discourse on the Origins and Foundations of Inequality)*, edited by Roger Masters and translated by Roger and Judith Masters, St Martin's Press, New York, 1964, p. 94.
[34] *Man and Citizen*, p. 90.
[35] *Leviathan*, p. 189.
[36] 'The Queen v. Dudley and Stephens', *Queen's Bench Division*, Volume XIV, 1884.

Dudley and Stephens were morally in the wrong. But, apparently, Hobbes would disagree. Hobbes would concur with the defence of necessity offered on behalf of Dudley and Stephens: the men could not have acted otherwise in preserving their lives, given the fear of their own death and, moreover, they were morally justified in what they did.

Whatever one may think of this as a moral judgement, the dual nature of Hobbes' concept – that saving one's life is a matter of empirical necessity and also is morally justified – creates logical puzzles. Holding that self-preservation is morally justified seems to imply that one morally ought to do what one can't help but do. Hobbes might try to save his argument by noting that a person might unreasonably seek to sacrifice his life for the sake of another, but this reply seems contradicted by the empirical claim that he couldn't even if he wished. Moreover, the claim yields the false conclusion that sacrifice of one's life for another is empirically impossible. Finally, one wonders: if self-preservation is morally right then is sacrifice of one's life to save another's morally wrong? Perhaps, as I suggest later, it is enough to say that it is not a moral duty.

A second obscurity is that Hobbes' concept of the right to one's life seems out of line with his general theory of rights. In general, Hobbes is insistent that the terms right, freedom and liberty are the contraries of law, obligation and duty.[37] To say that someone has a right to do something is to indicate the *absence* of a law, moral or positive. That is, for Hobbes, rights in general do not entail duties; they entail their absence. To have a right is not to have a duty and, correspondingly, to have a duty is not to have a right. However, the natural right to life seems to be an exception to Hobbes' general rule in being both a right and a duty.

For on the same page on which he describes the right to one's life as natural and as a liberty, he describes it as a natural law and a duty:

> A Law of Nature . . . is a . . . generall Rule, found out by Reason, by which a man is forbidden to do, that, which is destructive of his life . . .[38]

Combining the two passages, self-preservation is both a right and a duty. Yet in the same paragraph from which the above is taken, Hobbes reiterates his argument that right and obligation are contraries and

---

[37] See *The Elements of Law*, p. 186; *Man and Citizen*, p. 274; *Leviathan*, pp. 189, 271 and 334.
[38] *Leviathan*, p. 189.

inconsistent: where you have the one, you don't have the other.

What this exception, if it is one, suggests is the importance Hobbes gives to the right of life. By making it both a natural right and an obligation of natural law, suicide seems proscribed. However, the general idea seems clear enough. The right to life does mean that there is no duty upon me to sacrifice my life for that of another or to do anything that imperils it. Self-sacrifice can never be a duty and one stands under no obligation with respect to it. One is obligated to respect the right to life of another but not at the cost of one's own.

Hobbes' most considered opinion, then, seems to be that self-preservation is both the fundamental right and duty of humans, that self-preservation necessitates a representative person, the sovereign, to protect it and that whatever he does to protect it, including not obeying the law, is fully justified. Any rational person rightly desires to preserve his life and therefore desires whatever is necessary to it. Hence the entitlement of the sovereign.

Now the expression 'Better dead than Red' current years ago suggests that Hobbes is mistaken about his fundamental principle. For it suggests that some people, perhaps many people, believe, or ought to believe, that there are other political values more important than self-preservation. One ought to be prepared, I presume it means, to lay down one's life rather than live under a tyrannical regime that denies individual liberty, justice, equality, etc.

However, there is a way of expressing Hobbes' argument which makes it worthy of the most serious reflection and which explains, in my view, the enduring importance of Hobbes' political philosophy. Other political philosophers, Rousseau among them, espouse the mutual compatibility of political values such as freedom, justice, equality, property and self-preservation. Yet it is arguable at least that they are not fully satisfiable together. Minimally, equality may necessitate a lessening of personal liberty, and vice versa. Alternatively, even societies that endorse all such values will rank them in order of priority for purposes of decision-making. Moreover, if, say, socialism and liberalism are viewed as political philosophies, then they will order the priorities differently. Socialism will give the highest priority to social justice and the lowest to free enterprise, and liberalism may do the opposite. Or, as the above suggests, socialism and liberalism may share the language of freedom, justice, equality, etc., but interpret them so as to turn them into contraries. Freedom, in the one, means freedom from economic oppression and necessitates state action. Freedom, in the other, means free enterprise, which necessitates state inaction.[39] What all these differences imply is profoundly different moral judgements concerning the role of the sovereign state and law. What should the state and law guarantee for its citizens?

It is in the context of such a confusing dispute that Hobbes' argument becomes most meaningful. For his contention is the basically simple one that *whatever else* may be thought to be the duty of rulers, all rational parties ought to agree that security and peace, including self-preservation, is *a* duty of rulers. But security is more than *a* duty, for security is *that condition which makes all other political values possible*. Without security of life; liberty, equality, justice, etc, cannot exist. Security, then, is what lawyers call a *sine qua non* condition, without which no other can be. This contention, and it is a powerful one, enables a modern-day Hobbesian to argue that however men may dispute the moral purposes of the state and law, no reasonable person should deny that the ultimate duty of those responsible for political and legal power is security of the people. The moral aspirations of socialists and liberals alike presuppose security of life for citizens. The other philosophers of politics claim moral superiority for their principles. Hobbes can be viewed as claiming logical priority for his. Without his, other principles cannot apply. Hobbes summarizes his position very neatly:

> All the duties of rulers are contained in this one sentence, the safety of the people is the supreme law.[40]

Safety is the *sine qua non* political value. Private men cannot provide it. The state must be given a monopoly of coercive power. The ruler has the duty to keep the peace, peace is the right and end of all which is entrusted to the ruler 'and whosoever has the right to the End, has right to the Means.'[41]

And to the 'good life'

So far I have presented Hobbes' argument in a way that might leave the reader with the impression that Hobbes sought to minimize the role of moral values in politics and law and perhaps even that he was opposed to the 'good life'. Properly understood, both are true.

---

[39] On the general idea of political parties expressing divergent moral values and concepts of freedom, see W. B. Gallie, 'Liberal Morality and Socialist Morality', in P. Laslett (ed.), *Philosophy, Politics and Society*, First Series, Blackwell, Oxford, 1956; and M. Cranston, *Freedom: A New Analysis*, Part 2, Longman's Green & Co., 1967.
[40] *Citizen*, p. 258.
[41] *Leviathan*, p. 232.

For one thing, like the latter-day Legal Positivists[42] who were influenced by him, Hobbes wishes to separate law and morals, at least to the extent that a determination of what the law is does not depend upon moral approval of particular laws. Valid positive law is simply the command of the duly authorized sovereign.

For another, Hobbes rejects the view of the ancients (Socrates, Plato and Aristotle) that human nature is constituted by a rational self which every individual ought to realize and which has the consequent that there is a universal supreme good life for man. According to Hobbes, there is no such universal absolute good, there is nothing that is simply good. Moreover, men quarrel over morals, perhaps more bitterly than over anything else. Such quarrels threaten the peace and security of all, and thus their right to life.

However, neither the necessity of identifying law separately from morality, nor the relativity of moral judgements, deny morality; nor do they exclude each from a good life. Indeed, I think Hobbes has two objectives regarding morality, which might be expressed as follows: One, law needs morality, as morality needs law. Two, the state ought to ensure the good life.

It is true that the law rules by fear, by the sword of the sovereign. But, as Rousseau concisely put it:

> The strongest is never strong enough to be master forever unless he transforms his force into right and obedience into duty.[43]

That is, it would be better if most citizens obeyed the law from a sense of moral duty. Law needs the support of morality. But it can obtain it only if law can be seen to serve a moral purpose. This it does by making morality practically possible. In Hobbes' state of nature, one from which the state and law are absent, men would know their moral duties but would not do them without sufficient reason to believe that others would as well.[44] The moral life needs a certain social stability, a certain modicum of mutual trust. It is this social stability that the law provides.

Moreover, law and morality are complementary in another sense, in that certain types of acts benefit all if they are done or not done. It is better if agreements are kept and gratitude shown, and if violent assault is

---

[42] See H. L. A. Hart, 'Positivism and the Separation of Law and Morals', in Feinberg and Gross (eds), *Law in Philosophical Perspective*, Dickenson, Encino, California, 1977, pp. 46–65.
[43] *Contract*, p. 48.
[44] *Leviathan*, p. 215.

discouraged. Rules prescribing and proscribing such acts appear both in morality and law, to the benefit of all, and command moral and legal obligation.

Hobbes describes the good life in terms of felicity (or happiness).

> Felicity is a continuall progresse of the desire, from one object to another; the attaining of the former, being still but the way to the later.[45]

As I interpret Hobbes, he means that it is not up to the sovereign or the law to decide in what various ways men will enjoy the good life. Each will decide for himself anyway. Consistently with this variety, the state ought to make possible as much liberty as possible. But the necessary condition of maximum liberty for all to enjoy the good life is minimum interference with the right to the good life of others. This minimum interference is best aided by a minimal morality, one that includes only such rules as are conducive to the right of life and the good life of all. Hobbes seems to concur with this interpretation when he complains that 'the Writers of Morall Philosophie' have not discerned 'wherein consisted (the) Goodnesse' of moral rules. Moral rules, he says are 'the *meanes* [my emphasis] of peaceable, sociable and comfortable living . . . These dictates of Reason, men use to call by the name of Lawes; but improperly: for they are but Conclusions, or Theoremes concerning what conduceth to the conservation and defence of themselves . . .'[46] Such means, as has been said, require the support of law and the state to control law-breakers. The good life, including the right to life itself, requires also that the hand that holds the sword be untied by laws.

Rousseau: The law shall make you free

Hobbes' right to life is conceptually obscure. The same is true of what Rousseau means by freedom and its relationship to law. In the passage from *Political Economy* where Rousseau praises the rule of law, he claims that one is *more* free under law.[47] Later, in *On the Social Contract*, he says that under law one is *as* free as before.[48] Both claims seem untrue together and indeed it is difficult to understand either. Part of the problem is uncertainty concerning the contrasting condition. As free as before; before what?

Hobbes' concept of the state of nature is a logical abstraction, a

[45] *Ibid.*, p. 160.
[46] *Ibid.*, pp. 216–7.
[47] *Contract*, p. 214.
[48] *Ibid.*, p. 53.

condition from which state and law are absent. It can apply to past, present or future.

Rousseau's concept of the state of nature is also a logical abstraction, but it applies to the past. It is a concept of the condition of man *before* the advent of the state and law. Rousseau sometimes refers to it as the original or primitive condition of man. According to Rousseau, primitive man was a solitary, nomadic animal who met others of his kind by accident. What complicates the problem is that Rousseau also refers to the condition of man in illegitimate states – those not ruled by the law of the general will – as a *new* state of nature.[49] Thus when Rousseau speaks of freedom he might be referring to any of three conditions: the original state of nature, the new one, and that under the general will.

Now if one thinks of the relation of freedom and law in Hobbes' terms then one is free in two senses: one, when you are free, to do as you want, from the interference of law, and two, freed by law from the interference of others. With Rousseau, the issue is more complicated. In an original state of nature, Rousseau holds that man is free in three senses: free from legal interference and from that by others, but also from the dominance of his own passions. However, man in this condition is not conscious of his freedom. He is, so to speak, objectively free in all these senses but freedom means nothing to him. Hence, if the comparisons of 'more' and 'as' free are applied to the original state, little of significance follows except that one cannot return to an original state of nature and man is not a moral being in it.

In the new state of nature, Rousseau claims that man is subject to the will of others, especially to rulers who rule the law, and to his own passion. He is subject to the will of others and not to his own reason. Now, if this is the contrast Rousseau is drawing, then clearly he means that man is *more* free under the sovereignty of the general will and not *as* free. Or one could argue, now that the contrasting conditions are clearer, that under the law of the general will, man is (in a sense) *as* and *more* free than in the original state of nature. As free, in that Rousseau claims that the three objective conditions are fulfilled. More free, in that one can experience the freedom of a moral agent; being free from the control of passion while subject to reason. However, 'more free' won't quite work in that it is plain that Rousseau attaches a higher value to moral freedom. 'More free' suggests a quantitative distinction, whereas Rousseau seems to mean that moral freedom is qualitatively superior. It is that which

---

[49] *Discourse on the Origins and Foundations of Inequality, op. cit.*, p. 177.

qualitatively distinguishes man. In a passage to which I will refer later, Rousseau says:

> To renounce one's freedom is to renounce one's status as a man, the rights of humanity and even its duties . . . Such a renunciation is incompatible with the nature of man, and taking away all his freedom of will is taking away all morality from his actions.[50]

On the basis of this attempt to make sense of what Rousseau means by 'as' and 'more' free, I wish to begin an exposition of what I take to be Rousseau's final reason; that rule by law is necessary to man's development as a moral being. As I interpret him, this places the emphasis on the freedom of the moral agent. An initial way of making this point is to note that Rousseau cites three senses of freedom in relation to law[51] – natural, civil and moral – and that Hobbes could agree with what he says of the first two.

Natural freedom is getting whatever you want by your own force and power. Hobbes and Rousseau agree in denying this freedom. Civil freedom is that freedom of action left to the subject by the law. Hobbes and Rousseau agree in accepting this freedom. Hence, the difference between Hobbes and Rousseau is over 'moral freedom, which alone makes man truly the master of himself. For the impulse of appetite alone is slavery, and obedience to the law one has prescribed for oneself is freedom'.[52]

The final reason which I wish to argue on Rousseau's behalf is that freedom – as a right and a duty, not alienated to any representative sovereign, but expressed in the law of the general will – is necessary to moral development and hence is expressible as a moral imperative. It is not the argument, as it is in Hobbes, that law ensures moral relations. It is rather that through the law, by being sovereign and subject of it, man becomes moral. But in setting this argument before the reader, I must admit two things: One, the argument, as an interpretation, is controversial. Two, the argument is only implicit in Rousseau.

However, one more preliminary point needs to be made. Rousseau's expression 'moral freedom' is ambiguous. It could mean the freedom of making moral choices and decisions, being able to choose to act morally as we think we ought. Rousseau's concept presupposes this but includes the idea that we are also free in doing what we morally ought to do.

---

[50] *Contract*, p. 50.
[51] *Ibid.*, *p. 56*.
[52] *Ibid.*, p. 56.

Freedom is both a right and a duty. In consequence, if we act from moral duty, if we do what we morally ought to do, we are free. The problem is to understand how one can be both free and obedient ('obedience to law . . . is freedom'). But, it can be suggested, freely choosing to do one's moral duty really is a matter of being both free and obedient.

Perhaps the shortest way of explicating these difficult ideas of Rousseau's is by contrast with Hobbes. We have noted that Rousseau speaks of the citizens of the state as passive when they are viewed as subjects of the law and as active when viewed as legislators. On this basis, one can argue that Rousseau's principal objection to any form of representative legislation – whether it be Hobbes' or that of present day legislators – is that citizens are treated as passive moral agents. This is not to deny that representatives do moral good for citizens. Hobbes' sovereign does a moral good in providing peace. Contemporary welfare states of various kinds provide many moral goods. But it still remains true that they are moral goods done for them.

Rousseau's criticism can be enlarged by saying that we have not yet found a way whereby political, including legal activity, engages the citizen in moral activity. The moral being is not merely one who should have moral good done for him. He is not merely the object of moral judgements; he must, if he is to develop as a moral agent, be author of them. He must himself make the moral judgements which govern his life.

Exponents of representative democracy by majority rule may argue that political activity does encompass moral activity in the determination of whom the representatives shall be. Rousseau presaged this criticism and replied to it:

> The English people thinks it is free. It greatly deceives itself; it is free only during the election of the members of Parliament. As soon as they are elected, it is a slave, it is nothing.[53]

Thus Rousseau's argument is that the people ought to be the authors of the laws to which all are obedient. To have them merely subject to laws is to treat them as moral patients and to deny their nature as moral agents. It is to deny them both their rights and their duties. Every citizen has a moral right to be a member of the sovereign legislator. To deny that right is to subject him to the wills of others who shall decide what is good for him. But sovereignty is also a moral duty in that it teaches morality, it

---

[53] *Ibid.*, p. 102.

teaches us to be concerned with the good of all and not with oneself alone. And more than that it teaches us moral respect, respect for ourselves as moral agents, as having the right and duty of moral decisions, and respect of a like kind for others. Rousseau's state is a sovereignty of equal moral agents in which each is called upon to make, and abide by, laws good for all. Some will not, of course, and therefore laws have sanctions. But at least, Rousseau argues, they are subject to law made by all for all, and not to the will of another. Even in suffering from such a law, Rousseau holds, one does as one wants. For one wants, or ought to want, to be obedient to laws for the good of all, including oneself. As subject of the law, I do not desire punishment. But as author, I recognize there must be punishments for legal disobedience.[54]

The usual objection to this reason why law ought to be above man is the boring and uninteresting one that Rousseau is 'too idealistic'. Of course, Rousseau supposes that the young could be educated to legislate for the common good. But by the same token, Hobbes thinks that the young could be educated to trust the sovereign.[55] Rousseau is perhaps unrealistic in presupposing a state of a size such that all would gather to legislate. But he is not idealistic in the sense of supposing men to be perfectly virtuous. Obviously, if men were that virtuous then law would be unnecessary.

There are other relevant differences between Hobbes and Rousseau. One might understand the expression 'The sovereign is above the law' to refer to (a) making, (b) repealing, or (c) interpreting the law, or (d) acting in the absence of law, or (e) acting illegally. In Hobbes' case, (a) and (b) are philosophically uninteresting since both presuppose law. They are both legal acts. Interpretation is a difficult matter but jurisprudents today are now agreed that it is not necessarily arbitrary.[56] The philosophically interesting cases for judging Hobbes seem to be (d) and (e). With regard to Rousseau and placing the law above man, (a) and (b) are accounted for by the sovereign legislative and neither the sovereign nor the government are entitled to act illegally (e). Magistrates, as agents of government, would be accountable for (c). Acting in the absence of law (d) is obscure. The sovereign people cannot act in the absence of law: their word is their law. The magistrates may, one supposes, have to act

---

[54] *On the Social Contract*, Book II, chapter 5, paragraph 3; *Ibid.*, p. 64.
[55] See *Man and Citizen*, pp. 262-3; *Leviathan*, p. 728.
[56] See H. L. A. Hart, *The Concept of Law, op. cit.*, chapter 7; R. Dworkin, *Taking Rights Seriously*, Harvard University Press, Cambridge, Mass., 1977; and Feinberg and Gross (eds), *Law in Philosophical Perspective, op. cit.*, pp. 181-93.

when there is no law to guide them. But, against this, there is Rousseau's general principle that the individual is only obligated by law.

Liberty or liberation?
This essay began with a mention of slogans. Although they are often inimical to rational thought, they may be of some value in summing up. Liberty or liberation? suggests at least one consideration which the reader can weigh. It is a way of expressing the basic question: What should be the moral purpose or end of law? With Hobbes, one purpose is that of permitting men liberty to do as they want. The price is that the sovereign himself is free of law. With Rousseau, lawmaking and lawobeying are themselves types of moral agency and development. It is not, as mainly it is with Hobbes, that law allows private moral relations. Law, with Rousseau, is primarily moral education; the content of which is one's rights and duties as a moral and social being.

Rousseau and Hume

Paul E. Corcoran

Rousseau and Hume in perspective
Jean-Jacques Rousseau (1712–78) and David Hume (1711–76) were exact contemporaries. As natives of Geneva and Scotland, each was in some ways a provincial, and each was deeply influenced by a need to be recognized in a neighbouring dominant culture. Both achieved fame as the result of an urge for celebrity, despite the Genevan facing periodic social and political ostracism, and the Scot being twice rejected and never appointed to a chair of philosophy. Each basked in the adulation of fashionable society in Paris and London, yet each prized long periods of obscure retreat. Both were important contributors to Enlightenment thought, but their lasting achievements were destructive of that tradition.

The contrasts are even more striking than the similarities. In temperament, Rousseau was by turns gracious and violently intolerant, but always insecure, passionate, inconsistent and finally, by the most sympathetic accounts, mad. Hume was a moderate man, restrained, thrifty and tolerant to a fault. Rousseau pleaded for the natural goodness in man's nature, but saw corruption everywhere: in himself, in society and in the very course of history. Hume, the justly famed sceptic, was convinced of man's sociable nature and peaceful inclinations. Rousseau scandalized the *philosophes* by criticizing art and science as forms of oppression; while Hume regarded them as the special dividends of freedom. Natural law was an essential tenet of Rousseau's theory of society, while Hume ended up depriving the laws of nature of any meaning and the social contract of any historical significance. Hume's political thought was influenced by the practical achievements and moral ambiguities of the English Revolution, while Rousseau's thought was profoundly pre-revolutionary.

Rousseau's *The Social Contract* is one of the greatest, as well as one of the last, accounts of the theory of popular consent. It is perhaps less well known that Hume was the first critic of social contract theory from within the liberal tradition; his attack on the contractarian account of the origins of society and government, and of justice and obligation, was developed and published years before *The Social Contract* was written.[1] His critique, like Rousseau's, was directed toward the well-established tradition of Hobbes, Locke, Spinoza and others in the natural law school, such as Pufendorf and Grotius. *Of the Original Contract*, first published in the 1748 edition of *Essays Moral, Political and Literary*, was Hume's fundamental reply to the contractarians.[2]

It would be mistaken, therefore, to interpret Hume's arguments as a critique of Rousseau.[3] In fact, he was attacking ideas expressed in Locke's *Second Treatise of Government* (1690) and adopted as a foundation of Whig political doctrine. Moreover, he was making a practical application of his own empiricist method to political theory in a way that Locke failed to do, apparently, in Hume's view, because he was 'actuated by party zeal'.[4] On the other hand, Rousseau was in no way equipped to meet Hume's arguments when he composed *The Social Contract* between 1756 and 1762. His philosophical grounding was sketchy, at best, and his preparation for an intended larger work, *Political Institutions*, of which *The Social Contract* was a part, was limited to a reading of Locke, Grotius, Pufendorf and several minor contemporary exponents of the natural law school. Rousseau's efforts should be seen against the background of Hume's critique as a revival of an already obsolete contractarian rationalism.

Hume's critique of contract and consent

Hume argues that the idea of a social contract can only be appreciated when it is placed alongside its rival 'speculative system of principles', the absolute power and divine right of kings. 'The one party, by tracing up Government to the Deity, endeavour to render it so sacred and inviolate, that it must be little less than sacrilege, however tyrannical it may become, to touch or invade it, in the smallest article.' The other party has

---

[1] These issues were first developed in Hume's *Treatise of Human Nature*, Book III, Part II, originally published in 1740.
[2] This work will be cited as *Essays*, from T. H. Green and T. H. Grose (eds), *Hume's Philosophical Works*, 4 vols, Longmans, London, 1875, Vol. III, based on the 1777 edition. Hume's revisions subsequent to the 1748 text will be noted.
[3] Hume revised his critique of the doctrines of contract, consent, obligation and origins of government throughout his life. *Of the Origins of Government*, written in 1774, did not appear in the *Essays* until the posthumous 1777 edition. See Duncan Forbes, *Hume's Philosophical Politics*, Cambridge University Press, 1975, pp. 76–7n.
[4] *Essays*, p. 443.

also 'reared up a fabric . . . to protect and cover that scheme of actions, which it pursues'. The Whigs, by 'founding government altogether on the consent of the People, suppose that there is a kind of *original contract*, by which the subjects have tacitly reserved the power of resisting their sovereign, whenever they find themselves aggrieved by that authority, with which they have, for certain purposes, voluntarily entrusted to him'.[5] By pairing the original contract with the Tory doctrine of divine right, and by insisting upon the purely political origins of these ideas, Hume establishes a new perspective for critical judgement.

He dismisses the divine right of kings in a single paragraph. Using the carefully aimed irony for which his essays are famous, Hume manages to avoid utterly outraging orthodox opinion. 'That the Deity is the ultimate author of all government, will never be denied by any, who admit a general providence . . . ' But Hume avers that since 'the omniscient Being' has created and guides the universe by a 'concealed and universal efficacy', a king cannot be 'his vice-regent, in any other sense than every power or force, being derived from him, may be said to act in his commission', including 'an inferior magistrate, or even a usurper, or even a robber and a pyrate'.[6]

In Hume's less peremptory analysis of the idea of original contract, the reader is immediately struck by the abrupt departure from the theological categories used in his royalist critique, and by his willingness to volunteer a series of concessions to the wholly secular views of the contractarians. Hume accepts 'how nearly equal all men are in their bodily force, and even in their mental powers and faculties, till cultivated by education'.[7] He admits that 'at first' such equals would never associate or subject themselves to 'any authority' except by 'their own consent'. If we trace the origins of government 'to its first origins in the woods and desarts', as Hume is willing to do, it follows that the people are the 'source of all power and jurisdiction', and would only leave their natural state voluntarily. They abandon 'their native liberty' for the sake of 'peace and order', and in doing so 'received laws from their equal and companion'.

---

[5] *Ibid*. The term 'party' is used by Hume, as well as Rousseau, to mean a spirit of faction, or a loose assemblage of persons holding to a set of ideas.
[6] *Essays*, p. 444.
[7] The natural equality of men was a radical doctrine espoused by the liberal thinkers, and given typical expressions by Hobbes and Locke, although Hobbes' exposition of physical and mental equality is laced with a good deal of sarcasm in *Leviathan*, Part I, chapter 13.

Hume is also willing to waive an obscurantist inquiry into the formalities of such an agreement by the inhabitants of the 'woods and desarts'.

> The conditions, upon which they were willing to submit, were either expressed, or were so clear and obvious, that it might well be esteemed superfluous to express them. If this, then, be meant by the *original contract*, it cannot be denied, that all government is, at first, founded on a contract, and that the most ancient rude combinations of mankind were formed chiefly by that principle.[8]

The first human groupings must have been in some way mutual and voluntary, but this can be nothing more than conjecture. 'In vain, are we asked in what records this charter of our liberties is registered. It was not written on parchment, nor yet on leaves or barks of trees. It preceded the use of writing and all the other civilized arts of life.' Where there is no force stronger than the roughly equal strength of men's limbs, nothing but consent, as well as a 'sense of the advantages resulting from peace and order', could induce one to the acceptance of combination and external authority.[9]

There Hume draws the line in conceding points to the 'philosophers who have embraced a party'. He is disdainful of how they take the contract both too seriously and too lightly. They assert 'not only that government in its earliest infancy arose from consent or rather the voluntary acquiescence of the people; but also, even at present, when it has attained its full maturity, it rests on no other foundation'. On the other hand, this contract is regarded as permanently provisional, the individual's allegiance extending no further than the obligation invited by his own promise, which is always 'conditional, and imposes on him no obligation, unless he meet with justice and protection from his sovereign'.[10]

The chief difficulty with this understanding, in Hume's view, is that it bears no resemblance to anything in the known world, past or present. The liberal idea of social contract is not only a deceptive mystification, but a parochial English one in the bargain. Whigs have taken the Magna Carta, the 1688 Revolution, the Bill of Rights and the English Parliament, and

---

[8] *Essays*, pp. 444–5.
[9] Hume added a paragraph in the 1777 edition qualifying this as 'imperfect consent', resulting from the dominance in time of war of a chieftain whose authority grew out of particular acts of exigency which, in their frequency, gradually produced habituation and voluntary acquiescence. *Essays*, pp. 445–6. Here Hume offers a psychological, rather than rationalist, account of the original contract.
[10] *Essays*, p. 446.

have spun out of them generalizations, even false in the English case,[11] about all nations and human nature itself.

> But would these reasoners look abroad into the world, they would meet with nothing that, in the least, corresponds to their ideas, or can warrant so refined and philosophical a system. On the contrary, we find, everywhere, princes, who claim their subjects as their property, and assert their independent right of sovereignty, from conquest or succession. We find also, everywhere, subjects, who acknowledge this right in their prince . . .[12]

In contrast to the rationalist derivation of political obligation, which attempts to explain a human reality through universal natural laws and innate qualities of mind (reason and will), Hume gives a pragmatic psychological analysis. 'Obedience or subjection becomes so familiar, that most men never make any enquiry about its origin or cause, more than about the principle of gravity, resistance, or the most universal laws of human nature.'[13]

The 'agreement by which savage men first associated and joined their force' may in the conjectural sense have been 'real', but this yields nothing to the present; 'being so ancient, and being obliterated by a thousand changes of government and princes, it cannot now be supposed to retain any authority'. If that original contract were to serve as a model, it must follow that every lawful government must have been founded on consent and voluntary compact, although this presupposes 'the consent of the fathers to bind the children', a serious embarrassment to a party opposed to patriarchalism. Such a model Hume dismisses as 'not justified by history or experience, in any age or country of the world'.[14]

The lesson of history that Hume draws is as blunt as Machiavelli's. 'Almost all the governments, which exist at present, or of which there remains any record in story, have been founded originally, either on

[11] Hume's *History of England* (1754–62) is devoted to a refutation of the Whig idea that English constitutional history in general, and the Whig party in particular, constitute a continuously unfolding tradition of freedom. A concise summary of Hume's historical writings is L. L. Bongie, *David Hume: Prophet of the Counter-Revolution*, Oxford University Press, 1965, pp. vii–xvii; a more detailed analysis is Forbes, *Hume's Philosophical Politics, op. cit.*, chapter 8. Hume himself displays a somewhat parochial outlook in his treatment of social contract as a peculiarly English invention, and his essays *Of the Rise and Progress of the Arts and Sciences* and *Of Refinement in the Arts*, both in *Essays*, betray a characteristically British viewpoint on 'innocent and vicious luxuries'. Hume's view that the more the 'arts advance, the more sociable men become' (*Essays*, 301) is diametrically opposed to Rousseau's argument in his *Discourse on the Moral Effects of the Arts and Sciences* (1751).
[12] *Essays*, p. 446.
[13] *Essays*, pp. 446–7.
[14] *Essays*, p. 447.

usurpation or conquest, or both, without any pretense of a fair consent, or voluntary subjection of the people.' If there was once a primordial 'voluntary acquiescence', the 'force, which now prevails, and which is founded on fleets and armies, is plainly political, and derived from authority, the effect of established government'.[15] This judgement is not offered with a low regard for the people, but with a keen understanding of the nature of public opinion and its shaping by the artful use of violence and the control of communication and assembly.[16]

Speaking of the 1688 Revolution, in which Parliament had one king beheaded and presented the throne to a foreigner, Hume attacks the primary precedent for the English contractarians.

> Let not the establishment of the *Revolution* deceive us, or make us so much in love with a philosophical origin to government, as to imagine all others monstrous and irregular . . . It was only the succession, and that only in the regal part of government, which was then changed: And it was only the majority of seven hundred, who determined the change for ten millions. I doubt not, indeed, but the bulk of the ten millions acquiesced willingly in the determination: but was the matter left, in the least, to their choice?[17]

Hume's intention is not to argue that all governments are illegitimate, or that popular consent is an absurd idea.[18] Rather, he is asking the reader to accept that the quality of his subjection and the moral character of a political constitution are matters of experience, custom and evolving opinion. Otherwise, the entire experience of mankind must be rejected. This is a demand to be realistic, not cynical or amoral. People are commonly dissatisfied with their governments, especially new ones, when fear and necessity, more than any idea of moral obligation, cause men to obey. 'Time, by degrees, removes all these difficulties, and accustoms the nation to regard, as their lawful or native princes, that family, which, at first, they considered as usurpers or foreign conquerors.'[19]

Hume finds no reason for interpreting this process as 'tacit consent', inferred from a subject's failure to withdraw from society by emigrating to another land, because 'such an implied consent can only have place,

---

[15] *Essays*, p. 445.
[16] *Essays*. pp. 447–8.
[17] Here Hume refers to the membership of Parliament, who resolved to invite William of Orange to the throne, and who passed the Bill of Rights in 1689. *Essays*, pp. 448–9.
[18] Hume added two paragraphs in the 1753–54 edition of *Essays* to assure the reader that the 'consent of the people' as a foundation of government 'is surely the best and most sacred of any' when it does occur. *Essays*, p. 450.
[19] *Essays*, pp. 450–1.

where a man imagines, that the matter depends on his choice'. The generality of a population, especially peasants and artisans, cannot be said to have a free choice to leave, or to adapt themselves to new customs and a foreign language. A wise prince will not allow them to go, but if he should, they will only find subjection to a new prince, rather than any recovery of their native freedom.[20]

Hume was well aware that this form of argument was historical, and that however sensible it might be to appeal to experience and custom, it was not a final answer to the contractarian view–which indeed was shared by the Tories–that mere mundane evidence cannot prevail against the higher truths discovered by reason and embedded in natural law (or, for the Tories, revealed religion and divine law). So he added a brief 'philosophical refutation' of legitimacy and obligation, which rests upon a novel distinction between two types of moral duties. The first are those to which 'men are impelled by a natural instinct', such as the 'love of children, gratitude to benefactors, pity to the unfortunate'. Men act on these duties without any reflection, without any idea of obligation, and free from any consideration of personal or public utility.

The second type of moral duties, justice and fidelity, are not instinctual or natural. They are 'performed entirely from a sense of obligation' when on reflection 'we consider the necessities of human society, and the impossibility of supporting it, if these duties were neglected'. They are 'natural' duties only in the sense that they arise by the force of necessity in human society. Justice ('a regard for the property of others') and fidelity ('the observance of promises') are therefore social duties. They emerge and become obligatory as the result of man's reflective and experiential control over the 'pernicious effects' of the natural instincts of self-love and a compulsion 'to extend his acquisitions as much as possible'. 'His original inclination, therefore, or instinct, is here checked and restrained by a subsequent judgement or observation.'[21]

This train of reasoning carries with it several startling rejections of the natural law tradition. Hume casually allows that justice, far from being a principle of an unchanging moral order discoverable by reason alone, is

---

[20] *Essays*, pp. 451–2. See Locke's account of tacit consent in *Second Treatise of Government*, paragraphs 119–21, in *Two Treatises of Government*, edited by Peter Laslett, Cambridge University Press, 1960.

[21] Hume's exposition of this point is very unclear. He states in adjacent paragraphs that justice and fidelity are 'natural duties' which 'are not supported by any original instinct of nature'. *Essays*, p. 455.

only a derivative moral duty. It obtains in and for society, a product of culture, flowing from a utilitarian calculation of the disadvantages resulting from not respecting the property of others. Most important of all, justice grows, or is learned, as a *feeling* of obligatory restraint as man becomes habituated to censoring his natural instincts. Justice, then, is a creature of habit and convention: in modern terms, 'socialization'. Hume does not even allude to the scholastic distinctions of *ius, iustidias* and *lex naturale* used by Hobbes and Locke to reconcile their doctrines, mechanistic and rationalist though they were, with the Christian conceptions of natural law and right.[22] For Hume, justice is simply a moral sense that is 'natural' only insofar as it is a learned response to coping with the demands, and pursuing the advantages, of political society.

Fidelity stands on precisely the same ground. No special higher law or sacred duty is attached to man's covenant, as Hobbes had allowed quite explicitly. Both obedience and fidelity 'become obligatory' and 'acquire' an authority over mankind. Hume has in effect secularized the natural law conceptions of moral duty and political obligation. Moreover, he has shifted the ground of moral philosophy away from speculation about man's innate nature and *a priori* axioms about universal causes to the historical investigation of human experience, with a view to discovering *inductive* principles of social behaviour. This explains what is otherwise seen as Hume's paradoxical optimism, for a sceptic, in his essay *That Politics May Be Reduced to a Science*.[23] It must be remembered that the subtitle of Hume's first publication, *A Treatise of Human Nature*, was *An Attempt to Introduce the Experimental Method of Reasoning into Moral Subjects*.[24]

Hume distinguishes allegiance, 'the political or civil duty', from fidelity solely to hammer home his point that moral duties are the product of experience and observation, and should not be 'traced up' to higher laws or speculative principles of human nature.[25] Allegiance does not 'derive' from a sacred promise, but results, in the same manner as fidelity, from 'reflection only, which engages us to sacrifice such strong

---

[22] See Forbes, *Hume's Philosophical Politics*, pp. 66–70, for a discussion of Hume's secular theory of natural law and political obligation.
[23] *Essays*, Part I, pp. 98–109.
[24] First published 1739–40. The edition cited here, as *Treatise*, will be that of Green and Grose (eds), 1875, Vols I and II.
[25] *Essays*, p. 455. Hume argues this point more explicitly in *Treatise*, II, Book III, Part II, Sec. VIII, 'Of the Source of Allegiance', 304–13.

passions' as unlimited freedom and 'dominion over others' to the 'interests of peace and public order'. This 'interest' in maintaining public authority, and this alone, is the source of allegiance. Hume disingenuously fails to acknowledge that universal *lex naturale* and divinely sanctioned covenants are the real targets of criticism. If we are bound to obey our sovereign because we have given a tacit promise, 'why are we bound to observe our promise?' If we are bound to be obedient to government because we are bound to keep our word, 'why are we bound to keep our word?' Hume avers that 'no body, till trained in a philosophical system, can either comprehend or relish' the circular logic involved in referring political allegiance to sacred fidelity – but he does not even hint at the orthodox, and indeed quite popular, understanding that covenants made on oath are believed to be sanctioned by God. Hume's answer is deadpan: 'the commerce and intercourse of mankind . . . can have no security where men pay no regard to their engagements'. The circle of inquiry is arrested when he states that the plain and simple rationale for obedience to government is *'because society could not otherwise subsist.'*[26]

Hume concludes that the doctrine of original contract and consent 'leads to paradoxes repugnant to the common sentiments of mankind, and to the practice and opinion of all ages . . . What authority any moral reasoning can have, which leads into opinions so wide of the general practice of mankind, in every place but in this single kingdom, it is easy to determine'.[27]

Rousseau on the original and social contract

We do not know with certainty that Rousseau had read Hume's criticism of popular consent and original contract, but at least there was no excuse for his being unaware of Hume's position by the time his *Social Contract* was published in 1762. Hume's *Political Discourses* was first sold in France in 1754, and the translator, Abbé Le Blanc, wrote to Hume[28] that

---

[26] *Essays*, p. 456 (emphasis in the original); cf. *Treatise*, II, 307–8.
[27] *Essays*, p. 460. Here Hume quotes directly from Locke, referring to him as 'the most notable of its partizans'.
[28] John Hill Burton, *Life and Correspondence of David Hume*, 2 vols, Wm Tait, Edinburgh, 1846, Vol. I, p. 458f. For a detailed account of Hume's works appearing in French prior to 1760, and to the great notoriety of the *Political Discourses* (the title given to several editions of the *Essays*), which caused many to regard Hume as the successor to Montesquieu as the most influential philosopher of the age, see Rudolf Metz, 'Les Amitiés françaises de Hume et le mouvement des idées', *Revue de littérature comparée* (1929), at pp. 654–8, 668–9 and 176–8.

the edition was so successful that it was selling like a novel. All we have as Rousseau's testimony that he was familiar with Hume's work is his first letter to him, in which he gives that impression. Speaking of a mutual acquaintance, Rousseau writes:

> ... he acquainted me with your virtues, as I had only known them until then by your talents. Your lofty views, your surprising impartiality, your genius would raise you too far above other men, if your kind heart did not unite you with them.[29]

Rousseau's *Social Contract*, whether or not it was written in the light of Hume's critique, was similarly intended as a correction of the English social contractarians. The *Discourse on the Origins and Foundations of Inequality* (1755) had been especially concerned to show how they failed to discover man in his truly 'natural state' in the 'embryo of his species'.[30] There Rousseau sought to reveal 'original man', although he equals Hume in his modesty, or ambivalence, on the question of the historical character of the original contract.

> For it is by no means a light undertaking to distinguish properly between what is original and what is artificial in the actual nature of man, or to form a true idea of a state which no longer exists, perhaps never did exist, and probably never will exist; and of which it is, nevertheless, necessary to have true ideas, in order to form a proper judgement of our present state.
>
> Let us begin then by laying all facts aside, as they do not affect the question. The investigation we may enter into, in treating this subject, must not be considered as historical truths, but only as mere conditional and hypothetical reasonings, rather calculated to explain the nature of things, than to ascertain their actual origins.[31]

The complexity of Rousseau's thoughts on 'origins' and the impetus to

---

[29] *The Letters of David Hume*, edited by J. Y. T. Grieg, 2 vols. Oxford University Press, 1932, Vol. II, p. 382, Rousseau to Hume, 19 February 1763 (my translation). Rousseau could not read or speak English at this time. In 1766 he tried to learn English by studying an English translation of his own *Emile*, borrowed from Hume, but he gave it up. Hume observed at the time: 'He has read very little during the course of his life, and has now totally renounced all reading.' (Burton, *Life and Correspondence*, Vol. II, pp. 314–16). On the friendship and eventual falling out between Hume and Rousseau, see Burton, *Life and Correspondence*, Vol. II, chapters XIV-XV; and E. C. Mossner, *The Life of David Hume*, Nelson, Edinburgh, 1954, chapter 35. Accounts more sympathetic to Rousseau are Henri Guillemin, *Les Philosophes contre Jean-Jacques, Cette affaire infernale*, Plon, Paris, 1942, and Henri Roddier, *J.-J. Rousseau en Angleterre au XVIII siècle*, Boivin, Paris, 1950.

[30] J.-J. Rousseau, *The Social Contract and Discourses*, edited and translated by G. D. H. Cole, Dent, London, 1973, pp. 45–7. (This excellent edition will be used for all Rousseau citations, unless otherwise noted.)

[31] *Origins of Inequality*, in Cole, *op. cit.*, pp. 39 and 58.

civil community is critical in distinguishing his thought from others in the contractarian tradition. Hobbes and Locke, as well as virtually every other contract theorist going back to the ancients[32], viewed the earliest association of men as an advancement of social life, even if only for mutual defence and material survival. Both the originality and the ambiguity of Rousseau's political thought stem from his profound disagreement on this point.

His forthright antipathy to society was, of course, the foundation of his personal and literary celebrity. In the planned second chapter of the *Social Contract*, which Rousseau deleted before publication, he argues that the very earliest tendencies to society pave the way to man's destruction through dependence, inequality, corruption and moral deformity. 'Thus the same causes which make us wicked also make us slaves; we are simultaneously subjected and depraved . . . Our needs bring us together at the same time as our passions divide us.' In this 'state of wretchedness', man perishes 'as the victim of this deceitful union which he expected would bring him happiness'. Rousseau struggles with the idea that man's first association, the 'origin' of government, is a subjugation, a departure from, rather than an advancement toward, general well-being. In one paragraph crossed out in the manuscript, he carried this idea too far for even his own tastes.

> When men first come together on a voluntary basis . . . they create a situation in which one's good fortune is another's misfortune. Once we are convinced of this, and once we recognize that, far from aiming at the general good, men only come together because they are moving away from it, then we shall come to feel that, even if such a state could exist, it would only be a source of crimes and misfortunes for men . . . [33]

In the next paragraph, left intact, Rousseau asserts that a 'happy life . . . could never really have existed for the human race. When men could have enjoyed it they were unaware of it; and when they could have understood it they had already lost it'. In a later deleted passage, his attack on natural law and the 'social treaty' is reminiscent of Hume.

> . . . the progress of society stifles humanity in men's hearts by arousing personal interest, and . . . the notion of natural law, which it would be more appropriate to call the law of reason, *only begins to develop when the earlier development of the passions* is making all its precepts powerless. From this it is

[32] Cole's Introduction to *The Social Contract and Discourses*, pp. xvii–xx.
[33] This chapter, which Rousseau entitled 'The General Society of the Human Race', has come to be known as *The Geneva Manuscript;* it is reproduced in full in the Cole edn, 1973; see also critical notes to the text, pp. xlviii–xlix, and p. 279ff; quotations from pp. 155–6.

apparent that this so called social treaty, dictated by nature, is a pure fantasy . . .[34]

Rousseau seems convinced of man's implacability in both the natural and social condition: '. . . there is no natural and general society among men . . . they become unhappy and wicked in becoming sociable'.[35] These are curious views to have been expressed, however privately, by the man who has since been credited with the romantically revolutionary ideas of the essential goodness of human nature and the moral salvation to be found in a new social contract.

The *Social Contract* in its published form is nevertheless devoted to portraying a form of compact that would transcend the fate of old 'associations'. There is no question that Rousseau believed in a *'première convention'*[36] but in affirming this he glosses over a major disagreement with Hume. His rhetorical flourish that there 'will always be a great difference between subduing a multitude and ruling a society', which Hume painstakingly denied, implies a distinction that leads Rousseau to use 'social contract' in two very different senses. Quoting Grotius on the issue of a compact between the people and a government, he concludes that if a 'people . . . can give itself to a king', it follows that 'a people is a people before it gives itself'. This act by which it becomes a people, 'being necessarily prior to the other, is the true foundation of society'.[37]

A careful reading of this text seems to show that Rousseau means an 'original contract', which he expresses as a *'convention antérieure'*, in the quite primitive sense conceded by Hume. The act of becoming a people appears to be the first coming together of a few, based on unanimous consent, to submit thereafter to a 'master'. Indeed, he claims that the motivation for departing the state of nature is physical necessity.[38] But there is a discontinuity here in Rousseau's thought. His account of the formation of the social compact is introduced as his solution to the 'obstacles' and 'resistances' of the state of nature, not of the wretched state of 'a people'. However, this solution is intended to associate men in a way that will leave them 'as free as before' – but before what? We must emphasize this sequence, because it shows that Rousseau has first

---

[34] *Geneva Manuscript*, p. 157 (emphasis added).
[35] *Geneva Manuscript*, p. 161. Rousseau nevertheless affirms the hope that we might 'extract from the evil itself the remedy which can cure it' by creating 'new associations'.
[36] This is the term used in the title to Book I, Chapter V, of *The Social Contract*. References to French terms are taken from the original text of *Du Contrat Social*, edited by R. Grimsley, Oxford University Press, 1972 edn.
[37] *Social Contract*, p. 173.
[38] *Ibid.*

brought up the idea of a 'prior' contract – by which a 'people' is formed – only to abandon it immediately. Chapter VI of Book I speaks of the 'solution' very much as had Grotius, Hobbes and Locke: men exist with difficulty in a state of nature, and then depart directly from it by means of a social compact. Thus Rousseau has left no room for either a period of primitive civility or of wretched sociability and the self-imposed chains of oppression, such as he had depicted in the *Origins of Inequality*[39], and still assumes is the 'problem' for which his *Social Contract* is boldly offered as the solution. The distinction between *'une première convention'* and *'le pacte social'* is unrealized, leaving in doubt the theoretical and historical significance of the 'prior contract'.[40] Is the social contract the solution to the physical necessities of the state of nature, or is it a means of renewing man's freedom by casting off the chains of corruption and tyranny?

Rousseau is curiously ambivalent on the distinction between the state of nature and civil society. Hobbes and Locke regarded these two conditions as mutually exclusive, however closely related they were by man's natural reason to enter into the security of a contract and by his natural appetites to violate and break it. If we take Book I, Chapter VI, as a convenient hypothetical construct and not a rejection of his argument on primitive society in the *Origins of Inequality*, Rousseau has consigned the state of nature to pre-historic oblivion, along with the rude but amiable savage who, like Montesquieu's earliest troglodytes, is 'liker beasts than men'.[41]* For Rousseau, like Hume, 'a people' has an

---

[39] *Origins of Inequality*, in Cole, *op. cit.*, pp. 82–3.

[40] This confusion is multiplied by Rousseau's changing terminology. For example, in Book IV, Chapter II, where the obvious antecedent is his proposed compact, and not some pre-historical conjecture, he refers to it as *'ce contrat primitif'*. *Social Contract*, p. 250.

[41] Montesquieu, *The Persian Letters*, X, several editions with Amsterdam or Cologne imprints published 1721.

* Charles-Louis de Secondat, Baron de la Brède et de Montesquieu (1689–1775), first of the great 'philosophes' of the eighteenth century, magistrate and president of the Bordeaux parliament. Reflecting interests other than legal, his first great work, *Les Lettres Persanes*, (1721) caught the public's interest. The letters, supposedly sent by two Persians travelling through Europe, to their friends in Persia, contain a satirical portrait of French life and of its social, religious and political conditions under the Regency.

Considérations sur les causes de la grandeur des Romains et de leur décadence, published in 1734, is generally viewed as a preparation for *The Spirit of the Laws*, his major work. From an investigation into the varieties of laws and customs, Montesquieu derives the principle of relativity; governments and laws, he argues, differ as a result of a kind of historical determinism – varying geographical, climatic, racial, economic and moral conditions. His preference is the English constitutional monarchy, which, according to him, guarantees freedom and liberty. In the same spirit, he recommends a separation of powers that was later to be embodied in the American Constitution. (Ed.)

existence in 'society' as a product of historical development. Whether the people, historically, were actually united by a primitive *convention antérieure* is necessarily conjectural. In any case, the main fact for Rousseau is that Frenchmen, not natural man, stand in need of a new association to redeem themselves from the oppression and depravity to which countless generations of society have brought them. Frenchmen are not obligated to the laws of nature, but are directly subject to Louis XV, obeying his whims as well as his laws. Rousseau makes no historical pretence that the king has somehow defaulted his right of obedience by breaking a contract with his subjects, thus returning them to a natural condition. Rather, he addresses himself to men in chains and offers his solution of a general and spontaneous expression of consent in a new compact, formed by reason, rather than forged by history. It is thus a uniquely revolutionary call. One set of bonds must be broken in fashioning a new allegiance that is the product of reason, liberated sentiment and a new force that is the redeeming artifice of the social contract: the *volonté générale*. Rousseau's contract is thus a break with, and a defiance of, history and its naturally debasing traditions. The contrast is not between the state of nature and civil society, but between a history of corrupt oppression and a new life of freedom and civic virtue.

In the context of other social contract theorists, three points of comparison are of special importance in understanding Rousseau's thought: (1) Although dubious of the historical status of a primitive social contract, he was willing to concede it on the basis of hypothetical reasoning and conjectural history. However, he insisted that all prior descriptions of that state of nature were widely inaccurate and laden with traits – such as language, property and warfare – that were necessarily acquired in society. (2) The social contract proper, such as he describes in Book I, Chapters VI-IX, is a common agreement among individual persons (*la personne particulière*) which creates 'a very remarkable change in man' such that each member becomes an indivisible part of the whole, that is, a 'public person', a *corps moral et collectif*.[42] This is, for Rousseau, the only act of the body politic deserving the name 'contract'.[43] (3) It follows that the institution of government is not a 'second' contract.

---

[42] *Social Contract*, pp. 175–7. See J.-J. Rousseau, *The Social Contract*, edited by Ernest Barker, Oxford University Press, 1947, pp. xxxvii–xl, for Rousseau's use of natural law terminology for the body politic (*corpus morale collectivum*), the individual will (*omnes ut singuli*) and the general will (*omnes ut universi*).
[43] Social Contract, p. 243.

Neither individually, as with Hobbes, nor collectively, as with Locke, does the corporate body make a covenant with a king or other instituted authority after its original compact of civil association. The people in their corporate capacity alone are sovereign, and can never give away or even appoint temporary representatives of its rights.[44] In effect, Rousseau's theory of government is radically 'provisional', a term he uses repeatedly. He emphasizes 'that the institution of government is not a contract, but a law; that the depositories of the executive power are not the people's masters, but its officers.' The sovereign may therefore by ' a simple act of the general will' establish itself as a democracy, or it may set up a monarchical or aristocratic administration, only to change it again, at will, in its periodic assemblies.[45] What the sovereign cannot do is bind itself irrevocably to anything, such as a 'fundamental law' or even the social contract itself.[46]

Apart from the provisional conception of politics implied in this view, we are struck by Rousseau's repeated references to the sacred and even miraculous nature of the social contract and its political consequences. It is as if the first modern democratic thinker is anxious to endow an otherwise temporal, secular and materialist conception of society with a *mysteria* of its own: to 'trace up', in Hume's phrase, a democratic government to a metaphysical order. In fact, Rousseau does this quite explicitly in his chapter on 'Civil Religion', where he sets out the need for 'a purely civil profession of faith' in a 'beneficent Deity'.[47] The spiritual intent of his language is even clearer in his discussion of the social compact and the sovereign. Often this theme is clouded in paradox, which may have been a literary strategy to avoid censorship, or it may have been his own indulgence in rhetoric – which was Hume's assessment of the *Social Contract*.[48] Rousseau affirms that 'the social order is a sacred right which is the basis of all right', although this right 'does not come from nature, and must therefore be founded on convention'.[49] The terms of the social compact, actually set off in the text as an oath of allegiance, are expressed in the form of a religious *credo*.

---

[44] *Social Contract*, Book I, Chapter VII, and Book II, Chapters I-II. See Locke's distinction between 'uniting' into civil community and 'putting themselves under government' in the *Second Treatise*, paragraphs 97–9, 124 and 134–5.
[45] *Social Contract*, pp. 244–5.
[46] *Social Contract*, p. 176.
[47] *Social Contract*, p. 276.
[48] Hume described Rousseau's opinion that the *Social Contract* was his greatest work as a 'preposterous judgement'. Grieg (ed.), *The Letters of David Hume*, Vol. II, p. 28.
[49] *Social Contract*, pp. 165–6.

> Each of us puts his person and all his power in common under the supreme direction of the general will, and, in our corporate capacity, we receive each member as an indivisible part of the whole.[50]

There is redemptive fervour in this 'mutual undertaking'. What were formerly individuals are miraculously transformed by this act of association which 'creates a moral and collective body . . . receiving from this act its unity, its common identity, its life, its will.' The strain of doctrinal casuistry is felt in his logic that 'each individual, in making a contract . . . with himself, is bound in a double capacity; as a member of the Sovereign he is bound to the individuals and as a member of the State to the Sovereign.' The sovereign draws 'its being wholly from the sanctity of the contract' and this sacred character is embellished with the surprising deduction that 'The Sovereign, merely by virtue of what it is, is always what it sould be.'[51] Thus Rousseau falls back upon natural law and rationalist abstractions to describe the sovereign and the general will.

The creation of the social compact is, nevertheless, more religious than legalistic, producing 'a very remarkable change in man, by substituting justice for instinct in his conduct'. The citizen is a person transformed. His actions now have a moral dimension, as they did not before. He now hears 'the voice of duty' and consults his reason. His mind is quickened and his feelings ennobled. The soul is uplifted. Savage simplicity is replaced by intelligence and manly courage. Man acquires moral liberty, and transcends the slavery of his appetites to attain true self-mastery.[52] The price of all this is one's loss of 'natural liberty', and the single and sufficient condition is one's total participation in the general will. Rousseau expresses his new form of association as if it were a spiritual act which transcends, rather than defies, rational analysis. The body politic seems almost possessed of magic powers, as when he describes how this corporate person, like a *trompe l'oeil*, can be two things at once.

> . . . there is revealed one of the astonishing properties of the body politic, by means of which it reconciles apparently contradictory operations; for this is accomplished by a sudden conversion of Sovereignty into democracy, so that, without a sensible change, and merely by virtue of a new relation of all to all, the citizens become magistrates and pass from general to particular acts . . .[53]

The *Social Contract* is, indeed, rich in paradoxes of 'double existence'.

---

[50] *Social Contract*, p. 175.
[51] *Social Contract*, pp. 175–7.
[52] *Social Contract*, pp. 177–8.
[53] *Social Contract*, p. 244.

Men are 'born free' but all are 'in chains'. The 'social order is a sacred right . . . founded on conventions'. A man's particular interests differ from his general interests. The general will remains pure and constant in a corrupt state. The opponents of the social contract become 'foreigners'.[54] Rousseau's vision of a dual reality, combined with his messianic romance of communal redemption, endows his thought with great potential as a revolutionary ideology and a vision of the future.[55]

Common and uncommon ground
The suprarational character of Rousseau's understanding of the social contract and the general will stands very much in opposition to Hume's 'new scene of thought'[56] and places Rousseau much closer to traditional contractarian thought than he would have liked. For Hobbes and Locke, as for such medieval thinkers as Thomas Aquinas and John of Salisbury, there was a supernatural aspect to the promises and covenants made by men, even relating to secular allegiance. Man's promise to man or to his prince carried with it a higher sanction, making that bond a part of his spiritual obligations under divine law. It was a commitment to keep faith, thus providing a moral foundation – instead of a utilitarian 'interest' – for the authority of the state and its right to individual obedience. It is clear that Rousseau was keen to invest his republic and its general will with this higher sanction. We see this aim in his insistence that the social compact is accompanied by a personal and collective moral transformation and the creation of a moral entity transcending merely particular interests. Hume would have none of this, and insisted that all promises and obligations repose on a 'natural' foundation of interests and experience. For Hume, political allegiance does not arise from one's sanctioned promise or original participation in a higher moral order of the Sovereign, *vox populi, vox dei*, but from one's interest in the benefits flowing from a stable political order and in the sense of moral duty to obey an authority which gradually arises through custom and habit.

---

[54] *Social Contract*, pp. 115–6, 182–5, 248 and 250.
[55] Donald W. Livingston, 'Hume's Historical Theory of Meaning', in D. W. Livingston and J. T. King (eds), *Hume: A Re-evaluation*, Fordham University Press, New York, 1976, p. 220, discusses the doctrine of double existence as a form of theoretical alienation, leading to a longing for some form of total revolution. In contrast to thinkers such as Descartes, Proudhon, Fourier and Marx, Hume resisted 'ontological language', preferring common language based on historical meaning.
[56] Letter to George Cheyne, 1734, in Grieg (ed.), *The Letters of David Hume*, Vol. I, p. 13.

The orientation of each thinker in relation to time is perhaps the most helpful comparison of Hume and Rousseau. Hume's argument is based upon actual human history, and the virtual lack of any real evidence or historical precedent for the social contract in establishing political authority. Rousseau's social contract, by contrast, is not an historical discovery, nor a proposition intended to reveal the meaning of any nation's political constitution. It is a manifesto for the future, a rhetorical appeal to a new generation to rise up and create a new republic. His many references to classical antiquity were in search of simple ideals to guide a rejection, not a recovery, of the past.

Still it is important to see the many similarities between Hume and Rousseau, even if the former is concerned with revealing the past with a non-ideological lucidity, and the latter offers the social contract as a vision of the future. Both quite clearly see political rights as the product of convention and social experience. Both speak of a natural man, and even of man as having certain universal and unshakable inclinations, and yet they are profoundly convinced that man's sense of justice and injustice, man's moral and intellectual capacities, and even man's need and capacity for sociability, are the products of experiential, rather than innately natural, attributes.

Hume and Rousseau, from practically diametrically opposed philosophical viewpoints, expressed a common sense of disillusionment with the Enlightenment. This is best shown in their tendency to emphasize the importance of tradition, and in their insistence upon a virtually organic sense of community.[57] They both represent an effort to criticize the rationalist and individualist tendencies of the modern contractarians, epitomized by Hobbes and Locke, who took a shallow view of man's social needs and his identity with a political culture. Indeed, Hume and especially Rousseau make extensive use of the 'organic metaphor' in portraying society. Hume was clearly reacting to the early liberal critique of tradition-bound corporate society, which had attacked royalist doctrine during the Great Revolution and depicted a new social compact made up of abstractly conceived, classless 'individuals' with no traditional ties or communal identity. With the Revolution well established, and the Whigs with it, Hume anticipates

---

[57] This point is made by Sheldon S. Wolin, 'Hume and Conservatism', in Livingston and King (eds), *Hume: A Re-evaluation*, pp. 254–5. Hume's emphasis on social interdependence is also discussed in Forbes, *Hume's Philosophical Politics*, p. 80. Rousseau's focus upon community, interdependence and shared patriotic sentiment is, of course, a pervasive theme of *Social Contract*.

Burke's 'new Whigs' by reviving a 'sense of society' and a renewed appreciation of gradual reform, stability and the grounding of values in custom and communal experience. Rousseau, on the other hand, depicts the abstract, free individual only to enable him to form a new, intimate social bond, making possible the recovery of true citizenship along classical rather than feudal lines.[58] All of Rousseau's writings condemn France for having no true citizens, no civic virtue, no genuine social sentiments. His emphasis upon the bonds of community has, in fact, been the object of vehement criticism. A measure of the vehemence of Rousseau's own criticism of the selfish egoism and ruthless ambition of the ruling classes is his view that some should 'be forced to be free' by the corporate power of the Sovereign.[59]

If Hume's sense of community is a good deal more calm and complacent than Rousseau's moral outrage, it is no less true that they both placed a higher value upon the community as a source of identity, moral character and genuine freedom than upon any abstract philosophical rights or natural faculties of individual man. The very substance of community, after all, was custom and sensibility. The great vices and virtues – love, war, courage, death, nobility – have less to do with reason than passion, a perception which led Hume to assert our inability to speak 'strictly and philosophically' unless we recognize that 'Reason is, and ought only to be the slave of passions, and can never pretend to any other office than to serve and obey them.'[60]

This introduces a second major contribution, which is more surprising to discover in Hume than in Rousseau. Each in his separate path prepared the way for romanticism. Their emphasis upon the priority of passion over reason in the texture of individual and social life is only one stream of this influence. This reversal of classical values, together with Rousseau's passionate eloquence – especially in *Emile* and his *Confessions* – constituted the seminal influence on the later romantic movement, but Hume's contribution was in some ways more profound, sweeping and permanent. Hume as well as Rousseau argued for the legitimacy of custom, sentiment and feeling, together with experience, as the actual ground of human knowledge. In this, they launched a powerful attack upon the primacy of reason in the moral and philosophical framework of

---

[58] See *Social Contract*, p. 175; and *Discourse on Political Economy* (1755), p. 127.
[59] *Social Contract*, p. 177.
[60] *Treatise*, II, 195. Rousseau echoed Hume by holding that knowledge 'is greatly indebted to the passions'; it is 'by the activity of the passions that our reason is improved.' *Origins of Inequality*, in Cole, *op. cit.*, p. 55.

the Enlightenment. Rousseau's writings were expressed in the romantic idiom of such a perspective, but Hume supplied the new philosophical system for it by demonstrating the weakness and limited scope of reason in the discovery of real knowledge.[61] In its place, exactly prefiguring the tenets of romanticism, Hume places impressions, sensation, memory and, most importantly, imagination. By the same token, his critique of causal inference struck down reason as the demonstrative and intuitive court of last resort for judging natural relationships and historical events. All values and moral standards, including justice itself, are artificial conventions, the product of a naturally inventive species.[62] Man is thus necessarily thrust back into his social and historical condition, the child of his times.

The elevation of custom, subjective experience and feeling as valid moral criteria, reinforced by Hume's critique of scholastic religion, unintentionally provided both a utilitarian and romantic rationale for the simplicity of faith, a view of religion that Rousseau gladly embraced.[63] Tradition, historical meaning and the importance of community became favourite themes of the English and German romantic movements at the turn of the nineteenth century, and the French in the 1820s. Rural life and the simple folk were idealized as models of social harmony and cultural purity. This yearning for the supposed goodness of small feudal communities may have been as much a romantic delusion as it was a distortion of Hume's own sense of historical realism. Yet it was certainly a manifestation of a renewed appreciation for custom and sensibility, unsullied by sophistication and – to use Voltaire's metaphor – the caustic acid of reason.

Despite their different approaches to the idea of a social contract, Hume and Rousseau stand on some common ground. It is significant that what they have in common is largely what made them original thinkers. Their critique of reason was a kind of iconoclasm, and it cut in both liberal and conservative directions. The *philosophes* and liberal contractarians on the left, as well as the *ancien régime* scholastics and Tories on the right, all believed that forms of government, law and political or religious institutions should pass the test of reason, and that truths – even the existence of God – could be established by rational

---

[61] Emotional intensity was not always foreign to Hume's writings, as is shown quite strikingly in his Conclusion to Book I of the *Treatise*, I, 548.
[62] *Treatise*, II, 258.
[63] *Social Contract*, pp. 275–6.

analysis. Hume and Rousseau, in their different manners, rejected this, and spoke of habit, custom, belief, sentiment and social interdependence as the foundation for institutions and the highest moral ideals. But they did not themselves, Hume less even than Rousseau, colour their own writings with the revived dogmatism and providential historicism which developed in the conservative reaction following the French Revolution.[64]

---

[64] Wolin, 'Hume and Conservatism', *op. cit.*, pp. 240–1, discusses this important distinction; see also Bongie, *David Hume, op. cit.*, pp. vi–xvii.

Hegel and Nietzsche

Wayne Hudson

Hegel (1770-1831) and Nietzsche (1844-1900) were nineteenth-century German philosophers who acquired notorious reputations, especially during the Nazi period, as enemies of liberal democracy. Modern scholarship and more accurate translations have made it clear that Hegel was not a reactionary philosopher of the absolute state, an authoritarian apologist for Prussia who can legitimately be regarded as a glorifier of the German militarism and nationalism which culminated in the catastrophe of the Nazi period; that Nietzsche was not a proto-fascist philosopher of irrationalism, an amoral advocate of racism, violence and war whose eugenic politics accelerated and helped justify malevolent developments on a tragic scale. Nonetheless, the fact remains that Hegel and Nietzsche are difficult thinkers to interpret and scholars continue to be divided over the exact nature and purport of their views. In a comparative context, therefore, it may be useful to concentrate first on the main differences in their approaches, and second on the extent to which they can be read as thinkers who raise problems with which contemporary political philosophy has still to come to terms, without entering into the *quaestiones disputatae* of Hegel–Nietzsche scholarship (including problems of periodization) or attempting a definitive exegesis of their respective philosophical systems.

Hegel is widely regarded as the greatest philosopher of the modern state, whereas Nietzsche remains a more peripheral figure who is often characterized as an apolitical thinker[1], albeit a thinker whose apolitical

---

[1] On the older debate about the nature of Hegel's political philosophy, see W. Kaufmann (ed.), *Hegel's Political Philosophy*, Atherton Press, New York, 1970. And on more recent themes, see Z. A. Pelczynski (ed.), *Hegel's Political Philosophy: Problems and Perspectives*, Cambridge University Press, 1971; S. Avineri, *Hegel's Theory of the Modern State*, Cambridge University Press, 1972; R. Plant, *Hegel*, Allen & Unwin, London, 1973; Charles Taylor, *Hegel*, Cambridge University Press, 1977, and *Hegel*

views have political consequences.[2] Both interpretations may be misleading. Hegel was a professional philosopher who developed a metaphysical system unparalleled in its range and complexity since Aristotle, and it is not only a mistake to isolate his political philosophy from his metaphysical system, of which it formed a part: it is also necessary to perceive the politics of his metaphysical system. Similarly, Nietzsche was only an apolitical thinker in the sense that he counselled detachment from the day-to-day politics of his time. In another, and perhaps more important sense, he was an essentially political thinker who developed a politics of philosophy intended to extend to 'A New Interpretation of the Universe'.

Both Hegel and Nietzsche were *metapolitical thinkers* who brought maximalist values and generalized philosophical visions to political questions, and it is ironic that modern scholars have spoken of Hegel's

---

and Modern Society, Cambridge University Press, 1979. For a different point of view, see G. A. Kelly, *Hegel's Retreat from Eleusis Studies in Political Thought*, Princeton University Press, 1978; and, more generally, A. MacIntyre (ed.), *Hegel: A Collection of Critical Essays*, Doubleday, New York, 1972; H. S . Harris, *Hegel's Development Towards the Sunlight 1770-1801*, Clarendon Press, Oxford, 1972; and J. N. Shklar, *Freedom and Independence: A Study of the Political Ideas of Hegel's Phenomenology of Mind*, Cambridge University Press, 1976. In German, see H. Ottmann, *Individuum und Gemeinschaft bei Hegel*, Vol. I, *Hegel im Spiegel der Interpretationen*, Walter de Gruyter, Berlin/New York, 1977. For an analysis of the history of Hegel interpretation, see J. Ritter's classic study, *Hegel und die französische Revolution*, Westdeutscher Verlag, Köln/Opladen, 1957; and M. Theunissen, *Hegels Lehre vom absoluten Geist als theologisch-politischer Traktat*, Walter de Gruyter, Berlin, 1970. See also *Hegel-Studien*, XI (1974): Kolloquium IV *Politische Philosophie*, 305-439, and Kolloquium, V *Marxistische Theorie*, 443-502.
On Nietzsche, see Walter Kaufmann's existentialist, almost Socratic Nietzsche, in his *Nietzsche: Philosopher, Psychologist, Antichrist*, 4th edn., Princeton University Press, 1974; and for a critical rejoinder, W. J. Dannhauser, *Nietzsche's View of Socrates*, Cornell University Press, Ithaca/London, 1974. See also R. J. Hollingdale, *Nietzsche*, Routledge & Kegan Paul, London/Boston, 1973; Robert Solomon (ed.), *Nietzsche: A Collection of Critical Essays*, Anchor Press/Doubleday, New York, 1973; T. B. Strong, *Friedrich Nietzsche and the Politics of Transfiguration*, University of California Press, Berkeley, 1975; J. P. Stern, *A Study of Nietzsche*, Cambridge University Press, 1979; B. Magnus, *Nietzsche's Existential Imperative*, Indiana University Press, Bloomington/London, 1978; M. Pasley (ed.), *Nietzsche: Imagery and Thought A Collection of Essays*, Methuen, London, 1978. In French, see J. Granier, *Le problème de la vérité dans la philosophie de Nietzsche*, Editions du Seuil, Paris, 1966; G. Deleuze, *Nietzsche et la Philosophie*, Presses Universitaires de France, Paris, 1962; and P. Klossowski, *Nietzsche et le cercle vicieux*, Mercure de France, Paris, 1969.

[2] For example, by K.-H. Ilting, 'The Structure of Hegel's *Philosophy of Right*' in Z. A. Pelczynski, *Hegel's Political Philosophy, op. cit.*, p. 90, and W. Kaufmann, *Nietzsche: Philosopher, Psychologist, Antichrist, op. cit.*, p. 412.

attempt at 'the transfiguration of politics' and of Nietzsche's 'politics of transfiguration' without seeking to bring their views into systematic conjuncture.[3] Both Hegel and Nietzsche implicitly challenged the relationship between 'political reason' and 'metaphysics' on which liberalism rests.[4] Liberalism bases its political theory on an occlusion of metaphysical questions as not directly relevant to problems of political philosophy. For liberals, 'reason' can guide men to the best set of political arrangements without their first needing to settle such grandiose questions as the meaning of life or the ultimate nature of the ontological order. But this view is open to challenge on the grounds, first, that the categories employed by 'political reason', as liberals interpret it, originate in earlier metaphysical systems; and second, that 'political reason', as liberals interpret it, is itself an implicit metaphysics with constitutive effects. As metapolitical thinkers, Hegel and Nietzsche were aware that there were dangers in accepting restricted conceptions of the political which embody characteristics of the political and social order to be assessed; they were also extremely critical of the abstract rationalism fathered by modern society and offered as its theoretical defence. Hegel saw clearly the loss of theoretical power implicit in any rationalism that separated reason from the world and from the objective processuality at work in it. He distinguished between 'understanding' (*Verstand*), which grasps things in isolation from the totality of relations of which they are a part and without regard to the underlying reason attempting to realize itself through them, and 'reason' (*Vernunft*), which grasped the thing in the totality of its mediations and immanent processuality.[5] For Hegel an adequate politics had to be based on a 'concrete' rationalism that grasped the processuality at work in political forms and recognized that reason was not simply a faculty of mind but something increasingly embodied in the world. He responded to the challenges of his time by developing a

---

[3] See R. Plant, *Hegel, op. cit.*, chapter 4, and T. B. Strong, *Friedrich Nietzsche and the Politics of Transfiguration, op. cit.*, especially chapter 7. For comparisons between Hegel and Nietzsche, see R. F. Beerling, 'Hegel und Nietzsche', *Hegel-Studien* I, Bonn, 1961, pp. 229–46, and Murray Greene, 'Hegel's "Unhappy Consciousness" and Nietzsche's "Slave Morality",' in D. E. Christensen (ed.), *Hegel and the Philosophy of Religion*, The Wofford Symposium, Nijhoff, The Hague, 1970, pp. 125-41.
[4] For background material on the relation between politics and metaphysics, see J. Ritter, *Metaphysik und Politik Studien zu Aristoteles und Hegel*, Suhrkamp, Frankfurt a.M., 1969; and M. Riedel, *Metaphysik und Metapolitik Studien zu Aristoteles und zur politische Sprache der neuzeitlichen Philosophie*, Suhrkamp, Frankfurt a.M., 1975.
[5] Hegel, *Logic* (Part 1 of the *Encyclopaedia of the Philosophical Sciences*), 1830, translated by W. Wallace, 3rd edn, Clarendon Press, Oxford, 1975, s. 45, 79–82 and notes to s.45.

powerful metaphysical system, based on rational necessity, which was designed to show that what was rational was actual (*wirklich*) and what was actual was rational.[6] This system was a form of absolute idealism for which the infinite was the truth of the finite and Spirit (*Geist*) posited the universe as its embodiment.

Nietzsche adopted a very different strategy. Where Hegel attempted to raise 'understanding' to a higher power capable of grasping the totality, Nietzsche attempted to go behind 'understanding': to show that 'reason' had always to be located in life and in power relations that furthered a form of life. Nietzsche rejected Hegel's all-encompassing ontological rationalism, for which rational concepts were present in the world and not only in thinking. He denied that there was any 'pure' or universal reason and argued that all the categories of logic were fictions that simplified and distorted reality for political ends.[7] Unlike Hegel, Nietzsche taught that 'life is, and is only, the will to power'.[8] Scholars remain divided about exactly what Nietzsche meant by 'the will to power', just as they are divided over what Hegel meant by Spirit (*Geist*), but however the doctrine is interpreted – as a psychological insight, an imperative to self transcendence, as a cosmological doctrine or as a 'last will' after which men would achieve a redemption beyond power orientated willing – its initial implications are clear. Nietzsche argued that it was necessary to go behind all human rationalizations and conscious purposes to an underlying attempt to assert power and domination over others. For Nietzsche the political was not so much a possible object to which reason could address itself as the underlying relation by which reason was constituted, and there was a vitalist politics of instinct and need that was more fundamental than the politics of institutions and economic interests that liberalism attempted to theorize.

Both Hegel and Nietzsche, from their very different standpoints, were critics of modern society and its constricted conception of the political, and both gained perspective on the ills of modern society from a comparison with classical Greece. Hegel saw in Greece the community and social integration lacking in modern society, while Nietzsche

---

[6] Hegel, *Philosophy of Right* (1821), translated by T. M. Knox, Oxford University Press, 1967, p. 10. Both 'actual' (*wirklich*) and 'actuality' (*Wirklichkeit*) are terms of art; the 'actual' is the unity of essence and existence, not the given at hand.

[7] Nietzsche, *Beyond Good and Evil* (1886), translated by R. J. Hollingdale, Penguin, Harmondsworth, 1973, s. 3 and 4.

[8] Nietzsche, *The Will to Power* (1901, 1904), translated by W. Kaufmann and R. J. Hollingdale, Random House, New York, 1967, s. 254 (revised transl.).

observed that the classical *agon**, which refracted the desire to dominate in a healthy manner, had no equivalent in modern politics, which was characterized by an elision of a genuine political space and by the use of the political sphere to pursue private ends.[9]

Both came to realize that modern conditions precluded any revival of the classical *polis* and demanded solutions that were essentially new, although the maximalism that both men associated with the highest achievements of the Greeks added to the metapolitical colouring of their subsequent views. Hegel responded to modern society by extending the definition of the political to include a more positive concept of 'the state'. He rejected the traditional theory of the state as the legitimate expression of self-interest and drew a famous distinction between *civil society*, or the realm in which men pursued their self-interest and treated others as means to their ends, and the state in the true sense or the realm of universality in which men pursued rational and consciously adopted ends present to consciousness.[10] Hegel accepted the necessity for civil society and emphasized that it involved an expansion of self-consciousness which made possible the higher articulation of the true state. Nonetheless, Hegel saw that civil society was a realm of atomism and egoism, that it tended to increasing specialization, an ever accelerating expansion of capital and the exploitation of overseas markets, and that the ideals of liberty, equality and fraternity could never be fully realized in a society that allowed civil society to operate unchecked without a reciprocal relation to the state, understood as something more than a reflection of civil society in the political sphere.[11]

Hegel's response was to develop a philosophy of the state designed to overcome both the use of the state as an instrument of arbitrary power and the liberal separation of the state and society which allowed the state to become an instrument for the pursuit of private ends. He attempted to rethink the idea of the state from the standpoint of a concrete rationalism which developed and articulated the rationality developing in the forms of life, legal arrangements, customs, institutions and social classes at

---

* In ancient Greek drama, *agon* was the name of a debate or argument between two characters, each of whom was supported by a chorus. In every kind of literature, *agon* refers to conflict and is a root appearing in such words as antagonist and protagonist. (Ed.)

[9] See J. Glenn Gray, *Hegel and Greek Thought* (1941), Harper Torchbooks, New York, 1968; and T. B. Strong, *Nietzsche and the Politics of Transfiguration, op. cit.*, chapters VI and VII.
[10] Hegel, *Philosophy of Right, op. cit.*, Part III, ii and iii.
[11] *Cf.* S. Avineri, *Hegel's Theory of the Modern State, op. cit.*, chapter 7.

hand. Hegel sought to show that the modern ideals of freedom, rationality and self-consciousness could be reconciled in a political community based on reason (*Vernunft*). He argued that the freedom of the individual and his rational self-consciousness could only be fully expressed in a community that was an *ethical* as well as political community: in a community based on *Sittlichkeit* or a shared ethical life embodied in social customs and institutions.[12] He rejected the concept of absolute freedom, or freedom from external restraint, in favour of a concept of situated freedom defined by rights and duties or obligations to the wider community of which the individual was a part.

Hegel set out his political philosophy in his *Philosophy of Right* (1821) and dealt with the family, civil society and the state as three departments of a single ethical life ascending in the universality of their ethical concerns.[13] Unlike Nietzsche, he made specific constitutional and legal arrangements central to his philosophical politics. The main features of his approach are well known – his stress on a constitutional monarchy which would symbolize subjectivity, on a bureaucracy which would be the universal class devoting itself to the implementation of universal rationality in the public sphere, on the security of property, on the rights to freedom of conscience, freedom of information and free speech, and on representation, not by direct universal suffrage, but by an assembly of 'estates' (*Stände*) in which men would be represented through the groups, voluntary associations or professional bodies to which they belonged. So far from being an advocate of totalitarianism, Hegel was a theorist of pluralism and differentiation, who attempted to combine the greatest possible degree of diversity at the appropriate level of mediation with the unity proper to an integrated community. Hence Hegel argued for a fully articulated, internally differentiated state, to which different estates with different levels of consciousness corresponding to their socio-economic roles different relations to power, were essential if political life was to be mediated in a way that preserved self-subsistent particularities instead of subjecting them to an all-powerful central bureaucracy or a wholly abstract general will.[14]

---

[12] *Cf.* Z. A. Pelczynski, 'The Hegelian Conception of the State', in Z. A. Pelczynski (ed.), *Hegel's Political Philosophy, op. cit.*, pp. 1–29; and C. Taylor, *Hegel, op. cit.*, chapters XIV, XV and XVI.
[13] For a modern discussion of Hegel's *Philosophy of Right*, see M. Riedel, *Studien zu Hegels Rechtsphilosophie*, Suhrkamp, Frankfurt a.M., 1970.
[14] *Cf.* S. Avineri, *Hegel's Theory of the Modern State, op. cit.*, chapters 5, 6, 7, and 8.

Nonetheless, Hegel's conception of the state was not a liberal one. Hegel held that the individual was an inadequate vehicle for the realization of Spirit (*Geist*) and his state was to be an organicist integrated *order*, not 'a heap' of isolated individuals, but the system of social integration through which the individual would know and recognize himself as Spirit (*Geist*).[15] In opposition to the liberal ideal of a political order that would allow men to develop their talents and pursue their legitimate interests, Hegel argued that it was necessary to supplement such a realm (civil society) with a further realm in which the individual would know and recognize the universal: a realm of 'concrete freedom' in which the freedom of the individual would become 'concrete' (that is, mediated) freedom:

> The state is the actuality of concrete freedom. But concrete freedom consists in this, that personal individuality and its particular interests not only achieve their complete development and gain explicit recognition for their right (as they do in the sphere of the family and civil society) but . . . they also pass over of their own accord into the interest of the universal, and . . . know and will the universal.[16]

Hegel's philosophy of the state was not only a therapy for the politics of civil society through which the atomism and egoism of civil society would be transcended: it was also central to the politics of his metaphysical system. Hegel had both a *philosophical politics* and a *politics of philosophy* but the nature of Hegel's metaphysical system meant that for Hegel these converged.[17] For Hegel the realized state was not simply an ideal but a rational teleological structure developing in the processuality of history itself, grounded in rational necessity. It was not merely a human political arrangement but a higher phase of the cosmic process of the embodiment of Spirit (*Geist*). Hence when Hegel argued that the realized state was the actuality (*Wirklichkeit*) of the ethical Idea: the substantial will knowing and thinking itself, an order in which men would consciously know and will the universal and in which the universal would be embodied in the content of political life[18], he was not merely characterizing the state, but legitimizing it on metaphysical grounds as a realization of the teleology of

---

[15] Hegel, *Die Vernunft in der Geschichte*, edited by J. Hoffmeister, Felix Meiner, Hamburg, 1955, s. 112.
[16] *Philosophy of Right, op. cit.*, s. 260.
[17] *Philosophical politics* – a politics inspired by philosophical ideas and/or intended to realize philosophical ends. *Politics of philosophy* – political aims furthered by advancing particular philosophical ideas.
[18] *Philosophy of Right, op. cit.*, s. 257.

the world process. For Hegel the state was 'divine', something bound up with God's 'way through the world'[19], and needed to be recognized and accepted as such, in accordance with his general programme of reconciling men to God's way in ruling the world through bringing them to a recognition of reason (*Vernunft*) as the rose in the cross of the present.[20] To this extent, Hegel's philosophy of the state was part of his politics of philosophy, which aimed to transfigure men's understanding of and reconciliation to their life in the universe. So far from accepting the liberal separation of political reason and 'metaphysics', Hegel developed a theory in which the political came to have 'metaphysical' status.

Nietzsche, in contrast, developed no political philosophy as such, partly because his philosophy subverted the grounds on which such a political philosophy could be constructed. Like Hegel, Nietzsche criticized the atomism of modern society which made men so many 'isolates' and observed that he lived in a period of 'atomistic chaos'.[21] Similarly, he saw that the division of labour tended to produce imperfect human beings who over-developed one aspect of their personalities. He also rejected a society based solely on the maximalization of wealth and production. Unlike Hegel, Nietzsche believed that the political problems facing modern humanity were too serious to allow any contemporary organizational solution. Nietzsche held that the life of modern Europe was 'sick' and needed to be 'healed'.[22] He claimed that Western civilization as it had developed since the Greeks was 'decadent' and coming to an end. He assessed political and social institutions according to whether they refracted and strengthened men's instincts or allowed them to atrophy and decline, and held that the instincts of modern Europeans had declined to such an extent that they preferred arrangements which tended to the dissolution of all political and social organization.[23] Moreover this decline of 'instincts', accelerated by liberal institutions that served to further weaken the will to power, had reached the point where European humanity lacked all the instincts out of which healthy institutions could be built:

---

[19] *Philosophy of Right, op. cit.*, addenda to s. 258 (revised transl.).
[20] *Ibid.*, p. 12.
[21] Nietzsche, *Untimely Meditations* (1873), translated by A. Collins as *Thoughts Out of Season*, Foulis, Edinburgh, 1909, III 'Schopenhauer As Educator', IV.
[22] *Ibid.*, II 'The Use and Abuse of History', X.
[23] Nietzsche, *Twilight of the Idols* (1889), translated by R. J. Hollingdale, Penguin, Harmondsworth, 1969, 'Expeditions of an Untimely Man', s. 39.

For institutions to exist there must exist the kind of will, instinct, imperative which is anti-liberal to the point of malice: the will to tradition, to authority, to centuries-long responsibility, to *solidarity* between succeeding generations backwards and forwards *in infinitum*.[24]

Because European humanity was no longer material from which a society in the true sense could be built, Nietzsche saw no solution in abstract attempts to 'change society'. Even if new institutions could be devised, they would not take proper effect as long as they were inhabited by instinctually defective humanity. Nietzsche's political vitalism led him to reject the modern attempt to understand politics in terms of 'society', construed as a system of social arrangements which could be isolated from the pathology of present humanity and from the political valuation system operative within it. He saw that such a perspective tended to preserve the problem by displacing it to the level of 'society', whereas the pathology to be overcome was present in the political and social theorists themselves and in their theories which often took the form of extensions or reversals of the existing order, rather than the *creation* of a genuine alternative to it. This was the basis of Nietzsche's attacks on the socialists whose psychology of resentment reflected the order they attacked, and who sought to continue slave morality society in a different institutional form.[25]

Nietzsche saw Hegel, and the tendencies popularly associated with him, as one of the obstacles in the way of a politics of philosophy that would help to overcome this 'decline'. He rejected the premises on which Hegel's political philosophy was based. Nietzsche distrusted all dialectics and decoded 'political reason' in terms of what furthered 'life'. He rejected any form of political rationalism and denied that a healthy society could be based on self-conscious rationalism. Where Hegel interpreted history as a teleological process towards the ever-increasing realization of freedom and self-consciousness, Nietzsche rejected the modern concept of progress as a false idea.[26] He denied that history could be understood as a causally determined rational process which developed to higher and higher stages. He rejected any teleological model of history and saw history, not as an objectivist process, but as a drama lived under

---

[24] *Ibid*.
[25] Nietzsche, *Human, All Too Human* (1878) translated by H. Zimmern, Foulis, Edinburgh/London, 1911, Part I, s. 473, *Beyond Good and Evil*, s. 202.
[26] Nietzsche, *The Anti-Christ* (1895), translated by R. J. Hollingdale, Penguin, Harmondsworth, 1969, s. 4. For an extended discussion, see H. P. Balmer, *Freiheit statt Teleologie, Ein Grundgedanke von Nietzsche*, Verlag Karl Alber, Freiburg/München, 1977.

the conditioning of a specific geneology which was only one possible form of human self-invention. Moreover, he opposed Hegel's theological conception of history and denied that history exhibited a quasi-logical teleological development based on rational necessity or that it could be interpreted as moral or just.[27] He also denounced Hegel for implanting in men's minds a worship of the power of history which terminated in an idolatory of the actual, and accused him of contributing to the modern European malady of 'an excess of history' which led to the rule of history over life and undermined the veil of illusion necessary for greatness.[28] Where Hegel believed that men came through the dialectical process of history to a higher realization and consciousness of the truth, Nietzsche insisted that untruth and illusion were conditions of life. He held that human beings needed to live within the limits of a horizon they believed to be absolute, and saw the 'historical sickness' afflicting modern Europe as a threat to the untruth and illusion without which men could not live:

> The unrestrained historical sense, pushed to its logical extremes, uproots the future, because it destroys illusions and robs existing things of the only atmosphere in which they can live . . . a thing can only live through a pious illusion. For man is creative only through love and in the shadow of love's illusions, only through the unconditional belief in perfection and righteousness. Everything that forces a man to be no longer unconditional in his love, cuts at the root of his strength.[29]

To overcome this malady of history Nietzsche argued for an 'unhistorical' attitude which forgot those parts of the past that did not further the current needs of humanity and a 'supra-historical' attitude which de-linearized human life by relating it to 'eternity'.[30]

Similarly, where Hegel assimilated the Enlightenment's belief in equality and universality and accommodated them in a hierarchical, qualitatively differentiated order, Nietzsche argued that both beliefs were harmful illusions which extended the decadence into which Western civilization had fallen. Nietzsche denied that men were equal in powers, capacities or needs. He rejected the modern doctrine of equality as unjust and as motivated by comparison and resentment.[31] In place of 'democracy', 'equal rights', 'compassion for those who suffer' and 'the happiness of the herd' which led to the dominance of 'the herd' and the

---

[27] *Untimely Meditations*, II 'The Use and Abuse of History', III.
[28] *Ibid.*, VIII, VII.
[29] *Ibid.*, VII.
[30] *Ibid.*, X.
[31] *Beyond Good and Evil*, s. 203.

'dwarfing' of human beings, Nietzsche argued for vitalist aristocracy: for the view that humanity is hierarchically differentiated into creative individuals who originate the achievements of culture and civilization and 'the mass' who are weak, incapable of creativity and prone to propagate their own powerlessness as a moral code. Consistent with this, Nietzsche rejected universality as a goal and insisted that the goal should be the creative individual and not 'the herd', and that the creation of great individuals required that the qualities of the elite not be extended to all.[32] He saw the idea that all men should live in the same way and be judged by the same standards as decadent. Moreover, he passed the same judgement on the modern idea of freedom and set up the counter ideal of the free man as a warrior whose will to self-responsibility did not imply any comparison with men generally or any ideal of a situation in which all men would be similarly free.[33] Finally, Nietzsche rejected Hegel's philosophy of the modern state outright. Confronted with the modern nationalistic state (admittedly not 'the state' as Hegel envisaged it), the '*coldest*' of cold monsters', he called for as little 'state' as possible.[34] Unlike Hegel, he did not believe that the modern state, however differentiated, could provide an antidote to the mediocrity and atomism of civil society. Where Hegel held that the egoism and self-seeking of civil society could be transcended in the universality of the state, Nietzsche, like Marx, held that the universality of the state itself became a means to the realization of self-seeking political ends. Similarly, where Hegel believed that the state could mitigate some of the harshest features of civil society by guaranteeing a minimum standard of living for all and countering the worst effects of economic inequality through taxation, Nietzsche denounced the idea of a state that would care for the welfare of its citizens as a manifestation of decadence which would deprive men of their inner worth.[35]

Unlike Hegel, Nietzsche separated his politics of philosophy from his philosophical politics. Nietzsche based his politics of philosophy on an analysis of the present which included both a geneology of the pathology which the present revealed and projections about likely future developments. Unlike Hegel, he held that the way out of this pathology required creationist interventions and placed his hope in 'new

---

[32] *Human, All Too Human*, Part I, s. 25.
[33] *Twilight of the Idols*, 'Expeditions of an Untimely Man', s. 38.
[34] Nietzsche, *Dawn* (1881), translated by J. Volz as *The Dawn of Day*, Fisher Unwin, London, 1903, s. 179.
[35] *Ibid*.

philosophers' who would subvert existing valuations, teach men that the future of humanity depended on changing human willing, and *create new values*:

> We, who have a different faith – we, to whom the democratic movement is not merely a form assumed by political organization in decay but also a form assumed by man in decay, that is to say in diminishment, in process of becoming mediocre and losing his value: whither must *we* direct our hopes? – Towards *new philosophers*, we have no other choice; towards spirits strong and original enough to make a start on antithetical evulations and to revalue and reverse 'eternal values'; towards heralds and forerunners, towards men of the future who in the present knot together the constraint which compels the will of millennia on to *new* paths. To teach man the future of man as his *will*, as dependent on a human will, and to prepare for great enterprises and collective experiments in discipline and breeding so as to make an end of that gruesome dominion of chance and nonsense that has hitherto been called 'history'.[36]

Nietzsche saw himself as one of the first of such 'forerunners' who would order an objectively meaningless world and legislate an *artistic* scheme of things as they *shall* be instead of bowing to an externally conferred objectivist order of things.[37] Nietzsche's famous doctrine of the 'eternal return' can be seen in this context: as a political doctrine designed to transform present humanity and its willing.[38] Nietzsche argued that man, in the sense of humanity up till now, was something that had to be surpassed.[39] It could be surpassed because human nature had changed over the centuries and could change again in the future if men acquired a second nautre which, when internalized, operated as a first nature.[40] To bring such a development about, men would need to embody new

---

[36] *Beyond Good and Evil*, s. 203.
[37] *Ibid.*, s. 211. For controversial interpretations of Nietzsche's philosophical views, see M. Heidegger's study, *Nietzsche* (2 vols.), Neske, Pfüllingen, 1961–62; and the chapter from *Holzwege*, Vittorio Klostermann, Frankfurt, 1950, 'The Word of Nietzsche: "God Is Dead"' in M. Heidegger, *The Question Concerning Technology and Other Essays*, translated by W. Lovitt, Harper Colophon Books, New York, 1977, pp. 53–112; and Karl Jasper's *Nietzsche: An Introduction to the Understanding of his Philosophical Activity* (1935), translated by C. F. Wallraff and F. J. Schmitz, Henry Regnery, Chicago, 1969, especially Book II, chapter 4: 'Great Politics'. For a comparison, see R. L. Howey, *Heidegger and Jaspers on Nietzsche: A Critical Examination of Heidegger's and Jasper's Interpretations of Nietzsche*, Nijhoff, The Hague, 1973.
[38] For two very different interpretations of Nietzsche's 'eternal return', see J. Stambaugh, *Nietzsche's Thought of Eternal Return*, Johns Hopkins University Press, Baltimore, 1972; and T. B. Strong, *Friedrich Nietzsche and the Politics of Transfiguration, op. cit.*, chapter IX.
[39] Nietzsche, *Thus Spoke Zarathustra* (1883, 1884, 1892), translated by R. J. Hollingdale, Penguin, Harmondsworth, 1961, Prologue, s. 3.
[40] *Untimely Meditations*, II 'The Use and Abuse of History', s. II.

knowledge until it became 'instinctive'. They would need to internalize new ideals and habits, including a new understanding of time. What was needed, Nietzsche argued, was a doctrine strong enough to have the effect of *breeding*.[41] For Nietzsche, this doctrine was the doctrine of the eternal return. Nietzsche held that the doctrine that everything returns eternally would change those who incarnated it by requiring and calling forth a stronger form of will; he also held that the doctrine would have a selective effect since 'the weak' would be unable to bear it. Moreover, he made the incarnation of this doctrine basic to the coming of the 'over-man' (*Übermensch*) with new instincts and habits, a Dionysian world affirming man who would love his fate (*amor fati*) and say 'yes' to his life in the world.[42] For Nietzsche the need for such a doctrine was made more urgent by the advent of nihilism.

Unlike Hegel, Nietzsche interpreted the history of Western civilization since the Peloponnesian wars as the rise and growth of nihilism. A time had come, he believed, in which the highest values were devaluating themselves and in which men would increasingly find the world objectively meaningless.[43] As long as men were governed by the will to truth, they would increasingly find no truth or value anywhere. Nietzsche, however, saw that it would be possible to overcome 'the will to truth' which lay at the base of Western civilization by completing nihilism in a way that derived a therapy from thinking through its consequences. Once it was accepted that there was no externally conferred objectivist meaning of life, but only perspectival and false schemas alleged to be true because they served human needs, the entire objectivist world conception could be undermined. Given that it was impossible for men to ever know 'reality' as it was because all human knowledge was perspectival, Nietzsche saw that it was possible to understand the work of interpreting the nature of reality as a political task. He saw that radical scepticism, especially a scepticism directed to the natural sciences with their evasion of basic causality[44], could release sovereign individuals from their servitude to the still 'theistic', ascetic ideal of objective truth which had outlived the 'death of God', and emphasized that men were under no obligation to accept as absolute an ontological schema which prevented them from realizing their highest

---

[41] *The Will to Power*, s. 862.
[42] Nietzsche, *Ecce Homo* (1888), translated by R. J. Hollingdale, Penguin, Harmondsworth, 1979, 'Thus Spoke Zarathustra', s. 6.
[43] *The Will to Power*, Book I, 'European Nihilism'.
[44] *Cf*, *Twilight of the Idols*, 'The Four Great Errors', 3.

potential. Here Nietzsche's views go to the central question of the scope of the political. For Nietzsche, politics should not confine its scope to practical questions such as the distribution of power or the organization of society. Instead, Nietzsche saw that there was a primacy of the politics of how men interpret life that determined the nature of the project under which more detailed political decisions took effect. Nietzsche believed passionately that the time had come for 'free spirits' who rejected every attempt to derive value and purpose from an inherently meaningful externally existing ontological order and sought to determine their will out of themselves. He envisaged not only the freedom of the masterful individual from society and the mediocrity of 'the mass', but men who made their own truth and values with an autonomy which no traditional world conception allowed: for sovereign individuals who imposed a meaningful aesthetic order on the world and affirmed this order in the full knowledge that it was an assertion of their will to power.[45]

In the same way, Nietzsche saw that a consistent moral nihilism could open the way for an ethics in which nihilism would be overcome. Once it was realized that there was no objective morality and that all moral evaluations were a form of politics, then it was possible to envisage a transvaluation (*Umwertung*) of all received values[46], based on the need for values which made men strong and which promoted a healthy instinctual life. Nietzsche's central insight was that men had come to mutilate their own natures by valuing the wrong things. Modern European humanity had become decadent, sickly and weak under the influence of 'morality', which made virtues out of the decline of instincts and condemned the qualities that were preconditions of a healthy life.[47] Moreover Nietzsche linked this development with the triumph of 'slave morality' or the negative morality of the weak, the prescriptive 'guilt' morality of 'good and evil' based on comparison and resentment, over 'master morality' or the positive morality of the strong, the aristocratic morality of 'good and bad' held by assertive men who were conscious that they determined values and felt no 'guilt' or 'consideration'.[48] Unlike Hegel, who saw the dialectical reversal in the relations between lord and

---

[45] *Beyond Good and Evil*, Part 2, 'The Free Spirit'.
[46] For a sophisticated discussion of Nietzsche's philosophy of values, see B. Bueb, *Nietzsches Kritik der praktischen Vernunft*, Ernst Klett Verlag, Stuttgart, 1970.
[47] *Beyond Good and Evil*, Part 5, 'On the Natural History of Morals'; and *Twilight of the Idols*, 'Morality as Anti-Nature'.
[48] *Beyond Good and Evil*, s. 260; and *The Geneology of Morals* (1887), translated by W. Kaufmann, Vintage Books, New York, 1967, s. 10 and 11.

bondsman as a moment in the history of consciousness, Nietzsche held that the triumph of 'slave morality' over 'master morality' since classical times had corrupted the whole of modern society. Nietzsche's solution was to annihilate 'morality': to reject the whole valuation pattern of guilt and to go 'beyond good and evil'. Because the supreme values of the present civilization were decadent values and encouraged men to admire and prefer what was harmful to 'life', it was necessary to engage in a work of destruction: the destruction of all received values and, in particular, the unmasking of Christian morality with its ethic of self-abasement.[49] In place of such 'decadent' values, Nietzsche sought to set up the counter-ideal of coming to oneself, of willing a self in order to become a self. He preached the new values of egoism and heroism, of 'war' rather than peace, of 'enmity' rather than compassion, of the healthy expression of the slandered instincts, of a new 'innocence' beyond the moral point of view, and envisaged a future extra-moral existence in which the value of an action would depend on what was unintentional in it.[50]

For Nietzsche, such a politics of philosophy was a necessary prelude to a future philosophical politics. Like Hegel, he accepted the ideal of a unity of philosophy and politics. Unlike Hegel, Nietzsche postponed a philosophical politics to the future. For Hegel, the future was not the proper concern of the philosopher, although Hegel himself made prescient remarks about future developments, including the crucial role of the United States. Nietzsche, in contrast, like the Young Hegelians, made the future a central philosophical concern. Nietzsche rejected modern politics as small politics concerned with unworthy ends and counselled non-involvement because the individual would inevitably be caught up in the mediocrity of 'the mass' and come to define his success by the herd's standards.[51] But he did not reject political involvement in principle. Instead, he looked forward to the 'great politics' which would become possible in the future, to a renewal of 'strong' politics on a global scale.[52] Nietzsche held that the democratization of Europe, including the abolition of the individual nations and the emergence of a mixed race of 'Europeans', would terminate in a period of great wars in which there would be a fight for men's minds and for the domination of the earth. He held that such a development, although it would make things worse at first, could also create the conditions for a breakthrough by exploding the

---

[49] *The Anti-Christ*, especially s. 6; and *Ecce Homo*, 'Why I Am A Destiny', 7.
[50] *Beyond Good and Evil*, 'What is Noble?' and s. 32.
[51] Cf. *ibid.*, s. 199.
[52] *Ibid.*, s. 208.

power structures of slave morality society.[53] Hence he welcomed such a development and argued that the levelling process taking place in Europe should be accelerated in order to bring such a development about.

In a similar apocalyptical vein, Nietzsche foresaw the emergence of a higher species of men, 'the lords of the earth', a class of aristocratic legislators who would use 'democratic' Europe to take the destiny of the world into their hands and to work on men as artists.[54] For the first time it would become possible to consciously breed the higher man, who previously had appeared in all cultures as an exception; an age of collective experiments involving whole portions of mankind could begin. In this context, Nietzsche envisaged the end of universal suffrage and a future philosophical politics based on aristocratic vitalism, a renewed 'order of rank', even perhaps a new caste system including a form of 'slavery'.[55] Granted that Nietzsche's projections were fragmentary and incomplete, unlike Hegel, he envisaged *a radical future transformation of the context and content of politics*, to which traditional political and social theories would be inappropriate.[56]

In a contemporary context Hegel and Nietzsche are important thinkers precisely because they are demanding and radically challenge our deepest assumptions, not least about philosophical method. Both were thinkers who opposed doctrines that triumphed despite them. Both were mistaken in many of their immediate projections and failed to provide an adequate appraisal of either nationalism or the proletariat. Where Hegel was an early critic of the modern industrial system with a remarkable understanding of the importance of production, labour and industry, Nietzsche compensated in part for his relative neglect of industry and political economy with outstanding psychological insights and an independent ethical outlook that challenged the confusion of moralism with political and social theory. Nevertheless, both Hegel and Nietzsche were dangerous thinkers who propounded doctrines liable to abuse and who neglected moral and political fallibilism at their peril; it is important to approach their ideas critically, to perceive their inadequacies and omissions, and to theorize the methodological implications of their failures. Neither Hegel nor Nietzsche developed an adequate philosophical anthropology or a coherent theory of action.

---

[53] *Ecce Homo*, 'Why I Am A Destiny', 1.
[54] *The Will to Power*, s. 960, (revised transl.).
[55] *Ibid.*, Book 4.
[56] *Ibid.*, s. 960 (revised transl.).

Neither provided an account of the individual which explained both his particularity and his immanence within biological and socio-economic systems. They both failed to solve the problem of the nature, sources and proper use of rationality. Hegel unified and rationalized his vision by adopting a speculative metaphysics and an ontological theory of concepts which rendered the crucial issues inaccessible; Nietzsche psychologized the problem of perspective and irrationalized the presentation of his critical insights by failing to move beyond rhetorical effects to a systematic theory of impostulates. Above all, neither Hegel nor Nietzsche provided a satisfactory theory of freedom based on procedural rules instead of idealized terminology and abstract principles.

Nonetheless, in a contemporary context, both Hegel and Nietzsche can be read as thinkers who raise problems with which contemporary political philosophy has still to come to terms. Hegel and Nietzsche were critics of the constricted modern conception of the political and of the liberal separation of 'political reason' and 'metaphysics'. Both were hostile to 'metaphysics' in the sense of an inaccessible beyond, but where Hegel developed a metaphysics of immanence and presented his politics as an illustration of it, Nietzsche spoke of annihilating 'the world of being' and of metaphysics as the science that deals with the fundamental errors of mankind as if they were fundamental truths.[57] Yet for all his anti-metaphysical polemics, Nietzsche can be seen as a thinker who transvalued metaphysics as well as values: as a thinker who developed post-metaphysical doctrines of 'the will to power', 'the eternal return' and 'the over-man' designed to transform the inner politics of men's relation to 'what there is'. To this extent Nietzsche, even more than Hegel, heralds a new post-liberal definition of the scope of the political. Nietzsche, however, failed to solve the problem of political community, although he left indications, including a crucial political role for art, which contemporary political philosophy has failed to take up. Hegel provided the elements of a political ontology of community which contemporary political philosophy needs to examine, not necessarily to agree with Hegel, but to think out more clearly the importance of the preservation of differentiations between (1) the individual, (2) the family, (3) the realm of economic associations, (4) the realm of rights, and (5) the realm of cultural and spiritual life, which in modern society are either heteronomously suppressed or eroded in what Nietzsche called a general 'formlessness'.

[57] *Ibid.*, s. 585; and *Human, All Too Human*, s. 18.

Similarly, both Hegel and Nietzsche raise the problem of a political theory of the will. Hegel made his theory of the rational will central to his political philosophy and analyzed social and political life in terms of the universality of the will which they embodied. In Hegel the problem of a political theory of the will was de-politicized by an ontological schema that ordained a coincidence of realized freedom, rationality and universality so that the free will was the will that determined itself by universal reason.[58] Nietzsche, on the other hand, rejected any rationalistic theory of the will and opted for 'the strong will' as a normative concept in political and social analysis. At the same time he did not succeed in reconciling his ideal of 'free spirits' who determined their own will with his underlying conviction that 'the strong will' only flourished in circumstances in which an elite of creative individuals were 'compelled' to be strong or 'go under'.[59] Both Hegel and Nietzsche suggest that the life history of the will under different political and social physiognomies requires further investigation in contemporary political philosophy.

Finally, both Hegel and Nietzsche raise the problem of a post-liberal, non-atomist theory of the free individual. Hegel held that the full development of the individual required his involvement in a community and in a trans-individual shared ethical life. But he also saw a need for the individual to be able to recognize an affirmation of his highest possibilities in the meaning structures found in the whole of reality – a political consideration lacking in modern liberalism with its doctrine that the interpretation of reality does not fall within the scope of politics. In contrast, Nietzsche held that reality had no meaning as such, but he went on to provide indications for 'a new interpretation of the universe' which, if accepted, would motivate and even coerce the strong individual to 'become a self'. Moreover, like Hegel, Nietzsche recognized that socially encoded valuation patterns were not neutral for the individual's ability to become a 'free self' but a central area of political concern. To this extent Hegel and Nietzsche raise the paradoxical question of whether the individual only becomes the 'free individual' in a trans-individual context of meaning and value. Against the tragic events of our century it would be reckless to prematurely answer this question in the affirmative, but it is a question that contemporary political philosophy needs to confront.

---

[58] Hegel, *The Philosophy of Right*, op. cit., s. 5–29.
[59] *Twilight of the Idols*, s. 38.

Calvin and Kropotkin

Vincent di Norcia

John Calvin, the Protestant reformer, and Peter Kropotkin, the anarchist revolutionary, are studies in contrasts. Man is evil, God alone good, Calvin felt, and revolution an abomination; while to Kropotkin man is good, religion evil, and revolution an ideal. Each criticized the foundations of modern society. After giving historical settings I will present their teachings on human nature and then on politics.

Historical settings

Religious and social revolution dominated Calvin's era, the sixteenth century. The Roman church and the feudal order were breaking apart; a new capitalist order and state were on the rise. Geneva was in the centre of this ferment. Luther, on the one hand, had not effected any social reforms and had allied himself with the princes in a bloody repression of the peasants. The Anabaptists and other communist–Christians, on the other hand, had revolted against their rulers. Calvin and the Swiss reformers took a middle position – of supporting social reform and avoiding the wholesale repression of their enemies. Calvin rejected the Anabaptists as 'spiritual anarchists and revolutionaries' who subverted 'not only religion but also all political order.' In contrast, in the Preface of his *Institutes of the Christian Religion,* Calvin proclaimed his support for all rulers, even the Catholic king of France.[1]

---

[1] For a summary of Calvin's life, see Georgia Harkness, *John Calvin: The Man and His Ethics*, Abingdon, Nashville, Tenn., 1948, p. 8f. The quotations are from André Biéler, *Le pensée économique et sociale de Calvin*, Georgia, Geneva, 1961, p. 75. The letter to the King of France constitutes the Preface of Calvin's *Institutes of the Christian Religion*. I have used the Library of Christian Classics edition, edited by J. T. McNeill and translated by F. L. Battles, SCM, London, 1960, p. 11. (Reference to it is by section; for example, 'I.2.3.' is Book I, chapter 2, section 3.)

Calvin arrived in Geneva in 1535 and except for an exile of three years stayed until his death in 1564. Throughout his work in Geneva he treated its government as independent when seeking its help in his reforms. These reforms were firstly to establish the true biblical religion in its churches and then to reform the morals of that 'wealthy, pleasure-loving medieval town'. He instituted public welfare programmes for the sick, the weak and the poor, and influenced the state to regulate prices, employment and work. He sought to moderate capitalism's excesses and direct its wealth towards public ends.[2]

Social revolution again dominated Europe from 1848 to 1917. Prince Peter Kropotkin (1842–1921), raised in a Russian aristocratic family, schooled in a military college and familiar with the Tsar's court, supported the revolutionary process till his death. He agitated for the abolition of the serfs. He volunteered for military duty in Siberia, where he studied geology, and directly observed the inefficiency of Moscow's centralized rule; he sympathized with local demands for autonomy. Such experiences led him to his scientific anarchism.[3] On returning to Moscow, Kropotkin worked in a secret revolutionary group, was arrested and imprisoned and escaped to Switzerland where he encountered many leading socialists and anarchists. After being imprisoned again he moved to England, where he stayed until his return to revolutionary Russia in 1917. He was an open critic of Lenin's state socialism to his death in 1921.[4]

Kropotkin's anarchism was based on his scientific theories about evolution and his direct experience of the centralized monarchic state and local autonomy. Social revolution, he felt, was rooted in evolution, spontaneously rising up from the people's needs, and realizing their principles of mutual aid and free association. The middle classes, he argued, were obstacles to full revolutionary freedom and equality.

Man and society

Human nature, Calvin's theology taught, is corrupt. The knowledge of human nature itself cannot be gleaned by man's unaided efforts but is

---

[2] Harkness, *op. cit.*, pp. 8 and 16; and Biéler, *op. cit.*, Introduction, Nos 1 and 3; In subsequent references the sources for quotations will be given first and then other topic references, with usually one note for each paragraph.
[3] See Kropotkin's *Memoirs of a Revolutionist*, Peter Smith, Gloucester, Mass., 1967, chapters II, III.
[4] See Kropotkin's *Memoirs*, chapters IV to VI; and P. A. Kropotkin, *Selected Writings on Anarchism and Revolution*, edited by M. A. Miller, MIT, Cambridge, Mass., 1973, pp. 324–39. (Hereafter this work will be referred to as '*Writings*'.)

revealed to us in the Bible, as read by the eyes of faith.[5] There God offers us the answers to our questions. Ignorance of God and His Word is due to our sinfulness; its knowledge, being a good, comes from God, whence all goods come.[6]

Before Adam's sin man's nature was not corrupt; but that pristine purity has been 'deranged' and 'almost blotted out' by the Fall.[7] Sin has been transmitted to the whole human species, becoming 'a hereditary depravity and corruption of our nature, diffused into all parts of the soul' and shows itself in pride and the sins of the flesh.[8] Since man's ruin was his fault alone and has led to every evil, man has been justly punished by God.[9] He has lost his free will and self-mastery by his enslavement to sin.[10] Obversely, any good men do comes from God alone.[11]

Man is alienated both from his nature and from nature itself, which is no longer a spontaneous source of the goods he needs to live. Rather man must toil to produce those goods, and his work is often unproductive. Chaos and scarcity only too often rule society. All social relations, from sex and the family into economics and politics, have been perverted by the Fall.[12]

The sum of Christian life, Calvin taught, must be self-denial and the affirmation of God; for He alone is 'the fountain of every good'.[13] Only God can restore us to our pristine innocence. God predestines the eternal fate of all, freely electing his elite and damning the rest. God is omnipotent. He rules all events by his providence, which directs all history to a final triumph over evil.[14] This might suggest his complicity in the evil men do.[15] The mystery here disclosed can only be reconciled by faith in God. It can be either a trial of the Christian's faith or a comfort to him in times of distress.[16]

---

[5] Calvin, *op. cit.*, I.1.1. For examples of torturous biblical commentary, see II.17.7–14 and IV.9.13 (on justification). I.13.3 (on the Trinity), and IV.17.21–25 (on the Eucharist).
[6] I.1.4.
[7] II.1.9, 10. The corruption does not 'flow from nature' but is 'adventitious' to it (II.1.10, 11).
[8] II.1.8.; *cf.* III.6–9.
[9] II.1.8.
[10] II.2.5.
[11] II.3.6–14.
[12] See Biéler, III.2.
[13] II.2.1.
[14] I.16.
[15] See Wilhelm Niesel, *The Theology of Calvin*, Westminster, Philadelphia, 1956, pp. 70f and 160–77; Harkness, p. 73; and Biéler, pp. 200 and 220f.
[16] I.17.10, 11.

Underlying Calvin's doctrine of human nature and indeed most Christian teaching, is a radical ontological dualism: the split between soul and body. It is also found in pre-Christian doctrines.[17] It takes religious form in the Two Worlds dialectic, according to which the visible, earthly, unstable city of man is a realm of death and misery. The heavenly, unchanging, internal kingdom of God is in contrast, a realm of goodness, grace, life and happiness; but it is invisible. It can be seen only by the eyes of faith. 'Christ's kingdom lies in the spirit,' Calvin wrote, 'we must forsake the world if we are to share in the Kingdom.'[18] History arises from the struggle of these two worlds.

Men are justified by their faith in God, not by any works of their own; for, being corrupt, men can do nothing to merit God's grace. Man is responsible only for his sins. The good men do is done by God acting in them.[19] The actions of the justified, however, are esteemed above their worth by God. They supplement faith and confirm justification. In addition, since morality arises from the law and laws command perfection, man, being imperfect, cannot be moral.[20] God alone is perfect. The law reinforces man's guilt.[21]

Even though an ethics implies the agent's freedom, responsibility and ability to act autonomously for ill or for good, Calvin proposed a moral code. Its first tenet is that man is responsible and voluntary in some of his acts, namely, his sins.[22] Second, Calvin repeatedly urged Christians to patience, humility, obedience, and especially to moderation instead of excess (too little or too much) in using the goods of this life.[23] The Christian, Harkness noted, should live a plain and honest life.[24] This doctrine of moderation is tied to Calvin's dual concept of Christian liberty. Internally the Christian enjoys an utter spiritual liberty of conscience, for this 'voluntary obedience' to God's will can emancipate him from enslavement to sin. Externally the Christian should be indifferent to physical goods and, therefore, free in their use. At no point does this teaching entail man's autonomous performance of good actions.[25]

[17] I.15.6–8.
[18] II.15.3; cf. II.10.17; III.1.2, III.9.4.
[19] II.5.13–15.
[20] II.5.12.
[21] II.7.3–5.
[22] II.1.4.; II.3.5.
[23] III.8.11; III.10.1, 2; III.12.6.
[24] Harkness, pp. 164f and viii.
[25] III.19.4–7, 15.

Property, moreover, is from God, its sole owner. Man is but God's steward. No one merits the property he owns because of his labour. All must use it well and increase it, but for the good of society and not just for themselves. Nonetheless, their property remains private and is not owned in common.[26] In addition Calvin denounced the effects of wealth: greed, idleness, and the sins of the flesh. He worked tirelessly to rid Geneva of them. He repeatedly condemned the abuses of wealth: fraud in commerce, high prices, monopoly, speculation, unemployment and usury. He demanded that the rich live up to their primary social obligation to aid the poor. He affirmed the dignity of all work, industrial and agricultural, as a service, a form of collaboration with God which is not to be exploited. Although he was the first to approve of interest rates on money loaned, he hemmed it about with many ethical restraints.[27]

'The Lord's calling' of each Christian to his occupation or work (*métier*), was the obverse of his election by God and 'the basis of our way of life'.[28] It implies no direct correlation of wealth to election. But it is allied to a religious concept of class: 'the very inequality of [God's] grace proves that it is free'.[29] Being free it is not comprehensible to us. Poverty is a mystery and social inequality inevitable. Both are due to man's sinfulness, which has perverted all social relations. All social institutions, moreover, are hierarchical, from a father's rule over his wife and household to the king's rule over his subjects. All replicate God's sovereignty over the cosmos. Class rebellion, therefore, is wrong.[30]

Calvin's social ethic expressed the values of the new middle classes, their resentment of the wasteful, oppressive rule of the old aristocracy and unreformed church. His moderation was theirs. It legitimized their dominance in the capitalist order of the new civil society.

Kropotkin's anarchism also 'embraces the whole of nature' and 'the life of human societies and their economic, political and moral problems.'[31] But he argued that religion was evil, that human nature evolves from an evolutionary process characterized deeply by ethical principles and culminating in social revolutions. There is no dualism of

---

[26] On property and the social duties of the wealthy, see Biéler, pp. 38–42 and chapter IV, sections I and V; and Harkness, pp. 169–85.
[27] On the critique of the abuses of wealth, see Biéler, pp. 316f, 412 and 417f; pp. 453–76 (on interest); and Harkness, pp. 170–7, 190 and 209f.
[28] III.10.6.
[29] III.21.6.
[30] See Biéler, pp. 258–65; p. 423f (on rebellion); pp. 403–7 (on calling as *métier*).
[31] *Kropotkin's Revolutionary Pamphlets*, edited by R. N. Baldwin, Dover, New York, 1970, p. 150; *c.f.* p. 46f. (Henceforth cited as *'Pamphlets'*.)

religion versus the world, spirit versus flesh. Man and nature are one. This is all known, moreover, not by faith, but scientifically: by the methodical use of one's intelligence and powers of observation; not by faith.

Kropotkin conceived man as a species within evolution. This implies that man is best understood in large groups, living through countless generations, and subject to discoverable laws. History is the history of the masses, not of elites. A society and its habitat are not ontologically opposed orders of reality. Rather, man is 'the result of the environment in which he grows up and spends his life' and which he shapes as well.[32]

Nature is the source of ethical values. 'Mutual aid is the predominant fact of nature' and history. 'It is more permanently at work in the social animals than even the purely egoistic instinct of direct self-preservation', competition and struggle. God did not reveal morality to us. 'The working out of moral principles', rather, 'was the creative effort of all humanity'. Those principles – of co-operation, equality, justice, free organization – are so inherent in social animals as to be 'a law of nature'.[33]

Evolutionary success does not imply ethical relativism, but the superiority of the mutual aid ethic to the internal divisiveness of an egoistic, competitive ethic of struggle for survival. Nature then contains the golden rule and shows us that how the individual and society's interests, being inseparable, can be harmonized.[34]

This theory is in sharp contrast to Calvin's judgement on human nature and to the related bourgeois myth of a pre-social state of nature in which free independent individuals are engaged in unrestrained mutual war. Societies, Kropotkin countered, preceded man, and individualism is not natural but acquired. He also rejected the more recent social Darwinist 'tooth and claw' model of natural selection in terms of competition and struggle. For it implies that human ethical principles originate solely in man, suddenly and inexplicably, with no roots in nature. This places science and ethics in opposition. It supports a religious theory of the divine origin of morality, such as Calvin's.[35]

---

[32] *Pamphlets*, p. 232; and Kropotkin's *Ethics: Origin and Development*, Blom, New York, 1968, p. 43; *Mutual Aid: A Factor of Evolution*, Extending Horizon, Boston, n.d., p. 116f; and *The Conquest of Bread*, Allen Lane, London, 1972, pp. 41 and 44. (Henceforth these works will be cited as '*Ethics*', '*Mutual Aid*' and '*Conquest*'.)

[33] *Ethics*, pp. 14–15, 137 and 286. See also chapters X, XI and XII, pp. 102–10, 149 and 158; and *Mutual Aid*, chapters I and II.

[34] *Mutual Aid*, Introduction and chapters I and II; *Ethics*, chapters II, XII and XIII.

[35] *Ethics*, p. 279 to end; *Mutual Aid*, chapter I and Appendix B.

Kropotkin often noted that there have been two theories about the origin of morality: the immanentist view, like his own, that ethics arises within nature; and the transcendental view, like Calvin's, that morality arises outside nature in God, that it is *supernatural*.[36] One Western philosophical current beginning with Aristotle has taken the immanentist position. It supports rationality and science. In contrast the transcendental view, found in non-religious form in Plato, has been used to support faith in God. It defines moral actions as springing from a unilateral duty to do good or obey the law, as Calvin did. This implies a radical ethical inequality: man must strive to do good, but God has no correlative duty to reciprocate or even to recognize man's achievements. Hence it is but a short step to Calvin's thesis that man is obliged to submit to all authority. Morality, moreover, is premised not on the free and intelligent use of one's faculties but on faith in a transcendent being, God – again, an authoritarian relation. It alienates man from his own competence.

Kropotkin's immanentist integration of ethics and science, man and nature, in contrast, implies that men are able to reform their societies; for such a project is continuous with the roots of ethics in both evolution and history. It is also demanded by the ethical injunction to extend the principles of human solidarity, justice and free association and constantly improve social relations, and, obversely, to narrow the domains of domination, competition, and struggle. Kropotkin recognized the existence of evil as a powerful current in history opposed to the mutual aid tendency and expressed in different social forms. He gave more play to the forces he opposed, such as the church and the state, than Calvin did to humanity. Both thinkers connected morality to the natural law principles of equity and justice; but where Calvin moderated their effect, Kropotkin sought to maximize their revolutionary potential.[37]

By Kropotkin's time Calvin's bourgeoisie were no longer revolutionary. Middle-class morality was 'double-faced', he felt; its talk of frugality 'nothing more or less than grinding the face of the poor'. Its moderation was suspect. Its critique of idleness was hypocritical; for the middle classes were the worst idlers, not the workers or peasants. Their dualistic split of religion and the world, of soul and body, joined to their belief in the superiority of mental to manual labour, all reinforce social inequality. And their philosophy of the free individual, Kropotkin

---

[36] *Ethics*, pp. 224f, 284f and 330f, and Conclusion; and *Pamphlets*, p. 98f.
[37] *Ethics*, pp. 18f, 49 and 258; on dualism, see *Pamphlets*, pp. 146f and 205f.

asserted, 'is not individualism at all'; for it does not lead to its goal, 'the complete development of individuality'.[38] Rather 'there are two classes in our modern society': the workers, who surrender more than half of what they produce to 'the monopolists of property' and 'the idler, the spoiler, hating his slave, ready to kill him'. In sum, Kropotkin concluded, 'everywhere the wealth of the wealthy springs from the poverty of the poor', not from the Fall of Adam. Capitalism furthermore is economically inefficient.[39]

Private property rights, moreover, are not sacred but are based on theft: 'Individual appropriation is neither just nor serviceable. All belongs to all. All things are for all men [Calvin would agree], since all men have need of them, since all men have worked in the measure of their strength to produce them.' [Here Calvin would disagree.] Consequently, the private ownership of the means of production was anachronistic, and the historic tendency to make all property common, to give all enterprises over to the control of their producers, and to make food, shelter and clothing free, was coming into its own. Such an economy would be far more productive, Kropotkin held, to the extent that people would have a great deal of free time to follow cultural pursuits and thereby develop their individuality and freedom.[40]

But this is possible only if all social institutions are structured according to the principles of free association and mutual aid. Only thus can all forms of inequality be eliminated and 'the fullest possible equality' in all things be realized. In his *Mutual Aid* Kropotkin gives many examples of such institutions in tribal societies, peasant villages and, especially, the free city or commune. It represented, on a larger scale than the village, 'a close union for mutual aid and support, for consumption and production, for social life altogether.' It was not subject to the authority of any ruler nor to the letters of the state. Its rise led to an era of unequalled economic, cultural and political progress.[41]

The decline of the medieval city was neither natural nor inevitable, Kropotkin maintained, but was the result of a struggle with forces dedicated to destroying it: the church, the aristocracy, the king, and the military. Their aim was 'to level the whole of society to a common submission to the master', to structure society on the principles of

---

[38] *Conquest*, p. 49; see p. 170f; *Writings*, p. 166 and 295; see pp. 164f, 293–307.
[39] *Writings*, p. 123; *Conquest*, p. 77; see *Pamphlets*, p. 48; and *Conquest*, p. 118; and pp. 52f, 118 and 165, and chapter 10.
[40] *Conquest*, p. 49; and see chapters 5, 6, 7, 9, 13 and 14, (also in *Writings*, pp. 160–209).
[41] *Writings*, p. 48; *Mutual Aid*, p. 186; see also chapters V and VI; and *Pamphlets*, p. 99.

dominion, authority and submission. Their victory meant economic, cultural and political regress, war and poverty. It produced a society, Kropotkin wrote, based on 'the spirit of voluntary servitude', such as Calvin's political theory proposes. To it we now turn.[42]

Politics: Dominion versus freedom

'God's dominion is absolute; it stands above our freedom,' Calvin wrote. 'Daily experience compels you to realize that your mind is guided by God's prompting rather than by your freedom to choose' even simple things.[43] The correlative to dominion, which means 'lordship', is slavery; it is a political concept, an old usage of empire. Dominion is total dependence. But where God is the lord, mastery extends into the depths of our inner being, our intelligence, will, mind, motives, and whole personality. 'We are not our master', therefore, 'but belong to God.'[44]

God's governance of the universe is total, Calvin held; for 'everything is done on the authority of God, who commands it.'[45] Absolute sovereignty is therefore the structure of being. God's dominion over all things is the foundation of authority, of man's dominion over man: 'The authority possessed by kings and other governors over all things upon earth is not a consequence of the perverseness of men but of divine providence and holy ordinance.'[46] A king's right to rule, Calvin added, is rooted in fact: 'it ought to be enough for us that they *do rule*; for they have been placed there by the Lord's hand.'[47]

The end of government is religious, the restoration of true religion and its support.[48] This does not entail theocracy, in Calvin's view, but the medieval theory of the Two Powers, a direct reflection of the Two Worlds doctrine. The spiritual domain of the church is distinct from the temporal domain of the state, as it was in Geneva. For 'man is under two kinds of government – one aspect is spiritual, whereby the conscience is instructed in piety and in reverencing God; the second is political, whereby a man is educated in the duties of humanity and citizenship.'[49] The dividing line may not always be clear. Nonetheless, in matters

---

[42] *Writings*,, pp. 235 and 258; see also *Mutual Aid*, p. 215f.
[43] II.4.7.
[44] III.7.1.
[45] IV.20.10.
[46] IV.20.4.
[47] In *Calvin on God and Political Duty*, edited by J. T. McNeill, Bobbs–Merrill, New York, 1956, p. 84 (on Romans 13.1.2). (Henceforth cited as *'Duty'*.)
[48] IV.20.2.
[49] III.19.15; *cf.* Biéler, pp. 124–32; and Harkness, p. 22f.

spiritual the state should have no authority over the church – as it does in England. However, the church has political missions: to pray for the state, to admonish authorities about the abuse of their powers, to defend the weak and the poor, and to have recourse to the state to enforce discipline.[50] The church's domain, then is the external outward forum. From this dualism and that of the doctrine of Christian liberty, each expressions of the Two Worlds doctrine, it follows that 'spiritual freedom can very well exist along with civil bondage'.[51]

Within in its own external forum, Calvin felt, the state is autonomous and supreme. Government is an institution 'far more excellent' than any private economic or social institution; for the ends it serves are public: the maintenance of peace and order, moral discipline, the security of property and commerce, and the restraint of abuses. In sum it must see that there be a 'public manifestation of religion among Christians and that humanity be maintained among men'.[52] It has the positive functions of promoting the public over the private good and regulating the economy in terms of social justice and equity.[53] It also has the monopoly of legal force, in whose use it must be both just and merciful, and promote peace rather than war.[54] These negative or coercive functions of the state arise from man's sinfulness. In contrast, the church's spiritual realm originates in God's goodness.

The best constitution of a 'civil government' is mixed, both aristocratic and democratic. Since human nature is corrupt no one man should have too much power. Calvin believed in a conservative democracy – even in the church, where most offices should be elective.[55] Liberty should be preserved and 'regulated with becoming moderation'; for 'once liberty is snatched away all is over.'[56]

There are three 'branches' to any government, Calvin taught: the magistracy, the laws and the people.[57] The office of the magistrate, or ruler, is the highest secular calling. It is his duty to secure the public ends to which the state is directed, to provide good government in a spirit of service to society, God, the law and the people, rather than seeking his own private advantage. Magistrates, being God's vice-regents, should be

[50] Biéler, pp. 292–301 and 378f.
[51] IV.20.3.
[52] IV.20.3.
[53] IV.20.16.
[54] IV.20.9–11.
[55] IV.4.15.
[56] *Duty*, pp. 100 and xxiv.
[57] IV.20.3.

examples of His benevolence, providence and justice. Integrity, prudence, gentleness, self-control, moderation and innocence should guide their rule.[58] They are accountable to both God and the people. 'No virtue is so rare in kings as moderation', Calvin wrote, for 'scarcely one king in a hundred . . . does not despise everything divine.'[59] He was a strong critic of tyrannical and wasteful rule.

The second branch of government is the law, the rules that regulate the power of the magistrate. The worth of all laws is rooted in the natural law of equity and justice, for 'equity alone must be the goal and rule the limit of all laws'.[60] It is apprehended by our conscience, is embodied in the moral law and the commandments, and ultimately grounded in God's law.[61] From such principles one could define crimes such as theft, adultery and murder.

The third branch of government is the people. Their first duty, Calvin felt, is to 'fear God, honor the king'. All rulers, no matter how bad, must be obeyed, for their authority appertains to their office. Obedience is the primary political virtue.[62] Political obligation is therefore unilateral. It is an expression of the hierarchical order of all authority, of rulers over rules, from within the family, to the state and church. While this does not mean that citizens should be apolitical,[63] they must in consequence accept corrupt and tyrannical rule and suffer injustices as a punishment of their sins or a test of their faith. They can hope that God will send some public figure to avenge them.[64] Obedience does not exclude passive legal resistance, but it does preclude the open class rebellion of the Anabaptists.[65] There is but one exception, Calvin argued. Where rulers 'command anything against true religion' disobedience is a duty; for here they exceed the limits of their office, and raise themselves above God.'[66]

Tyranny, like rebellion, is a product of man's sinfulness. Both are wrong. Calvin believed emancipation from sin has already begun in the church; but it is spiritual and invisible. Nonetheless, its presence on earth begins the godly work of restoring the original communal and harmonious society of Eden. As this latent emancipation comes only

---

[58] IV.20.6–9.
[59] *Duty*, pp. 91 and 94.
[60] IV.20.16.
[61] IV.20.16; *cf.* IV.20.14, 16; II.2.22–4; II.7.2, 8; II.8.1.
[62] IV.20.22, 23.
[63] *Duty*, p. 101; Biéler, p. 285f; Harkness, p. 223.
[64] IV.20.24–32.
[65] IV.20.1, 3.
[66] IV.20.32; *cf. Duty*, pp. 90–102; Harkness, p. 233; and Biéler, p. 423f.

from God, it conflicts with man's continuing need for authority. The full restoration of Eden, Calvin taught, will come from God at the end of history. It will not be the work of man. Our present situation is therefore profoundly ambiguous.[67]

Kropotkin's political theory, in contrast, arose from his opposition to 'the mutual alliance between the lord, the priest, the soldier, and the judge, which we call "the state".' It extended to all authoritarian institutions but focused on the state, which in his view maintains the authority of the rest. For the state, as a form of government, is constituted by a double 'concentration of powers', in the control of a definite territory, and the centralization of 'many functions of the life of society in the hands of a few'. It is this concentrated autonomous 'power above society' that the state stands for.[68]

Its roots are ancient. They lie, he wrote, in the centralized Roman empire and its unified legal code. The ancient glories of Rome legitimized the modern state's hard-fought ascendancy over its feudal lords, village communes and free cities. Its harbingers were the religious, military and other elites within the tribes, village and communes – whose powers were later concentrated in the state.[69]

The state is in principle opposed to the free city. It saw the institutions of free association, such as guilds, as threats to its sovereignty, for there could be no 'state within the state'. Similarly French governments, both during the Revolution and later in 1871, opposed the creation of independent democratic communes, especially in Paris. For by its nature the state cannot 'recognize a freely formed union operating within itself; it only recognizes *subjects* . . . Consequently the state must, perforce, wipe out cities based on the direct union between citizens. It must abolish all unions within the city, as well as the city itself, and wipe out all direct union between the cities. For the federal principle it must substitute the principle of submission and discipline.' The rise of the centralized state has meant social regress: the private company and public welfare have replaced mutual aid.[70]

The church's dominion over souls and its teaching 'that all that comes from human nature is sin, and that all good in man has a supernatural origin' reinforced the authority of the state; for, Kropotkin wrote, it made men fall 'in love with authority' and blinded them to their own

[67] See Biéler, pp. 202f, 211f, and 251-69.
[68] *Writings*, pp. 213 and 250.
[69] See *Writings*, pp. 213-35; *Mutual Aid*, pp. 226f and 283f.
[70] *Writings*, pp. 245 and 251; see *Mutual Aid*, pp. 210f, 265, 271 and 277.

capabilities. Kropotkin interpreted the Two Powers doctrine in this light, as representing the church's failure to create a theocracy and need to come to terms with the rising monarchical states. This she did by bestowing 'her sanctity' upon kings, crowning 'them as God's representatives on earth'. In her schools and pulpits she preached the need of the centralized state and the right of its rulers to use any amount of force to protect the public good. When Luther sought the aid of princes to suppress peasant rebellions he restated and reinforced the Two Powers teaching on the autonomy of the state.[71]

But the state was a dangerous ally, as Calvin had intuited. After it destroyed the free cities and allied itself with the new capitalist elites it began to turn against the church. England expropriated the monasteries and established the church under the state's control. The internal divisions that the Protestants created in Christianity weakened it in relation to the new nation state. This process culminated in the French Revolution's expropriation of the church, to pay state debts and, following the Americans, its secularization of the state.[72] The church/state alliance was at root competitive. Both were seeking dominion; but as Calvin noted, only one Lord can rule.

The rise of the new capitalist bourgeoisie meant not only an attack on the old church but also on its old ally, the monarchy. Parliament gradually became sovereign instead of the monarch. The individualist foundations of this new state were, however, not radical. Just as Protestantism had asserted the individual's direct relationship to God without the need of the priest as mediary, so, Kropotkin wrote, 'the State demands from its subjects a direct, personal submission without intermediaries; it demands equality within slavery.' This strengthens the coercive function of the state, as Hobbes' social contract myth implied; for, Kropotkin noted, it holds that 'the natural state of man is war of all men against all men. The State protects the life and property of its subjects at the price of their absolute obedience' – as Calvin had taught. 'The will of the State is supreme law. The submission to the power of the omnipotent "Leviathan State" is the basis of sociality.'[73] The secular state itself has become God, the supreme authority.

---

[71] *Mutual Aid*, p. 278; *Writings*, pp. 228 and 240; *cf.* pp. 238f, 243–5 and 305; and *Mutual Aid*, p. 217f.
[72] In Peter Kropotkin, *The Great French Revolution*, Schocken, New York, 1971, pp. 169f and 185; *cf.* chapter XXII. (Henceforth cited as '*Revolution*'.)
[73] *Writings*, p. 251; *Ethics*, p. 153; *cf. Mutual Aid*, pp. 77f and 251f; on parliament, see *Pamphlets*, pp. 185 and 238f, and *Revolution*, p. 7.

Its absorption of all social functions and services and concentration of powers reinforces the new possessive individualism; for (as Calvin, too, had sensed) it relieves citizens of their social duties.[74] It freed them to pursue their private interests unrestrainedly. In consequence modern individualism requires the strong state. The task of protecting property against an unbridled individualism reinforces its coercive function. The law, the police, the army and the prisons are even more essential to meeting its social contract.

Kropotkin was only too familiar with the state police's repression of internal dissent and uncontrolled power. Like the FBI and RCMP even in 'democracies', the state police is a threat to the government itself. Its existence shows vividly that the state is based on force and fear – the state's fear of the people and the people's fear of the state. Law is said to legitimize and restrain the might of the state within basic moral principles like equity and justice, as Calvin held. But legal codes, Kropotkin argued, merely serve to support the ruling class's dominion over the people. The origin of law is neither in morality or God (as Calvin taught), but in sheer power. The might of the state is not made moral by laws. Rather, laws legitimize rule by force; they make might right.

Crime is the obverse of law. It does not arise from a corrupt human nature but, Kropotkin reasoned, is mostly economic in origin. Few crimes are caused by personal vengeance. Prisons do not deter criminals but are schools of crime. Crimes (like sin in Calvin's Pauline teaching) are created by laws. We would be better, Kropotkin felt, to follow many non-Christian cultures and treat crimes as accidents beyond the control of the individual.[75]

War and armies are natural to the state, which arose from the military class. Wars and armies are legal because of the state's monopoly of force and the absence of laws governing the relations among states. War in addition, is inevitable, Kropotkin argued, because the state is rooted in the control of territory and the dynamic of increasing its powers. It must therefore increase its territory, like an empire. This unavoidably leads to conflicts with other states which provoke war.[76]

The legitimacy of the elective state is rooted in its claim to be a representative form of government, to 'represent the interests of society', to be neutral in respect to different groups' demands, and to treat all

---

[74] *Mutual Aid*, p. 227; cf. C. B. Macpherson, *The Political Theory of Possessive Individualism: Hobbes to Locke*, Oxford. London, 1962, p. 3.
[75] See the chapters on law and prisons in *Pamphlets*, pp. 195–235.
[76] *Ethics*, pp. 317 and 79; *Writings*, pp. 246 and 258.

equally. This classless ideology veils the real mission of the modern state, which, Kropotkin held, has been to consolidate and maintain the power of the capitalist classes over society. This is done by a double standard: the rule of *laissez faire* for capital and the denial of the right to combine and strike for workers.[77]

Thus France's revolutionary government represented the new bourgeoisie not only in opposing the royalists and abolishing feudalism – albeit often half-heartedly – but also, Kropotkin showed, in preventing the peasants, the urban workers and the communes from gaining political power and economic equality. It suppressed popular uprisings mercilessly and encouraged monopolists and speculators. Its Declaration of the Rights of Man barely mentioned economic rights, such as the rights to subsistence, to work and limits on property. Finally it distinguished between 'active' and 'passive' citizens, each with different voting powers, on the basis of the property they owned. Political class was a direct expression of economic class.[78]

Kropotkin attacked the principle of 'electing representatives to replace the people in their political tasks'. This not only 'saps their initiative' but also creates an explicitly political class. Parliamentary sovereignty over the king, moreover, meant not only that an elected legislature increased its powers but also that a parliamentary executive replaced the crown. This meant parliamentary rather than popular sovereignty. France, Kropotkin wrote, here modelled itself on the English constitutional principle, 'to concentrate all governmental power in the hands of a central executive authority, strictly controlled by the parliament, but also strictly obeyed in the state and combining every department – taxes, law, courts, police, army, schools, civic control, general direction of commerce and industry – everything.' To this the modern state has added the control of cultural functions, social welfare, transport, and communications.[79]

The rapid growth of the state has required large revenues to finance these functions. It raises taxes unequally: more from the poor than from the rich. In this it continues the church's previous system of tithing. The modern state also runs monopoly enterprises of its own. Thus the state itself produces wealth. It is itself a major economic force. Simultaneously

---

[77] *Mutual Aid*, p. 265; *Writings*, p. 50; *Revolution*, p. 9f, *Pamphlets*, p. 183f; and *Conquest*, p. 148.
[78] See *Revolution*, chapters II and LVI–LXI; on political class, pp. 164, 191, 212 and 217.
[79] *Pamphlets*, p. 238f; *Revolution*, p. 7; cf. *Writings*, pp. 213, 245 and 257f.

it also acts to support the capitalist corporation's private accumulation of wealth. The state, in sum, means economic inequality.[80]

But religion no longer serves to make the state legitimate; for the secular state has replaced the church. Yet it must be legitimate. It cannot have constant recourse to force to maintain its power. This would reveal its true foundations, might and inequality. Today the state directly seeks the support and trust of the people. Legitimacy is the essence of its power. Since it cannot rely on religion to gain legitimacy, Kropotkin saw, it must itself create a new religion, 'the religion of government side by side with the religion of property' and dominant over the old religion. The state itself is providence, it has become God.[81] Society turns to it to solve all its problems. In Roman fashion the modern state is the sole idol of a new public and secular religion. It has won total victory.

In its time the state was historically necessary. Now, Kropotkin argued, its abolition is equally necessary. His identification of the state with all forms of government, with a power independent of those on whom it is exercised, led him to the simple anarchist demand: 'no government!' Since government is the greatest obstacle to freedom, it cannot be the force which will destroy the present structure of power. The state must be abolished if we are ever to create 'free organizations and free federations in all those . . . areas of social life once considered part of the state.' 'Revolution and government', therefore, are 'incompatible'.[82]

The principles of this revolution have already been stated. The Anabaptists of the sixteenth century, Kropotkin noted, asserted the freedom of the individual conscience and supported the peasant struggle to communalize the land. He praised communal groups such as the Moravian brethren. The eighteenth-century French philosophers of revolution, he also noted, showed an 'eminently scientific' and 'moral spirit', trusted 'the intelligence, strength and greatness of the free man among equals', and opposed despotism.[83]

Kropotkin's immanentist ethics, springing from nature and the people, were also revolutionary. For, unlike the transcendental religious morality or Two Worlds dualism, and the bourgeois ethic of moderation

---

[80] See *Writings*, pp. 257f; *Revolution*, pp. 22f, 36f, 105–25 and 132f; on the state as a capitalist, see *Pamphlets*, p. 183; *Writings*, p. 50.
[81] *Writings*, p. 132; *Conquest*, p. 67; see also *Writings*, p. 245.
[82] *Pamphlets*, pp. 237 and 243; cf. *Conquest*, p. 65; *Writings*, pp. 211f, 256 and 261; and *Pamphlets*, pp. 63, 131 and 165–71.
[83] *Revolution*, p. 9; *Writings*, pp. 242–44; *Pamphlets*, 149; *Mutual Aid*, p. 225.

and duty, it implied that men can and have lived without the various forms of dominion that have inhibited their freedom and destroyed the institutions of mutual aid. That is to say, there is a historical tendency or tradition of co-operation, freedom and equality.[84] It bears the seeds of the anarchist critique of the church, the state, and capitalism.

That critique entails a complete social revolution inasmuch as 'all is interdependent in a civilized society.' Thus 'the smallest attack on property' will free society to expropriate private property and totally reorganize the economy on communal principles. Just as dominion was total so must freedom be. Because communism requires the transference of production and distribution to the effective control of the workers and the community, it entails a complete, and usually violent, revolutionary struggle. Kropotkin added, however, that this cannot be done, as the state socialists argue, by making a centralized bureaucratic state the owner of all social wealth. For communal ownership of all property means that it must not be controlled by a power above society, but by the workers and the community. Communism, therefore, is only possible 'without government'. It means a society based on 'free agreements', such as those that underlay the international railroad system of Kropotkin's day.[85]

The urban commune of a free city would be the central political institution of such a society. Having arisen from federations of villages and being internally self-administrating and self-legislating, the free city alone can embody anarchist principles in the political realm. The medieval free cities, for example, performed many of the international functions of the state – negotiation, alliance, treatymaking and federation – without themselves being states. They were constituted by 'a double federation: of all householders united into small territorial unions – the street, the parish, the section – and of individuals united by oath into guilds according to their professions.' Unlike states they were externally and internally decentralized and democratic.[86]

Clearly only a social revolution could create such a social order. That revolution, Kropotkin argued, would itself have to embody the communal forms it sought to realize. It could not be directed by a secret party nor governed by a centralized state, however socialist. Rather,

---

[84] See *Pamphlets*, pp. 59, 141, 146f, 158, 169 and 256; *Ethics*, pp. 17f, 49 and 256; *Conquest*, pp. 41f, 61 and 65; and *Revolution*, chapter I, p. 581.
[85] *Conquest*, pp. 80 and 65; see chapters 3 and 11.
[86] *Mutual Aid*, pp. 174 and 181; see also pp. 169–86; *Writings*, pp. 221–35; *Pamphlets*, p. 168f; *Revolution*, chapters XXIV–XXV and XXXVI–XLIX.

revolution must 'begin with the people' and express their aspirations and needs and insights; for 'the people will be right'. Kropotkin, for example, noted the surprising political competence of peasants. The people or masses to which he referred are, specifically, the rural peasantry, the urban workers, and the radical intellectuals.[87] This model has been prophetic. It fits the Russian, Algerian, Chinese and Iranian revolutions better than does Marx's focus on the proletariat.

Revolution will be spontaneous, Kropotkin held, when the initial conditions are present: general dissatisfaction, unbearable misery, a weak regime unwilling to make reforms and viciously repressing all progressive forces, and a pervasive readiness among the people to risk their lives in order to gain their rights and demands – often merely for adequate wages, food and shelter. Although small minorities may prepare the way, only the people themselves can make the revolution and bring it to fruition. Finally, the revolution itself will educate society in the new free and communal forms of social life which it seeks to create.[88]

Conclusions

The lives and theories of Calvin and Kropotkin do indeed constitute radical contrasts. Calvin was one of the chief spokesmen of the middle class to which he himself belonged; while Kropotkin, an aristocrat, was one of its most radical critics. Calvin lived in the city of Geneva, but believed in the state; Kropotkin lived in the Tsarist state, but believed in the free village and city. To the Geneva of Calvin, Kropotkin would oppose the commune of Paris. Each sought to be politically effective; but Calvin gained power and sought to implement moderate reforms, while Kropotkin rejected the power he could have enjoyed and worked to implement revolutionary changes.

Man, Calvin wrote, could only do evil; for his nature is corrupt; all good comes from God. Kropotkin rejected this religious idolization of God and degradation of humanity. He saw in natural evolution and human history actual embodiments of the highest ethical principles.

---

[87] *Pamphlets*, pp. 190 and 173; *cf. Conquest*, pp. 81 and 90; and *Writings*, pp. 71 and 83; and on populism and the revolutionary classes, see *Writings*, pp. 100, 103, 110f, 143f, 219, 272 and 278f; and *Revolution*, chapters III–VIII and XIV–XVI; on the peasantry's competence see *Writings*, pp. 157 and 206.

[88] On the conditions of revolution, see *Writings*, pp. 575–80, 91, 178 and 258f; on revolutionary minorities, see *Writings*, pp. 53, 138 and 146f; and *Memoirs*, pp. 210–30; on the revolution as education, see *Writings*, pp. 80, 83 and 113; and for the essay on 'Expropriation', see either *Writings* pp. 160–210 or *Conquest*, chapters 4–7.

Calvin, too, noted the natural roots of the values of equity and justice but felt that man's imperfection prevented him from realizing them. Neither believed man is perfect; but Calvin inferred hence that man is corrupt, while Kropotkin tried to show that men could and had created ethically sound institutions. Both had a pronounced sense of evil; both were profound social critics of their times. But they differed on the roots and remedies of social evils.

Both believed in liberty. Since Calvin felt it was primarily spiritual he drastically moderated its public expression, while Kropotkin sought to realize the fullest possible spiritual and social freedom for all. Calvin's theology and Kropotkin's ethics were, however, each appropriate ideological expressions of the principles underlying the social ferment of their times. Calvin could not have been as secular a theorist as Kropotkin nor Kropotkin as religious as Calvin, if each were to be as seminal and influential as they have been.

Each proposed an objective, universal ethics, explicitly intended to permeate all of social life. Each saw ethics, religion, society and politics as an interconnected whole. But Calvin's morality of moderation was opposed by Kropotkin's revolutionary ethics. Both theorists were consistent, comprehensive, idealistic, and given to exhortations to action. But Calvin's theology was rooted in St Augustine's and St Paul's pessimism about man and utter faith in God. In contrast Kropotkin adopted a scientific and rational approach, rooted in methodical observation and generalizations, and open to independent confirmation. This to my mind makes Kropotkin's philosophy truer, more accessible and applicable to the contemporary world. In its critique of the allegedly natural roots of human greed, aggression and competitiveness, and its almost ecological vision of man's roots in nature it is directly relevant to us.

Both nonetheless perceived the close relationship of religion and politics, but in opposite ways. Calvin abandoned his moderation in proposing utter submission to the authority of the state, which Kropotkin equally totally opposed. New authoritarian religious sects, furthermore, have arisen. Their total control of their members' lives and minds was unknown even in Calvin's Geneva; but their dualistic Two Worlds and soul/body doctrines are continuous with Calvin's theology.[89]

---

[89] On the new sects, see R. Enroth, *Youth, Brainwashing and the Extremist Cults*, Zondervan, Grand Rapids, Mich., 1977.

On the other hand religion is again becoming a revolutionary force, as it was among the Anabaptists, whom Calvin damned and Kropotkin praised. I refer to worker priests in Europe, to the theology of liberation in Latin America and to revolutionary Iran. Kropotkin clearly underestimated the revolutionary potential of religion.

Despite his sound analysis of the class forces essential to revolution, Kropotkin did not perceive the revolutionary impact of nationalism; nor did Calvin. Kropotkin nonetheless would not have been surprised at its statism. The state's connection to empire, familiar to Kropotkin, is again evident, from Moscow and Washington to Peking. Finally, although both Calvin and Kropotkin were perceptive critics of modern capitalism, neither foresaw the emergence of the large, multinational corporation – though each, I imagine, would not be surprised at its concentration of power and its uneasy alliance with the state.

Such phenomena raise in new form the old issues of legitimacy and force, the varying conjunctures of religion and politics, and the morality of the concentration of power. On such matters, despite their differences, Calvin and Kropotkin remain our insightful guides.

Rousseau and Marx

Patricia Springborg

Commentators on the works of Rousseau have come increasingly to see him as a precursor to Marx. Thus a number of contributors to the 1962 Dijon Studies on *The Social Contract* have seen in Rousseau's condemnation of the peculiar evils of modern society and his distinction between '*bourgeois*' and '*citoyen*' the rudiments of a case against capitalism as a specific mode of production.[1] Lucio Colletti in his excellent bibliographical essay 'Rousseau as Critic of "Civil Society"'[2] articulates this shift in Rousseau scholarship, which Goldschmidt's thorough analysis of Rousseau's political and economic principles serves to confirm.[3]

There is a basis in Rousseau's writings for such a reading. In his condemnation of co-operative labour, the institution of property, government as the guarantor of property rights and class divisions, the arts and sciences as class phenomena, we see constituents of a Marxist analysis. In Rousseau's first and second Discourses we have in outline a picture of the alienation that civilization is said to produce which approaches the dark picture of Marx's 1844 Manuscripts and *Capital* itself.

It has been common to assume that Rousseau was a wholesale critic of society, an advocate of the noble savage, and a supporter of the landed peasant in his attempt to reverse the trends of urbanization and corruption. In fact, as a host of recent commentators have shown, such a view seriously misrepresents Rousseau's position; even the first

---

[1] See *Etudes sur le Contrat Social de J.-J. Rousseau* (Proceedings of the Dijon Seminar, 3-6 May 1962), Paris, 1964.
[2] Lucio Colletti, 'Rousseau as Critic of "Civil Society"', in Colletti (ed.), *From Rousseau to Lenin*, New Left Books, London, 1972.
[3] Victor Goldschmidt, *Anthropologie et Politique, Les Principes du Système de Rousseau*, Vrin, Paris, 1974.

Discourse on the arts and sciences, relentless though it is in its criticisms of civilization and the corruption of morals that accompanies progress, makes it clear that sociability is an innate human trait. 'The mind, as well as the body has its needs', Rousseau declares; 'those of the body are the basis of society, those of the mind its ornaments.'[4]

The subject proposed by the Academy of Dijon (to which the second Discourse is addressed) – 'What is the origin of inequality among men and is it authorized by natural law?' – poses more directly the question whether society as it has developed has a basis in human nature. Rousseau's choice of the text by Aristotle on the title page is revealing: 'We should consider what is natural not in things which are depraved but in those which are rightly ordered according to nature.' In other words, he hopes to distinguish the fundamental attributes of human nature from the accretions or deviations that a certain form of social development has produced. The quotation from Aristotle could well have been in a Stoic text, suggesting as it does the valorization of nature in the concept of 'the life according to nature', and the possibility of distinguishing between things to be found in nature that are 'indifferent' and those that represent the uniform and universal features constitutive of the structure of the physical and moral universe. This text alerts us to the necessity to see Rousseau's concept of natural man in a special light: he is not referring to human traits as they are found in nature in the loose sense, since these may well be morally indifferent, but rather to those constitutive of human nature. True Rousseau constantly obscures this distinction himself, by talking about the natural needs found in primitive man, moving from descriptions of the chronological state of nature to hypothetical statements about universal tendencies of human nature. It represents a basic and unresolved ambivalence in his thought.

On the one hand, we have Rousseau the primitivist who, assuming that the natural state of affairs was the true state of affairs, draws the unwarranted inference that this was therefore the uncivilized state, confusing the two concepts of nature that he had already distinguished. On the other hand, we have the Rousseau who is insistent on distinguishing between nature in a descriptive sense (whatever may be found in nature) and nature in a normative sense (things in accordance with nature rightly ordered), and who is careful to distinguish between

---

[4] J.-J. Rousseau, *The Social Contract and Discourses*, Everyman edn, Dent, London, 1913, p. 120. (Translations of the first and second Discourses are taken from this edition, except where noted.)

the attributes of man in the natural state and those that are constitutive of human nature as such.

It is the latter Rousseau who prevails in the end, I think, for two reasons. First of all, Rousseau does conclude that the golden age of mankind – that is, the age in which man most closely approximated his true nature – was not that of the essentially solitary primitive, but rather that of the early community of households. Secondly, despite himself, Rousseau admits a mutual dependence between the development of man's innate potentialities and the creation of society. Here again Rousseau is forced reluctantly to concede in the concept of human perfectibility that progress is endemic and, moreover, that it produces benefits as well as losses. Here too Rousseau postulates a mutual dependence between the development of man's innate potentialities and the creation of society. There is therefore, in his account of human nature, a basis for whatever the hazards of progress produce. Rousseau spells out the mutual dependence of man's cognitive development and the growth of new needs and their objects, as well as the development of such societal institutions as language, the family and co-operative labour. Moreover, he admits that the dynamics of progress and the strengthening of an interlocking dependency between the individual and society are processes which once set in motion cannot easily be halted.

Rousseau postulates Hobbes' 'perpetual and restless desire of power after power, that ceaseth only in death'[5] as the source of human virtue, as well as vice. 'The passions too originate in our wants and their progress depends on that of our knowledge', he argues.[6] The savage man, 'being destitute of every species of intelligence', is one whose 'desires never go beyond his physical wants.' Like an animal his instincts adapt to and are restricted by the means of satisfaction that his environment naturally provides. Were it not for the growth of knowledge, the development of technology and the provision of new objects for our expanding desires, man could never have departed from the 'stupid' and 'brutish' natural state in which 'the only goods he recognizes . . . are food, a female and sleep.'[7]

Since Rousseau does show in his account of human nature the need for society as a precondition for perfectibility, we are forced to conclude that it is not society as such that he condemns, so much as a specific form of

---

[5] Thomas Hobbes, *Leviathan*, edited by Michael Oakeshott, Blackwell, Oxford, 1960, p. 64.
[6] Rousseau, *Discourse on Inequality*, p. 171.
[7] *Ibid*.

society: that governed by the pursuit of luxury and ephemeral goods, characterized by inequality, consumerism, corruption and so on – what Marx came subsequently to condemn as the specific evils of bourgeois society.

The case for Rousseau's recognition of Western culture as a specific cultural phenomenon is strengthened by an understanding of what Rousseau saw correctly ordered human nature to be and how it related to society. As I have argued, from a careful reading of the second Discourse we see that it was not the primitive, asocial condition of man that Rousseau identified with the golden age of mankind, but the communal society of self-sufficient households.

It is in the causes and progress of the departure from this happy condition that we see the greatest similarity between the Marxist accounts and the Rousseauean accounts of exploitation and alienation. Inequality and the institution of property are seen to be the systemic basis of modern society. In distinguishing between natural or physical inequality (which comes from differences of strength and ability) and moral or political inequality (which he argues is conventional), Rousseau asserts that only the first is natural, and that it is generally insignificant and far surpassed in importance by the artificial inequalities that society itself establishes; these inequalities are a direct consequence of the growth of artificial needs and the monopoly of resources through the institution of property, which allows the needs of some to proliferate without limit and the basic needs of others to go unsatisfied. True to his characterization, in the first Discourse, of needs of the mind and needs of the body, Rousseau distinguishes between physical needs, or the need for commodities to satisfy the physical appetites, and psychological needs, or the need for goods for purely symbolic purposes in the competition for status and honour. The latter are far more insidious.

Rousseau's specific indictment of modern society and where it went wrong focuses not so much on the waste, injustice and physical hardships that inequality produces, as on the moral corruption that stems from abandoning the 'life according to nature' and the voice of conscience in favour of conventional mores and popular opinion as a guide to behaviour. Social life generated reciprocal needs, and of these the need for approbation or *amour-propre*, the recognition of others – which Rousseau describes in note 15 of the *Discourse on Inequality* as 'relative, artificial, born in society' – is the root of evil. For he shows that by expanding their range of commodities and physical comforts men lost their natural hardiness and even allowed these luxuries 'to degenerate into real needs'. But becoming soft in this way was by no means as dangerous as becoming morally corrupt through a dependence on psychological needs for self-esteem and approbation; goods then acquired a surrogate value as currency in the competition for honour and power, which became all-consuming and which destroyed the natural basis for morality, compassion, setting egoism and the pursuit of gain in place of all other considerations.

In the Preface to his comedy *Narcissus, or the Lover of the Self*, written in 1753, a year before the *Discourse on Inequality*, Rousseau wrote of the hazards of 'fastening the knots of society by personal interest', putting men 'in mutual dependence, giving them reciprocal needs and common interests and obliging each of them to contribute to the good of others in order to ensure his own'.[8] The satisfaction of needs becomes subject to competition, which encourages dissembling, cheating and betrayal. It becomes necessary 'to take care that no-one sees what we are like; because for every two men whose interests agree, those of ten thousand perhaps are opposed, and there is no other way to succeed than to cheat or ruin all those people. Here is the fatal source of violence, cheating, lies and all the horrors necessarily brought about by a state of affairs where each pretending to work for the fortune or reputation of others can only raise his own above theirs at their expense.'[9]

In the second Discourse, Rousseau embellishes this picture of the servitude to which men are subjected by 'a multiplicity of new wants' by which they are 'brought into subjection ... to all nature, and particularly to one-another'. Whether victor or vanquished in the competition for power, their dependence is just as great. 'Insatiable ambition, the thirst of raising their respective fortunes, not so much from real want as from the desire to surpass others, inspired all men with a vile propensity to injure one another, and with a secret jealousy, which is the more dangerous, as it puts on the mask of benevolence.'[10] What were these evils but 'the first effects of property, and the inseparable attendants of growing inequality', Rousseau concludes.[11] Property and a growing awareness of the advantages of co-operative labour are seen as the foundation of civil society.[12]

---

[8] J.-J. Rousseau, *Narcissus*, in *Oeuvres complètes*, Gallimard, Paris, Bibliotheque de la Pléiade, Vol. II, p. 969. (All references to the complete works are to this edition.)
[9] *Ibid*.
[10] *Discourse on Inequality*, p. 203.
[11] *Ibid*.
[12] *Ibid*.

... from the moment one man began to stand in need of the help of another; from the moment it appeared advantageous to any one man to have enough provisions for two, equality disappeared, property was introduced, work became indispensable, and vast forests became smiling fields, which man had to water with the sweat of his brow, and where slavery and misery were soon seen to germinate and grow up with the crops.[13]

In *Emile*, Rousseau explicitly linked the expansion of needs with the generation of a surplus and the problems of the division and distribution of labour:

So long as only physical needs are recognised man is self-sufficient; the introduction of a surplus necessitates the division and distribution of labour; for although one man working alone earns only one man's subsistence, a hundred working together can earn enough for two hundred to subsist.[14]

Metallurgy and agriculture, 'the two arts which produced this great revolution', were by no means accidental discoveries; they presupposed a disposition to co-operative labour that was postulated by Rousseau in the initial undertaking to live and work together in communities – by that stage well established. The development of metallurgy and agriculture permitted a division of labour that increased the efficiency of co-operative labour, while bringing in train the perils of exploitation of the individual and tightening the knots of dependence between the individual and the group. While toolmakers were indispensable for the development of agricultural implements, they were also dependent on farmers to produce a surplus so that they could eat. Dependence of the individual on the group was increased at the time when individual property, through enclosure of the land, came to be introduced, bringing a tension that was to become a major source of social conflict. As Rousseau showed, the concept of property had already been established in the community of households, but this was property on the basis of use, which neither permitted the unlimited accumulation of goods, nor was the source of much contention, as long as it was kept on this basis.[15] It was with the enclosure of land and the development of a surplus, made possible by the technologies of metallurgy and agriculture, that individual property, the peculiar basis of civil society, was instituted and all its attendant evils came into play.

---

[13] *Ibid.*, p. 199.
[14] *Emile*, in *Oeuvres complètes*, Vol. IV, p. 456.
[15] *Discourse on Inequality*, p. 195.

In his glorification of manual labour; in his claim in *Emile* that 'the value set by the general public on the various arts is in inverse ratio to their real utility'[16]; his suggestion in the second Discourse that labour is the source of value[17]; that wages are driven down to the barest minimum for subsistence because of the exigencies of supply and demand[18]; Rousseau enumerates elements of the labour theory of value. There is a conceptual connection between the emphasis on needs as an objective category and utility as an economic criterion that is already made by Rousseau. Interestingly enough, he relates the distinction between true and false needs to the propensity of men to seek happiness in appearance rather than in reality. And because, after the Greeks, he associates true needs with the requirements of nature, he feels safe in referring to them as an objective standard in economics.

Despite the striking similarities between the picture Rousseau paints of the dialectic of civilization and the critique of bourgeois society of Marx, we should not be blind to its antecedents. Surprisingly enough we have in both Seneca and Lucretius, known to be formative influences on Rousseau, an account of the development of civilization and its evils which also focuses on the development of metallurgy and agriculture, the institution of individual property, and so on.

Apart from Rousseau's obvious references to various Stoic philosophers, such as Diogenes, Cato, Epictetus and Seneca, Georges Pire and Peter Jimack have shown conclusively that his moral philosophy as a whole is greatly influenced by the Stoics, and in particular by Seneca.[19] 'The theses of the two Discourses are already completely those of Seneca', Jimack claims[20]; and according to Pire the two authors share 'principles fundamentally identical'.[21] One could easily exaggerate this influence, but, as Pire is careful to point out, Seneca is only one bibliographic source among a host of others.[22] The work of Pire, Jimack and Jean Morel alone has documented Rousseau's indebtedness to the Epicurean Lucretius, on progress from the state of nature to advanced

---

[16] In *Oeuvres complètes*, Vol. IV, pp. 456-7.
[17] In *Oeuvres complètes*, Vol. III, p. 173.
[18] *Emile*, in *Oeuvres complètes*, Vol. IV, pp. 456-7.
[19] Georges Pire, 'De l'influence de Sénèque sur les théories pédagogiques de J.-J. Rousseau', *Annales de la Société J.-J. Rousseau*, 33 (1953-55); and P. D. Jimack, 'La Genese et la rédaction de *l'Emile* de J.-J. Rousseau', *Studies in Voltaire and the Eighteenth Century*, 13 (1960). See also Kennedy F. Roche, *Rousseau: Stoic and Romantic*, Methuen, London, 1974, chapter 1, 'The Stoic Origins'.
[20] Jimack *op. cit.*, p. 350.
[21] Pire, *op cit.*, p. 73.
[22] *Ibid.*, p. 83ff.

civilization[23]; to Diderot, on the infinity of possible fictitious needs compared with limited natural needs[24]; to Condillac, on the growth of needs and desires due to the ability to make comparisons[25]; to Locke, for his account of the genesis of ideas in the individual[26]; to Condillac, Buffon and Helvétius, for elements of sensationalist psychology, taken in turn from Locke[27]; and to Plutarch, Montaigne, Grotius and Pufendorf on natural law.[28] All of these were important themes in the second Discourse.

The Stoics were known advocates of proto-socialist principles: the essential equality of man, the ideal of communally owned goods, the exhortation to treat all men as brothers – tenets of Cynic philosophy, which had been handed down to them through Zeno. In Seneca's account of the life according to nature – which was also, incidentally, that of primitive man – in his Letter on Progress, we see these principles implicit:

> The earth herself, untilled, was more productive, her yields being more than ample for the needs of peoples who did not raid each other . . . All was equally divided among people living in complete harmony. The stronger had not yet started laying hands on the weaker; the avaricious person had not yet started hiding things away, to be hoarded for his own private use, so shutting the next man off from actual necessities of life; each cared as much about the other as about himself . . . What race of men could be luckier? Share and share alike they enjoyed nature. She saw to each and every man's requirements for survival like a parent. What it all amounted to was undisturbed possession of resources owned by the community . . . Into this ideal state of things burst avarice, avarice which in seeking to put aside some article or other and appropriate it to its own use, only succeeded in making everything somebody else's property and reducing its possessions to a fraction of its previously unlimited wealth.[29]

Lucretius' account of the development of society out of the state of nature follows the same successive stages as Rousseau's: from the hardiness of a solitary existence in nature, to the institution of the family group, and the development of language and covenants. As Rousseau notes, for the poet it was gold and silver 'which first civilized man and ruined humanity',

---

[23] See J. Morel, 'Récherches sur les sources du *Discours de l'Inégalité*', *Annales de la Société J.-J. Rousseau*, 5 (1909), 163ff.
[24] *Ibid.*, p. 140
[25] *Ibid.*, p. 146.
[26] Jimack, *op. cit.*, p. 289.
[27] *Ibid.*, chapter 13.
[28] Morel, *op. cit.*, p. 160ff.
[29] Seneca, Letter 90, from *Letters from a Stoic*, Penguin, London, 1969, pp. 174–5.

where for the philosopher it was iron and corn[30] – referring undoubtedly to Lucretius.[31] Nevertheless, for Lucretius, too, metallurgy and agriculture were significant developments in the history of progress, precisely because of the growth of needs that attended them:

> For what is ready to hand, unless we have known something more lovely before, gives pre-eminent delight and seems to hold the field, until something found afterwards to be better usually spoils all that and changes our taste for anything ancient. So men grew tired of acorns, so were deserted those old beds strewn with herbage and leaves piled up . . . Therefore mankind labours always in vain and to no purpose, consuming its days in empty cares, plainly because it does not know the limit of possession, and how far it is ever possible for real pleasure to grow, and this little by little has carried life out into the deep sea, and has stirred up from the bottom the great billows of war.[32]

For Lucretius the source of evil was not so much progress as such, as the intentions of men who allow themselves to be overridden by insatiable desires which they have the capacity and the duty to hold in check. Even though Rousseau, like Epicurus and the Stoics, linked needs and the expansion of knowledge as mutually determining facts, he, like them, was unwilling to argue that needs were therefore socially *determined*, their ineluctable expansion something over which we have no control or for which we bear no responsibility. A number of recent authors have argued that Rousseau sees in society the source of evil, shifting the theodicy problem from man, and his individual fall from grace, to society and its peculiar propensity to develop in him false needs.[33]

But Rousseau subscribes to certain Stoic axioms that make such a simple position impossible for him. As Epictetus claimed, it is not things themselves that disturb men, but their judgements about them[34]; and Rousseau too upheld the role of the faculty of judgement, admitting the intervention of the human will between sensation and desire. In *Emile* we have a number of reflections on the subject, some with explicit reference to the Epicurean view of sensation, where he insists that the sensationalist psychology of the Epicureans, which sees judgement itself as a species of sensation and our judgements therefore naturally determined, is false. In the *Discourse on Inequality*, Rousseau argues quite specifically against deterministic theories of human motivation. What

---

[30] *Discourse on Inequality*, p. 199.
[31] See Lucretius, *De Rerum Natura*, Book 5, 1113–14.
[32] *Ibid.*, Book 5, 1412–35.
[33] *Cf.* Colletti, *op. cit.*, pp. 144–5.
[34] Epictetus, *Encheiridion*, (Loeb edn of the *Discourses*, Vol. II, p. 487).

distinguishes men from animals is not intelligence as such, but 'the...quality of free agency':

> Nature lays her commands on every animal, and the brute obeys her voice. Man receives the same impulsion, but at the same time knows himself at liberty to acquiesce or resist: and it is particularly in his consciousness of this liberty that the spirituality of his soul is displayed. For physics may explain in some measure, the mechanism of the senses and the formation of ideas; but in the power of willing or rather of choosing, and in the feeling of this power, nothing is to be found but acts which are purely spiritual and wholly inexplicable by the laws of mechanism.[35]

Interestingly, Rousseau links the capability of free agency to the ability of man to vary the form that his needs take. He sees 'nothing in any animal but an ingenious machine, to which nature hath given senses to wind itself up' – language that bears a striking similarity to Locke's account of the human instincts. The difference between the animal who 'chooses and refuses by instinct' and man, who chooses 'from an act of free will'; is that 'the brute cannot deviate from the rule prescribed to it, even when it would be advantageous for it to do so; and, on the contrary, man frequently deviates from such rules to his own prejudice.'[36] Rousseau gives his famous, though inaccurate, example of the pigeon who would 'starve to death by the side of a dish of the choicest meats, and a cat on a heap of fruit or grain; though it is certain that either might find nourishment in the foods which it thus rejects with disdain, did it think of trying them'.[37] Man, by contrast, not only is able to vary the form that his basic physiological needs take, but also invents fictitious needs to take over where these leave off. 'Hence, it is that dissolute men run into excesses which bring on fevers and death because the mind depraves the senses and the will continues to speak when nature is silent.'[38]

But whatever Rousseau has to say about the natural needs of primitive man cannot lead us to associate innocence with virtue. Man's nature is such that once his cognitive and moral faculties have been developed (which already involves a departure from the natural state), all needs and desires involve a degree of assent, an element of judgement. Morality depends not on nature but on how we bring our will into accordance with its principles. The 'life according to nature' in this sense is far from being the life of the primitive in which, as for the beast, instinct rules.

---

[35] *Second Discourse*, p. 170.
[36] *Ibid.*, p. 169.
[37] *Ibid.*, pp. 169–70.
[38] *Ibid.*, p. 170.

Rousseau, like the Stoics, defined freedom as the ability to adopt a rule of behaviour and follow it: the ability to subjugate superfluous desires. This is a moral act which can only be undertaken by man already aware of choice and the range of options of which primitive man is innocent. Virtue is not a product of nature but of moral capability. No-one expressed this better than Seneca, in the closing lines of his ninetieth letter. Speaking of the primitive man, he declares:

> But however wonderful and guileless the life they led, they were not wise men; this is a title that has come to be reserved for the highest of all achievements ... though they all possessed a character more robust than that of today, and one with a greater aptitude for hard work, it is equally true that their personalities fell short of genuine perfection. For nature does not give a man virtue: the process of becoming a good man is an art ... the fact remains that their innocence was due to ignorance and nothing else. And there is a world of difference between, on the one hand, choosing not to do what is wrong and, on the other, not knowing how to do it in the first place. They lacked the cardinal virtues of justice, moral insight, self-control and courage. There were corresponding qualities in each case not unlike these, that had a place in their primitive lives; but virtue only comes to a character which has been thoroughly schooled and trained and brought to a pitch of perfection by unremitting practice. We are born for it, but not with it. And even in the best of people, until you cultivate it there is only the material for virtue, not virtue itself.[39]

Rousseau's thesis in the first and second Discourses that evil is a social phenomenon related directly to the emergence of artificial needs, which accompanies the expansion of inquiry, technological innovation and economic development, belongs to a genre of writings that was well established by the time he wrote. This genre, the critique of civilization, may claim such works as Lucretius' *De Rerum Natura*, Seneca's Ninetieth letter on Progress, Diderot's *Supplement to Bougainville's Voyage* and various Cynic and Stoic writings that are less famous. There is in these works a primitivist tendency, the propensity to judge the evils of civilization by comparing the life of advanced society with that of the simple life, which dates back as far as Plato's *Republic* and his nostalgic portrayal of the 'genuine and healthy city' where men limit their desires to the real 'neccessaries' of life.[40]

The appeal of the life 'according to nature', as I have tried to show in the case of Rousseau, has two senses which are often confused: it may be an appeal to nature in the descriptive sense – that is, to nature before

---

[39] Seneca, *op. cit.*, pp. 176–7.
[40] Plato's *Republic*, 372e and 373a.

man's influence through society was brought to bear on it, which is associated with the earliest chronological period of man's development. Or it may be an appeal to nature in the normative sense – that is, to the principles of nature, or the laws constitutive of man's nature and the physical universe at large. These principles as uniform and universal tendencies operate in all historical epochs and are always accessible to man through reason, and so an appeal to the life according to nature in this sense is not necessarily associated with the 'state of nature' or primitivism at all. Rousseau, like the Stoics, tended to vacillate between these two meanings; although capable of distinguishing between them, they were nevertheless disposed to think that the simple life of primitive man did accord better with the correct ordering of nature than the life of advanced civilization.

Even though the primitivist tendency is strong in these writings it did not entail naturalism. Both Rousseau and the Stoics were doubtful whether the life of the primitive man, the man who knew nothing but his natural needs, was in itself virtuous, because virtue involves moral choice and innocence is a natural goodness that knows no choice, assuming as it does ignorance of evil. Their position is therefore considerably more sophisticated than at first appears: they do not appeal to the life of natural man as the most perfect form of existence. Nor do they recommend man in advanced society to return to that form of existence. Rather, what they advocate is that civilized man should re-establish the harmony and tranquillity that primitive man enjoyed naturally, by consciously ordering his life according to the principles constitutive of human nature through exercise of his reason and will. This is a moral project and not the restitution of some primitive state and, as a consequence, even the 'natural' needs of man can no longer be seen simply as those basic needs for survival found in primitive man. Thus Rousseau made it clear that to want to abandon advanced society and return to the primitive state is a conclusion that only his detractors would wish to draw from what he has said.[41] Not only is it not feasible to put back the clock, as Seneca and most other critics of civilization realized, but it would achieve nothing. The problem of evil was the responsibility of the individual and his moral choice. Although having historical origins these were not problems susceptible to an historical solution.

[41] See *Discourse on Inequality*, note IX.

There are passages in Marx's 1844 Manuscripts, as Lucio Colletti[42], Iring Fetscher[43] and others have pointed out, that are highly reminiscent of the account Rousseau gives in the second Discourse of alienation due to property and artificial needs. Marx contrasts socialism geared to the satisfaction of 'human' needs, with capitalism which promotes 'inhuman' needs. Under socialism, 'the *wealth* of human needs' signifies 'a new manifestation of the forces of *human* nature and a new enrichment of human nature'. [44]

> Under private property their significance is reversed: every person speculates on creating a *new* need in another, so as to drive him to fresh sacrifice, to place him in a new dependence and to seduce him into a new mode of *enjoyment* and therefore economic ruin. Each tries to establish over the other an *alien* power, so as thereby to find satisfaction of his own selfish need. The increase in the quantity of objects is therefore accompanied by an extension of the realm of alien powers to which man is subjected, and every new product represents a new *potentiality* of mutual swindling and mutual plundering . . . Subjectively, this appears partly in the fact that the extension of products and needs becomes a *contriving* and ever-*calculating* subservience to inhuman, sophisticated, unnatural and *imaginary* appetites. Private property does not know how to change crude need into *human* need.[45]*

One cannot fail to notice the similarity to Rousseau's argument: advanced society creates needs of mutual dependence which are such that men cannot satisfy their personal needs without seeming to guarantee others the satisfaction of theirs; but this simply lays society open to massive dissembling that reduces them all to enemies. Marx, like Rousseau and a number of early socialists, believes that competition for the satisfaction of needs that society engenders is unnecessary and due only to the inequalities that it establishes. Society, through the institutions of property and money, creates artificial inequalities that are themselves the source of the greater powers of some over others and the gap between the inflated needs of the rich and the crude needs of the poor. Under alienated society,

---

[42] Colletti, *op. cit.*
[43] Carl J. Friedrich, 'Rousseau's Concepts of Freedom in the Light of his Philosophy of History', in Friedrich (ed.), *Nomos IV, Liberty*, Lieber–Atherton, New York, 1962, pp. 29–56.
[44] Marx/Engels, *Collected Works*, Lawrence & Wishart, London, 1975–, Vol. III, p. 306.
[45] *Ibid.*, pp. 306–7.
* See P. Springborg, 'Karl Marx on Needs', in R. Fitzgerald (ed.), *Human Needs and Politics*, Pergamon Press, Sydney, 1977. (Ed.)

Every product is a bait with which to seduce away the other's very being, his money; every real and possible need is a weakness which will lead the fly to the glue-pot . . . every need is an opportunity to approach one's neighbour under the guise of utmost amiability and to say to him: Dear friend, I give you what you need, but you know the *conditio sine qua non*; you know the ink in which you sign yourself over to me; in providing for your pleasure, I fleece you.[46]

All the institutions of bourgeois society contrive to maintain or increase the inequality of needs, because the expansion of capital – by means of a surplus accruing to some while others are exploited – depends on it. Thus, Marx argues, if 'industry speculates on the refinement of needs' for some, 'it speculates . . . just as much on their *crudeness*' for others 'but on their artificially produced crudeness'; the irony of advanced society lies in 'civilization contained *within* the crude barbarism of need'.[47] Under these conditions money needless to say, is the arbiter, the pimp, between the artificially inflated needs of the rich and the artificially diminished needs of the poor. Not only can money change needs into their opposite, but it can also create needs where none existed before: 'If I have no money for travel I have no need – that is, no real and realizable need – to travel'[48]; and vice versa. Lack of money has the power to deprive men of their capacities, transforming 'the *real essential powers of man and nature* into . . . merely abstract notions'[49], just as having money can transform all incapacities into their opposite; so the ugly can procure beautiful women, and the lame furnish themselves with the means of locomotion.

But Marx's invective against money, highly reminiscent though it is of Rousseau's argument that property reverses natural inequalities of strength and intelligence, is to a somewhat different effect. He does not condemn money as wealth, or even so much as the purveyor of false needs. It is money as 'the general distorting of *individualities*', the frustration of '*real essential powers* and *faculties*'[50], 'the general *confounding* and *confusing* of all things – the world upside down – the confounding and confusing of all natural and human qualities'[51], that he condemns. This is a judgement made with reference to his conception of the human essence and of the constitution of things in general. Money,

[46] Marx/Engels, *Collected Works*, p. 307.
[47] *Ibid.*, p. 311.
[48] *Ibid.*, p. 325.
[49] *Ibid.*
[50] *Ibid.*
[51] *Ibid.*, p. 326.

because as a manifestation of alienation it contravenes the human essence, frustrating the unfolding of man's latent needs and powers, is an evil. But Marx, unlike Seneca, Rousseau, Babeuf and the rest, does not argue that wealth and the fruits of civilization are bad in themselves; on the contrary, he is scornful of the old prejudices against luxury, believing that culture improves on nature, and he has nothing against wealth, seeing it, when its 'bourgeois form is stripped away', as 'the universality of needs, capacities, pleasures, productive forces . . . the full development of human mastery over the forces of nature . . . the absolute working out of [man's] creative potentialities'.[52] Money is, in fact, the 'alienated *ability of mankind*', and private property the only medium that permits the 'ontological essence of human passion come into being, in its totality as well as in its humanity', as he had already claimed in the 1844 Manuscripts.[53] This means that civilization with all its trappings, far from being an unqualified evil, is actually responsible for the development of productive forces which want only the removal of certain fetters for man's powers to be realized fully.

It is a curiosity of Marx's theory of human nature that there is a close association between the concepts of needs and powers. This has to do with the belief in a reciprocal dependence between progress of knowledge, new needs and the availability of objects for their satisfaction that we have already noted in Rousseau as presuppositions for the development of man's latent potentialities. Marx's materialism, which is more thoroughgoing than that of Rousseau, makes this mutual dependence explicit in his theory of objectification. Needs, and the passions in general, Marx claimed, are 'not merely anthropological phenomena in the [narrower] sense, but truly *ontological* affirmations of our being . . . and . . . they are only really affirmed because their *object* exists for them as a *sensual* object.'[54] Man's species–activity is such, Marx argues, that his capabilities exist *in potentia* as needs that require the material world as their field; thus man's potential powers are characteristically expended in creating a world of objects. This is not only a precondition for man's self-realization in a metaphysical sense, but it is also a precondition for survival. Man is a being whose nature it is to require objects outside himself in order to subsist. 'Man *lives* on nature . . . Nature is man's inorganic body . . . with which he must remain in

---

[52] Marx, *Grundrisse*, edited by Martin Nicolaus, Penguin, London, 1973, p. 488.
[53] *Collected Works, op cit.*, Vol III, pp. 325 and 322.
[54] *Ibid.*, p. 322.

continuous interchange if he is not to die.'[55]

But this dependence of man on the objects of his needs is not confined to the requisites for survival; it characterizes all other aspects of the maintenance and development of the self. In this way Marx subsumes under the class of human sensuous needs – the activities that presuppose a material object – not only the five senses, 'seeing, hearing, smelling, tasting, feeling,' but even the peculiarly cognitive activities, 'thinking, observing, experiencing, wanting, acting, loving', which he refers to as 'so-called practical senses'.[56]

The emergence of all these capabilities depends on a culture being able to provide appropriate objects for their exercise; so the emergence of a musical ear awaits the emergence of music, and so on. Subscribing to principles of sensationalist psychology, Marx argues after Feuerbach that, since 'sense–perception must be the basis of all science', and since the scientific understanding of behaviour is one that 'proceeds from sense–perception in the twofold form of *sensuous* consciousness and *sensuous* need', the scientific understanding of society is one that sees that 'all history is the history of preparing and developing *"man"* to become the object of *sensuous* consciousness, and turning the requirements of "man as man" into his needs.'[57]

This is far from being a mechanistic materialism. Indeed, Marx differentiates man from other animals who also depend on nature for the object of their needs, and who also produce some of their means of subsistence (that is, their dwellings) on the grounds of freedom and consciousness: an animal 'produces only under the domination of immediate physical need, whilst man produces even when he is free from physical need and only truly produces in freedom therefrom.'[58] While the animal produces at the behest of instinct, as in the case of the bird building its nest, man can freely choose the goals for his production.

This view of objectification as the vehicle of human creativity accompanies an expressivist tendency in Marx that can be traced back to Hegel, where man's unfolding powers over nature, actualized as needs, are seen as manifestations of man's innate characterological traits.[59] Far from being a deterministic mechanism in the form of instinctual urges as they are in animals, needs in man are expressive of his ability to transcend

[55] *Ibid.*, p. 276.
[56] *Ibid.*, pp. 299–300.
[57] *Ibid.*, p. 303.
[58] *Ibid.*, p. 276.
[59] See Charles Taylor, *Hegel*, Cambridge University Press, 1975, who develops the concept of an 'expressivist tendency' in Hegel.

the limits of material existence and leave his own mark on the external world by shaping it in accordance with his elected ends. Marx in this way avoids in his conception of man's relation to the objects of his existence the mechanical determinism of eighteenth-century materialism and its man–machine theories of human nature. Needs are symptomatic, not so much of the power of physical objects and processes over man, as of his own powers over the physical world. The concept of needs functions in Marx's philosophy rather like the concept of desire in Hegel's: to express an awareness of the limits and finitude of human existence that man as a creature reaching out for mastery of the given necessarily experiences.

It is not too much to claim, then, that the concept of needs has a primarily ontological function to perform in Marx's writings, since Marx already suggested as much himself. Needs represent basic human motivations and they represent the form in which man's relation to the world is actualized; but more than that they are tangible manifestations of an underlying human nature. So much is this so that one is justified in asking whether we are to understand Marx's concept of needs in a literal sense at all. In other words, Marx so characteristically refers to the whole range of human powers in the abstract as needs that we are prompted to ask whether these have to be concretely expressed as needs to count as such or not. The free attribution of needs in the construction of theories of human nature that we have seen since Marx and Freud poses a general dilemma, in that it now becomes open to anyone to attribute to man, in general, and men, in particular, needs irrespective of what they themselves feel they need.

This poses problems in the case of Marx, in that from *The German Ideology* on, when he develops more systematically his theory of historical materialism, the concept of needs has a specific role to play as the motor of progress. Here it is inconceivable that needs could refer to anything less than concrete or expressed needs. Marx enumerates the 'four basic moments of human existence' as (1) the satisfaction of basic subsistence needs ('eating, drinking, clothing', etc.); (2) the creation of new needs emerging from the satisfaction of basic subsistence needs; (3) the social relations which the organization of everyday life throws up; and (4) co-operative labour as a further development of this process.[60] In other words, Marx generates his theory of the dynamics of culture as a tissue of structures and institutions built up around the creation and satisfaction of needs.

[60] *The German Ideology*, in *Collected Works*, Vol. V, pp. 41–3.

One cannot but be struck by the similarities between Marx's account of the 'four moments' in the development of civilization and the classic account of Seneca, Lucretius, Rousseau, etc. There is an important difference, however, and that is in the much tighter relation that Marx draws between environmental factors and needs. The classic account had taken note that needs are such that the object must be within conceivable reach for one to conceive a need for it, and thus the mutual dependence between the growth of knowledge, technical proficiency and new needs. Nevertheless, needs, although occasioned by environmental factors, were not seen to be caused by environmental factors. From the Stoics and Epicureans to Rousseau, although sensitive to the material conditions of behaviour, these philosophers nevertheless argued that the attraction of material goods, however great, could still be controlled through moral purpose. Their indictment of progress was made on the assumption that men could still choose not to succumb to a life governed by the pursuit of an ever wider range of material benefits. This marks the difference between Marx and his antecedents. Marx argues that those who attribute to moral purpose the capability of distinguishing between true and false needs simply fail to recognize the causal origins of needs in society:

> Whether a desire becomes fixed or not, i.e., whether it obtains exclusive [power over us] – which, however, does [not] exclude [further progress] – depends on whether material circumstances, 'bad' mundane conditions permit the normal satisfaction of this desire and, on the other hand, the development of a totality of desires.[61]

The communists, Marx argues, are the only ones who recognize this 'empirical connection'.[62] And,

> Since they attack the material basis on which the hitherto inevitable fixedness of desire and ideas depended, the communists are the only people through whose historical activity the liquefaction of fixed desires and ideas is in fact brought about and ceases to be an impotent moral injunction as it was up to now with all moralists 'down to' Stirner.[63]

For Marx (and Rousseau), genuine needs, compared with the artificial needs of advanced society, are not 'fixed' or 'natural' in the obvious sense. They are genuine not because they are in fact fixed, since all needs have that propensity, or because they are found in cultures least altered by civilization, but because they are constitutive of human nature as such. Marx reserves the term 'human need' for this special normative

[61] *Ibid.*, p. 255.
[62] *Ibid.*, p. 256n.
[63] *Ibid.*, p. 255n.

sense of the term in the same way that Rousseau uses the term 'natural needs'. But unlike Rousseau, whom he condemns in the *Grundrisse* as a 'Robinsonade', or primitivist, Marx never confuses those characteristics constitutive of human nature as such, with those to be found in nature.

In Marx we have a different difficulty, and that is that while he retains the notion of a proper human nature, a human nature properly constituted, by which, for instance, the man of capitalism is judged, nevertheless at the same time this human nature is open to history to determine. Thus he claims that which needs will be changed and which needs will be eliminated by the communists will be decided in a practical way, and not on the basis of theoretical principles; in the same way that in the second of the *Theses on Feuerbach* he claims that the question of truth is not a theoretical but practical question – man 'must prove the truth, i.e., the reality and power, the this-sidedness of his thinking in practice'.[64]

Now only if history conforms to rational laws uniform with those of the universe as a whole can we accept the idea that we can leave it to history to decide which needs and which truth claims are genuine and which are not. This suggests a teleological, if not, indeed, an eschatological, concept of history which sits badly with Marx's avowed secularism and rejection of all theological positions.

Marx always tried to avoid the problem of values, but by his use of the concept of needs to express conditions for the actualization of the human essence he demonstrated that he could not. Moreover, his penchant for explaining man's function in terms of human needs shares in the confusion between needs as imputed attributes of human nature in general and concrete or expressed needs, which has become a feature of some forms of need theory ever since. Wherever there is a gap between the ideal picture of human nature and that of human reality, a need is inserted – hence needs for love, security, relatedness, creativity, etc. There is nothing wrong with this way of talking about human nature as such, as long as it is recognized for what it is – metaphorical.

In other words, the imputation of needs produces a theory of human nature at a metaphysical level that cannot at the same time do service as an account of the motivation of particular men. This is a mistake that can be seen whenever a move is made from theory of human nature in terms of imputed needs, to the analysis of the behaviour of individuals as need-based, on the assumption that imputed needs and expressed needs

[64] In *Collected Works*, Vol. v. p. 6.

are the same thing, or indeed that a need can be imputed even when it is not felt. This becomes more dangerous when people get the idea of bringing people's concrete needs into line with needs imputed to them according to a theory of human nature; the theory of environmental conditioning from the early socialists to the Skinnerians has provided a basis for doing this. Marx, who commended the communists for seeing the solution to the problem of man in terms of a transformation of needs and of society at large, was not immune from making this link.

Rousseau's election of an individual moral solution to the problem of freedom was unacceptable to Marx for various reasons. Hegel's influence had left its mark on Marx, in his conception of needs as the ontological expression of man's characteristic powers over a world of objects. The Hegelian philosophy of history, which saw man's nature as unfolding in time, put an emphasis on the growth of these latent powers as new sciences and technologies provided objects for them. In a curious way, however, Marx shares with the Stoics a view of the correct relation between man as subject and the objects of his existence – that they are for enjoyment and use and not to possess, nor should man be possessed by them – which puts him closer to Rousseau than one might otherwise think. Marx shared with the Stoics the ideals of equality, the community of goods and the universal brotherhood of man, an ethic that rejected individual property and the appropriation of goods except on the principle of use. One can see in Marx's declamations against the passion for 'having', similarities with Epictetus' conception of man's correct attitude to material objects in the allegory of the ball-player, on which Marx, in his theory of activity and production, however, does not quite follow through. The good ball-player, says Epictetus, lavishes his attention on the ball, not because of any intrinsic merits in the object, but because it provides the opportunity for him to display his skill. In his 'struggle for possession' the ball-player does not really want to keep or own the ball, but only to establish mastery. Man's relation to the material world in this way constitutes the durable framework within which he plays out the characteristic traits of his nature: an ability to humanize the world by the exercise of moral purpose.

It is, of course, a moral purpose which Marx will not recognize as such; and yet if we think of the significance of the doctrine of the fetishism of commodities and the various forms in which he foreshadowed it, we can see that the whole point of Marx's insistence that men need not feel terrorized by the material artifacts they have created, and that they can destroy the alien power of commodities through correct understanding and right disposition towards them, suggests a concept of moral purpose as it was traditionally understood. Epictetus' parable states very well a central Marxian theme:

> So ought we also to act, exhibiting the ball-player's carefulness about the game, but the same indifference about the object played with, as being a mere ball. For a man ought by all means to strive to show his skill in regard to some of the external materials, yet without making the material a part of himself, but merely lavishing his skill in regard to it, whatever it may be . . . It is, indeed, difficult to unite and combine these two things — the carefulness of the man who is devoted to material things and the steadfastness of the man who disregards them, but it is not impossible.[65]

In this sense Epictetus expresses the logic of Marx's position where, although sometimes drawing on the distinction between natural and artificial needs, Marx ultimately sees all needs as indifferent, the link with material existence that gives man the opportunity to develop his human potential. As we have seen, however, this was a logic to which Marx was not always faithful.

The difference between Marx, on the one hand, and Epictetus, Rousseau and the Stoics, on the other, is that the latter conceived man's relation to material objects negatively, while Marx conceived it positively. On the whole the Stoics saw the use of material goods as an unavoidable necessity, their attraction posing a distraction from moral purpose. But Marx saw the creation of a world of material objects as a positive expression of man's species nature — and if these artifacts sometimes created an obstacle to man's further advancement, it was one the very overcoming of which increased his power. We have only to look at the opening lines of Epictetus' *Encheiridion* to see the difference:

> Some things are under our control, while others are not under our control. Under our control are conception, choice, desire, aversion, and in a word, everything that is our own doing; not under our control are our body, our property, reputation, office, and in a word, everything that is not our own doing. Furthermore, the things under our control are by nature free, unhindered, and unimpeded; while the things not under our control are weak, servile, subject to hindrance, and not our own. Remember, therefore, that if what is naturally slavish you think to be free, and what is not your own to be your own, you will be hampered, will grieve, will be in turmoil, and will blame both gods and men; while if you think only what is your own to be your own, then no one will ever be able to exert compulsion upon you, no one will hinder you, you will blame no one, will find fault with no one, will do absolutely

---

[65] Epictetus, *Discourses*, Book II, chapter 5 (Loeb edn, Vol. I, pp. 243 and 239).

nothing against your will, you will have no personal enemy, no one will harm you, for neither is there any harm can touch you.[66]

This is a concept of freedom that could hardly be more diametrically opposed to the Promethean view of Marx. Freedom as he saw it was precisely the ability to subject the material world to human needs, to exert an increasing power over nature. Not only did Marx not foresee the constant obstacles to its own end that such a process necessarily throws up, as Rousseau had explained; but he held that a transformation of society, or a widespread change in the relation of man to his external environment, is the only true criterion for freedom, which is not to be sought in the state of the perfect will, as Rousseau and Kant maintained, or any moral condition arrived at through introspection and understanding, as Hegel and the ancients had declared.

It is here, of course, that we see the greatest difference between Rousseau and Marx, in the conclusions they draw from the same premises, that emphasis on similarities in their thought to some extent obscures. Rousseau's critique of civilization is ultimately pessimistic; only a spiritual rejection of the ethos of economic expansion and competition for material goods can lead to restoration of the moral tranquillity from which man through progress has departed; this is a morality that harks back to the Stoics and early Christian thought. Marx, by contrast, is optimistic in his criticisms of the evils of capitalism, foreseeing in the expansion of human powers over nature and the material world the obsolescence of a morality that forces man to deny his expanding desires and the possibility of the harmonious gratification of all under socialism, 'to each according to his needs'.

---

[66] Epictetus, *Encheiridion*, (Loeb edn of the *Discourses*, Vol. II, p. 483).

Mill and Marx

Graeme Duncan

It is clearly a very difficult matter to compare, in general terms, the writings of two complex, active and prolific political thinkers. However, that task may be carried out with vigour, cogency and a readiness to define an essential contrast at all costs. In the case of Mill and Marx, the sharpest – and in my view, the most misleading – dichotomies have been drawn within political or ideological frameworks which are closely related to the divisions and conflicts that preoccupy the interpreter in his own day. Mill and Marx are presented commonly as protagonists of rival and incompatible social types and, anachronistically, as champions of the modern forms of liberal and communist society – though such forms of society are diverse internally, and are as a rule characterized very differently by social theorists. A few deny any fundamental difference between modern societies, focusing instead upon the pressures imposed upon them by a high level of industrial development, bureaucracy or some other common feature of modernity, which leads to significant if not overbearing similarities between societies of apparently different political complexion. But to the traditional liberal or Marxist, liberal and communist societies differ substantially, and those differences can be observed – through a glass darkly, perhaps – in the classical writings of the respective traditions. Thus, to the liberal, J. S. Mill is a champion of pluralism, diversity, freedom in history, choice, the full flowering of the individual; while Marx is a monist, a determinist, an historicist, a champion of totalitarian democracy and collectivized man. To the Marxist, Mill is likely to be seen as an airy-fairy preacher of liberties and reason, who accepted as tolerable if not desirable, institutions that bred basic inequality, whereas Marx fought for full human emancipation, identified those institutions and arrangements that were incompatible with freedom, and defined the conditions of social change. My own view, which I have elaborated elsewhere[1], is that the liberal Mill and the anti-liberal and post-liberal – but not totalitarian – Marx are reasonable shorthands, but careful selection makes it possible to radicalize or illiberalize Mill, and to soften and de-radicalize Marx, so that Mill becomes dogmatic or totalitarian or socialist, and Marx the forerunner of the placid Bernstein, or an anguished, moralistic humanist, not a rigorous scientist of society, or the father of Western sociology.

Rather than trying to cover everything, which is impossible within such a short compass, I propose to limit the dimensions of my comparison to the theories of human nature that are present in the writings of Mill and Marx, though this will naturally force me to touch upon their views on social organization, the physical or material environment, epistemology, etc. At that point I will simply indicate the bearings and draw boundaries.

At the heart of political theory lies the effort to establish a relationship between the state, or political institutions, or institutional arrangements, and man's nature, in whatever terms that might be expressed, and to engage in political advocacy – and perhaps more direct action – on that basis. Political theory is not pure, monastic, unsullied, but both arises out of particular social and political circumstances, especially situations of conflict, and advocates solutions or responses: it may be elevated, abstract, remote, learned, distinguished, but it is advocacy nonetheless, and it advocates on the basis of certain assumptions about the powers and limits of human beings. Crudely, a view of human nature is a view of what human beings actually – or normally or naturally – are, or what they distinctively, truly or ideally are, or what they are potentially. It is expressed basically in terms of needs (biological as well as cultural), interests or drives, standards, and potentialities or capacities – man needs political authority, a power out of himself, or he is a calculating egotist, or naturally aggressive; man is a rational animal; man has the power, within appropriate social conditions, to be a creative, versatile and communal being. These are all difficult notions, which overlap, and are therefore neither always nor easily separated out: a view of human nature may contain elements of each. Such views are set commonly within a particular account of history; for example, the conservative will see human nature as revealed in past history and actual human behaviour (in the interpretation of which there may be a strong element of selection and

[1] G. Duncan, *Marx and Mill: Two Views of Social Conflict and Social Harmony*, Cambridge University Press, 1973.

idealization), whereas the radical will tend to present history as a systematic suppression or violation of human nature.

I should state at this point that I am suspicious of the term 'human nature'. Most statements or facts about 'human nature' seem to me statements or facts about human societies or human beings. 'Human nature' may suggest something fixed or common, an essence. My own preference is for human potentialities or powers or capacities, the appropriate question being: Of what are men capable, or incapable, in such and such circumstances? 'Such and such circumstances' calls for a further word. Political theory, as I understand it, contains three basic elements or parts as it deals with the world (as distinct from how it deals with or approaches the world; for example, appropriate methods of understanding, etc.). These are views of human nature or whatever that signifies, of social and other structures and arrangements, and of the natural or physical environment, although that is increasingly man-made. Human nature cannot reside in a vacuum, theoretical or actual, and arguments about human nature must be related to arguments about social and environmental circumstances and frameworks: the ideal circumstances for human nature to unfold may not be achievable for social/structural or environmental reasons, and hence structures and environments may constitute limiting or even destructive conditions.

John Stuart Mill (1806–73) and his contemporary Karl Marx (1818–83) wrote in the aftermath of violent political change – the French Revolution – and in the midst of rapid and far-reaching economic change – commonly referred to as the Industrial Revolution. Traditions, established routines, even orderly living seemed to be under substantial threat, especially according to conservative thinkers. Edmund Burke, writing of political dissolution rather than of the economic changes which were clear to other observers by the turn of the eighteenth century, complained of a new, fragmented, differentiated, contractual and individualistic world, and distinguished between a true community, united by common feelings, accepted hierarchy and habitual ways, and a competitive, loose association, in which people were divided, lonely, insecure, with each struggling against all. Mill and Marx shared elements of that critique, contrasting existing fragmentation and conflict with a more harmonious and cohesive order, but neither accepted the social arrangements which seemed natural to Burke. Each defined a realized or fulfilled human nature which served as a critical and normative instrument in terms of which existing societies might be analyzed and evaluated, though other instruments of analysis and evaluation were also used. Each thought that men and women were less than they might and could be, elaborated the strategies that would bring them closer to true humanity, and roughly sketched the kind of social arrangements that might support their ideal conceptions of man.

Yet the differences are great. Liberals need not say that human nature is all of a piece, and will generally recognize and incorporate a particular vision of existing social differences or principles of stratification in their accounts of man's nature as it is. The bulk of mankind, the masses, the working class, may be deficient in the relevant political or cultural capacities or gifts, and part of the political problem becomes that of ensuring the influence and authority of those who are politically impartial, competent or expert. (Another part of that problem may be how to restrain rulers and to raise the level of the – perhaps temporarily – subordinate groups.) It is not surprising that we should find that one of the several crucial conflicts or uncertainties in Mill's thought should be between a genuine desire to raise the virtue and increase the powers of everybody and a fear that a too-rapid extension of political and other rights might challenge what were, for the time being, institutions and arrangements necessary to civilization. While we may take as his central moral goal the increase of the general capacity for self-determination, we cannot leave things there. Was Mill able to combine liberal and democratic values, the modified market society and the entitlement of all men to civilized and full lives? Was his doctrine blighted by elitism, a disguised or subtle class bias, in that the style, drift and substance of his liberalism was above all relevant to the few, and took little account of the resources, economic and otherwise, of the bulk of mankind?

On the face of it, Mill offered a clear and appealing account of the human qualities he valued, and it was largely in terms of their promotion that he supported liberal political and economic institutions. But before we can accept this, two lines of criticism, each of which relates Mill to aspects of his philosophical heritage, must be noted. The first connects Mill to his utilitarian background, and particularly to the idea that there are no qualitative distinctions between pains and pleasures. Pushpin is as good as poetry as long as the amount of pleasure is equal. Such an apparently soft or democratic doctrine has been condemned because it seems that, in its terms, a society of contented slaves, or one of masochists and sadists, or a Brave New World, might produce the greatest sum total of satisfaction. Whether or not this is the case – and none of these are anything like the kind of society actually recommended by Jeremy Bentham* or by his father James Mill† – the younger Mill clearly rejected such uncritical and possibly low conceptions of man. In his writing on Utilitarianism and elsewhere, he rejected the inherited doctrine both descriptively and morally. According to his firm liberal vision of self-development, dissatisfied human beings were much superior to ever so satisfied pigs.

The second doubt cast on the firmness of Mill's view of human nature concerns the relationship between his theory of cognition and his social and political doctrines. Ellen Wood has argued recently that Mill's allegedly empiricist conception of the self as simply a series of sensations or possibilities of response cannot sustain a principle of extreme importance to him – that of 'individuality' based upon individual spontaneity, autonomy and the primacy of the self. Again, she finds his theory of cognition not really compatible with a conception of liberty which 'emphasizes the precedence of the self, the individual, the idea of self-development and spontaneity'.[2] A simple reply is that even if Mill did work with such a crude cognitive theory – and he did puzzle over exactly what potentialities and natural bents man might have – he nonetheless was committed undoubtedly to a view of man that stressed and valued his capacity for autonomy and self-development; the basic aim of social policy was to remove bad influence and place people under the sway of institutions and arrangements that conduce to their betterment.

Of what, then does this betterment consist? Mill was at his most ebullient in describing the liberal society and the human excellences he expected it to encourage. He thought that it could be most favourable to the emergence of persons who were critical, rational, thoughtful, active, bold, individual, autonomous, and socially conscious and disinterested.

---

* Jeremy Bentham (1748–1832), English jurist and philosopher; one of the chief expounders of utilitarianism. (Ed.)

† James Mill (1773–1836), Scottish philosopher, historian, and economist in England; father of John Stuart Mill. Met Jeremy Bentham (1808), adopted his principles, became his companion and chief promulgator of Bentham's utilitarian philosophy in England. Known as founder of philosophical radicalism. (Ed.)

[2] E. M. Wood, *Mind and Politics: An Approach to the Meaning of Liberal and Socialist Individualism,* University of California Press, Berkeley, 1972, p. 41. Along with John Gray, I have criticized Ellen Wood's effort to force Mill into a strait-jacket of liberal-empiricism, in 'The Left Against Mill', in a collection of essays on Mill edited by Kai Neilsen, (forthcoming).

These terms are not necessarily distinct from each other and, in any event, require some elaboration and placing within the institutional context that Mill recommended. They do not refer to what are, so to speak, free virtues, exercised at the mere whim of the agent, independently of historical conditions. The bold, active, critical lover of liberty, who refuses to bend the knee, is the foe of irrational and constricting authority: his role, at certain historical stages, may be to help define and defend a rational authority. The rational person is prey to neither passion nor prejudice. State intervention, based on rational Malthusian assumptions, might be used legitimately to limit the size of poor families – which might ultimately help reduce the potency of the sensual desires, despised by Mill for both their effects and their nature. The political prejudice most feared by Mill was that of 'the uncultivated herd who now compose the labouring masses'[3] though he was also critical of many of their masters. Given their prejudice, ignorance and caprice, their immediate accession to political power would make bad laws almost inevitable – for example, laws for a minimum wage or a tax on machinery, laws founded on mistakes in political economy. 'They believe that they are ground down by the capitalist. They believe that his superiority of means, and power of holding out longer than they can, enables him virtually to fix their wages. They ascribe the lowness of those wages, not, as is the truth, to the overcompetition produced by their own excessive numbers, but to competition itself.'[4] Class conflict was irrational, and a militant proletariat was suffering from false consciousness, to use the Marxian term. Whereas to Marx the sharpening of class-consciousness was crucial to its eventual abolition, and hence to human liberation, to Mill it was destructive and unnecessary, rooted in ignorance and immaturity. Mill's sympathy with a socialism of small, competing, co-operative associations rested upon the assumption that they would be moralizing bodies, expanding social or public feeling and undermining class division: his goal was 'the healing of the standing feud between capital and labour; the transformation of human life, from a conflict of classes struggling for opposite interests, to a friendly rivalry in the pursuit of good common to all'.[5]

[3] J. S. Mill, *Autobiography*, Oxford University Press, 1958 edn, p. 197.
[4] Mill, 'Reorganization of the Reform Party', in *Essays on Politics and Culture*, G. Himmelfarb (ed.), New York, 1963, p. 292.
[5] J. S. Mill, *Principles of Political Economy*, Vols II and III, in *The Collected Works of John Stuart Mill*, University of Toronto Press, 1965, IV.vii.2, p. 763.

Mill drew limits to the innumerable and conflicting directions in which men might develop. The restrictive principle assumes that freedom – and the right to the rights that it requires – presupposes some notion of what to do, and that the lack of an existing capacity for freedom creates a need for restraint in the time being, perhaps along with the exercising of freedom in areas not dangerous to rational social arrangements. This leads on to a more positive or developmental principle – that people should be encouraged, by education, example, exhortation, political and other participation, to develop their faculties so that ultimately they might become full members of the society. Mill's efforts for the emancipation of women – which he described, with co-operative production, as 'the two great changes that will regenerate society'[6] – are well known. Mill did not take 'the sum total of the existing generation' for granted: certain paths were dangerous and should be barricaded, and others were desirable and should be fostered. Certain forms of self-assertion – notably, bold radical collective action on the part of workers – were rejected as manifestations of human excellence in terms of the assumptions, themselves ideological, Mill made about the nature of the most fruitful and practicable social order in his own time.

Mill thus accommodated his vision of a widespread unfolding of human nature to a down-to-earth awareness of present possibilities and constraints. As dreamer, social critic, reformer, even social engineer, he was quite unprepared to accept existing behaviour, attitudes and beliefs, existing 'human nature', as universal and inescapable, as 'inherent in Man and Society'. This was an error with which he charged the classical political economists:

> the principal error of narrowness with which they are frequently chargeable, is that of regarding not any economical doctrine, but their present experience of mankind, as of universal validity; mistaking temporary or local phases of human character for human nature itself; having no faith in the wonderful pliability of the human mind; deeming it impossible, in spite of the strongest evidence, that the earth can produce human beings of a different type from that which is familiar to them in their own age, or even, perhaps in their own country![7]

This denial that there were firm limits to human nature – such as those suggested by the conservative slogan 'You can't beat human nature' – hints at the possibility of far-reaching change. But there were limits set

---

[6] Letter to Parker Goodwin, 1 January 1869, in *Letters of John Stuart Mill*, edited by Hugh S. R. Elliott, London, 1910, Vol. II, p. 172.

[7] Mill, *Auguste Comte and Positivism*, University of Michigan Press, 1961, pp. 82–3.

by the existing development of human nature. Communism might be possible in some future state of enlightenment and virtue, but in the meantime the major need was to publicly defend private property, 'that primary and fundamental institution', against increasing working-class attacks upon it.

> We may, without attempting to limit the ultimate capabilities of human nature, affirm that the political economist, for a considerable time to come, will be chiefly concerned with the conditions of existence and progress belonging to a society founded on private property and individual competition; and that the object to be principally aimed at in the present stage of human improvement, is not the subversion of the system of individual property, but the improvement of it, and the full participation of every member of the community in its benefits.[8]

The private property or market system needed purification – for example, through the limitation of rights of inheritance and bequest – but the social principle had not yet penetrated man, and self-interest and individualism remained vital and positive forces. Mill could argue this while hoping for the eventual disappearance of the competitive and selfish attitudes and institutions of his own society, and expressing revulsion at much of liberal culture and market morality, especially the ideal of 'a society only held together by the relations and feelings arising out of pecuniary interests.'[9]

Mill's recommendations rest upon a belief in the growing power of reason in social life, as through education and closer communication it touches more and more people. In his view, ignorance bred division and knowledge encouraged cohesion, and hence he was able to establish a conceptual linkage between wisdom, virtue and social unity. This clearly underlay his confidence in the peaceful emergence of an educated, harmonious and tolerant community.

One of the standard conflicts between interpreters of Marx is between those who deny and those who assert that he had a theory of human nature. My own view is that he had such a theory and that it forms a crucial element of his total social theory. I claim this notwithstanding the fact that he did at times deny there was such a thing as human nature, by which he meant that there was no essential, classless, ahistorical human nature, something that transcended the boundaries of historical epochs and social groupings. He came to attack those who talked about Man, or man as such, or the human essence – all abstractions divorced from an

---

[8] *Principles of Political Economy*, II.i.4, p. 214.
[9] *Ibid.*, IV.vii.1, p. 760.

historical context. The discussion of human nature by the German True Socialists was politically reactionary as well as wrong – their concern was 'not the interests of the proletariat, but the interests of Human Nature, of Man in general, who belongs to no class, has no reality, who exists only in the misty realm of philosophical fantasy.'[10] A universal and undiscriminating love of mankind replaced practical social analysis. One part of Marx's critique of ideology was that particular human qualities and social institutions were dignified as natural, so that, for example, Carlyle could treat the cult of genius as an eternal law of nature, or the calculating egoist of classical political economy could be perceived as authentic man. What kind of human nature did the pedantic Bentham, much abused by Marx, come up with? 'With the dryest naivety he takes the modern shop-keeper, especially the English shop-keeper, as the normal man. Whatever is useful to this queer normal man, and to his world, is absolutely useful.'[11] But all this being said, Marx's indictment of the capitalist society which he loathed rested heavily upon a moral vision of a truly human life, though the conditions for its fulfilment were not yet there, its dimensions could not be described adequately, and it could not be brought into being by fiat or by choice. In the future 'realm of freedom', the condition of human beings is spoken of as that 'most favourable to, and worthy of, their human nature'.[12]

In arguing that Marx worked with a conception of what was humanizing and what dehumanizing, what human and what inhuman or subhuman, I am not denying that it is possible to develop a predictive social theory that is independent of notions of a truly human life. Such a theory could rest upon the imagined nature and development of structures – for example, a crisis of capitalism – with the relevant assumptions being those about the dynamics of the economic system and how people might be expected to react – as determined heteronomous creatures, or calculating pursuers of pleasure, or whatever. No judgements are made about how human beings ought to act or react in such circumstances or why. A bare social theory of this character could be elaborated, but it is not Marx's, at any stage of his life. Capitalism may contain certain forces driving it towards destruction, but it needs to be destroyed because of what it does to human beings, and if it is to be

[10] Karl Marx, 'The Communist Manifesto', in *Selected Works*, Progress Publishers, Moscow, 1958, Vol. I, p. 58.
[11] Marx, *Capital: A Critique of Political Economy*, 3 vols, Foreign Languages Publishing House, Moscow, 1957–62, Vol. I, p. 609, note 2.
[12] *Ibid.*, Vol. III, p. 800.

destroyed, it will be because of the chosen action of people, aware at last of its effects upon them.[13] The system is not merely disintegrating, but is bad.

According to Marx, the human labour process – as distinct from that of animals – is characterized by the use and fabrication of instruments of labour. Human labour is planned, conscious and purposive. In labouring, man acts upon and changes nature, thereby putting a human stamp upon it, and he is thus able to contemplate himself in a world he has created. Economic reproduction changes not only the objective conditions, nature, but man and his communities as well. 'By thus acting on the external world and changing it, he at the same time changes his own nature. He develops his slumbering powers and compels them to act in obedience to his sway.'[14] The producers change 'by the emergence of new qualities, by transforming and developing themselves in production, forming new powers and new conceptions, new modes of intercourse and new speech'.[15] Or, putting it more baldly, 'all history is nothing but a continuous transformation of human nature.'[16] Under industrial capitalism, however, man's distinctive powers were exercised within a crippling framework. Capitalist 'human nature' was not man fulfilled.

Marx indicated – sometimes directly, but more often indirectly, in indicting man's dehumanization – the powers of the fully human being, insofar as he was capable of perceiving them in his time. The writings on alienation, both in the early 1840s and in the *Grundrisse*, articulate a conception of human nature through a critical analysis of particular, concrete social conditions, which divided men within and from each other, and enslaved them to alien and destructive forces. Alienation arose within the process of labour, especially owing to the division of labour. As Marx wrote in *Capital*, manufacture revolutionized labour and converted the labourer 'into a crippled monstrosity, by forcing his detail dexterity at the expense of a world of productive capabilities and

---

[13] I have argued in more detail elsewhere that Marx made it quite clear that the objective tendencies of social development led towards a future which was desirable in terms of his own conception of human nature. (*Marx and Mill*, p. 98) Agitation and propaganda were to help awaken people to what was wrong with their world, rather than to embrace the inevitable.
[14] *Capital*, Vol. I, p. 177.
[15] Marx, *Pre-Capitalist Economic Formations*, edited by E. J. Hobsbawm, translated by Jack Cohen, Lawrence & Wishart, London, 1964, p. 93.
[16] Marx, *The Poverty of Philosophy*, Foreign Languages Publishing House, Moscow, 1956, p. 165.

instincts; just as in the states of La Plata they butcher a whole beast for the sake of his hide or his tallow'.[17] Alienation was expressed in his relationship to the diverse things, objects and institutions he produced, in that his creations became themselves creators, objects of worship, to which man subordinated himself. Religion, commodities and money, and the state, were all the work of men, but the relationship was systematically misconceived, and men were emptied in the process. Under bourgeois domination, with the immense expansion of man's productive power, men were more than ever subjected to 'the violence of things'.[18] A further form of alienation is that in which man experiences separation from his fellows. The authentic man of liberal society – the egoistic and anti-social individual – 'treats other men as means, degrades himself to the role of a mere means, and becomes the plaything of alien powers'.[19] He, and especially the proletarian, is excluded from true social life. 'What sort of society is it, in truth, where one finds several millions in deepest loneliness, where one can be overcome by an inevitable longing to kill oneself without anyone discovering it. This society is not a society: it is, as Rousseau says, a desert populated by wild animals.'[20]

The theory of alienation, and scattered comments throughout Marx's works, hold that man is deprived of his humanity because of the crippling and restricted character of his labour, which denies his freely creative capacity (which is part of what Marx understood by universal or species-being, or *Gattungswesen*), because he is controlled by outside or alien forces which are in fact his own products, and because he is divided from and hostile to other men. All of this suggests a standard of human nature or, at least, an account of powers and needs that are taken to be truly human (rather than deformed, limited or debased). To be distinctively human in the Marxian sense is to be free and self-determining, creative and versatile (a whole man) and social or communal, enjoying genuine human relationships. Some of these notions are difficult and their meaning is disputed, and they can only be understood adequately in relation to an elaboration of the economic, social and political institutions and arrangements within which they

---

[17] *Capital*, Vol. I, p. 360.
[18] Marx, *The German Ideology*, Progress Publishers, Moscow, 1964, p. 94.
[19] Marx, 'On the Jewish Question', in *Early Writings*, translated by T. B. Bottomore, Watts, London, 1963, p. 35.
[20] Quoted in Eugene Kamenka, *The Ethical Foundations of Marxism*, Routledge & Kegan Paul, London, 1962, p. 36, note 1.

might be embodied, or which might promote them. And it was just such an elaboration that Marx generally – and on principle – avoided.

To be free, man had to be master in his own universe, to dominate his own creations rather than being dominated by them. Marx's humanist anthropology demanded the destruction of religious and other illusions in order that man could become the highest being for man. 'The criticism of religion ends with the doctrine that man is the supreme being for man. It ends, therefore, with the categorical imperative to overthrow all those conditions in which man is an abused, enslaved, contemptible creature.'[21] Now those conditions, whose historical function and imminent weakening Marx was to analyze carefully in his major works, were very substantial and deep-rooted, and are held by many of his critics to be inseparable parts of civilization. They include money, commodities, the market or free enterprise system, surplus value, wage labour, the division of labour, classes, the state and ideology, including religion and moral philosophies. The capitalist economic system, combining features unique to it with others shared by previous class societies, was incompatible with human liberation: it was compatible, to a point, with political emancipation, that is liberal political institutions, including the representative state. The form of society in which all people might realize fully their human potentialities – potentialities inevitably squandered or denied outlet within capitalism – was clearly very different institutionally and morally from any with which we are familiar historically. Within it, the greatest possible creativity and versatility[22] would develop. And the need for society would be satisfied within genuine communities. The new sociality was already prefigured in the meetings of French socialist workers. 'Smoking, eating and drinking are no longer simply means of bringing people together. Company, association, entertainment which also has society as its aim, is sufficient for them; the brotherhood of man is no empty phrase but a reality, and the nobility of man shines forth upon us from their toil-worn bodies.'[23] Given such powerful social feelings, the government of men might be replaced by the administration of things, public life might lose its political character, and free and close associations emerge out of the

[21] 'Contribution to the Critique of Hegel's Philosophy of Right', in *Early Writings*, p. 52.
[22] Marx had difficulties with the division of labour; his hatred of it was deep-rooted, as his whole vision of man conflicted absolutely with crippling specialization. But while, in some of the writings of the 1840s, he suggested that the division of labour might be abolished or sharply curtailed, a realm of necessity is accepted later. (*Capital*, Vol. III, p. 800) Upon that restricting basis a true realm of freedom might blossom.
[23] In *Early Writings*, p. 176.

divided, class-ridden and coercive societies of the past. Perhaps human nature itself is not a bar to such achievements; whether or not they are feasible if societies are to remain large, complex and industrial, and to face serious resource problems, is another question.

At one level – and not the deepest – it is possible to focus upon the apparent affinities between the two conceptions of man. It has been suggested that Marx and Mill shared essentially the same commitment to freedom, the same ultimate goal of society 'in which the free development of each would be the condition of the free development of all',[24] and Arnold Kaufman has claimed that 'Mill's ideal of the good life is more like Marx's conception of unalienated man than it is like Bentham's happy man.'[25] I have argued that Mill presented a firm, critical and developmental conception of man, ascribing distinctive virtues to the good man, and it is true also that some of the qualities in man that Mill valued were also valued by Marx. Each wanted human nature to develop in innumerable and conflicting directions, and praised resolution, determination, boldness and the transcendence of narrow or selfish individualism. Mill's attack upon market morality, upon the primitive liberal vision of society as a collection of self-absorbed calculators, and his preoccupation with the creation of a cohesive society, along with the strength of Marx's feeling for individualism in the right conditions, suggest that it is wrong to counterpose an individualist Mill to a socialist or communally oriented Marx. Each – but in different ways – tried to combine the virtues of individuality and a deep feeling of community in their free or fulfilled man.

But this is only part of the story. The nature of an ideal cannot be comprehended adequately without an awareness of the thinker's attitudes to existing institutional structures, his views of the processes and purposes of change, and his accounts of imagined and valued alternative states. There may be substantial differences between superficially similar images of man once those images are tied into the theories of which they are part. According to one social theorist, another conception of man may be appealing but denuded because arrangements are assumed, implicitly or openly, which put it beyond the mass of the people.

---

[24] Felix Oppenheim, *Moral Principles in Political Philosophy*, Random House, New York, 1968, p. 54.
[25] A. S. Kaufman, 'Wants, Needs and Liberalism', in *Inquiry*, XIV:(3) Autumn 1971, 202.

Mill, unlike Marx, stressed the basic importance of consciousness or ideas in social life. 'It is how men think that determines how they act, and though the persuasions and the convictions of average men are in a much greater degree determined by their personal position than by their reason, no little power is exercised by the persuasions and convictions of those whose personal position is different, and by the united authority of the instructed.'[26] The gradual reform of social institutions and the gradual uplifting of the masses, fostered and led by rational and moral persons, would lead eventually to a reformed private property system and some democratization of the political system. This could lead to the withering of competitive and selfish attitudes and institutions and a merging of social classes. The stationary state that Mill envisaged when men made peace with their world was characterized by

> a well-paid and affluent body of labourers; no enormous fortunes, except what were earned and accumulated during a single lifetime; but a much larger body of persons than at present, not only exempt from the coarser toils, but with sufficient leisure, both physical and mental, from mechanical details, to cultivate freely the graces of life, and afford examples of them to the classes less favourable circumstanced for their growth.[27]

Such a vision of steady change inspired by a kind of classless reason seemed to Marx unrealistic, and the accepted institutional framework seemed incapable of realizing the values to which Mill explicitly adhered. Marx's analysis is materialistic: political and other ideological forms, including the claims of reason, can only be understood when related to 'the anatomy of civil society'. Those forms serve, more or less precisely, the demands of the capitalist productive system, namely accumulation and exploitation. Although it is not a simple one-way relationship, in which political and ideological forms immediately and straightforwardly express the needs of the economic system, the roots of change lie within the relations of production. Relationships of ownership and non-ownership to the means of production constitute the structural basis of class division and conflict, which has a positive role in Marxian theory.

> The very moment civilization begins, production begins to be founded on the antagonism of orders, estates, classes and finally on the antagonism of accumulated labour and actual labour. No antagonism, no progress. This is the law that civilization has followed up to our days. Till now the productive forces have been developed by virtue of this system of class antagonisms.[28]

[26] Mill, *Considerations on Representative Government*, London, 1960, p. 184.
[27] *Principles of Political Economy*, IV.vi.2, p. 755.
[28] *The Poverty of Philosophy*, p. 68.

Social conflict was not to be left dormant. The suppressed class was awakening but needed to be further awakened: the objective roots of class conflict were present but Marxism, as active proletarian science, was to aid the process of class maturation and class war. And in the – perhaps protracted – revolutionary transformation of society, the proletariat rids itself of 'the muck of ages and become fitted to found society anew'.[29] And that means a new and not simply reformed society.

There are two significant differences between the two positions that require comment here. The first is that, from a Marxian standpoint, the liberal appeal to reason and morality is ill-conceived, in that generally these are not the sources of change, and specifically that capitalist interests, within a tightening economic system allow little flexibility. Mill was preaching to deaf ears, however much verbal adherence there was to his high ideals. The more relevant difference concerns whether or not the recommended institutional structures are compatible with, or supportive of, the declared ideals. The basic Marxian criticism at this point is that the actual social and economic order recommended by Mill is incapable of realizing liberalism's own promise and values, because of the inequalities, biases and restrictions that are integral to it. Marx discerned a contradiction between the traditional economic dogmas and the modern tendencies of men such as Mill[30]; while C. B. Macpherson finds a clash for liberals, including Mill, between the vision of 'the fullest development and enjoyment of men's faculties' and 'the necessary requirements of the market economy, the essentials of which they did not fully see'.[31] Capitalist property institutions, and especially the market economy, are seen as important sources of unfreedom for the non-owning classes. I myself have no doubt that the market system, in its historical forms, has been a significant source of unfreedom and frustration for large numbers of people, but I am yet to be convinced, by cogent argument and probing speculation – adequate demonstration being clearly out of the question – that this and other equally powerful sources of unfreedom can be removed in large modern societies.

No clinching answers are possible. The best that we can do, in evaluating different conceptions of human nature, is in the first place to consider the following elements of the larger social theories in which they are set: the account of existing reality; the explanation of it; the

[29] *The German Ideology*, p. 86.
[30] *Capital*, Vol. I, pp. 610–11, note 2.
[31] C. B. Macpherson, 'Post-Liberal-Democracy?', in *Democratic Theory: Essays in Retrieval*, Clarendon Press, Oxford, 1973, p. 179.

evaluations of existing and alternative or imaginable polities, and of the costs of change and stasis; models for the future; strategies of action and supporting conditions for a different order; and the elaborations or pictures of the society within which men are expected to find fulfilment or themselves. In other words, the view of human nature needs to be displayed within its total theoretical context, although that may remain at points opaque or obscure, because of the changes that are presupposed. But that, at least, gives us theories – rather than merely assertions, polemics or prophetic utterances – to meet. However, given that there are no commonly agreed criteria for appraising political beliefs, including beliefs about human nature – that, as is often said, there are no proofs of political beliefs, only good and bad defences – what can we say about the means of appraising beliefs and the kind of susceptibility they should have to criticism? Theories can be confronted in at least three ways: by evidence relevant to their basic tenets; by logical and empirical analysis concerned essentially with the internal consistency of the theory; and by moral and descriptive critique which is concerned with the evaluation of images of society in what is taken to be their concrete or practical meaning.

Relevant evidence does not sit waiting to be accommodated. There is no 'accurate empirical assessment' of the real world with which political theorists can be confronted indiscriminately. The gap between fact and value, between the existing and the ideal society, may not be unbridgeable, but the impact of the evidence remains to be mediated theoretically, and that will be done in quite different ways by those who want to change the world and those who wish to keep it. The preponderance of a certain human type within a particular society may be taken as an exemplification of human nature or as a result of bad social institutions. Both Marx and Mill took a very critical attitude to the dominant behaviour and values of their own time, while taking cognizance of facts which seemed, from other perspectives, counter-evidence.

The clear specification of the object of analysis – an account of human nature, for example – will enable the critic to explore the inner consistency of the theory, through a mixture of conceptual and empirical analysis. Are all the valued or human potentialities compatible with each other? Are the means of realization and the assumed institutional structures compatible with the values that are enunciated?

This form of critical investigation links up with the effort to identify what counts as an embodiment or concretization of the relevant ideal.

The question 'what would it look like in institutional terms?' is a perfectly proper one, although the answer given will depend upon the social and ideological background and assumptions of the interpreter. Different assumptions about human capacities or desires may lead to the same thinker being seen as an optimistic voluntarist and as a repressive totalitarian. Hence, while it is vital that the actual meaning, the social shape, of political recommendations and visions of life or of realized human nature should be rigorously and thoroughly explored, we must remain conscious of the dangers of reading them from rival or contradictory perspectives and changing them into an alien currency which distorts them. The totalitarian side of Marx's theory can be highlighted by disregarding his assumptions about the process of change and his belief in freedom and by introducing conservative views about what would be required to create such a radically different social order. The sociological weakness of Mill's analysis can be emphasized by concentrating upon the alleged effects of a market system, and disregarding the economic reforms and the general improvements he favoured.

A choice between Marx and Mill on human nature will need to be made, finally, not on the basis of their explicit statements about the best type of human character and the society most befitting man's nature, but in relation to the realism of their ideals in relation both to their other theoretical postulates and to what we ourselves regard as the possibilities of our own social orders. Mill's ideal differed less from the world he saw than did Marx's ideal, but each exaggerated the degree of rationality, disinterestedness and community possible in large, complex and diverse societies where people are placed differently. The major problems for the more optimistic social theorists arise because of the inevitability of difference, division, and social and political structures in modern societies, and not because 'you can't beat human nature'.

Herbert Marcuse and Christian Bay

Ross Fitzgerald

Although discussion about human needs in intellectual inquiry is as old as Plato and Aristotle, recently there has been a marked revival of need theory, especially in relation to politics. Herbert Marcuse and Christian Bay are two of the most important contemporary scholars who have constantly and consistently related talk about human needs, not only to the explanation of political behaviour, but also to the evaluation of political ends and purposes.

There are striking similarities between Marcuse, the German-born Hegelian philosopher[1], and Bay, the Norwegian-born political scientist now resident in Canada. Both are influenced by Marx and Freud; both are vocal critics of so-called liberal democracies and the 'liberal-make-believe'; both are crucially concerned with the promotion of 'positive' freedom. Most importantly, both attempt to ground political morality on a notion of human needs, Marcuse by making a distinction between 'true' and 'false' needs, Bay by distinguishing 'needs' from 'wants, desires and demands'.

Marcuse makes the notion of needs central to his analysis of the defects of advanced industrial society.[2] A fundamental thesis of his work is that, guided and controlled by the imperatives of technical rationality, contemporary industrial society – both Soviet and Western – has succeeded in satisfying the needs perceived by most of its members: these perceived needs are primarily material needs. However, this satisfaction is at the expense of the vital needs for liberty, for non-alienation, and for individual fulfilment without repression, which Marcuse had identified on the basis of his reading of Hegel, Marx and Freud. For Marcuse, the

[1] Marcuse died on 31 July 1979, as this essay was being written.
[2] See especially Herbert Marcuse, *One Dimensional Man*, Beacon Press, Boston, 1964, chapter 1 and pp. 241–5; *Eros and Civilization*, Beacon Press, Boston, 1955, p. 96ff; and *Negations: Essays in Critical Theory*, Beacon Press, Boston, 1968, pp. 189–90.

satisfaction of men's material needs via technological progress is part of a whole system of domination. This is because such satisfaction eliminates conflict and extinguishes the desire for social change among groups who in earlier forms of society would be revolutionaries and dissenters. Instead of being the precondition of all other freedoms – as Marx believed – the satisfaction of material needs has been transformed into a process that reinforces servitude.

Aware of the apparently paradoxical claim that in satisfying the needs of individuals the contemporary system may dominate them, Marcuse attempts to distinguish between 'true' and 'false', or alien, needs. The former, he maintains, begin with 'the vital ones – nourishment, clothing, lodging at the attainable level of culture'[3]; only these needs have an unqualified claim for satisfaction because, as Marx held, the satisfaction of these needs is the precondition for the realization of all needs, true and false. 'False needs' are those that are 'superimposed upon the individual by particular social interests in his repression: the needs which perpetuate toil, aggressiveness, misery and injustice'.[4] Most of the prevailing needs to relax, to have fun, to behave and consume in accordance with the advertisements, to love and hate what others love and hate, belong to this category of false needs; their gratification is at the expense of the person's, and others', true needs for liberty and self-determination. For Marcuse, in contemporary industrial society most *perceived* needs are false needs; moreover such needs are determined by external powers over which the individual has no control. Therefore, no matter how much 'false' needs may have become the individual's own, not matter how much he identifies himself with them and finds himself in their satisfaction, they continue to be what they were from the beginning – products of a society whose dominant interest demands repression and domination. Marcuse maintains that advanced industrial society (note that he always uses the singular) is to be judged not simply as undesirable but as 'impossible' – so antithetical to the (true) needs of man in society that it must be transcended if humanity is not to be destroyed.[5]

Although Marcuse claims that human needs are historical needs (in the sense that they are the product of historical social conditioning), he holds

---

[3] *One Dimensional Man*, pp. 4–5.
[4] *Ibid.* See also *Negations*, pp. 189–96.
[5] But what can it mean, asks David Kettler, to say that the 'impossible' is existent and stable and seemingly invincible? See 'Herbert Marcuse: Alienation and Negativity', in Anthony de Crespigny and Kenneth Minogue (eds), *Contemporary Political Philosophers*, Dodd, Mead & Co., New York, 1975, pp. 1–48.

that the existence of needs is a matter of truth and falsehood, and that their satisfaction

> ... involves standards of *priority* – which refer to the optimal development of the individual, of all individuals, under the optimal utilization of the material and intellectual resources available to man.[6]

These resources, he maintains, are calculable. The 'truth' or 'falsehood' of needs, designate objective conditions 'to the extent to which the universal satisfaction of vital needs and, beyond it, the progressive alleviation of toil and poverty are universally valid standards'.[7]

Marcuse holds that individuals are not necessarily the arbiters of what they truly need.

> In the last analysis, the question of what are true and false needs must be answered by the individuals themselves, but only in the last analysis; that is, if and when they are free to give their own answer. As long as they are kept incapable of being autonomous, as long as they are indoctrinated and manipulated . . . their answer to this question cannot be taken as their own.[8]

This position, and – as we shall see – that of Christian Bay, raises the charge of elitism and authoritarianism. It allows, and in fact encourages, the possibility of rulers 'forcing men to be free' and 'indoctrinating a *real* concensus'. This is because while human beings all know what they want or desire, they may not know what they (truly) need. 'How', asks Alasdair MacIntyre, for example, 'has Marcuse acquired the right to say of others what their true needs are? How has he escaped the indoctrination which affects others?'[9] These questions underline what MacIntyre takes to be inescapable elitist consequences of Marcuse's viewpoint.

A fundamental thesis of Marcuse's *One Dimensional Man* is that by producing material affluence, the technology of advanced industrial society has the effect of eliminating protest and dissent, and at the same time fostering identification with the established order. As MacIntyre says, 'If the worker and his boss enjoy the same television program and visit the same resort places, if the typist is as attractively made up as the daughter of her employer, if the Negro owns a Cadillac, if they all read the same newspaper, then this assimilation indicates not the disappearance of classes, but the extent to which the needs and satisfactions that serve the

---

[6] *One Dimensional Man*, p. 6 (his emphasis.)
[7] *Ibid.*
[8] *Ibid.*
[9] Alasdair MacIntyre, *Herbert Marcuse: An Exposition and a Polemic*, Viking Press, New York, 1970, p. 72.

preservation of the Establishment are shared by the underlying population.'[10] Because of its all-persuasive technological rationality, Marcuse argues that contemporary industrial society is 'totalitarian'; he explains that the word 'totalitarian' applies not only to a terroristic political co-ordination of society, but equally to a non-terroristic economic–technical co-ordination that operates through the manipulation of needs by vested interests, thus precluding the emergence of an effective opposition against the whole system.[11] For Marcuse, it is this totalitarian productive apparatus that determines individual needs and aspirations. Moreover, totalitarian technology 'obliterates the opposition between private and public existence, between individual and social needs' and serves to 'institute new, more effective, and more pleasant forms of social control and social cohesion'.[12]

For Marcuse, the fact that individuals seem 'happy' being satisfied with material goods and services handed down by the system is beside the point. Such people are suffering from false consciousness. They are fulfilling false needs. Moreover, their false and alien needs (and possibilities) are imposed upon them by the system itself. Marcuse makes it clear that this happiness is not true happiness; this false happiness, like 'repressive affluence', is part of the 'democratic unfreedom' that Marcuse (and also Christian Bay) castigates. The same applies to 'sexual satisfaction' and 'sexual freedom' in advanced industrial society. Just as the satisfaction of false needs is part of the system of servitude, so Marcuse argues in *One Dimensional Man* and later works that the permissiveness of modern society is also an instrument of domination. So-called 'sexual liberation' is part of democratic unfreedom: it distracts attention from revolutionary possibilities.

In *Eros and Civilization*, Marcuse had optimistically argued for a revision of the orthodox Freudian position that all civilization must be based on repression. The two most important concepts he developed in his attempt to synthesize Marx and Freud were 'surplus repression' and 'the performance principle'. Marcuse's terminology reveals that the first concept was to be identified with Marx's 'surplus value' – that is, the *quantitative* measure of human exploitation under capitalism; 'surplus repression', a set of restrictions necessary to maintain a particular form of social domination, is distinguished from 'basic repression', the set of restrictions upon the instincts necessary to found and maintain civilization

---
[10] *Ibid.*, p. 8.
[11] *One Dimensional Man*, p. 3.
[12] *Ibid*, p. xvi.

per se.[13] Marcuse insisted that a large portion of sexual repression was repression in the service of domination.[14] His argument went as follows: As technical and material progress removes the obstacles that scarcity placed in the path of civilized development, repression is more and more surplus to the task of maintaining civilization and more and more a matter of maintaining specific and removable forms of social dominations – that is, advanced capitalism.[15] Given Marcuse's revision of Freudianism, modern society might in theory be relieved of its repressive character without relapsing into chaos and barbarism.[16]

While Marcuse accepted Freud's distinction between the pleasure principle and the reality principle (this corresponded to the distinction between unrepressed behaviour and repressed civilized behaviour), he argued that under capitalist domination the reality principle takes a particular, and a particularly repressive, form which he termed 'the performance principle'. This concept which corresponded to Marx's *qualitative* characterization of existence under capitalism – that is, alienation and reification – involved the repression of libidinal energies and their expression only in controlled forms of work and of limited monogamic sexuality. Marcuse argued that the repression of sexuality contributed significantly to maintaining the general order of repression[17], but it was a repression of *eros*, rather than of genital sexuality, with which Marcuse was concerned. In fact, he was strongly opposed to 'genital tyranny', which he regarded as yet another expression of the performance principle and the turning of human beings into things. He argued that genuine liberation would involve a return to the state of 'polymorphous perversity', in which the entire body would become a source of sexual pleasure. (As Marcuse explained in his pessimistic 'Political Preface' to the 1966 edition of *Eros and Civilization*: '"Polymorphous sexuality" was the term which I used to indicate that the new direction of progress would depend completely on the opportunity to activate repressed or arrested *organic*, biological needs: to make the human body an instrument of pleasure rather than labor. The

---

[13] See Paul A. Robinson *The Sexual Radicals*, Paladin, London, 1972, pp. 114–82, especially p. 153, for a useful exposition of the difference between surplus repression and basic repression.
[14] See *Eros and Civilization*, p. 185.
[15] *Ibid*.
[16] See Robinson, *op. cit.*, pp. 114–82.
[17] For a similar argument, see Wilhelm Reich, especially *The Sexual Revolution*, Vision Press, New York, 1962; and *The Function of the Orgasm*, Farrar, Straus & Groux, New York, 1961.

old formula, the development of prevailing needs and faculties, seemed to be inadequate; the emergence of new, qualitatively different needs and faculties seemed to be the prerequisite, the content of liberation.'[18])

When *Eros and Civilization* was first published in 1955, Marcuse optimistically believed that erotic liberation and 'non-repressive sublimation' were possible, and that the life instinct (Eros) would triumph over the death instinct (Thanatos) – one of whose representations, via the performance principle and surplus repression, was the alienation of man from his sexuality.[19] However, in his later works Marcuse has stressed the constant increase in aggression and destructiveness in advanced industrial society as a result of the combination of the performance principle and surplus repression.[20]

In *One Dimensional Man*, and in his works since then, he has argued that desublimation has already occurred in contemporary society, but that the forms in which it occurs are as repressive as ever sublimation was. The release of libido is so controlled that the 'sexuality' that saturates the surface of social life – in advertising, for example – satisfies human beings without restoring to them the proper enjoyment of their true organic sexuality.[21] The channelled release of libidinal energy also diverts them from revolutionary activity, and from 'negative' critical thinking that is necessary for challenging the system. In many ways Marcuse, like Freud, has a conception of sexuality and libido – that involves a notion of energy that 'builds up' and the 'pressure' of which has to be 'released'. What is important to stress here is that contemporary sexual freedom is, for Marcuse, a wrong road and yet another example of the domination of the system.

For Marcuse all human liberation depends on the consciousness of servitude; the emergence of this consciousness is greatly hampered by the predominance of false needs and satisfactions which, to a great extent, have become the individual's own. Because Marcuse emphasizes that all needs are historical needs – he insists that even human instincts must be seen as a historical product – the historical process always replaces one system of preconditioning by another. The optimal goal of political activity is the replacement of false needs by true ones (or the

---

[18] *Eros and Civilization: A Philosophical Inquiry into Freud*, Allen Lane, 1970, p. 13 (his emphasis).
[19] There is not space here to deal with a criticism of Marcuse's reinterpretation of Freud, but for a trenchant critique, see MacIntyre *op. cit.*, pp. 43–58.
[20] See 'Aggressiveness in Advanced Industrial Society', in *Negations*, p. 256.
[21] See MacIntyre, *op. cit.*, p. 74.

inculcation of true needs rather than false ones) and the abandonment of repressive satisfactions. This must involve, Marcuse tells us, the redefinition of needs: the needs that human beings possess at the moment must undergo a 'qualitative change' if they are to be liberated.[22] But in Marcuse's good society who is to do the redefining and inculcation of needs? Who is to do the liberating? And what is the price of such 'liberation'?

When Marcuse wrote *One Dimensional Man* he was markedly pessimistic about radical change. In fact, he saw contemporary industrial society as one in which 'all counter-action is impossible' because of the pervasiveness of technical rationality. But four years later after hearing of the student uprising in Paris in the spring of 1968, he quickly wrote his *Essay on Liberation* (published 1969) in which, as Geoffrey Hawthorn explained, 'although his diagnosis remained the same he was markedly more optimistic about the possibilities of "negation" from outside the society – from the Third World, from the stubborn refusals of students and other rebels, not, or not yet, incorporated into the pervasive unidimensionality, from dropouts, from necessarily unconventional art, and from the "unconscious", ex *hypothesi* immune to all social influence. But he never explained in what way any of these constituted or even pointed towards the positive promise of new order.'[23]

In his essay 'Liberation from the Affluent Society'[24] Marcuse explains that the 'problem' is that because contemporary capitalism (in defiance of Marxist theory), delivers the goods to an ever larger part of the population, far too few people want the kind of 'liberation' of which he dreams – or which as some of his critics suggest, he so longs to impose. Marcuse consequently contrasts 'objective need' – what he thinks people ought to want – with 'subjective need' – people actually wanting what they ought to want. The latter, alas, 'does not prevail. It does not prevail precisely among those parts of the population that are traditionally considered the agents of historical change.' The subjective need is repressed, Marcuse argues, 'firstly, by virtue of the actual satisfaction of needs, and secondly, by a massive scientific manipulation and administration of needs'.[25]

[22] See *One Dimensional Man*, pp. 6–7, 100 and 245–6.
[23] Geoffrey Hawthorn, *Enlightenment and Despair: A History of Society*, Cambridge University Press, 1976.
[24] In D. Cooper (ed.), *The Dialectics of Liberation*, Penguin, Harmondsworth, 1968, pp. 175–6. For a similar argument, see Marcuse, *Counter Revolution and Revolt*, Beacon, Boston, 1972.
[25] 'Liberation from the Affluent Society', in Cooper, *op. cit.*, p. 182.

Throughout his work Marcuse is never quite clear about who are to be the agents of radical transformation and liberation. Sometimes he talks about the proletariat (but rarely: the working class cannot be a revolutionary force as they have been 'bought off with golden chains'); sometimes he considers the likely revolutionary force to be radical students and social outsiders; sometimes deeply repressed erotic instincts; and sometimes intellectuals. But in 'Liberation from the Affluent Society' and in an essay with the 'newspeak' title of 'Repressive Tolerance', Marcuse makes it clear (as clear as he ever makes anything) that it is the intelligentsia who are to be the catalyst of historical change and that the revolution requires 'the dictatorship of an elite over the people', albeit an 'educational dictatorship', which will 'force men to be free'.[26] Indeed, one of Marcuse's main grievances against the 'late' capitalist order is that, because of the satisfaction of material needs, the silent minority does not want, and has no interest in, such a revolution. 'By the same token, those minorities which strive for a change in the whole . . . will be left free to deliberate and discuss . . . and will be left harmless and helpless in the face of the overwhelming majority, which militates against qualitative social change. The majority is firmly grounded in the increasing satisfaction of needs.'[27]

In 'Repressive Tolerance' Marcuse argues that the tolerance of the advanced industrial democracies is a deceit. The expression of minority views is allowed just because it cannot be effective; indeed the only type of expression it can have renders it ineffective. The major premise of his argument is that the majority are effectively controlled by the system and so moulded that they cannot hear or understand radical criticism. It follows, says MacIntyre, that the people have no voice, and the alternatives are not between genuine democracy and the rule of an elite, but between rival elites, the repressive elite of the present and the

---

[26] See 'Liberation from the Affluent Society', p. 180; and 'Repressive Tolerance', in H. Marcuse, B. Moore, Jnr., and R. Wolff, *A Critique of Pure Tolerance*, Cape, London, 1969, pp. 95–137.

[27] 'Repressive Tolerance', pp. 107–8 and 134; quoted in Antony Flew's superb critique of Marcusian need theory, 'Wants or Needs, Choices or Commands?', in Ross Fitzgerald (ed.), *Human Needs and Politics*, Pergamon Press, Sydney, 1977, pp. 213-28, especially pp. 222-4. For other critiques, see, from a Marxist viewpoint, Paul Mattick, *Critique of Marcuse*, Horder and Herder, New York, 1972; and from a liberal viewpoint, David Spitz, 'Pure Tolerance', in *Dissent*, 13 (1966): 510-25. See also Maurice Cranston's long polemical essay, 'The Pessimism of Herbert Marcuse', in *The Mask of Politics and Other Essays*, Allen Lane, London, 1973, pp. 157-85; and Gad Horowitz, *Repression, Basic and Surplus Repression in Psychoanalytic Theory: Freud, Reich, and Marcuse*, University of Toronto Press, 1977.

liberating elite of the Marcusean future. Freedom of speech is not an overriding good, for to allow freedom of speech in the present society is to assist in the propagation of error, and 'the telos of tolerance is truth'. The truth is carried by the revolutionary minorities and their intellectual spokesmen, such as Marcuse, and the majority have to be liberated by being re-educated into the truth by this minority, who are entitled to suppress rival and harmful opinions. This is perhaps the most dangerous of all Marcuse's doctrines, for not only is what he asserts questionable but his is a doctrine which, if it were widely held, could be an effective barrier to any rational progress and liberation. As MacIntyre suggests, 'To make men objects of liberation by others is to assist in making them passive instruments, it is to cast them for the role of inert matter to be molded into forms chosen by the elite'.[28]

Marcuse's implicit elitism is made explicit in *An Essay on Liberation*.[29] His position is, as MacIntyre says, that the human nature of inhabitants of advanced industrial society has been 'molded so that their very wants, needs, and aspirations have become conformist – except for a minority, which includes Marcuse. The majority cannot voice their true needs, for they cannot perceive or feel them. The minority must therefore voice their needs for these, and this active minority must rescue the necessarily passive majority'.[30] This passive majority includes even the 'new (technically skilled) working class' who 'by virtue of its position, could disrupt, reorganize, and redirect the mode and relationships of production. However, they have neither the interest nor the vital need to do so.'[31] They are well integrated and well rewarded by the system. But who, asks MacIntyre, are the minority who are to rescue the majority by transforming them: the same old ratbag of students, blacks, 'flower-power', or an educational elite?[32]

The answer is that Marcuse's utopia *must* involve an educational dictatorship. In *One Dimensional Man* Marcuse asked a key question: how can the people who have been the object of effective domination create by themselves the conditions of freedom?[33] His answer is honest and direct: to the degree to which the slaves have been preconditioned to exist as slaves and be content in that role, their liberation necessarily

---

[28] See MacIntyre, *op. cit.*, pp. 102-3 and 105.
[29] *An Essay on Liberation*, Beacon Press, Boston, 1969.
[30] MacIntyre, *op. cit.*, p. 100-1.
[31] *An Essay on Liberation*, p. 11.
[32] In MacIntyre, *op. cit.*, p. 101.
[33] *One Dimensional Man*, p. 6.

appears to come from without and from above. They must, in Rousseau's famous words, be 'forced to be free', to 'see objects as they are, and sometimes as they ought to appear', they must be shown the 'good road' they are in search of. Marcuse continues:

> But with all its truth, the argument cannot answer the time-honoured question: who educates the educators, and where is the proof that they are in possession of 'the good?'[34]

This position, as with Bay's, contains terrible dangers: of authoritarianism and the erosion of personal freedom.

Of the writings of contemporary theorists, that of Christian Bay best exemplifies the recent revival of need theory and especially the idea of politics being put in the service of human needs. His important work, the *Structure of Freedom*, first published in 1958, was an attempt to combine the behavioural and the normative approaches to the study of politics and to unify research in all social sciences.[35] Since then, Bay has constantly argued that the social sciences should be used to help mankind, and specifically that our increasing knowledge should be placed in the service of the satisfaction of human needs.

Like other contemporary need theorists[36], Bay's more recent work involves an attempt if not to *ground* political prescriptions on a theory of human needs, then at least to connect and relate value-statements in an intelligible way to allegedly empirical evidence about a hierarchy of human needs.

According to Bay's normative position, a government's only acceptable justification, which also determines the limits to its legitimate authority, is its task of serving human needs — serving them better than would be done without any government. The only acceptable justification of a particular form of government is that it serves to meet

---

[34] *One Dimensional Man*, p. 40. See Rousseau, *The Social Contract*, Book I, chapter 7, and Book II, chapter 6. '[T]he only possible excuse (it is weak enough!) for "educational dictatorship" is that the terrible risk which it involves may not be more terrible than the risk which the great liberal as well as the authoritarian societies are taking now, nor may the costs be much higher.' *One Dimensional Man*, pp. 40–1.

[35] See Christian Bay, *The Structure of Freedom*, Stanford University Press, 1970, (first published 1958).

[36] See, for example, C. B. Macpherson, *The Real World of Democracy*, Clarendon, Oxford, 1966; Charles Reich, *The Greening of America*, Random House, New York, 1970; James C. Davies, *Human Nature in Politics*, Wiley, New York, 1973.

human needs better than other forms of government. Once we develop a conception of man and his needs, the natural consequence is to insist that a political system should have our allegiance only if and to the extent that it serves human needs in the order of their importance to individual survival and growth, and does so better than alternative systems. Thus Bay submits that to meet human needs is the ultimate purpose of politics.[37]

While, in substance, Bay thinks that Marcuse's distinction between true and false needs dramatizes a most important insight – that, as Plato taught, there is a radical difference between reality and appearance in human affairs – Bay also maintains that the concepts of true and false needs are misleadingly facile, for they suggest a clear empirical distinction, even an easy classification. Bay's preferred alternative is to make a distinction between needs (which, by definition, are genuine) and wants, desires and demands (which may, or may not, correspond to needs). Bay also differs from Marcuse in that he talks about universal human needs, and opposes the historicizing of all needs.

In a recent paper, Bay reaffirms that his need/want distinction is quite different from the distinction between true and false needs proposed by Marcuse.[38] Marcuse, he says, is too quick to construe the true/false needs dichotomy as if there were a clear empirical distinction between true and false needs. Bay argues that this involves a premature reification with dangerously authoritarian policy implications[39]; but, as we shall see, so does Bay's use of the notion of needs, especially in relation to politics.

Bay is concerned that, under the influence of behaviouralism and empirical political science, the term 'politics' has become debased. No longer does politics refer, as it did for Plato and Aristotle, to the promotion of justice or the search for the common good of the political

---

[37] See Bay, 'Needs, Wants and Political Legitimacy', in *Canadian Journal of Political Science*, 1: September 1968, 241–60, especially 241-2. See also Bay, 'The Cheerful Science of Dismal Politics', in T. Roszak (ed.), *The Dissenting Academy*, Penguin, Harmondsworth, 1969, pp. 187-205.

[38] Human Needs, Wants and Politics: Abraham Maslow meet Karl Marx, unpublished paper presented to International Society of Political Psychology, Washington, May 1979. Bay also thinks that some of Marcuse's 'false needs' – needs induced by advertising or propaganda – can become as compelling, in a psychological sense, as many needs that are authentic in the individual. See also William Leiss, *The Limits to Satisfaction: An Essay on the Problem of Needs and Commodities*, University of Toronto Press, 1976, pp. 49–71.

[39] See Bay's new book *Strategies of Political Emancipation*, Peacock, Itasca, Ill., 1980, chapter 4.

community.[40] In the main, the term refers to 'who gets what, when, how', or to some similar concept that focuses not on justice but on power. This focus makes political science more quantifiable and political scientists more pliable and useful for the powers that be. At the same time, it severs the study of politics from any direct bearing on the task of developing institutions and organizations in the service of human needs.

As a beginning towards a more appropriate political theory, Bay spells out a distinction between authentic 'politics' (in the classical sense) and what he regards as 'pseudopolitics'. By 'political' Bay means all activity aimed at improving or protecting conditions for the satisfaction of human needs and demands in a given society or community, according to some universalistic scheme of priorities, implicit or explicit.[41] 'Pseudopolitical', on the other hand, refers to activity that resembles political activity, but is exclusively concerned with either alleviating personal neuroses or promoting private advantage or private-interest group advantage, deterred by no articulate or disinterested conception of what would be just or fair to other groups; thus, to Bay, pseudopolitics is the counterfeit of authentic politics. In terms of Bay's distinction between political behaviour and pseudopolitical behaviour, it is the concept 'needs' that provides the key criterion. This is because the former is activity based on human needs, whereas the latter, while resembling political activity, merely satisfies group wants and private interests. An adequate *political* theory, he maintains, is one that deals with basic human needs as well as overt desires and other observable aspects of behaviour.

To Bay, current empirical research has little bearing on the fundamental problem of the needs of human beings.[42] While Bay's specialized definition of 'politics' has been criticized on the grounds of being too restrictive[43], Bay makes it clear that he is supportive of the

---

[40] To Aristotle, political science was the master science which drew upon the rest of the sciences. This was because 'the end of politics is the good of man . . . which itself is the highest good attainable by action.' See *Nichomachean Ethics*, Book I; *Politics*, Book I, i–iii.

[41] 'Priorities' refers to norms for guiding the choice between conflicting needs or demands.

[42] For the above, see especially Bay, 'Politics and Pseudopolitics: A Critical Evaluation of Some Behavioural Literature', *American Political Science Review*, 59:1 (March 1965), 39–51; and 'Needs, Wants and Political Legitimacy', *op. cit.*, 244–60.

[43] Heinz Eulau, for example, argued that 'much political activity throughout history has been directed toward the achievement of goals that were eminently evil. To neglect this kind of politics would deprive the study of politics of some of its most perplexing

study of what he regards as 'pseudopolitical behaviour'. But he is highly critical of what he takes to be the almost exclusive focus on pseudopolitical activities (that is, on private wants and desires and on group demands) in much behavioural literature, and the virtual exclusion of the study of human needs.

If Bay is going to place such primacy on the notion of needs, he has to face – as he does – the questions of how one determines what people need and how one differentiates needing from associated notions like wanting, desiring or demanding. Clearly one can determine what people want by asking them or by observing their behaviour. But this is not so with needs. We know that, in common language people can 'want' something they do not 'need' and 'need' something they do not 'want'. Bay has therefore to attempt to develop an empirically useful concept of needs, as compared with wants, desires, or demands.

In four important papers published between 1965 and 1970, Bay addressed himself to this problem.[44] In these papers, and in his work up to the present, the concept 'want' refers to a perceived or felt need that may or may not correspond to or overlap with a real need, while 'demand' refers to a politically activated want.

He began by defining 'needs' negatively via pathology; using empiricist terminology, he regarded as a 'human need' any behaviour tendency whose continued denial or frustration leads to pathological responses. Granting that there were problems in defining the terms 'pathological responses' and 'behaviour tendency', he maintained that it made sense to say that the most obviously pathological kinds of behaviour indicated that relatively crucial needs have been denied or frustrated.

---

problems.' *Behaviouralism in Political Science*, Atherton Press, New York, 1969, p. 13. In a similar vein, Howard Ball and Thomas P. Lauth, Jr, argued that Bay's definition 'substantially narrows the range of what is generally considered political activity. Particularistic and essentially self-serving interests pursued by groups of individuals would seem, according to Bay, to be not only dysfunctional for "the satisfaction of human needs", but, also an improper focus for political science investigation.' *Changing Perspectives in Contemporary Political Analysis*, Prentice Hall, Englewood Cliffs, New Jersey, 1971, p. 66.

[44] See Bay, 'Politics and Pseudopolitics: A Critical Evaluation of Some Behavioural Literature', *American Political Science Review*, *op. cit.*; 'Needs, Wants and Political Legitimacy', *op. cit.*; 'The Cheerful Science of Dismal Politics', *op. cit.*; and 'Human Development and Political Orientations: Notes Toward a Science of Political Education', *Bulletin of Peace Proposals*, 1 (1970): (2) 177–86.

The following categories of behaviour, he suggested, were clearly pathological: (1) suicide, and homocide, or serious attempts at either; (2) psychosis; (3) severe neuroses; and (4) severe addiction to alcohol or other drugs.[45] Obviously there were many problems with the above. Is suicide necessarily pathological? What about rational suicide – for example, the unattached elderly person who decides to terminate a life of pain caused by incurable cancer? Moreover, 'pathology', like 'health', was clearly a value-laden and problematic term. Bay recognized that the problems of pathology and mental illness were extremely complex, and that the political theorist cannot enter deeply into this territory without help. Moreover, he acknowledged distinct disadvantages with this negative approach to defining 'need', especially its implication that need-frustration cannot readily be recognized before it has led to pathologies of one kind or another. Also, his catalogue of pathologies was by his own admission restrictive; what, he asked, of the person doomed by early deprivation to become the perfect accountant but be incapable of doing anything warm and impulsive and playful in his whole life? This approach must be supplemented by other lines of approach, based on theoretically more meaningful concepts of 'need'. The shortcoming of the approach to defining 'need' via pathology was that it suggested neither a hierarchy of needs nor a developmental scheme. It hardly began to suggest a model of actual or potential man. Nor did it answer a fundamental question: according to what order of priorities is the satisfaction of human needs important for individual survival and growth?

Bay therefore rejected the idea of defining needs negatively via pathology and switched to another approach; namely, to defining 'needs' in terms of a positive model of man.

Bay, along with many other contemporary need theorists, believes that the late Abraham Maslow's scheme (as outlined in his 1943 article, 'A Theory of Human Motivation'[46]) still provides the best available point of departure for establishing a theory of a hierarchy of human needs. In his work, Maslow listed five categories of universal human needs in the order of their assumed priority: (1) physical (biological) needs; (2) safety needs – assurance of survival and of continuing satisfaction of basic needs; (3)

---

[45] See 'Needs, Wants and Political Legitimacy', *op. cit.*, pp. 241–60; and 'The Cheerful Science of Dismal Politics', *op. cit.*
[46] See A. H. Maslow, *Motivation and Personality*, Harper & Row, New York, first published 1954, revised edn 1970, chapter 4.

affection or belongingness needs; (4) esteem needs – by self and others; and (5) self-actualization or self-development needs. While, for simplification, I refer to five basic needs, it is important to realize that Maslow's need hierarchy is based on five need *areas* (so that the physiological level, for example, refers to a variety of specific needs, such as air, water, food, sleep, sex, etc.) and does not rest on a simplistic assumption that man's motivational patterns could be defined in terms of five single needs.[47]

These need-areas are arranged in a hierarchy of prepotency. Thus for Maslow, 'higher' needs (belongingness, esteem, self-actualization) cannot become activated unless the 'lower' needs are met, or at least have been reasonably well met at some time in a person's life – particularly in childhood. However, once higher needs are activated, they are not necessarily extinguished by subsequent deprivation of lower or more basic needs. For example, some individuals, provided they have known satisfaction of physiological and safety needs, will sacrifice the former for love, for self-esteem, or for truth; thus a person such as Gandhi may deny himself food because higher needs have become more important. But according to Maslow, a person who has never had enough to eat or has never felt safe could not activate or articulate his higher needs.[48]

It is important to realize that Maslow does not clearly differentiate between 'needs' and the related concepts of 'wants', 'drives', 'motives' or 'desires', and that he regards 'needs' as a trouble-free and empirical notion. But, as I have argued in detail elsewhere, the notion of 'need' can be rendered empirical only by relating it to some specified end, most obviously that of human goodness or a model of human excellence.[49] Bay maintains that a simple model of man, if it is realistic and open-ended, is better than no model at all. Thus while he accepts that there are difficulties with Maslow's need-hierarchy, he suggests that it be tentatively adopted for the purpose of indicating what the priorities of politics should be – assuming that the most basic needs have first claim on political guarantees.

Given an allegedly empirical theory of human needs, Bay argues that

---

[47] See Jeanne Knutson, *The Human Basis of the Polity*, Aldine-Atherton, Chicago, 1972, p. 23.
[48] See Maslow, *op. cit.*, chapter 4. See also Ross Fitzgerald, 'Abraham Maslow's Hierarchy of Needs – An Exposition and Evaluation', in Fitzgerald (ed.), *Human Needs and Politics, op. cit.*, pp. 36–51.
[49] See Ross Fitzgerald, 'The Ambiguity and Rhetoric of "Need" ', in *Human Needs and Politics, op. cit.*, pp. 195–212.

certain political prescriptions follow: namely that governments ought to answer the needs of human beings in the order of their assumed priority. This sounds unproblematically praiseworthy; but there are many difficulties with Maslow's need-hierarchy as it stands, let alone in its application to politics.

It is important to realize that Maslow was working up to a scientific ethics based on universal human needs. In a similar way, Erich Fromm (whose ideas Bay also draws on) claimed that it was for psychology to discover the principles of a universal ethics tuned to the universal needs of man.[50] Both Maslow and Fromm argued that a knowledge of human needs could enable us to establish values that have objective validity.[51] As an extension of this position it therefore follows, for theorists such as Bay, that one can ground a political morality on allegedly empirical statements asserting the needs of human beings. But the unambiguously empirical status of need statements is precisely what is in dispute.

One way of making it clear that the concept of human needs employed by Bay cannot be purely empirical is to understand that concepts of what people 'need' are tied to concepts of human excellence and the nature of man. Different concepts of human nature and different models of excellence will generate different needs. Thus one model of man might stress the 'needs' for ambition, power and competition, while another might emphasize the 'needs' for trust, co-operation and mutuality. Because different concepts of what is good and desirable generate different needs, any concept of what is a 'human need' cannot of itself be purely empirical. The only way in which the concept of need can be made empirical is to spell out in detail a particular model of human excellence and then talk about needs in order to achieve this goal or end. But then there is the fundamental problem of how one determines the end or goal or model of excellence to which man's needs are relative.

Despite cultural variations in human behaviour, there do appear to be certain basic propensities, other than bodily ones, which all or most human beings share. The problem is therefore not that of making universal statements about human *propensities* as such. Rather the problem is the selection of some of these propensities, on the basis of some criteria of goodness or health or human excellence, and the

---

[50] See Erich Fromm, *Man for Himself: An Enquiry into the Psychology of Ethics*, Routledge & Kegan Paul, London, 1975 (first published 1949).
[51] See Maslow and Fromm's contribution to *New Knowledge in Human Values*, Maslow, (ed.), Harper & Row, New York, 1959, especially pp. 123 and 151.

labelling of them as 'needs'. If 'need' is merely a concept referring to certain physiological and psychological processes and nothing else, there is no way of regarding these processes as desirable or undesirable without introducing some normative premise or some notion of human excellence. Disagreement on these normative premises or notions will lead to the development of a different set of 'needs'. To attribute *needs* to people presupposes certain standards or norms as to which among human propensities or characteristics it is desirable to foster; this selection will be culture-bound and dependent on different ethical preferences. This applies to even allegedly physiological needs. As R. F. Dearden puts it, 'If you say that in my emaciated condition I need food, I may refuse to attach any importance to the norms of health that you are presupposing, pointing out that I am engaged in a religious exercise.'[52] Obviously if I am fasting I do not need food. And if I intend to commit suicide I do not need to breathe.

It is the notion of 'a need for self-actualization' that most clearly highlights the problems confronting Bay (and Maslow). It is impossible to make such a metaphysical notion empirical at all. Human selves have many potentialities; we have many things in us. This raises the problem of which selves and which potentialities are to be realized. The answer to the question 'What sort of self does Bay want actualized or realized' is simple: it is a good self. Similarly, it is good potentialities that he wants to be developed or expressed. Likewise the answer to the often unasked question 'What are the needs that ought to be satisfied, fulfilled or promoted' is good needs. This is precisely why it sounds strange to talk about a need for destruction or punishment or a need to be sadistic, while talk in terms of a need for love, affection or knowledge sounds fine. And this is why Bay and Marcuse are compelled to distinguish between 'real' needs and mere 'wants' (Bay) or 'false' or 'artificial' needs (Marcuse). It hardly has to be pointed out that 'real needs' or 'genuine needs' come to equal 'good needs'.

If by self-actualization is meant whatever a person can be motivated to act out or express, it provides us with no way of distinguishing between desirable and undesirable forms of self-expression. This, of course, theorists like Bay who use Maslow's scheme do not intend. Manifestly the murderer, the sadist, fascist, rapist, incendiarist, does not fit in with their notion of a person developing his or her potentialities. Bay and

[52] See R. F. Dearden, 'Needs in Education' in Dearden, P. H. Hirst and R. S. Peters (eds), *Education and the Development of Reason*, Routledge & Kegan Paul, London, 1972, p. 55.

Maslow must, and by implication do, set up standards of what the individual ought to become or express, and what he or she ought not to become or express.[53] To speak of a 'need for self-actualization' is either tautological or unequivocally normative. The criteria used to specify what sort of self is to be realized must be thoroughly value-laden, and notions of the self to be actualized will vary according to different estimates of things that are worth doing and propensities that are worth developing. Self-actualization is merely another way of referring to what one ought to do and what one ought to be or become.[54] Fundamentally the notion of 'need' itself simply substitutes for 'good' or for 'what ought to be'. Any talk about human needs must involve value-judgements about which of our many propensities it is desirable to foster and which forms of human development are good. As we are aware, these judgements differ markedly even in Western industrial society: such differences are dramatically compounded when we compare this society with other past and present societies. For example, are competition and rivalry, anger and aggression, human goods? Are incestuous and polyandrous relationships evil? Do human beings who become soldiers, shamans, accountants, bookmakers, stockbrokers or priests exhibit examples of desirable personal development? Many would disagree. And what of surfers, poets, commune dwellers, transvestites, Trotskyites, fortune-tellers? What forms of human development people consider desirable, and what human beings value in general, vary enormously. And even if human beings did agree on what they considered good or valuable, agreement or consensus *cannot* validate judgements of value, any more than agreement on the statement that the world is flat would validate that allegedly factual proposition. This point is of the utmost importance for a theory of human needs, because any such theory is ultimately dependent upon a series of judgements about what is good and valuable for human beings and for human society. When one is talking about human needs such value-judgements cannot be escaped.[55]

In his very recent work, Bay has restructured Maslow's need-hierarchy – affirming three general categories or classes of needs, in this order of urgency: (1) basic physical needs for sustenance and safety; (2)

---

[53] See Ross Fitzgerald, 'Abraham Maslow's Hierarchy of Needs', *op. cit.*, pp. 49–50.
[54] *Ibid.*
[55] For a more detailed argument, see Ross Fitzgerald, 'Human Needs and Political Morality', in Richard Lucy (ed.), *The Pieces of Politics*, Macmillan, Sydney, 1979. See also K. R. Minogue's superb demolition of the doctrine of needs, *The Liberal Mind*, Methuen, London, 1963, especially p. 103 ff.

community needs, most notably the needs for love, belongingness and esteem; and (3) individuality or subjectivity needs, which include needs for individual identity and dignity, freedom of choice, and self-development.[56] While this involves a restatement, Bay is clearly following Maslow's model.

As in his earlier work, Bay argues that human need priorities must come to be seen as the only legitimate basis for priorities of human liberties. While there are innumerable human wants in a society saturated with commercial advertising and consumerism, he now argues that there are only three categories of basic needs, the satisfaction of which should be the first principle of politics. Physical survival is the most basic need, followed by the need for security against violence – violence grievous enough to lead to possible injuries. In terms of humam rights, physical survival, or the right to life, obviously must take precedence over competing claims; for example, the execution of a criminal is totally impermissible, at least unless it can be proved that failure to apply the death penalty will lead inevitably to an increase in homicides. Bay thus argues that needs must take precedence over wants or demands; and that the most basic needs of all must be satisfied before the less basic needs of the few.

He argues that there are *universal* human needs, despite differing ways of satisfying them, and that there is a *universal hierarchy* in the sense that basic physical needs precede community or social belongingness needs, which have priority over subjectivity needs. In this, Bay differs radically from Marcuse, and even more from Marcuse's pupil William Leiss, who historicizes all needs.[57] Their approach loses sight of what Bay assumes to be the basic biological–psychological unity of the human species: 'While universal basic needs and propensities to be sure are hard to establish empirically, let alone with any degree of exactitude, I think we must reject the notion that, of all species, mankind is the one that is entirely without instinctual equipment or species-wide psychological characteristics of any kind.'[58] Bay's position is that human right

---

[56] Human Needs, Wants, and Politics: Abraham Maslow meet Karl Marx, *op. cit.* Bay speaks of three 'tiers' of needs in a paper presented earlier, Acquisitive Liberties for Some: Toward a Constructive Critique of the Pluralist Persuasion, presented to the Study Group on Social and Economic Problems of Pluralism, International Political Science Association, Paris, 27–29 April 1978, Section IV; and of three 'ranges of needs' in *Strategies of Political Emancipation, op. cit.*, chapter 4.
[57] See Leiss, *The Limits to Satisfaction, op. cit.*
[58] *Strategies of Political Emancipation, op. cit.*, chapter 4.

priorities must be based on our knowledge of priorities among universal human needs; and that a legitimate government must honour and promote human rights as effectively as possible, in the order of these priorities. On the basis of priorities among human needs, it follows that the most oppressed persons in any social order must have first claim on protection, support, and redress of grievances, from any government that claims political legitimacy.

Bay draws a sharp distinction between a human rights approach to politics, based on need-priorities, and a liberal–democratic approach, based on wants and desires (and demands) which may be artificially created.

In his latest book, *Strategies of Political Emancipation*, 'human need' refers to

> any and all minimum requirements for every individual's health and well being, as distinct from the needs of specific categories of individuals or needs that are shared by all or most people within a given social order, and/or culture. By definition, when a person becomes psychosomatically sick, or commits suicide, or becomes dependent on health-destructive drugs, some of his or her individual needs are not being met; if such things happen to many in a given class or culture, then class-shared or culturally imprinted needs are not being met; if in the study of sickness in this broad sense we begin to find regularities across cultures and across generations, then we may develop tentative empirical generalizations about human need priorities in general. We can also study conditions under which, in various societies, high levels of public health are achieved.[59]

But who determines what constitutes 'health'? That is a key question.

In a paper presented at the Annual Meeting of the International Society for Political Psychology in Washington in May 1979, Bay suggested that 'want' should be an empirical term, referring to every kind of verbally stated or otherwise manifest wish, preference, demand, desire, interest, etc., that indicates a felt or alleged need; any given want may or may not reflect a human need. 'Need' should be reserved, then, for what Marcuse would consider true or genuine needs – that is, requirements for life, health and/or basic freedom of the living person.[60] Bay accepts that needs are not readily visible, except at the lower extreme of 'dire needs'. Yet, he argues, all needs are real; they exist; by definition

---

[59] *Ibid.*
[60] Human Needs, Wants and Politics: Abraham Maslow meet Karl Marx, *op. cit.* p. 19.

they must be met if human health and well-being are to be assured.[61]

In another recent paper, Bay has defined human rights as 'all categories of individual claims (including claims on behalf of individuals or groups) which *ought to have* legal protection, as well as social and moral support, *because* the protection of these claims *is essential to meet basic human needs*.'[62] For Bay, human right priorities ought to be ordered according to objective human need priorities. He constantly stresses that priorities of rights ought to be determined by the best available knowledge of human need priorities. But the vital question is who knows, and how? Who is to determine what are needs, and what are mere wants? Wants, desires, and demands are ascertainable facts; we ascertain what people want by asking them, or (more indirectly) by observing their behaviour. But this is not so with needs, which are hypothetical constructs. This, Bay admits, makes it difficult to disentangle authentic human needs from, for example, alienated wants that result from high powered promotion and programming. In *Strategies of Political Emancipation*, Bay does maintain that it will not do to take the course so easily suggested by Marcuse's terminology, and simply hold that politicians must choose to serve the people's 'true' needs while ignoring or suppressing or explaining away their 'false' needs. This he agrees could indeed come to vindicate Plato's republic, or Stalin's Politbureau: 'To do people good against their own will is to serve people badly.'[63] But he never explains how *he* can avoid the authoritarianism implicit in a politics based on needs.

In fact, while Bay pays continual lipservice to respecting the (often manipulated) wants and desires of individuals – for example, 'wants and demands are not to be ignored'[64] – he places primacy on needs. The 'dilemma' of resolving the conflict between wants and needs is always decided in favour of the latter. Despite Bay's protestations, in his schema it is not individuals who 'validly' determine what they need, for under capitalism individuals are often misled; ultimately the people who know, and come to determine what human needs really are, are intellectual experts – in Bay's case, social scientists. Like Marcuse's intellectual elite

---

[61] 'The Right to Peace and the Right to Critical Political Knowledge', paper prepared for the Panel on Fundamental Rights in a Democratic Order, at the International Political Science Association Congress, Moscow, 12–18 August, 1979, p. 5.
[62] 'A Human Rights Approach to Transnational Politics', *Universal Human Rights*, 1 (1979): (1) 9–14 (his emphases).
[63] *Strategies of Political Emancipation*, chapter 4.
[64] 'The Right to Peace and the Right to Critical Political Knowledge', *op. cit.* p. 8.

who will force people to be free, the individuals and groups who know are in essence Platonic experts. Bay hints at this connection by saying 'As every political theory requires a model of the human being, so it requires a conception of human need priorities, which in a given society to be sure will be influenced by history and culture, but still retain some universal aspect. Much before Marx and Marcuse, Plato was preoccupied with the difference between what benefits men and what men on spurious grounds may come to desire.'[65]

Such a distinction can have extremely dangerous consequences. It leaves the way open for an elite of experts, or other 'representatives' of the State, to 'objectively' pronounce upon what people, or 'The People', need, despite the fact that the individuals said to have such needs want something quite different. This situation resembles Rousseau's theory of the General Will – which is not what all or the majority of people actually want or demand, but what they would will if they were true to their essential (good) natures. Actual support of real people becomes unnecessary.

The allegedly 'objective' and scientific nature of 'needs' is what makes needs talk of the Bay–Marcuse variety so fashionable, especially in educational circles. Of all human beings in our society, children are in the least authoritative position to pronounce upon what they want or desire, or to resist the findings of 'experts'. The current welter of literature about the 'educational needs' and 'curricula needs' of those who cannot 'legitimately' speak for themselves is a dramatic example of the grave danger of applying a theory of human needs to politics. As a consequence, the British philosopher Antony Flew argues that, in political discussion, references to people's supposed needs, as opposed to their actual or expressed wants, are often the mark of the authoritarian. The famous slogan, 'From each according to his abilities, to each according to his needs' ought, he suggests, for that reason, to make liberals and those who are committed to individual freedom shudder.[66]

For all their differences, Herbert Marcuse and Christian Bay are united in the seductive pursuit of a politics based on true or genuine or real needs as opposed to false or alien ones, or as opposed to mere wants, desires and demands. From the perspective of those who value individual freedom, they are also linked in their implicit authoritarianism. To highlight the dangers that the contemporary emphasis on needs in

[65] 'Human Needs, Wants, and Politics', *op. cit.*, p. 19.
[66] 'Wants or Needs, Choices or Commands', *op. cit.*, pp. 213–28.

politics poses for personal autonomy, it is appropriate to close this comparison with a quotation from Yevgeny Zamyatin's great antitotalitarian novel *We:* 'I want to want myself – I do not want others to want for me.'[67] Despite its current appeal, need theory in relation to politics, as exemplified by Marcuse and Bay, has profoundly authoritarian, even totalitarian implications.

---

[67] Yevgeny Zamyatin, *We: A Novel of the Future,* translated by Mirra Ginsberg, Viking Press, New York, 1972, p. 5.

John Rawls and Robert Nozick

M. W. Jackson

Imagine Mr Bruce Ocker to possess some outstanding talent issuing from the consilience of his endowments, education, experiences and efforts. During the week he works at an occupation quite dissociated from the talent in question, but on weekends Ocker exercises his talent. Initially, he uses his savings to organize and advertise his performances, charging spectators a mere 20c fee. On opening night and on every subsequent night, large crowds greet Ocker's displays. Every last man, woman and child comes away from the performances delighted. All the while Ocker continues to fulfil the duties of his ordinary occupation. The nominal fee accumulates so that Bruce Ocker finds himself to have considerable wealth.

Is Ocker's new found wealth just? Such a fortune does not long evade the notice of the Argus-eyed authorities who administer the taxation laws or the indefatigable legislators who make them. Having espied the glitter of Ocker's treasure, these administrators and legislators ponder, first, the justice of Ocker's possession of it and, second, the justice of the public's interest in it, most likely in the form of taxation. This is a matter of distributive justice, which is the subject of this comparison.

First, the subject of distributive justice is introduced; then John Rawls' theory of distributive justice is outlined, with particular emphasis on his concept of the 'original position'. Robert Nozick's critical alternative to Rawls' theory, which is called 'entitlement', is detailed; then Rawls and Nozick are contrasted on the justice of entitlement, which Rawls treats partly under the heading of 'natural liberty'. This comparison leads to a conclusion that Rawls' most telling argument against natural liberty, or entitlement, stems from the focus of his theory on the basic structure of a society and not on the individual cases within it. Consequently, Rawls' arguments concerning the basic structure are examined. In conclusion, I suggest that Rawls' arguments concerning the basic structure are inadequate because they cannot comprehend community. Nozick's position, though different, offers no advantage over Rawls on this score, for his theory is even more individualistic.*

The example of Mr Ocker is modified from one mooted by Robert Nozick in his book *Anarchy, State, and Utopia*[1] to serve as a reference for several parts of the ensuing discussion. In considering his example, Nozick implies that John Rawls' *A Theory of Justice*[2] indicates that Ocker's wealth is unjust and that taxation of 100 per cent on the earnings of his talent would be just. For his own part, Nozick declares wealth such as Ocker's to be just in acquisition and, therefore, to be free from any and all taxation. In this conflict, Rawls represents the liberal tradition within political theory according to which distributive justice involves positive state activity; Nozick represents the libertarian position according to which such activity is deemed to be unjust redistribution.

How does Rawls conceive of distributive justice? Rawls' theory of distributive justice takes society as a self-sufficient co-operative venture for mutual advantage.[3] Consequently, it is marked by a conflict and confluence of interests. A basic identity of interests exists adequate to make social co-operation mutually beneficial. Society leads to a better life for all than would be possible if each person were left to individual action. To further their differing individual aims, persons are assumed to be likely to prefer a larger to a smaller share of the benefits of that better life secured by social co-operation. As a result people are not indifferent as to how the benefits produced by their sharing of burdens are distributed among themselves.

Distributive justice is a set of principles by which to judge the basic structure of a society. This standard, additionally, allows for the assessment of alternative social arrangements which might be instituted to distribute the benefits yielded by co-operation. All in all, the principles of distributive justice promote a consensus concerning the proper shares of the burdens and benefits of a given society.

---

* John Rawls, born Baltimore, 21 February 1921; Robert Nozick, born Brooklyn, 16 November 1938. (Ed.)
[1] See Robert Nozick, *Anarchy, State and Utopia*, Basic Books, New York, 1974, pp. 161–4.
[2] John Rawls, *A Theory of Justice*, Harvard University Press, Cambridge, Mass., 1971.
[3] See Rawls, 'Distributive Justice', in Peter Laslett and W. G. Runciman (eds), *Philosophy, Politics and Society*, third series, Blackwell, Oxford 1967, pp. 58–9.

Rawls' study offers the systematic presentation of many ideas that have been taken for granted in the study of ethics and politics in the English-speaking world for the past thirty years. For instance, his book accepts and justifies individualism, limited government, self-realization, moral beneficence, welfare measures, civil disobedience, and the like. These subjects are handled with great verve and sophistication.

No aspect of Rawls' theory more clearly sums up conventional wisdom in a single stroke and carries it to its logical conclusion than his concept of the 'original position'.

Ethical theory makes the basic distinction between meta-ethics and normative ethics: normative ethics consists of the moral prescriptions offered to guide and judge conduct; meta-ethics refers to the method by which these prescriptions are adduced – this method includes the epistemological and ontological assumptions of any particular moral theory. By using this distinction, reactions to moral prescriptions can be distinguished from evaluations of the rational or empirical origin and content of the statements. It was widely agreed that much of the inherent controversy of normative ethics could be alleviated if attention turned to meta-ethics. More than one writer argued that the undisputed meta-ethical position was marked by three qualities: independence, benignity and rationality. It was argued that the most worthy morality would be that formulated from a detached perspective free from repercussions, with kindly intentions towards those whose conduct is to be guided, and following the canons of formal rationality. The original position is Rawls' construction of such a perspective.

Capping its academic and popular reception, *A Theory of Justice* was named as one of the five most significant books of 1972 by *The New York Times Book Review*. The editors concluded from a passage of Rawls' book proclaiming that the talented may gain from their good fortune only on terms that improve the situation of those who have lost out, that 'Rawls' arguments for this proposition are persuasive; its political implications may change our lives.'[4]

Rawls' theoretical arguments are outlined in Part I of *A Theory of Justice*. The lodestar of his initial argument is the concept of fairness; his 'two principles of justice' are derived from fairness by means of the 'original position'. In Part II of his book, institutional arrangements compatible with the existence of the two principles of justice are considered, first in terms of liberty, then in terms of distributive shares,

---

[4] *New York Times Book Review*, 3 December 1972, p. 1.

and finally in terms of duties and obligations. Part III offers the reader a glimpse of the life of a society in which the basic structure of institutions passes the tests set by the two principles of justice.

What is the relation of fairness and justice in Rawls' theory? In his view, justice is what would be unanimously chosen in a fair decision-making procedure by the persons to be governed by justice. The 'original position' is devised by Rawls as such a fair procedure. He then argues that his two principles of justice would be chosen by persons in such a position. The procedure is fair because the participants are morally equal.

How is moral equality attained by persons in the original position? Rather than being innocent, as in classical contract theory, the persons of Rawls' original position are conceived of as being behind a veil of ignorance that makes them unaware of their particular self-interest. The principles it would be rational to choose in ignorance are those of justice, according to Rawls.

What is the nature of the preterhuman beings in the original position? An understanding of the original position requires that we conceive of each decision-maker as unaware of 'his fortune in the distribution of natural assets and abilities, his intelligence and strength, and the like.'[5] In addition to these subjective qualities, certain objective qualities characterize persons in the original position, such as having a full knowledge of social and economic facts and the need for justice.[6] Because they are ignorant, the persons in the original position are independent; because they are each deciding on standards to govern themselves, they are benign; and because they have empirical knowledge and are independent and benign, they will be rational.

How then do these unidentified, unaffiliated persons in the original position form a community? Rather than considering their own personal talents, persons in the original position must take into account the assets and abilities any citizen may have. Furthermore, these talents cannot be thought of as the possession of identified individuals, yet they must be taken into account as the basis of the just community; they are regarded as the property of the community of individuals as a whole. Rawls' persons in the original position would be led to principles of justice that reward only the use of individual assets and abilities for the common good.

---

[5] *A Theory of Justice*, p. 137.
[6] *Ibid.*, and *cf.* pp. 146–7.

How is Rawls' ethical communism expressed politically in the principles of justice? Communal ownership of individual talents is expressed within the original position by an additional ingredient, styled the 'maximin' rule, which is agreed will lead to the 'difference principle' as one of the main principles of justice.

Maximin is a rule of choice.[7] Not only is a person in the original position unaware of her or his own identity, but also the person is ignorant of the statistical probability of being one thing rather than another. Behind the veil of ignorance of the original position, Bruce Ocker would know neither that he is male nor that the probability of being male is 0.5. Therefore, in the original position Bruce Ocker would not be rational if he decided on principles of justice discriminating between the sexes, since he would not know his own sex. To be rational he must favour the universal interest because he might be anyone. Rawls holds that this double ignorance makes it rational to adopt the conservative strategy of *maximum minimorum* or 'maximin'. Maximin compares alternatives at their worst possible (not probable) outcomes. The choice between rival theories of justice would be made by the comparison of worst outcomes, and not the best, average or total outcomes as a utilitarian theory of justice would dictate.

How does the rational desire to make the worst possible outcome as good as possible lead to the 'difference principle' in Rawls' theory? The difference principle directs the communal assets and abilities to make maximum the minimum position. This principle offers the sole justification for inequality in Rawls' theory[8], because it is to the common good. The difference principle allows citizens to harvest unequal social and economic benefits if, and only if, the exercise of their talents advantages those citizens otherwise receiving the worst outcome consistent with the theory.[9] These citizens comprise the least-advantaged class.[10]

For the insurance that the difference principle represents to be effective, some consideration has to be given to the terms in which persons assess better and worse outcomes. To this end, Rawls introduces a set of primary goods as the benefits of social life – consisting of liberty

---

[7] *Ibid.*, p. 152.
[8] *Ibid.*, p. 276. Need is acknowledged as a special case and added to, but not integrated with, the theory.
[9] *Ibid.*, p. 302.
[10] For a more detailed explanation, see M. W. Jackson, 'The Least Advantaged Class in Rawls's Theory', *Canadian Journal of Political Science*, September 1979.

and self-respect, powers and opportunities, and income and wealth. These three kinds of goods are nominated on the grounds that they are the 'things that every rational man is presumed to want.'[11] These goods are taken to be morally neutral, in that they are consistent with and equally conducive to all manner and means of living. Unlike a utilitarian theory devoted to the maximization of utility, the theory of 'justice as fairness . . . does not look behind the use to which persons make of the "primary goods" in order to measure, much less to maximize, the satisfactions . . . [citizens] achieve.'[12] The distinction between the neutral primary goods and all other goods allows for justice to be determined short of the interminable controversy about the good ends of life.[13] Our ideas of the good are diverse and lead to conflict, but our ideas of justice do not so vary, in Rawls' judgement.[14]

Is the moral neutrality attributed to the primary goods unqualified? A moment's reflection suggests that they cannot be taken as read. At the very best they are relatively neutral; indeed they may be as neutral as possible, but absolute neutrality is neither required nor achieved by Rawls' formulations. Such neutrality is not achieved because the primary goods named are not consistent with all reasonable ways of life. A person committed to the life of an ascetic votary or to fulfilment through a labouring craft may find the provision of income and wealth a positive temptation to foresake the calling. Rawls might contend that the primary goods are more general and more important than any alternative candidates. If this is so, they can be taken as the most probable motivation for persons in the original position, knowing no more about themselves than they do.

Such recognition of probability would imply that no theory of justice can be unexceptional. There would be exceptions to be determined by the political process. Rawls would not welcome this alternative, for his characterization of the political process in a society employing his principles is not marked by sectional interests. Rather Rawls presents a depoliticized technocracy.[15] Unlike other contract theorists, Rawls requires justice to be determined in perpetuity before the advent of

---

[11] *A Theory of Justice*, p. 62.
[12] *Ibid.*
[13] *Ibid.*, p. 331.
[14] Rawls has returned to the reconciliation of goodness and justice in 'Fairness to Goodness', *Philosophical Review*, 84 (1975): 536–54.
[15] M. W. Jackson, 'La science et la dépolitisation', *Impact: science et société*, 28 (1978): 383–92.

government and the initiation of politics. His justice is literally beyond politics.

How does Rawls depoliticize his idea of a well-ordered society? For Rawls, 'in the ideal procedure, the decision reached is not a compromise, a bargain struck between opposing parties to advance their ends.'[16] Even the legislative process 'must be conceived not as a contest between interests, but as an attempt to find the best policy as defined by the principles of justice', so that 'an impartial legislator's only desire is to make the correct decision.'[17] Moreover, the legislative process in 'the ideal procedure bears a certain analogy to the statistical problem of pooling the views of a group of experts to arrive at a best judgment.'[18]

Yet it is also acknowledged by Rawls that 'a society in which all can achieve their complete good, or in which there are no conflicting demands and the wants of all fit together without coercion into a harmonious plan of activity, is a society in a certain sense beyond justice.'[19] This caution is implicit in the discussion of civil disobedience.[20] Not ordinary political processes but only civil disobedience is left to those whose interests are overlooked by the depoliticized technocracy of the Laodicean political institutions that Rawls traces from his theory.

What then are Rawls' two principles of justice?

> First, each person is to have an equal liberty to the most extensive total system of liberties compatible with a similar system of liberty for all. In part, liberty is given first priority because it is held to be the key to self-respect. Knowing that one is as free as the next person, Rawls argues, produces self-respect.
>
> Second, social and economic inequalities are to be arranged so that they are: attached to offices and positions open to all under the conditions of fair equality of opportunity covering the primary goods of powers and opportunities and, last in priority, to the greatest benefit of the least advantaged class consistent with the just savings principle for future generations.[21]

The order of priority imposed on these principles means that there can be made no trade-offs among them. First the liberty principle must be

---

[16] *A Theory of Justice*, p. 357; and *cf.* p. 28.
[17] *Ibid.*
[18] *Ibid.*, p. 358.
[19] *Ibid.*, p. 281.
[20] *Ibid.*, pp. 363–94.
[21] *Ibid.*, pp. 302–3. On Rawls' treatment of self-respect, liberty, and the worth of liberty, see Norman Daniels, 'Equal Liberty and the Unequal Worth of Liberty', in Daniels (ed.), *Reading Rawls*, Blackwell, Oxford, 1975, pp. 253–82.

satisfied, then the opportunity principle, and finally the difference principle. Assuming a minimum level of income, no amount of liberty can be sacrificed for the greatest gains to opportunities or incomes. Nor can opportunities be sacrificed to increase wealth. Only those inequalities of income and wealth occasioned by the difference principle are permitted.

Rawls himself describes his book as an effort to present a conception of justice that generalizes and carries to a higher level of abstraction the familiar theory of social contract found, say, in Locke, Rousseau, and Kant[22], as antidote to the dominance of utilitarianism over so much recent moral and political theory.[23] Unlike teleological utilitarianism, Rawls' deontological theory does not construe justice as maximizing the good.[24] Aligning himself most particularly with Kant, Rawls opts for an hypothetical rather than historical state of nature, such as that attributed to Locke and Rousseau. Thanks to the self-ignorance of Rawls' original position, each person must think of every person as an end in her or himself, as Kant requires.

In sum, Rawls hopes to have derived substantive conclusions – the principles of justice – from the formal procedure of the original position. These principles recommend themselves to us because they are the rational conclusions of a fair procedure. Rawls' argument is that the principles are rational and that is why we would choose them, and not that because we would choose them the principles are right. Rationality, not choice, is the independent variable.

How does Nozick's theory differ from that of Rawls? Nozick places exclusive emphasis on actual consent rather than on rationality as the basis of political justice.[25] Nozick takes it as his unargued premise that 'individuals have rights, and there are things no person or group may do to them.'[26] These rights are imprescriptible, but they are not inalienable. The fullest realization of individual rights in Nozick's utopia would permit persons selling themselves into slavery.[27] So complete is Nozick's

---

[22] *Ibid.*, p. 3.
[23] *Ibid.*, pp. 3, 22, and 26.
[24] *Ibid.*, pp. 30 and 31.
[25] See T. Scanlon, 'Nozick on Rights, Liberty, and Property', *Philosophy and Public Affairs*, 6 (1976): 3.
[26] *Anarchy, State and Utopia*, p. ix.
[27] *Ibid.*, p. 331.

reliance on individual rights that he declares all taxation to be theft.[28] Yet according to Nozick, Rawls' theory implies just such taxation.

Rawls' theory aims at a certain end-state pattern, in Nozick's assessment, namely equality. This is absolutely true of the liberty and opportunity principles, and partly true of the difference principle. Despite the fact that every step in Bruce Ocker's career was wholly voluntary by himself and his customers, in Nozick's view Rawls' end-state theory would justify the complete taxation of Ocker's proceeds, for Ocker's activities do not benefit the least-advantaged class. In contrast, Nozick offers an historical theory of justice that emphasizes the production of benefits through the assumption of burdens. If no injustice incurs in the acquisition of benefits, as is true in Ocker's case, then there are no just grounds for interference. The only grounds for just distribution is the labour of acquisition and skill in transfer. The only grounds for redistribution is a claim of injustice, force or fraud, in acquisition or in transfer.

The matter of distributive justice lies at the centre of Nozick's book, though it is logically independent of much else in it. *Anarchy, State and Utopia* divides into three parts, addressed to each of the topics named in the title. In Part I Nozick argues against anarchism. He maintains that there is a moral justification for the minimal state, which is nothing else than the 'night-watchman state' of classical liberal political economy. This state is committed only to the protection of the sanctified rights of the individual against murder, assault, battery, fraud, theft, rape and the like[29]; these rights are sometimes called absolute moral side-constraints.[30] Nozick describes how such a minimal state might come into existence out of the Lockean state of nature through a process by which the unco-ordinated actions of separate individuals brings about the result none of them intended – as if by an invisible hand. Motivated only by a desire for protection from one another, the persons in Nozick's state of nature join to form a state to protect, not to sacrifice, their rights as individuals. An anarchist might but declare that, in fact, no state has ever come about in the way described.[31]

Like Rawls, Nozick draws part of his inspiration from Immanual Kant. The rights enshrined in Nozick's minimal state are deemed just in his view, because they are the necessary and sufficient condition to affirm

[28] *Ibid.*, p. 169.
[29] *Ibid*, p. 162.
[30] *Ibid.*, p. 33.
[31] T. Nagel, 'Liberalism without Foundation', *Yale Law Journal*, 85 (1975): 139, note 4.

Kant's dictum that no one person ought ever to be dealt with purely as a means to the ends of another.[32] To tax Ocker, so Nozick would have it, uses him as a means to the ends of the other benefited by that taxation.

In Part II Nozick holds that only such a night-watchman state is just, contrary to those who, like Rawls, advocate a more extensive state.[33] For Nozick there are only absolutely autonomous individuals with no basis for sharing, from the state of nature, through the minimal state, to utopia. At one early point in the book he writes that 'there is no social entity', there are only discrete individuals.[34] Against misguided attempts to justify the enlargement of the state, Nozick offers his own theory of justice. It is termed 'entitlement'.

In Part III utopia is discussed. Because Nozick's people are autonomous and begin by being different they will remain different. A utopia for such persons would be an arrangement where, their rights protected, individuals could seek out like-minded others to form associations.[35]

The first necessary step for entitlement theory is to establish property as a natural right on a par with the other natural rights of life and limb. To accomplish this, the entitlement theory proffers three principles of justice; these principles comprise Nozick's equivalent to the pure procedure of Rawls' original position. Nozick's principles of justice are:

(1) A person who acquires a holding in accordance with the principle of justice in acquisition is entitled to that holding.
(2) A person who acquires a holding in accordance with the principle of justice in transfer, from someone else entitled to that holding, is entitled to that holding.
(3) No one is entitled to a holding except by (repeated) applications of 1 and 2.[36]

Holdings inconsistent with principles 1 and 2 are to be rectified by principle 3. For Nozick, both of the first two principles impose an historical orientation, rather than the end-state focus of Rawls' theory. Nozick declares that 'whatever arises from a just situation by just steps is itself just.'[37] Naught else is to be considered.

---

[32] *Anarchy, State and Utopia*, pp. 30–3. *Cf.* Immanual Kant, *The Groundwork of the Metaphysics of Morals* (1785), translated by H. J. Paton, and published as *The Moral Law*, Hutchinson, London, 1956, p. 96.
[33] *Anarchy, State and Utopia*, p. 149.
[34] *Ibid.*, p. 32.
[35] *Ibid.*, pp. 318–9.
[36] *Ibid.*, p. 151.
[37] *Ibid.*

An end-state theory, such as typified by Rawls', will constantly be upset by the free and not unjust actions of individuals and will lead to constant interference within the lives of citizens, says Nozick.[38] In contrast, the rights guaranteed by Nozick's theory are absolute and not *prima facie*.[39] They never come into conflict, because they are based on property, so they may be absolute. No two claims to a concrete piece of property are ever both just historically. Claims to abstract rights may conflict precisely because they are abstract, like a right to well-being or meaningful employment.

How does Nozick establish acquisition as the first principle of justice? To do this he returns to the political theory of John Locke, expressed in the *Second Treatise*.[40] Locke holds that property was a natural fact for men and beginning with the ownership of their own bodies as a trust placed in them by God.[41] Locke's God gave the world to mankind in common.[42] Discrete individuals take possession of parts of the divine apanage as one mixes one's labour with things in the world.

Is Locke's right of possessive individualism unlimited? Each of Locke's men is morally free to draw into possession as much of nature as one's labour permits, with three qualifications. First, the acquisition of each individual finds a natural limit in spoilation; to acquire more perishable goods than one can use before they rot is unjust to Locke.[43] Second, Locke assumes that individual appropriation of the common entitlement is to the benefit of mankind as a whole, because it provides the incentive for each individual to work on nature to produce benefits.[44] Third, the acquisition of each individual is just, provided that enough bounty remains as yet unclaimed in nature to satisfy the concupiscence and labours of others.[45] This last qualification has been termed the 'Lockean proviso', and it alone does not evade Nozick.

---

[38] *Ibid.*, p. 163. *Cf.* A. Buchanan, 'Distributive Justice and Legitimate Expectations', *Philosophical Studies*, 28 (1975): 419–25.
[39] See L. Francis and J. Francis, 'Nozick's Theory of Rights', *Western Political Quarterly*, 29 (1976): 634–6.
[40] John Locke, *The Second Treatise on Government: An Essay Concerning the True Original, Extent, and End of Civil Government* (1690). Several writers have examined Nozick's use of Locke, but none with more vigour than V. Held, in 'John Locke on Robert Nozick', *Social Research*, 43 (1976): 169–95.
[41] *Second Treatise*, section 27.
[42] *Ibid.*, sections 25, 26 and 27.
[43] *Ibid.*, section 30.
[44] *Ibid.*, section 34.
[45] *Ibid.*, section 33.

Students of political theory have long been puzzled by Locke's proviso. How one mixes one's labour with nature is by no means clear. Picking an apple may qualify to claim an apple, but is fencing the land adequate to claim the land, the apple trees on it, or the apples themselves?[46] Nozick interprets Lockean ownership to consist in the right to determine the use of things, starting with our bodies and continuing to that over which our bodies give us power.[47] In a brilliant stroke Nozick extends his use of Kant's principle of autonomy to encompass Locke's right of property.

What are the implications of Nozick's synthesis of Kant and Locke on autonomy and property? Interpreting Locke's proviso as an expression of individual right allows Nozick to alter its character considerably as a limitation on acquisition. Simply put, for Nozick all acquisition is just, provided it does not harm others by violating their rights.[48] Scarcity for Nozick then, unlike for Locke, is no limit to just acquisition. Indeed, the ownership of the total supply of a necessary good does not entail that this ownership places others in a worse position than they would otherwise be. 'A medical researcher who synthesizes a new substance that effectively treats a certain disease and who refuses to sell except on his terms does not worsen the situation of others by depriving them of whatever he has appropriated', namely the raw and unsynthesized materials that were mixed with the researcher's mental and physical endeavours.[49]

In a divertissement, Rawls considers an alternative similar to Nozick's entitlement theory which he styles a system of natural liberty.[50] Under a system of natural liberty, the principle of equality of opportunity 'is understood as an open social system in which . . . careers are open to talents.'[51] Natural liberty does not appear on the agenda of the original position[52], because 'there is no effort to preserve an equality, or similarity, of special conditions, except insofar as this is necessary to

---

[46] See J. Exdell, 'Distributive Justice – Nozick on Property Rights', *Ethics*, 82 (1977): 146.
[47] *Anarchy, State and Utopia*, p. 171.
[48] *Ibid.*, pp. 176 and 179.
[49] *Ibid.*, p. 181.
[50] *A Theory of Justice*, p. 66ff.
[51] *Ibid.*, p. 66.
[52] *Ibid.*, p. 124.

preserve the requisite background institutions.'[53] The initial distribution is the product of natural and social contingencies. Rawls assumes a linear relation between contingent starting points and eventual rewards. 'Intuitively', for Rawls, 'the most obvious injustice of the system of natural liberty is that it permits distributive shares to be improperly influenced by these [contingent] factors so *arbitrary from a moral point of view*.'[54] Rawls goes so far as to say that even 'character depends *in large part* upon . . . circumstances'.[55] Thus Rawls rejects as arbitrary any distribution related at all to individual actions (except via the difference principle).

Nozick disputes Rawls' assumption of linearity because it portrays individuals as the helpless products of their environment, with no consideration '*at all* of how persons have chosen to develop their natural talents'.[56] More importantly, for Rawls to deny completely the moral importance of human action is to deny to the very Kantian autonomy he wishes to achieve.[57] If it is true that we are not morally responsible for our virtues, then once in a just basic structure will we not go on being determined by the environment? We will have justice without autonomy.

Rawls' theory aims at the basic structure of society and not the justice of each event within it – like Ocker's case.[58] Persons in the original position, after all, are conceived of as choosing principles of justice to guide conduct. They are not choosing a society in which to live, for that is not a matter of choice. Once accepted, the principles of justice are applied to whatever society we inhabit.

In Rawls' account the basic structure is 'the way in which the major social institutions distribute fundamental rights and duties and determine the division of advantages from social cooperation'.[59] Examples of such institutions include 'the political constitution and the principal economic and social arrangements', such as 'the legal protection of freedom of thought and liberty of conscience, competitive markets, private property in the means of production, and the

---

[53] *Ibid.*, p. 72.
[54] *Ibid.*, (my emphasis).
[55] *Ibid.*, p. 104 (my emphasis); and *cf.* pp. 311-2 and 36. See also M. W. Jackson, 'A Contradiction in Rawls: Desert, Determinism, and Justice', *Australian Society of Legal Philosophy Bulletin*, No. 4 (1977).
[56] *Anarchy, State and Utopia*, p. 214.
[57] *Ibid.*
[58] *A Theory of Justice*, p. 7; and *cf.* pp. 54 and 84.
[59] *Ibid.*, p. 7.

monogamous family'.[60] At day's end it is the basic structure that 'shapes the wants and aspiration . . . citizens come to have'.[61]

In a recent article Rawls claims that the basic structure of a society is sociologically unique, because 'society as a whole has no ends in the sense that associations and individuals do'.[62] Rawls concludes that individuals can make no particular claims for benefits.

Rawls advances two arguments. The first is an argument of membership. The voluntary membership of sub-societal organizations is the basis for determining the goals of such an organization. Were Bruce Ocker to join a football club it would be expected that he was interested in football; it would be a surprise if he were to suggest that the club become a choir. Membership in the community, however, is an accident of birth.[63]

Is society unique in that we are born into it? Are we not also born into all manner of groupings, such as races, languages, religions and classes? It would suffice for Rawls to claim that the difference in degree between involuntary social membership and other involuntary or voluntary sub-societal memberships is so great in its foreclosure of alternatives as to be a difference in kind. This qualification is adequate for Rawls to conclude that 'there is no question of the parties [in a dispute] comparing the attractions of other societies'.[64] We do, in fact, compare the burdens and benefits of different families, sexes, languages, races, religions, classes and individuals within a community, but we do not compare the attractions of other societies in this way. An Australian pipefitter, say our exemplary Mr Ocker, does not press a wage claim by saying that were he a German pipefitter he would be worth the claim at stake, and that the fact that he is Australian and not German is morally arbitrary. Yet a female pipefitter would argue just this vis-à-vis a male within either nation.

Moreover, even if genetically determined, 'abilities and talents cannot come to fruition apart from social conditions and as realized they always take but one of many possible forms'.[65] Rawls seems to be saying that a community can have any one of an unknown number of basic structures.

---

[60] *Ibid.*
[61] *Ibid.*, p. 259.
[62] Rawls, 'The Basic Structure as Subject', *American Philosophical Quarterly*, 14 (1977): 162.
[63] *Ibid.*
[64] *Ibid.*
[65] *Ibid.*, p. 160. Cf. *A Theory of Justice*, pp. 103–4 and 310–5.

The one it does have is morally arbitrary, determined by history and geography, and not by moral rationality as exemplified by the original position. To illustrate his point, elsewhere Rawls uses the example of a singer.[66] Let us assume that Bruce Ocker is a weekend singer. In the case of a tenor like Ocker, Rawls argues that his worth depends on the morally indifferent mechanisms of supply and demand. Ocker and another singer may be identical in musical endowment and effort, and yet differently rewarded because Ocker lives in a community that prizes song while the other singer does not. According to Rawls, Ocker is not justly entitled to his earnings; his talent is profitable due to the morally arbitrary conventions of the society.

Rawls' second argument addresses contributions. Because the basic structure is so diffuse, it shapes citizens. A football team can assess the potential contributions of each prospect in a way that a community cannot. Apart from community, none of us have assessed talents, schooled virtues, inspired interests, or disciplined habits. One cannot claim to be worth something to one's community on the basis of the possession of these qualities, for one would not have them nor be rewarded for them but for the existence of the community. Rawls writes that 'there is *no* way to identify potential contribution to society as an individual not yet a member of it'.[67] Of course, Rawls concedes, we can judge the performance of institutional roles by an individual as spouse, pipefitter, trade unionist, amateur singer, parent, and so on. These roles are located in different institutions and are neither additive nor transitive. Even if Ocker performed all of these roles well, we would not be correct to say that he is a good citizen – though the good performance of each such role grants the person a legitimate expectation of some specified entitlement. But 'the sum of an individual's entitlements, or even of their uncompensated contributions to associations within society, is not to be regarded as a contribution to society'.[68] Therefore, one can give citizen contribution 'no meaning' because there is 'no clear or useful notion' of contribution.[69]

For Rawls, then, we are involuntary members of a community which shapes us and assigns value to our activities. It might be supposed that one candidate for a community goal would be justice itself; however,

---

[66] *A Theory of Justice*, p. 311.
[67] 'The Basic Structure as Subject', p. 162.
[68] *Ibid.*, p. 163.
[69] *Ibid.*

Rawls excludes this goal by declaiming that 'this is not an aim that ranks their [citizens] expected contributions'.[70] In the absence of any goals, Rawls opines, 'insofar as we compare the worth of citizens, all their worth in a well-ordered society is always equal'.[71] Even those motivated by the difference principle to bear a burden beneficial to the least-advantaged class must be content with a material reward alone. Rawls states that no moral connotations are to be attached to such persons.[72] Elsewhere he implies that the self-appointed vocation of counting blades of grass is as worthy an activity for a citizen as the greatest feats of supererogation.[73] All activities are equal – productive or not – so that all people may be equal.

Nozick finds Rawls' disinterest in the ways and means of the production of benefits through the distribution of burdens to be a manna-from-heaven model.[74] The model assumes that benefits such as Rawls' primary goods are there to be distributed. Indeed, it is 'incredible' in Rawls' theory to picture an individual being called upon to make any sacrifice to shoulder some communal burden.[75] On the other hand, Nozick's exclusive preoccupation with individual motivation ignores community. And as parts of Rawls' analysis of the basic structure shows, community cannot be ignored in matters of justice.

The one primary good conspicuously absent from the firmament of the original position, and equally removed from Nozick's ken, is community itself. It is the first benefit and the first burden. Nonetheless it does seem to be true that Rawls assumes that the benefits (the primary goods) of liberty, self-respect, opportunities, powers, income and wealth will exist to be distributed. No explicit attention is allowed to the social organization and distribution of the burdens of work that would bring about these benefits. Although Nozick's night-watchman state would be minimal in its aim, it would not necessarily be minimal in the powers required to that end. More than one state devoted to the free market and opposed to (re)distributive justice has been a police state.

---

[70] Ibid., p. 162.
[71] Ibid., p. 163. Cf. A Theory of Justice, p. 485.
[72] A Theory of Justice, p. 536.
[73] Ibid., p. 432.
[74] Anarchy, State and Utopia, p. 198.
[75] Ibid., p. 178.

A political theory that takes the isolated individual as its basic normative unit cannot find just those necessary burdens that make mutually beneficial community life possible. The passage of arms in defence is only the most obvious of such burdens. Unlike Rawls and Nozick, individualist writers have confronted the burden of defence directly, as when Hobbes wrestles irresolutely with conscription.[76] For his part, Locke considers obedience in warfare and declares that the citizen soldier must give absolute allegiance, even 'to march up to the mouth of a canon'.[77] Locke contradicts his absolute priority of individual rights in the ownership of one's own body. There is a discussion of conscription in *A Theory of Justice*, to be sure, but it is couched more in terms of a matter of labour relations than the life and death struggle of a community.[78]

To study the theories of John Rawls and Robert Nozick is to look at a map upon which the names of all the cities, the waterways and the districts are clearly lettered, but not the name of the country itself. Only when having foresaken the attempt to espy the name is it perceived quite as large as life, spread across the entire surface. For all the difficulty in locating it, the name turns out not to be unknown, but only forgotten momentarily because it is too common to make a point of remembering. It is a country one seldom sets out to visit, a place infrequently mentioned in world's events and yet familiar for all of that. In this case, it is the land of the political theory of individualism.

It is oblivious of the most fundamental and puzzling matter to explain and to justify, namely that we do live together in political communities, that we do think of ourselves in this way, and that we seldom think of ourselves in any other way. Yet to read these two books one would never know that this is so. Individuals come first and last. When community is discussed it is to elevate the level of generality at which the concerns of individuals are discussed. There is no change in the content of the discussion. At no point in either work is culture discussed. In passing, Rawls suggests that a just government might not subsidize art, learning, drama or opera, since they have no utilitarian value.[79] For his repeated references to history, Nozick means the history of isolated individuals and not of communities or members of communities. Like Hobbes'

---

[76] Thomas Hobbes, *Leviathan*, Part II, chapter 20.
[77] Locke, *Second Treatise*, section 149.
[78] *A Theory of Justice*, p. 380ff.
[79] *Ibid.*, p. 332.

citizens, Nozick's citizens would each be left to make a separate peace with a conqueror without a thought to obligations and duties to the cultural heritage and living distinctiveness of their community.[80] Insofar as women and men do not act in this way, they are as yet unlike the cormorant people depicted by Rawls and Nozick.[81]

---

[80] See *Leviathan*, Part II, chapter 20.
[81] Consider Jean-Paul Sartre, 'La république du silence', *Situations* III, Gallimard, Paris, 1949 [1944], pp. 11–13.